Raymond Williams

and the City

Paladin

Granada Publishing Limited
Published in 1975 by Paladin
Frogmore, St Albans, Herts AL2 2NF

First published in Great Britain by Chatto & Windus Ltd 1973
Copyright © Raymond Williams 1973
Made and printed in Great Britain by
Cox & Wyman Ltd
London, Reading and Fakenham

For the country workers
who were my grandparents
James Bird
Mary Ann Lewis
Joseph Williams
Margaret Williams

Contents

Acknowledgements

Earlier versions of parts of this book have appeared in *Stand, The Listener, The Critical Quarterly, Eighteenth Century Studies* and *Novel*; in introductions to the second volume of the *Pelican Book of English Prose*, the Penguin edition of *Dombey and Son* and the MacGibbon & Kee reissue of *Hodge and his Masters*; and in the lectures published as *The English Novel from Dickens to Lawrence.*

Since some of the early work was published I have had many opportunities, in different capacities, of working with others on parts of its subject, including a good deal of detailed research. I ought especially to mention, with this reciprocal learning in mind, Dr G. T. Cavaliero, Dr J. P. Parrinder and Mr Adrian Poole. I have also had the advantage of discussions with Dr T. F. Eagleton, Dr H. H. Erskine-Hill, Dr S. C. Heath, Dr M. D. Long, Mr Charles Swann, Mr John Fekete and many others of my colleagues and students.

My wife's help with the book has been sustaining and irreplaceable. I am also especially indebted to Dr Merryn Williams, author of *Thomas Hardy and Rural England*, who was kind enough from her special experience to read the manuscript and the proofs.

I have to make the following acknowledgements for the use of copyright material: to Faber & Faber Ltd and Harcourt Brace Jovanovich, Inc. for extracts from poems in *Collected Poems, 1909–1962* by T. S. Eliot. © 1936 by Harcourt Brace Jovanovich, Inc. and © 1963, 1964 by T. S. Eliot; The Trustees of the Hardy Estate, The Macmillan Company of Canada, St Martin's Press, Inc. and Macmillan, London and Basingstoke for extracts from *Tess of the d'Urbervilles* by Thomas Hardy; and the Trustees of the Hardy Estate, The Macmillan Company of Canada, The Macmillan Company, New York, and Macmillan, London and Basingstoke, for an excerpt from *Collected Poems* by Thomas Hardy.

R. W.

1 Country and City

'Country' and 'city' are very powerful words, and this is not surprising when we remember how much they seem to stand for in the experience of human communities. In English, 'country' is both a nation and a part of a 'land'; 'the country' can be the whole society or its rural area. In the long history of human settlements, this connection between the land from which directly or indirectly we all get our living and the achievements of human society has been deeply known. And one of these achievements has been the city: the capital, the large town, a distinctive form of civilization.

On the actual settlements, which in the real history have been astonishingly varied, powerful feelings have gathered and have been generalized. On the country has gathered the idea of a natural way of life: of peace, innocence, and simple virtue. On the city has gathered the idea of an achieved centre: of learning, communication, light. Powerful hostile associations have also developed: on the city as a place of noise, worldliness and ambition; on the country as a place of backwardness, ignorance, limitation. A contrast between country and city, as fundamental ways of life, reaches back into classical times.

Yet the real history, throughout, has been astonishingly varied. The 'country way of life' has included the very different practices of hunters, pastoralists, farmers and factory farmers, and its organization has varied from the tribe and the manor to the feudal estate, from the small peasantry and tenant farmers to the rural commune, from the *latifundia* and the plantation to the large capitalist enterprise and the state farm. The city, no less, has been of many kinds: state capital, administrative base, religious centre, market-town, port and mercantile depot, military barracks, industrial concentration. Between the cities of ancient and medieval times and the modern metropolis or conurbation there is a connection of name and in part of function, but nothing like identity. Moreover, in our own world, there is a wide range of settlements between the traditional poles of country and city: suburb, dormitory town, shanty town, industrial estate. Even the idea of the village, which seems simple, shows in actual history a wide variation: as to size and character, and internally in its variation between dispersed and nuclear settlements, in Britain as clearly as anywhere.

In and through these differences, all the same, certain images and associations persist; and it is the purpose of this book to describe and analyse them, to see them in relation to the historically varied experience. For practical reasons I take most of my examples from English writing, though my interests go much wider. It ought in any case to be clear that the English experience is especially significant, in that one of the decisive transformations, in the relations between country and city, occurred there very early and with a thoroughness which is still in some ways unapproached. The Industrial Revolution not only transformed both city and country; it was based on a highly developed agrarian capitalism, with a very early disappearance of the traditional peasantry. In the imperialist phase of our history the nature of the rural economy, in Britain and in its colonies, was again transformed very early: dependence on a domestic agriculture dwindled to very low proportions, with no more than four per cent of economically active men now engaged in farming, and this in a society which had already become the first predominantly urban-dwelling people in the long history of human settlements. Since much of the dominant subsequent development, indeed the very idea of 'development' in the world generally, has been in these decisive directions, the English experience remains exceptionally important: not only symptomatic but in some ways diagnostic; in its intensity still memorable, whatever may succeed. For it is a critical fact that in and through these transforming experiences English attitudes to the country, and to ideas of rural life, persisted with extraordinary power, so that even after the society was predominantly urban its literature, for a generation, was still predominantly rural; and even in the twentieth century, in an urban and industrial land, forms of the older ideas and experiences still remarkably persist. All this gives the English experience and interpretation of the country and the city a permanent though of course not exclusive importance.

This importance can be stated, and will have to be assessed, as a general problem. But it is as well to say at the outset that this has been for me a personal issue, for as long as I remember. It happened that in a predominantly urban and industrial Britain I was born in a remote village, in a very old settled countryside on the border between England and Wales. Within twenty miles, indeed at the end of a bus route, was in one direction an old cathedral city, in the other an old frontier market town but only a few miles beyond it the first industrial towns and villages of the great coal and steel area of South Wales. Before I had read any descriptions and interpretations of the changes and variations of settlements and ways of life, I saw them on the ground, and working, in unforgettable clarity. In the course of education I moved to another city, built round a university, and since then, living and travelling and working, I have come to visit, and to need to visit, so many great cities, of different kinds, and to look forward and back, in space and time, knowing and seeking to know this relationship, as an experience and as a problem. I have written about it in other ways but also I have been slowly collecting the evidence to write about it explicitly, as a matter of social, literary and intellectual history.

This book is the result, but though it often and necessarily follows impersonal procedures, in description and analysis, there is behind it, all the time, this personal pressure and commitment. And since the relation of country and city is not only an objective problem and history, but has been and still is for many millions of people a direct and intense preoccupation and experience, I feel no need to justify, though it is as well to mention, this personal cause.

Thus at once, for me, before the argument starts, country life has many meanings. It is the elms, the may, the white horse, in the field beyond the window where I am writing. It is the men in the November evening, walking back from pruning, with their hands in the pockets of their khaki coats; and the women in headscarves, outside their cottages, waiting for the blue bus that will take them, inside school hours to work in the harvest. It is the tractor on the road, leaving its tracks of serrated pressed mud; the light in the small hours, in the pig-farm across the road, in the crisis of a litter; the slow brown van met at the difficult corner, with the crowded sheep jammed to its slatted sides; the heavy smell, on still evenings, of the silage ricks fed with molasses. It is also the sour land, on the thick boulder clay, not far up the road, that is selling for housing, for a speculative development, at twelve thousand pounds an acre.

As I said, I was born in a village, and I still live in a village. But where I was born was under the Black Mountains, on the Welsh border, where the meadows are bright green against the red earth of the ploughland, and the first trees, beyond the window, are oak and holly. Where I live now is in the flat country, on a headland of boulder clay, towards the edge of the dikes and sluices, the black earth of the Fens, under the high East Anglian skies.

That physical contrast is continually present to me, but it is not the only contrast. Within that Black Mountain village, as again here, there is a deep contrast in which so much feeling is held: between what seems an unmediated nature – a physical awareness of trees, birds, the moving shapes of land – and a working agriculture, in which much of the nature is in fact being produced. Both kinds of hedgerow, there on its earthbank, here on the flat or with a lining ditch, together with the oaks and hollies or the elms and thorns that follow their lines, have been seen and planted and tended by men. At the end of the lane by the cottage where I was a child, there is now a straight wide motor road where the lorries race. But the lane also has been set, stoned, driven over: it is a mark on the land of no more than two generations, since a young builder married the daughter of a farmer and was given a corner of a field on which to build their house, and then his workshop with the lane to it, and then neighbouring houses, and then successive workshops converted to new houses; the first workshop was my parents' first home. In the field with the elms and the white horse, behind my own present home, there are faint marks of a ninth-century building, and a foot below the grass there is a cobbled road, that resists the posts being driven, today, for a new wire fence.

This country life then has many meanings: in feeling and activity; in region and in time. The cobbles under the field are older than the university to which the bridletrack leads, five miles under thin thorn hedges, across the open and windy fields, past Starvegoose Wood. The foot of earth over them is a millennium, in one kind of reckoning. But the lane in that Black Mountain village, now so different both from the motor road and from the shaded lane I remember, is recent: about as far back as when my father, at twelve, went to work as a boy on a farm. I have the farmer's reference when he left: the shaky, rounded writing that he was honest and willing; and what he left for was to be a boy porter on the railway: that line of four through the valley, old road, tramroad, new road, railway: the cuttings and embankments moving like foothills; settled and familiar, laid a hundred years ago. When I was born he was a signalman, in the box in the valley: part of a network reaching known named places, Newport and Hereford, and beyond them London, but still a man in the village, with his gardens and his bees, taking produce to market on a bicycle: a different network, but it was a bicycle he went on, to a market where the farmers came in cars and the dealers in lorries: our own century. He had been as much born to the land as his own father, yet, like him, he could not live by it. That man, Joseph, my grandfather, was a farmworker until middle age, when he lost his job and with it his cottage, and became a roadman: cutting and clearing along a length of the road that led away to the Midlands, to other cities. One uncle lived in London; another in Birmingham; we moved, as a family, on visits and holidays, between country and city, in our own direct relationships. We were a dispersed family, along the road, the railway, and now letters and print. These were the altering communications, the altering connections, between country and city, and between all the intermediate places and communities, the intermediate or temporary jobs and settlements.

So this country life had its meanings, but these changed in themselves and changed in relation to others. In the south-west, at nights, we used to watch the flare, over the black ridge of

Brynarw, of the iron furnaces of industrial South Wales. In the east now, at nights, over the field with the elms and the white horse, I watch the glow of Cambridge: a white tinged with orange; and in the autumn here, the stubble fields are burned, sometimes catching the thorn hedges, and when I saw this first at night I took it as strange accidental fire. My own network, from where I sit writing at the window, is to Cambridge and London, and beyond them to the postmark places, the unfamiliar stamps and the distant cities: Rome, Moscow, New York.

The lights of the city. I go out in the dark, before bed, and look at that glow in the sky: a look at the city while remembering Hardy's Jude, who stood and looked at the distant, attainable and unattainable, Christminster. Or I remember Wordsworth, coming from high country to London, and saying from Westminster Bridge:

> Earth has not anything to show more fair:
> Dull would he be of soul who could pass by
> A sight so touching in its majesty:
> This city now doth, like a garment, wear
> The beauty of the morning; silent, bare,
> Ships, towers, domes, theatres and temples lie
> Open unto the fields, and to the sky;
> All bright and glittering in the smokeless air.

It is true that this was the city before the rush and noise of the working day, but the pulse of the recognition is still unmistakable, and I know that I have felt it again and again: the great buildings of civilization; the meeting-places; the libraries and theatres, the towers and domes; and often more moving than these, the houses, the streets, the press and excitement of so many people, with so many purposes. I have stood in many cities and felt this pulse: in the physical differences of Stockholm and Florence, Paris and Milan: this identifiable and moving quality: the centre, the activity, the light. Like everyone else I have felt also the chaos of the metro and the traffic jam; the monotony of the ranks of houses; the aching press of strange crowds. But this is not an experience at all, not an adult experience, until it has come to include also the dynamic movement, in these centres of settled and often magnificent achievement. H. G. Wells once said, coming out of a political meeting where they had been discussing social change, that this great towering city was a measure of the obstacle, of how much must be moved if there was to be any change. I have known this feeling, looking up at great buildings that are the centres of power, but I find I do not say, 'There is your city, your great bourgeois monument, your towering structure of this still precarious civilization', or I do not only say that; I say also, 'This is what men have built, so often magnificently, and is not everything then possible?' Indeed this sense of possibility, of meeting and of movement, is a permanent element of my sense of cities: as permanent a feeling as those other feelings, when I look from the mountain at the great coloured patchwork of fields that generations of my own people have cleared and set in hedges; or the known living places, the isolated farms, the cluster of cottages by castle or church, the line of river and wood and footpath and lane; lines received and lines made. So that while country and city have this profound importance, in their differing ways, my feelings are held, before any argument starts.

But then also, specifically, I came from a village to a city: to be taught, to learn: to submit personal facts, the incidents of a family, to a total record; to learn evidence and connection and altering perspectives. If the walls of the colleges were like the walls of parks, that as children we had walked round, unable to enter, yet now there was a gate, an entry, and a library at the end of it: a direct record, if I could learn to read it. It is ironic to remember that it was only after I came that I heard, from townsmen, academics, an influential version of what country life, country literature, really meant: a prepared and persuasive cultural history. I read related things still, in academic books and in books by men who left private schools to go farming, and by others who grew up in villages and are now country writers: a whole set of books, periodicals, notes in the newspapers: country life. And I find I keep asking the same question, because of the history: where do I stand in relation to these writers: in another country or in this valuing city? That problem is sharp and ironic in its cultural persistence.

But there was more to Cambridge than that. An ambivalence

certainly: a university of scholars and teachers but also of coaches and placemen, on their way to higher places; a world of men extending human knowledge and bringing light to nature and to the lives of others; a world of other men contracted in sympathy, telling their qualifying paradigms inside the walls, in an idle and arrogant observation and consumption. The university, to my family, had been equally foreign, whether it was Cambridge or Bologna. But there was also the Cambridge of Stourbridge Fair, once the leading market of the country: 'the prodigious resort of the trading people of all parts of England' as Defoe described it in the 1720s; 'a prodigious complex of people' and also a model, to Bunyan, for Vanity Fair. When I returned much later, as a Fellow of a College, I found I was by virtue or default of an intellectual appointment an aspect, an unwilling member, of a collective and perpetual landlord, and I was asked, politely, to attend tenants' lunches, which I could never stomach. I remembered Arthur Young on the University of Cambridge:

its revenue £16000 a year and for 1s 6d a member can sit down to a dinner such as a gentleman with £1000 a year cannot often give with prudence.

Defoe had followed one road out:

on the edge of the Fenns, to Huntingdon, where it joins the great north road; on this side it is all an agreeable corn country, as above, adorned with several seats of gentlemen.

Young, in 1791, had followed another:

Taking the road from Cambridge to St Neot's, view six or seven miles of the worst husbandry, I hope, in Great Britain ... There seems somewhat of a coincidence between the state of cultivation within sight of the venerable spires of Cambridge and the utter neglect of agriculture in the establishment of that University.

That is the road I now drive on, coming home from the university. The fields are well farmed now. But in the next village west, Cobbett saw, in 1822, something

which very much resembles almost a village of the same size in Picardy, where I saw the women dragging harrows to harrow in the corn. Certainly this village resembles nothing English except some of the rascally rotten boroughs in Cornwall and Devonshire, on which a just Providence seems to have entailed its curse. The land just about here does seem to be really bad. The face of the country is naked. The few scrubbed trees that now and then meet the eye, and even the quick-sets are covered with a yellow moss. All is bleak and comfortless; and, just on the most dreary part of this most dreary scene, stands almost opportunely, 'Caxton Gibbet', tendering its one friendly arm to the passers-by. It has recently been fresh-painted, and written on in conspicuous characters, for the benefit, I suppose, of those who cannot exist under the thought of wheat at four shillings a bushel.

That, too, is different now, but whenever I consider the relations between country and city, and between birth and learning, I find this history active and continuous: the relations are not only of ideas and experiences, but of rent and interest, of situation and power; a wider system.

This then is where I am, and as I settle to work I find I have to resolve, step by slow step, experiences and questions that once moved like light. The life of country and city is moving and present: moving in time, through the history of a family and a people; moving in feeling and ideas, through a network of relationships and decisions.

A dog is barking – that chained bark – behind the asbestos barn. It is now and then: here and many places. When there are questions to put, I have to push back my chair, look down at my papers, and feel the change.

2   A Problem of Perspective

The initial problem is one of perspective. A few years ago I was sent a book for review; a country book, in a familiar idiom, that I would normally have enjoyed reading. But there in front of the experience was a formula:

A way of life that has come down to us from the days of Virgil has suddenly ended.

In detail, certainly, this was curious. From Virgil? Here? A way of country life?

But in outline, of course, the position was familiar. As it is put in a memorable sentence, in the same book:

A whole culture that had preserved its continuity from earliest times had now received its quietus.

It had happened, it seemed, in the last fifty years: say since the First World War. But this raised a problem. I remembered a sentence in a critically influential book: Leavis and Thompson's *Culture and Environment*, published in 1932. The 'organic community' of 'Old England' had disappeared; 'the change is very recent indeed'. This view was primarily based on the books of George Sturt, which appeared between 1907 and 1923. In *Change in the Village*, published in 1911, Sturt wrote of the rural England 'that is dying out now'. Just back, we can see, over the last hill.

But then what seemed like an escalator began to move. Sturt traced this ending to two periods: enclosure after 1861 and residential settlement after 1900. Yet this at once takes us into the period of Thomas Hardy's novels, written between 1871 and 1896 and referring back to rural England since the 1830s. And had not critics insisted that it was here, in Hardy, that we found the record of the great climacteric change in rural life:

the disturbance and destruction of what one writer has called the 'timeless rhythm of agriculture and the seasons'? And that was also the period of Richard Jefferies, looking back from the 1870s to the 'old Hodge', and saying that there had been more change in rural England in the previous half-century – that is, since the 1820s – than in any previous time. And wasn't George Eliot, in *Mill on the Floss* (1860) and in *Felix Holt* (1866), looking back, similarly, to the old rural England of the 1820s and early 1830s?

But now the escalator was moving without pause. For the 1820s and 1830s were the last years of Cobbett, directly in touch with the rural England of his time but looking back to the happier country, the old England of his boyhood, during the 1770s and 1780s. Thomas Bewick, in his *Memoir*, written during the 1820s, was recalling the happier village of his own boyhood, in the 1770s. The decisive change, both men argued, had happened during their lifetimes. John Clare, in 1809, was also looking back –

> Oh, happy Eden of those golden years

– to what seems, on internal evidence, to be the 1790s, though he wrote also, in another retrospect on a vanishing rural order, of the 'far-fled pasture, long evanish'd scene'.

Yet still the escalator moved. For the years of Cobbett's and of Bewick's boyhood were the years of Crabbe's *The Village* (1783):

> No longer truth, though shown in verse, disdain,
> But own the Village Life a life of pain

and of Goldsmith's *The Deserted Village* (1769):

> E'en now, methinks, as pondering here I stand
> I see the rural virtues leave the land.

And by ordinary arithmetic, in the memory of Sweet Auburn –

> loveliest village of the plain,
> Where health and plenty cheer'd the labouring swain,
> Where smiling spring its earliest visit paid,
> And parting summer's lingering blooms delay'd;
> Dear lovely bowers of innocence and ease,
> Seats of my youth, when every sport could please

– back we would go again, over the next hill, to the 1750s.

It is clear, of course, as this journey in time is taken, that something more than ordinary arithmetic and something more, evidently, than ordinary history, is in question. Against sentimental and intellectualized accounts of an unlocalized 'Old England', we need, evidently, the sharpest scepticism. But some at least of these witnesses were writing from direct experience. What we have to inquire into is not, in these cases, historical error, but historical perspective. Indeed the fact of what I have called the escalator may be an important clue to the real history, but only when we begin to see the regularity of its pattern.

It is worth, perhaps, getting on the escalator again, since all we have done so far is to move 'Old England' and its timeless agricultural rhythms back from the early twentieth century to the middle of the eighteenth century. When we remember 'our mature, settled eighteenth century', we may not, after all, have made very much difference to the ordinary accounts. Shall we then go back to Philip Massinger, in the early 1620s, in *The City Madam* and *A New Way to Pay Old Debts*? Here the new commercialism is breaking the old landed settlement and its virtues. Here is the enclosing and engrossing Sir Giles Overreach. Here is the corruption of an older rural civilization:

> Your father was
> An honest country farmer, goodman Humble,
> By his neighbours ne'er called Master. Did your pride
> Descend from him?

We can't say, but we can go on back to Bastard's *Chrestoleros*, in 1598, where the same complaints are being made, or, if we are asked to assume that the disturbance occurred at the turn of the century, to Thomas More's *Utopia*, in 1516, where another old order is being destroyed:

For looke in what partes of the realme doth growe the fynest and therfore dearest woll, there noblemen and gentlemen, yea and certeyn abbottes, holy men no doubt, not contenting them selfes with the yearely revenues and profytes, that were wont to grow to theyr forefathers and predecessours of their landes, nor beynge content that they live in rest and pleasure nothinge profiting, yea much noyinge the weale publique, leave no ground for tillage, thei inclose all into pastures; thei throw doune houses; they plucke downe townes, and leave

20

nothing standynge, but only the churche to be made a shepehouse. And as though you lost no small quantity of grounds by forestes, chases, laundes and parkes, those good holy men turne all dwellinge places and all glebeland into desolation and wildernes.

Except that then, of course, we find ourselves referred back to the settled Middle Ages, an organic society if ever there was one. To the 1370s, for example, when Langland's Piers Plowman sees the dissatisfaction of the labourers, who will not eat yesterday's vegetables but must have fresh meat, who blame God and curse the King, but who used not to complain when Hunger made the Statutes. Must we go beyond the Black Death to the beginning of the Game Laws, or to the time of Magna Carta, when Innocent III writes:

the serf serves; terrified with threats, wearied by corvees, afflicted with blows, despoiled of his possessions?

Or shall we find the timeless rhythm in Domesday, when four men out of five are villeins, bordars, cotters or slaves? Or in a free Saxon world before what was later seen as the Norman rape and yoke? In a Celtic world, before the Saxons came up the rivers? In an Iberian world, before the Celts came, with their gilded barbarism? Where indeed shall we go, before the escalator stops?

One answer, of course, is Eden, and we shall have to look at that well-remembered garden again. But first we must get off the escalator, and consider its general movement.

Is it anything more than a well-known habit of using the past, the 'good old days', as a stick to beat the present? It is clearly something of that, but there are still difficulties. The apparent resting places, the successive Old Englands to which we are confidently referred but which then start to move and recede, have some actual significance, when they are looked at in their own terms. Of course we notice their location in the childhoods of their authors, and this must be relevant. Nostalgia, it can be said, is universal and persistent; only other men's nostalgias offend. A memory of childhood can be said persuasively, to have some permanent significance. But again, what seemed a single escalator, a perpetual recession into history, turns out, on reflection, to be a more complicated movement: Old England, settlement, the rural virtues – all these, in fact, mean different things at different times, and quite different values are being brought to question. We shall need precise analysis of each kind of retrospect, as it comes. We shall see successive stages of the criticism which the retrospect supports: religious, humanist, political, cultural. Each of these stages is worth examination in itself. And then, within each of these questions, but returning us finally to a formidable and central question, there is a different consideration.

The witnesses we have summoned raise questions of historical fact and perspective, but they raise questions, also, of literary fact and perspective. The things they are saying are not all in the same mode. They range, as facts, from a speech in a play and a passage in a novel to an argument in an essay and a note in a journal. When the facts are poems, they are also, and perhaps crucially, poems of different kinds. We can only analyse these important structures of feeling if we make, from the beginning, these critical discriminations. And then the first problem of definition, a persistent problem of form, is the question of pastoral, of what is known as pastoral.

3 Pastoral and Counter-Pastoral

(i)

> No longer truth, though shown in verse, disdain,
> But own the Village Life a life of pain.

This couplet of Crabbe's, which opens the second book of *The Village*, is a significant introduction to the character of the general problem. Where did it come from, that tone of apology about verse? Who was it aimed at, that insistence on the truth? Crabbe's poem, *The Village*, needs to be read between these questions.

> By such examples taught, I paint the Cot,
> As Truth will paint it, and as Bards will not.

Truth again, and against poetry. Whatever we may later ask about Crabbe's England, it is clear that the contrast in his mind is not between rural England past and present, but between true and false ways of writing. More generally, the contrast he is forcing is between a tradition of pastoral poetry and his own intention of realism. He assumes, certainly, that there was once a basis for what he knew as pastoral, but in classical times, not in his own or recent England:

> Fled are those times, when in harmonious strains
> The rustic poet praised his native plains:
> No shepherds now, in smooth alternate verse,
> Their country's beauty or their nymphs' rehearse.

It is a literary tradition, that of neo–classic pastoral, that is being formally rejected: 'mechanick echoes of the Mantuan song'. Or, as Crabbe originally wrote, before Johnson's amendment of his lines:

> In fairer scenes, where peaceful pleasures spring,
> Tityrus the pride of Mantuan swains might sing;
> But, charmed by him, or smitten with his views,
> Shall modern poets court the Mantuan muse?
> From Truth and Nature shall we widely stray,
> Where Fancy leads, or Virgil led the way

Johnson weakened this by amending the last lines to 'where Virgil, not where Fancy, leads the way'. It would have been better if Crabbe had not needed, as in practice he did, Johnson's help.

'A way of life that has come down to us from the days of Virgil.' But if it is the continuity of a settled agriculture, it is from very much earlier than that. The literary reference, for a presumed social fact, is the really significant structure. It is symptomatic of the confusion which surrounds the whole question of 'pastoral'.

For if we look back into literature for significant writing about country life, we are taken many centuries beyond Virgil to the *Works and Days* of Hesiod, to the ninth century before Christ. And what we find there, in a very particular structure of customs and beliefs, is an epic of husbandry, in the widest sense: the practice of agriculture and trading within a way of life in which prudence and effort are seen as primary virtues. The recommendations are made within the mythical structure of the loosing of evils, among them the evil of hard work, from Pandora's jar, and the influential chronology of the five ages, from the first golden age in which:

remote and free from evil and grief ... (mortal men) had all good things, for the fruitful earth unforced bare them fruit abundantly and without stint.

We shall see the long influence of this myth of the Golden Age, but for Hesiod, at the beginning of country literature, it is already far in the past. Three other ages have intervened, and it is the character of his own 'iron age' that determines his recommendation of practical agriculture, social justice and neighbourliness. It is from the 'life of pain' that these practices can deliver a working community.

The Greek bucolic poets are very much later: some six centuries. It is in the Hellenistic world of the third century before Christ that 'pastoral', in any strict sense, emerges as a literary form. Its landscape is not the Boeotia of Hesiod, but the Sicily of Theocritus and Moschus, the Greek islands, and Egypt; the literary centre of the movement is Alexandria. Thus 'pastoral' already has a different base: the tenth Idyll of Theocritus has a background of sowing and harvesting, but this is an exception; the normal work is the herding of goats, sheep and cattle. The working year of Hesiod, ploughing, tending vineyards, keeping pigs and sheep and goats, is thus already significantly altered. It is generally assumed that literary pastoral developed from singing competitions in local peasant communities; but as it emerges in Theocritus, though this form is often retained, a degree of elaboration and artifice, most evident in the use of literary dialects, is evident everywhere. At the same time the working context of the Idylls is recognizable and at times insistent. Thus we read on the first appearance of the long figure of Lycidas:

He was a goatherd, nor could one that saw him have mistaken him, for beyond all he looked the goatherd. On his shoulders he wore the tawny skin of a thick-haired shaggy goat reeking of fresh curd, and round his breast an aged tunic was girt with a broad belt; in his right hand he grasped a crooked club of wild olive.

The Rustic Singers of Idyll IX only begin their songs when they have

set the calves beneath the cows and the bulls to run with the barren heifers.

The couch of fair skins, by the cool stream, on which Daphnis lies, is made from the herd driven over a cliff by a gale. This is the oxherd's 'ease', and the goatherd's 'wealth of dreamland' is

many a ewe and many a she-goat, and fleeces, from them lying at my head and my feet. And on my fire of oaklogs puddings boil, and dry acorns roast there in wintry weather.

Wolves, foxes, locusts and beetles are as much part of the experience as balm and rockrose and apples and honey. The herdsman who goes to the festival, in Idyll IV, leaves thin bulls and calves, for he has 'fallen in love with cursed victory'. Within the beautiful development of the pastoral songs this sense of a simple community, living on narrow margins and experiencing the delights of summer and fertility the more intensely because they also know winter and barrenness and accident, is intensely present:

as spring is sweeter than winter, as apple than sloe; as the ewe is deeper of fleece than her lamb.

Of course, as the tradition developed, it was possible to extract, for their evident delight, the invocations of summer: from Hesiod –

> When the cardoon flowers and the loud cicada sings
> perched on a tree . . .
> > . . . O give me then
> the shade of a rock, with Biblis' wine set by,
> and bread of the best, and the milk of goats drained dry;

or from Theocritus:

> All rich delight and luxury was there:
> Larks and bright finches singing in the air;
> The brown bees flying round about the well;
> The ring-dove moaning; everywhere the smell
> Of opulent summer and of ripening-tide:
> Pears at our feet and apples at our side
> Rolling in plenteousness; in piles around
> Branches, with damsons burdening to the ground
> Strewn for our feast.

At a very much later date, this could be seen, by false extraction, as the essence, the only essence, of pastoral. But as we move from Theocritus to Virgil, two centuries later, in the first century before Christ, we find a continuity of pastoral which in and through its literary elaboration maintains its contact with the working year and with the real social conditions of country life. Virgil's *Eclogues* are in one sense more idealized, as they are also more elaborate, than the idylls of Theocritus; but the rural disturbance of his own Italy often breaks through into the poetically distant Arcadia. Thus in Eclogue I, Meliboeus' familiar invocation –

Ah fortunate old man, here, among hallowed springs
And familiar streams you'll enjoy the longed-for shade, the cool shade.
Here, as of old, where your neighbour's land marches with yours,
The sally hedge, with bees of Hybla sipping its blossom,

Shall often hum you gently to sleep. On the other side
Vine-dressers will sing to the breezes at the crag's foot;
And all the time your favourites, the husky-voiced wood pigeons
Shall coo away, and turtle-doves make moan in the elm tops

is in explicit contrast to his own condition, as an evicted small
farmer:

But the rest of us must go from here and be dispersed –
To Scythia, bone-dry Africa, the chalky spate of the Oxus,
Even to Britain – that place cut off at the very world's end.
Ah, when shall I see my native land again? after long years,
Or never? – see the turf-dressed roof of my simple cottage,
And wondering gaze at the ears of corn that were all my kingdom.
To think of some godless soldier owning my well-farmed fallow.
A foreigner reaping these crops! To such a pass has civil
Dissension brought us . . .
No more singing for me.

Again, in Eclogue IX, the pastoral singing is directly related to
the hopes and fears of the small farmers under threat of confiscation of their land:

Oh, Lycidas, that I should have lived to see an outsider
Take over my little farm – a thing I had never feared.
And tell me, 'You're dispossessed, you old tenants, you've got to
    go'.
We're down and out. And look how Chance turns the tables on us –
These are *his* goats (rot them) you see me taking to market.

Poetry itself might seek to protect the land and its customary
farmers, but under the pressure of violence and the consequences
of war, as the ex-soldiers are resettled by large-scale confiscation,

poems such as ours, Lycidas, stand no more chance than doves if an
eagle comes.

And we remember that Virgil himself was the son of a smallholder whose land was threatened by just such a confiscation.
    Thus the contrast within Virgilian pastoral is between the
pleasures of rural settlement and the threat of loss and eviction.
This developed, in its turn, into a contrast already familiar from
some earlier literature, in times of war and civil disturbance,
when the peace of country life could be contrasted with the
disturbance of war and civil war and the political chaos of the

cities. It depends very much how this contrast is made. It can be a present fact, as in Eclogues I and IX. It can be a living retrospect, as in the sad memories of Meliboeus. Or it can begin to be built into a wider system of ideas: a scheme of the past or of the future. In some passages of the *Georgics*, for example at the end of Book 2, there is the note of idealization, of extended retrospect, which was to become so characteristic. The pastoral landscape of Theocritus had been immediate and close at hand: just outside the walls of the city. The Golden Age of Hesiod had been a mythical memory, contrasting with the iron time of modern men, in which labour is necessary and is admired. A transmutation occurs, in some parts of Virgil, in which the landscape becomes more distant, becomes in fact Arcadia, and the Golden Age is seen as present there, at once summoned and celebrated by the power of poetry:

> For them, far from the strife of arms, the earth, ever just, pours an easy living on the land of its own accord . . . By their own will the trees and the fields bear produce, and he picks it. His peace is secure and his living cannot fail.

It is only a short step from a natural delight in the fertility of the earth to this magical invocation of a land which needs no farming. But it is a step that is sometimes taken, though only in isolated passages, in the complicated movement of the *Georgics*: that prolonged and detailed description and celebration of the farmer's year; of his tools, his methods, his dangers, his enemies, his skills and his lifetime's efforts. What needs to be emphasized is not only the emergence of the idealizing tone, but also that it is not yet abstracted from the whole of a working country life. Yet at the same time the idyllic note is being sounded in another context: that of the future: of a restoration, a second coming, of the golden age; one that is even politically imminent, as in Eclogue IV:

> Goats shall walk home, their udders taut with milk, and nobody
> Herding them; the ox will have no fear of the lion . . .
> . . . Then shall grapes hang wild and reddening on thorn trees
> And honey sweat like dew from the hard bark of oaks . . .
> . . . The soil will need no harrowing, the vine no pruning-knife
> And the tough ploughman may at last unyoke his oxen.

28

This magical Utopian vision is a prophecy: 'run looms and weave the future'. And it thus includes within its celebration the consciousness of the very different present from which the restoration will be a release.

So that even in these developments, of classical pastoral and other rural literature, which inaugurate tones and images of an ideal kind, there is almost invariably a tension with other kinds of experience: summer with winter; pleasure with loss; harvest with labour; singing with a journey; past or future with the present. The achievement, if it can be called that, of the Renaissance adaptation of just these classical modes is that, step by step, these living tensions are excised, until there is nothing countervailing, and selected images stand as themselves: not in a living but in an enamelled world. Thus the retrospect of Meliboeus, on the life he is forced to leave, becomes the 'source' of a thousand pretty exercises on an untroubled rural delight and peace. Even more remarkably, the famous second Epode of Horace – the *Beatus Ille* to which a thousand poems of happy rural retreat are confidently traced – had its crucial tension commonly excised. The celebration of herds and honey and fruit and clear streams, far from war and the city and the cold practice of usury, had been in Horace the sentimental reflection of a usurer, thinking of turning farmer, calling in his money and then, at the climax of the poem, lending it out again. The first conscious and then conventional excision of this irony is a fact even more important than the nominal and thematic continuity.

All traditions are selective: the pastoral tradition quite as much as any other. Where poets run scholars follow, and questions about the 'pastoral' poetry or the poetry of 'rural retreat' of our own sixteenth to eighteenth centuries are again and again turned aside by the confident glossing and glozing of the reference back. We must not look, with Crabbe and others, at what the country was really like: that is a utilitarian or materialist, perhaps even a peasant response. Let us remember, instead, that this poem is based on Horace, Epode II or Virgil, Eclogue IV; that among the high far names are Theocritus and Hesiod: the Golden Age in another sense.

It is time that this bluff was called. Academic gloss has made such a habit of tracing influences that it needs the constant correction of a Coleridge, to those

who seem to hold, that every possible thought and image is traditional; who have no notion that there are such things as fountains in the world, small as well as great; and who would therefore charitably derive every rill they behold flowing, from a perforation made in some other man's tank.

(Preface to *Christabel*)

And how much more is this necessary when the presumed sources, the other men's tanks, have been so altered and simplified that nobody can easily see what has happened, meanwhile, to the water.

(ii)

We must therefore use some illusion to render a Pastoral delightful; and this consists in exposing the best side only of a shepherd's life, and in concealing its miseries.

When Pope could say that, the 'tradition' had been altered. 'No longer truth, though shown in verse.' The long critical dispute, in the seventeenth and eighteenth centuries, on the character of pastoral poetry had this much, at least, as common ground. What was at issue was mainly whether such an idyll, the delightful Pastoral, should be referred always to the Golden Age, as Rapin and the neo-classicists argued; or to the more permanent and indeed timeless idea of the tranquillity of life in the country, as Fontenelle and others maintained. In the former case, because it was the Golden Age, there was really peace and innocence. In the latter, there could still be an idea of these, a conventional literary illusion in native and contemporary scenes:

exposing to the Eye only the Tranquility of a Shepherd's Life, and dissembling or concealing its meanness, as also in showing only its Innocence, and hiding its Miseries.

It is with this in mind that we can understand Crabbe:

> But when amid such pleasing scenes I trace
> The poor laborious natives of the place,
> And see the mid-day sun, with fervid ray,
> On their bare heads and dewy temples play;
> While some, with feebler heads and fainter hearts,

Deplore their fortune, yet sustain their parts:
Then shall I dare these real ills to hide
In tinsel trappings of poetic pride?

The question 'shall I dare?' carries the felt outrage, at one of those critical moments, a crisis of perspective, when habits, institutions and experiences clash. Who are they, who dare in this way, to whom Crabbe addresses himself?

Oh trifle not with wants you cannot feel,
Nor mock the misery of a stinted meal;
Homely, not wholesome, plain, not plenteous, such
As you who praise would never deign to touch.
Ye gentle souls, who dream of rural ease,
Whom the smooth stream and smoother sonnet please;
Go! if the peaceful cot your praises share,
Go look within, and ask if peace be there.

They are a numerous company, these pretenders to simplicity. It is possible to follow a direct line from Virgil, at the end of which, as in the English 'Augustans', the eclogue has become a highly artificial and abstracted form: its simplicities wholly external. But the line runs also from the *Georgics*, and in Politian and Alamanni, for example, in the late fifteenth and early sixteenth centuries, there is inspiration as well as imitation: the verse of Politian's *Rusticus* is in Latin but the working year he describes is that of the Tuscan peasant; Alamanni's *La Coltivazione* is a modern Italian equivalent to the working descriptions of country life of the *Georgics*.

Yet 'pastoral', with its once precise meaning, was undergoing in the same period an extraordinary transformation. Its most serious element was a renewed intensity of attention to natural beauty, but this is now the nature of observation, of the scientist or the tourist, rather than of the working countryman. Thus the descriptive element in original pastoral could be separated out, and a whole tradition of 'nature poetry', strong and moving in these separated ways, could be founded to go on its major course, over several centuries into our own time. The other main element was very different: pastoral became theatrical and romantic, in the strict senses. The pastoral romance, from Boccaccio to Sannazzaro's *Arcadia* (*c.* 1500), was a new form, in which the eclogue and natural description were absorbed into the essentially different world of an idealized romantic love. That the shepherds in pastoral had sung love-songs was the nominal basis, but the shepherds and nymphs who now begin to appear are lay figures in an aristocratic entertainment. The pastoral drama, beginning with Tasso's *Aminta* (1572), is similarly the creation of a princely court, in which the shepherd is an idealized mask, a courtly disguise: a traditionally innocent figure through whom, paradoxically, intrigue can be elaborated. This filigree game, which continued as a form of aristocratic entertainment as late as Marie Antoinette, and which has left its physical legacy in its thousands of painted porcelain figures, has more connection, obviously, with the real interests of the court than with country life in any of its possible forms.

Yet this was not always realized. Pope took the game for the fact, in his essay on pastoral, and recommended description

not . . . as shepherds at this day really are but as they may be conceiv'd to have been; when the best of men follow'd the employment.

If courtiers played shepherd long enough, original shepherds must have been aristocrats.

But the offered simplicity was not only this kind of fancy dress. A second real interest of the time found its way into pastoral: the medieval and post-medieval habit of allegory. Puttenham in 1589 argued that the Eclogue was devised

not of purpose to counterfeit or represent the rusticall manner of loves or communications: but under the vaile of homely persons, and in rude speeches, to insinuate and glance at great matters.

He went on to say that this was true of Virgil, and this is the exact process of selective cultural adaptation: Virgil, like Hesiod, could raise the most serious questions of life and its purposes in the direct world in which the working year and the pastoral song are still there in their own right. What happened in the aristocratic transformation was the reduction of these primary activities to forms, whether the 'vaile' of allegory or the fancy dress of court games. It is a significant change, but it has been so prepotent – though its impulses, one would think, had been so long dead – that the ordinary modern meaning of pastoral, in the critical discourse of otherwise twentieth-century writers, has been derived from these forms, rather than from the original substance or from its more significant successors. 'Pastoral' means, we are told, the simple matter in which general truths are embodied or implied: even a modern proletarian industrial novel can be pastoral in this sense! But while as a critical procedure for understanding, say, Spenser, this is fair enough, its extension is absurd, and the absurdity has a point. As in so many other areas of English literary thought, there has been an effective and voluntary congealment at the point of significant historical transition, from a feudal to a bourgeois world. If pastoral is only a disguise or an allegory, Crabbe's question has no point; it is no more than a rude noise. But Crabbe's is a question which has to be answered, if the reality of a major transition is to be acknowledged and understood.

For the pastoral of the courts and of the aristocratic houses was not, as it came through, the really significant development. Isolated in time and in status, its modes and its realities are quite easily understood. What is much more significant is the internal transformation of just this artificial mode in the direction and in the interest of a new kind of society: that of a developing agrarian capitalism. Neo-pastoral as a court entertainment is one thing; neo-pastoral in its new location, the country-house and its estate, is quite another. We must follow the development of the artificial eclogue and idyll, but we shall only arrive at the decisive transition when these have been relocated, in a new ideology, in the country-house.

(iii)

Poets have often lent their tongues to princes, who are in a position to pay or to reply. What has been lent to shepherds, and at what rates of interest, is much more in question. It is not easy to forget that Sidney's *Arcadia*, which gives a continuing title to English neo-pastoral, was written in a park which had been made by enclosing a whole village and evicting the tenants. The elegant game was then only at arm's length – a rough arm's length – from a visible reality of country life.

There were, of course, other pastoral metaphors. The good

shepherd was a permanently available Christ-figure, the loving pastor, who could be set against the corruption of the church. There are English examples of this in the May and July and September eclogues of Spenser's *The Shepherd's Calendar*. More generally, by what seems an obvious association, the life of the shepherd could be made to stand for the life of nature and for natural feeling. This convention was worked to a thread, in the late sixteenth and early seventeenth centuries, but in some of the shorter poems there is a freshness which is only rarely present in the elaborated figures and devices of drama and romance; it is still a known country, and not merely Arcadia.

> In the merry month of May,
> In a morn by break of day,
> Forth I walk'd by the wood-side,
> When as May was in his pride.

But this verse of Nicholas Breton's, in which the lovers by the wood are suddenly Phillida and Coridon is less characteristic than the crystal fountains, the scorched vales, and the madrigal birds which are the ordinary neo-pastoral setting. The metaphor holds, in feeling, in the conscious ambiguity of Marlowe's

> belt of straw and ivy-buds
> With coral clasps and amber studs.

But there is a more permanent interest in the way in which the neo-pastoral metaphor tries to authenticate itself in observed nature. The court toy and the hyperbole of feeling are returned, with some loss and some gain, to the country walk. It is at this point, more significantly than when the neo-pastoral convention was a total literary artifice, that the difficult inquiry begins.

There had of course already been counter-pastoral, of a kind. The working shepherd, already present in the Towneley *Secunda Pastorum* in his figurative and in his actual role above Bethlehem, was present again in the winter song in *Love's Labour's Lost*. But the ordinary counter was Raleigh's to Marlowe: the relentless intrusion of time on that endless neo-pastoral May:

> But Time drives flocks from field to fold,
> When rivers rage and rocks grow cold.

34

Had joys no date, nor age no need, the pastoral appeal would convince.

What is then interesting is the movement beyond romantic love, the perpetual neo-pastoral May, to the way of life as a whole: a new metaphor, in the English country, for the oldest rural ideal. Not the nymphs and shepherds of neo-pastoral romance, in their courtly love in the parks and gardens; but the quiet, the innocence, the simple plenty of the countryside: the metaphorical but also the actual retreat. Traditional images were of course immediately available: the Golden Age and Paradise. It is interesting to see Michael Drayton in his poem *To the Virginian Voyage* locating both in a colony:

> *Virginia,*
> Earth's only paradise.
>
> Where nature hath in store
> Fowl, venison, and fish,
> And the fruitfull'st soil
> Without your toil
> Three harvests more,
> All greater than your wish . . .
>
> . . . To whom the Golden Age
> Still nature's laws doth give,
> No other cares attend,
> But them to defend
> From winter's rage
> That long there doth not live.

This kind of vision becomes a commonplace. There is a very pure form of it in an anonymous late seventeenth-century poem:

> How beautiful the World at first was made
> Ere Mankind by Ambition was betray'd.
> The happy Swain in these enamell'd Fields
> Possesses all the Good that Plenty yields;
> Pure without mixture, as it first did come,
> From the great Treasury of Nature's Womb.
> Free from Disturbance here he lives at ease
> Contented with a little Flock's encrease,
> And covered with the gentle wings of Peace.
> No Fears, no Storms of War his Thoughts molest
> Ambition is a stranger to his Breast;
> His Sheep, his Crook, and Pipe, are all his Store,
> He needs not, neither does he covet more.

35

Here we can see the simple vision of natural plenty reabsorbed into a moral attitude with social implications: transferred from its classical sources to the 'enamell'd Fields'. And country life, as traditionally, is an innocent alternative to ambition, disturbance and war. There are countless poems which offer this view, sometimes dreamy, sometimes rapt. As in these lines from Charles Cotton's aptly named poem *The Retirement*:

> Good God! how sweet are all things here!
> How beautifull the Fields appear!
> How cleanly do we feed and lie!
> Lord what good hours do we keep!
> How quietly we sleep!
> What peace! What unanimity!

This is a form of that persistent desire to get away from what is seen as the world, or from what, more interestingly, is seen as other people. The 'we' of the lines quoted is by the end of the same poem 'I':

> Lord! would men let me alone,
> What an over-happy one
> Should I think my self to be.

This note can be heard again in Abraham Cowley's *The Wish*, in an explicit contrast with 'this great *Hive, the City*':

> Oh, *Fountains*, when in you shall I
> My self, eas'd of unpeaceful thoughts, espy?
> Oh *Fields*! Oh *Woods*! when, when shall I be made
> The happy Tenant of your shade?

And it is then interesting to see the steady inclusion, in what at one extreme is a simple unlocalized reverie, of another quality from contemporary social experience and desire.

Cowley sees the realized self as the 'happy tenant'. This is partly the absorption of actual social and economic relations into the natural vision, as in John Hall's *Pastoral Hymne*:

> Great Lord, from whom each Tree receaves,
> Then pays againe as rent, his leaves.

There is a strange poem by Richard Lovelace, *Elinda's Glove*, in which the romantic compliment is made wholly from this kind of imagery:

36

> Thou snowy Farme with thy five Tenements!
> Tell thy white Mistris here was one
> That call'd to pay his dayly Rents:
> But she a gathering Flowers and Hearts is gone,
> And thou left void to rude Possession.
>
> But grieve not pretty *Ermin* Cabinet,
> Thy Alabaster Lady will come home;
> If not, what Tenant can there fit
> The slender turnings of thy narrow Roome,
> But must ejected be by his owne doome?
>
> Then give me leave to leave my Rent with thee;
> Five kisses, one unto a place . . .

Here, through the elaboration of the conceit, we see moment-
arily more of actual seventeenth-century country life than in the
poems of retirement. Yet an increasing location in an actual
social estate can be seen in some of the later poems: it is that of
the small independent freeholder. There is Nahum Tate's

> Grant me, indulgent Heaven! a rural seat
> Rather contemptible than great.

Or Pomfret's:

> I'd have a clear and competent estate
> That I might live genteely, but not great:
> As much as I could moderately spend:
> A little more, sometimes, t'oblige a friend.
> Nor should the sons of poverty repine
> Too much at fortune, they should taste of mine.

Or Pope's unqualified version of Horace:

> Happy the man whose wish and care
> A few paternal acres bound
> Content to breathe his native air
> In his own ground.
>
> Whose herds with milk, whose fields with bread,
> Whose flocks supply him with attire;
> Whose trees in summer yield him shade,
> In winter fire.

The unworked-for providence of nature, that mythical or
utopian image, is now, significantly, acquiring a social dimension:

a 'clear and competent estate', well supplied with hired help. As in Matthew Green's

> A farm some twenty miles from town
> Small, tight, salubrious and my own:
> Two maids, that never saw the town,
> A serving man not quite a clown,
> A boy to help to tread the mow,
> And drive, while t'other holds the plough ...

When economic reality returns, it is again absorbed into the natural vision:

> And may my humble dwelling stand
> Upon some chosen spot of land ...
> Fit dwelling for the feather'd throng
> Who pay their quit-rents with a song.

What we can see happening, in this interesting development, is the conversion of conventional pastoral into a localized dream and then, increasingly, in the late seventeenth and early eighteenth centuries, into what can be offered as a description and thence an idealization of actual English country life and its social and economic relations. It was against this, as well as against the conventional simplicities of literary neo-pastoral, that Crabbe was making his protest.

(iv)

For it is not only a question of formal or informal pastoral, which, as I have said, are quite easily recognized. There is a more difficult case, in some important poems which have been commonly read as describing an actual rural economy: an existing social base for the perpetual peace and innocence of the neo-pastoral dream. These are the poems of country houses, which Cowley had celebrated as a part of Nature, in *Solitude*:

> Hail, old Patrician Trees, so great and good!
> Hail, ye Plebeian under wood!
> Where the Poetique Birds rejoyce,
> And for their quiet Nests and plenteous Food,
> Pay with their grateful voice.

> Hail the poor Muses richest Manor Seat!
> Ye Country Houses and Retreat,
> Which all the happy Gods so Love,
> That for you oft they quit their Bright and Great
> Metropolis above.

Here the wood, the birds, the poets and the gods are seen literally
(the figure is so complete) as the social structure – the natural
order – of seventeenth-century England. It is interesting to
compare Fanshawe, writing directly of the actual situation,
when the gentry were being ordered back to their estates in
1630. What he sees is

> one blest Isle:
> Which in a sea of plenty swam
> And Turtles sang on ev'ry Bough,
> A safe retreat to all that came,
> As ours is now.

That is the familiar image of a smiling country.

> Yet we, as if some Foe were here,
> Leave the despised fields to Clowns,
> And come to save ourselves as 'twere
> In walled Towns.

And so they must go back:

> The sap and blood o' th' land, which fled
> Into the Root, and choakt the Heart,
> Are bid their quick'ning power to spread,
> Through ev'ry part.

It is the image that Milton more generously developed, drawing
on the associated image of culture as natural growth, in his appeal
for a national education: 'communicating the natural heat of
Government and Culture more distributively to all extreme
parts, which now lie num and neglected'. Fanshawe, in his
return, foresees the breeding of another Virgil (that reference
was dominant), but his main appeal is more direct:

> Nor let the Gentry grudge to go
> Into those places whence they grow.

It is a way of seeing the crisis of seventeenth-century rural

England, but of course it also reminds us that Cowley's 'bright and great metropolis' was not quit as often or as naturally as all that.

Yet at the centre of the structure of feeling which is here in question – a relation between the country houses and a responsible civilization – are the poems to actual places and men: notably Ben Jonson's *Penshurst* and *To Sir Robert Wroth*, and Thomas Carew's *To Saxham*. These are not, in any simple sense, pastoral or neo-pastoral, but they use a particular version of country life as a way of expressing, in the form of a compliment to a house or its owner, certain social and moral values.

> How blest art thou, canst love the countrey, Wroth,
> Whether by choice, or fate, or both;
> And, though so neere the citie, and the court,
> Art tane with neither's vice, nor sport.

The life of a country gentleman is thus celebrated as an explicit contrast to the life of the court and the city. The figures of city lawyer, city capitalist, and courtier, are brought in to point the moral.

In Wroth's rural economy, as the poem proceeds and as

> the rout of rurall folke come thronging in

there is an emphasis on the absence of pride and greed and calculation. And then Jonson can turn, positively, to identify and localize the pastoral convention:

> Such, and no other, was that age of old,
> Which boasts t'have had the head of gold.

But is it really so, past the lattice of compliment? Has a neo-pastoral vision acquired a social base, in a Tudor country house? Some critics have taken it so, but the complexity of *To Penshurst* would in any case make us pause. For what is most remarkable about it, in any open reading, is its procedure of definition by negatives:

> Thou art not, Penshurst, built to envious show
> Of touch, or marble; nor canst boast a row
> Of polish'd pillars, or a roofe of gold:
> Thou hast no lantherne, wherof tales are told;

> Or stayre, or courts; but stand'st an ancient pile,
> And these grudg'd at, art reverenc'd the while . . .
> . . . And though they walls be of the countrey stone,
> They' are rear'd with no man's ruine, no mans grone,
> There's none, that dwell about them, wish them downe . . .
> . . . Now, Penshurst, they that will proportion thee
> With other edifices, when they see
> Those proud ambitious heaps, and nothing else.
> May say, their lords have built, but thy lord dwells.

This declaration by negative and contrast, not now with city and court but with other country houses, is enough in itself to remind us that we can make no simple extension from Penshurst to a whole country civilization. The forces of pride, greed and calculation are evidently active among landowners as well as among city merchants and courtiers. What is being celebrated is then perhaps an idea of rural society, as against the pressures of a new age; and the embodiment of this idea is the house in which Jonson has been entertained.

This is where the comparison with Carew's *To Saxham* is particularly relevant. For there too, as it happens, there is a definition by negatives, though now in a different house:

> Thou hast no Porter at the door
> T'examine, or keep back the poor;
> Nor locks nor bolts; thy gates have been
> Made only to let strangers in.

Or again, more subtly:

> The cold and frozen air had sterv'd,
> Much poore, if not by thee preserv'd,
> Whose prayers have made thy Table blest
> With plenty, far above the rest.

The island of Charity is the house where the poet himself eats; but that it is an island, in an otherwise harsh economy, is the whole point of the successive compliments.

We need not refuse Jonson and Carew the courtesy of their lucky exceptions: their Penshurst and Saxham 'rear'd', unlike others, 'with no man's ruine, no mans grone'; with none, 'that dwell about them', wishing them 'downe'. There were, we need not doubt, such houses and such men, but they were at best the gentle exercise of a power that was elsewhere, on their own evidence, mean and brutal. The morality is not, when we look into it, the fruit of the economy; it is a local stand and standard against it.

It is of course clear that in each of the poems, though more strongly and convincingly in Jonson, the social order is seen as part of a wider order: what is now sometimes called a natural order, with metaphysical sanctions. Certainly nothing is more remarkable than the stress on the providence of Nature, but this, we must see on reflection, is double-edged. What kind of wit is it exactly – for it must be wit; the most ardent traditional-ists will hardly claim it for observation – which has the birds and other creatures offering themselves to be eaten? The estate of Penshurst, as Jonson sees it:

> To crowne thy open table, doth provide
> The purpled pheasant with the speckled side:
> The painted partrich lyes in every field
> And, for thy messe, is willing to be kill'd.

Carew extends this same hyperbole:

> The Pheasant, Partridge, and the Lark
> Flew to my house, as to the Ark.
> The willing Oxe, of himselfe came
> Home to the slaughter, with the Lamb,
> And every beast did thither bring
> Himselfe to be an offering.
> The scalie herd, more pleasure took
> Bath'd in the dish than in the brook.

In fact the wit depends, in such passages, on a shared and conscious point of view towards nature. The awareness of hyper-bole is there, is indeed what is conventional in just this literary convention, and is controlled and ratified, in any wider view, by a common consciousness. At one level this is a willing and happy ethic of consuming, made evident by the organization of the poems around the centrality of the dining-table. Yet the possible grossness of this, as in Carew (a willing largeness of hyperbole, as in so many Cavalier poems, as the awareness of an alternative point of view makes simple statement impossible) is modified in Jonson by a certain pathos, a conscious realization of his situation:

> And I not faine to sit (as some, this day,
> At great men's tables) and yet dine away.
> Here no man tells my cups; nor, standing by,
> A waiter, doth my gluttony envy:
> But gives me what I call, and lets me eate.

It is difficult not to feel the relief of that. Indeed there is more than a hint, in the whole tone of this hospitable eating and drinking, of that easy, insatiable exploitation of the land and its creatures – a prolonged delight in an organized and corporative production and consumption – which is the basis of many early phases of intensive agriculture: the land is rich, and will be made to provide. But it is then more difficult to talk, in a simple way, of a 'natural order', as if this was man in concert with nature. On the contrary: this natural order is simply and decisively on its way to table.

Of course, in both Jonson and Carew, though again more convincingly in Jonson, this view of the providence of nature is linked to a human sharing: all are welcome, even the poor, to be fed at this board. And it is this stress, more than any other, which has supported the view of a responsible civilization, in which men care for each other directly and personally, rather than through the abstractions of a more complicated and more commercial society. This, we are told, is the natural order of responsibility and neighbourliness and charity: words we do not now clearly understand, since Old England fell.

Of course one sees what is meant, and as a first approximation, a simple impulse, it is kindly. But the Christian tradition of charity is at just this point weak. For it is a charity of consumption only, as Rosa Luxemburg first pointed out:

The Roman proletarians did not live by working, but from the alms which the government doled out. So the demands of the Christians for collective property did not relate to the means of production, but the means of consumption.

And then, as Adrian Cunningham has argued, this version of charity – of loving relations between men expressed as a community of consumption, with the Christian board and breaking of bread as its natural images, and the feast as its social consummation – was prolonged into periods and societies in which it became peripheral or even damaging. A charity of production – of loving relations between men actually working and producing what is ultimately, in whatever proportions, to be shared – was neglected, not seen, and at times suppressed, by this habitual reference to a charity of consumption, an eating and drinking communion, which when applied to ordinary working societies was inevitably a mystification. All uncharity at work, it was readily assumed, could be redeemed by the charity of the consequent feast. In the complex of feeling and reference derived from this tradition, it matters very much, moreover, that the name of the god and the name of the master are significantly single – our Lord.

Any mystification, however, requires effort. The world of Penshurst or of Saxham can be seen as a moral economy only by conscious selection and emphasis. And this is just what we get: not only in the critical reading I have referred to, but in Jonson's and Carew's actual poems. There were of course social reasons for that way of seeing: the identification of the writers, as guests, with the social position of their hosts, consuming what other men had produced. But a traditional image, already becoming complicated, was an indispensable poetic support. It is not only the Golden Age, as in Jonson to Sir Robert Wroth, though Penshurst, in its first positive description, is seen through classical literature: the woods of Kent contain Dryads and Pan and Bacchus, and the providing deities of the charity are Penates. More deeply, however, in a conventional association of Christian and classical myth, the provident land is seen as Eden. This country in which all things come naturally to man, for his use and enjoyment and without his effort, is that Paradise:

> The early cherry, with the later plum,
> Fig, grape and quince, each in his time doth come:
> The blushing apricot, and woolly peach
> Hang on thy walls, that every child may reach.

Except that it is not seen as Paradise; it is seen as Penshurst, a natural order arranged by a proprietary lord and lady. The manipulation is evident when we remember Marvell's somewhat similar lines in *The Garden*:

> The Nectaren, and curious Peach
> Into my hands themselves do reach;
> Stumbling on Melons, as I pass,
> Insnar'd with flowers, I fall on grass.

Here the enjoyment of what seems a natural bounty, a feeling of paradise in the garden, is exposed to another kind of wit: the easy consumption goes before the fall. And we can then remember that the whole result of the fall from paradise was that instead of picking easily from an all-providing nature, man had to earn his bread in the sweat of his brow; that he incurred, as a common fate, the curse of labour. What is really happening, in Jonson's and Carew's celebrations of a rural order, is an extraction of just this curse, by the power of art: a magical recreation of what can be seen as a natural bounty and then a willing charity: both serving to ratify and bless the country landowner, or, by a characteristic reification, his house. Yet this magical extraction of the curse of labour is in fact achieved by a simple extraction of the existence of labourers. The actual men and women who rear the animals and drive them to the house and kill them and prepare them for meat; who trap the pheasants and partridges and catch the fish; who plant and manure and prune and harvest the fruit trees: these are not present; their work is all done for them by a natural order. When they do at last appear, it is merely as the 'rout of rurall folke' or, more simply, as 'much poore', and what we are then shown is the charity and lack of condescension with which they are given what, now and somehow, not they but the natural order has given for food, into the lord's hands. It is this condition, this set of relationships, that is finally ratified by the consummation of the feast. It is worth setting briefly alongside this a later description of a country feast, by one of the labourers: Stephen Duck, in the late 1720s:

> A Table plentifully spread we find,
> And jugs of huming Ale to cheer the Mind,
> Which he, too gen'rous, pushes round so fast,
> We think no Toils to come, nor mind the past.
> But the next Morning soon reveals the Cheat,
> When the same Toils we must again repeat;
> To the same Barns must back again return,
> To labour there for Room for next Year's Corn.

45

It is this connection, between the feast and work, that the earlier images significantly obscure, taking the passing moment in which anyone might forget labour and acquiesce in 'the Cheat', and making it 'natural' and permanent. It is this way of seeing that really counts. Jonson looks out over the fields of Penshurst and sees, not work, but a land yielding of itself. Carew, characteristically, does not even look:

> Though frost, and snow, lock'd from mine eyes
> That beauty which without door lyes . . .
> . . . Yet (Saxham) thou within thy gate
> Art of thy selfe so delicate,
> So full of native sweets, that bless
> Thy roof with inward happiness:
> As neither from, nor to thy store,
> Winter takes ought, or Spring adds more.

So that here not only work, but even the turning produce of the seasons, is suppressed or obscured in the complimentary mystification: an innate bounty: 'native sweets'. To call this a natural order is then an abuse of language. It is what the poems are: not country life but social compliment; the familiar hyperboles of the aristocracy and its attendants.

The social order within which Jonson's and Carew's poems took conventional shape was in fact directly described, in another kind of country poem, of which Herrick's *The Hock-Cart* (1648) is a good example. Here the fact of labour is acknowledged:

> Come Sons of Summer, by whose toile
> We are the Lords of Wine and Oile:
> By whose tough labours, and rough hands,
> We rip up first, then reap our lands.
> Crown'd with the eares of corne, now come,
> And to the Pipe, sing Harvest home.

But this is that special kind of work-song, addressed to the work of others. When the harvest has been brought home, the poem continues:

> Come forth, my Lord, and see the Cart.

This lord is (in the poem's address) the 'Right Honourable Lord Mildmay, Earle of Westmorland', and Herrick places himself between the lord and the labourers to make explicit (what in Jonson and Carew had been implicit and mystified) the governing social relations. The labourers must drink to the Lord's health, and then remember all to go back to work, like the animals:

> Ye must revoke
> The patient Oxe unto the Yoke
> And all goe back unto the plough
> And Harrow (though they're hang'd up now)
> And, you must know, your Lord's word's true,
> Feed him ye must, whose food fills you.
> And that this pleasure is like raine
> Not sent ye for to drowne your paine
> But for to make it spring againe.

It is crude in feeling, this early and jollying kind of man-management, which used the metaphors of rain and spring to see even the drink as a way of getting more labour (and more pain) But what is there on the surface –

> Feed him ye must, whose food fills you

– is the aching paradox, which is subsumed in the earlier images of natural bounty. It is perhaps not surprising that *The Hock-Cart* is less often quoted, as an example of a natural and moral economy, than *Penshurst* or *To Saxham*. Yet all that is in question is the degree of consciousness of real processes. What Herrick embarrassingly intones is what Jonson and Carew mediate. It is a social order, and a consequent way of seeing, which we are not now likely to forget.

4   Golden Ages

But there is still a crisis of perspective. When we moved back in time, consistently directed to an earlier and happier rural England, we could find no place, no period, in which we could seriously rest.

Yet the backward reference has its own logic. If we take a long enough period, it is easy to see a fundamental transformation of English country life. But the change is so extended and so complicated, to say nothing of its important regional variations, that there seems no point at which we can sharply distinguish what it would be convenient to call separate epochs. The detailed histories indicate everywhere that many old forms, old practices and old ways of feeling survived into periods in which the general direction of new development was clear and decisive. And then what seems an old order, a 'traditional' society, keeps appearing, reappearing, at bewilderingly various dates: in practice as an idea, to some extent based in experience, against which contemporary change can be measured. The structure of feeling within which this backward reference is to be understood is then not primarily a matter of historical explanation and analysis. What is really significant is this particular kind of reaction to the fact of change, and this has more real and more interesting social causes.

Thus in the poems we have been looking at there is no historical reference back. What we find, nevertheless, is an idealization of feudal and immediately post-feudal values: of an order based on settled and reciprocal social and economic relations of an avowedly total kind. It is then important that the poems coincide, in time, with a period in which another order – that of capitalist agriculture – was being successfully pioneered. For behind that coincidence is a conflict of values which is still crucial. These celebrations of a feudal or an aristocratic order –

> And you must know, your Lord's word's true,
> Feed him ye must, whose food fills you

– have been widely used, in an idealist retrospect, as a critique of capitalism. The emphases on obligation, on charity, on the open door to the needy neighbour, are contrasted, in a familiar vein of retrospective radicalism, with the capitalist thrust, the utilitarian reduction of all social relationships to a crude moneyed order.

This leads to an evident crisis of values in our own world. For a retrospective radicalism, against the crudeness and narrowness of a new moneyed order, is often made to do service as a critique of the capitalism of our own day: to carry humane feelings and yet ordinarily to attach them to a pre-capitalist and therefore irrecoverable world. A necessary social criticism is then directed to the safer world of the past: to a world of books and memories, in which the scholar can be professionally humane but in his own real world either insulated or indifferent. But also, and more important, this kind of critique of capitalism enfolds social values which, if they do become active, at once spring to the defence of certain kinds of order, certain social hierarchies and moral stabilities, which have a feudal ring but a more relevant and more dangerous contemporary application. Some of these 'rural' virtues, in twentieth-century intellectual movements, leave the land to become the charter of explicit social reaction: in the defence of traditional property settlements, or in the offensive against democracy in the name of blood and soil.

Yet many draw back before those points are reached. In Britain, identifiably, there is a precarious but persistent rural-intellectual radicalism: genuinely and actively hostile to industrialism and capitalism; opposed to commercialism and to the exploitation of environment; attached to country ways and feelings, the literature and the lore. But the point of decision, within any such feelings, is on the nature of the capitalist transition. As in every kind of radicalism the moment comes when any critique of the present must choose its bearings, between past and future. And if the past is chosen, as now so often and so deeply, we must push the argument through to the roots that are being defended; push attention, human attention, back to the natural economy, the moral economy, the organic society, from which the critical values are drawn.

There is an early complication. The most evident opponents of just this position are certain metropolitan intellectuals of an again identifiable kind. I mean not only the people who have never known rural settlements and whose ignorance can therefore be identified, but all those who have inherited a long contempt, from very diverse sources, of the peasant, the boor, the rural clown; who then have as their currency the accumulated hoard of party impersonations and accepted mimings of a truly rural distance; milk and straw and beasts and dung as the quick cues to parody and laughter. And they might be left to their amusements if they did not include and overlap with more serious possible positions. How many socialists, for example, have refused to pick up that settling archival sentence about the 'idiocy of rural life'? Until very recently, indeed until the peasant socialist revolutions of China and Cuba, this reflex was habitual among the metropolitan socialists of Europe. And behind it, all the time, was a more serious position, near the centre of historical argument. For it has been commonplace since Marx to speak, in some contexts, of the progressive character of capitalism, and within it of urbanism and of social modernization. The great indictments of capitalism, and of its long record of misery in factories and towns, have co-existed, within a certain historical scheme, with this repeated use of 'progressive' as a willing adjective about the same events. We hear again and again this brisk, impatient and as it is said realistic response: to the productive efficiency, the newly liberated forces, of the capitalist breakthrough; a simultaneous damnation and idealization of capitalism, in its specific forms of urban and industrial development; an unreflecting celebration of mastery – power, yield, production, man's mastery of nature – as if the exploitation of natural resources could be separated from the accompanying exploitation of men. What they say is damn this, praise this; and the intellectual formula for this emotional confusion is, hopefully, the dialectic. All that needs to be added, as the climax to a muddle, is the late observation, the saving qualification, that at a certain stage – is it now?; it was yesterday – capitalism begins to lose this progressive character and for further productive efficiency, for the more telling mastery of nature, must be replaced, superseded, by socialism. Against this powerful tendency, in which forms of socialism offer to complete the capitalist enterprise, even the old, sad, retrospective radicalism seems to bear and to embody a human concern.

But in the end it cannot do this, cannot be what it suggests. Between the simple backward look and the simple progressive thrust there is room for long argument but none for enlightenment. We must begin differently: not in the idealizations of one order or another, but in the history to which they are only partial and misleading responses.

Take first the idealization of a 'natural' or 'moral' economy on which so many have relied, as a contrast to the thrusting ruthlessness of the new capitalism. There was very little that was moral or natural about it. In the simplest technical sense, that it was a 'natural' subsistence agriculture, as yet unaffected by the drives of a market economy, it is already doubtful and subject to many exceptions; though part of this emphasis can be readily accepted. But the social order within which this agriculture was practised was as hard and as brutal as anything later experienced. Even if we exclude the wars and brigandage to which it was commonly subject, the uncountable thousands who grew crops and reared beasts only to be looted and burned and led away with tied wrists, this economy, even at peace, was an order of exploitation of a most thoroughgoing kind: a property in men as well as in land; a reduction of most men to working animals, tied by forced tribute, forced labour, or 'bought and sold like beasts'; 'protected' by law and custom only as animals and streams are protected, to yield more labour, more food, more blood; an economy directed, in all its working relations, to a physical and economic domination of a significantly total kind. 'The churl, like the willow, sprouts the better for being cropped.' That bailiff's maxim is in all essential respects the principle of this 'natural' and 'moral' economy.

Through the long generations men had been clearing and establishing their settlements, and at the edges and at intervals, always, they had lived for a time in these direct ways, with their corresponding imperatives and virtues. As we look back, at the earliest Britain, we have always to remember how few people there were, and how possible, locally, were their immediate settlements. The widely scattered Celtic farms; the villages of the Roman period, cultivating two or three per cent of today's land; the total population of the country rising in the historical millennium from just under to just over a million; these facts remind us how much early settlements can be seen as a direct struggle with nature, the clearing of wild land. But that is never the whole story. The tribal settlements were under the power of the sword and of tribute; the Celtic and Saxon and Scandinavian kingdoms were based on general and local seizure. And the pressure, even then, was for others to keep moving in; in conquest and in the flight from bad land, or from famine or terror. Or as the simplicities of local defence were built and developed into a military system, there was another kind of invasion: an altered distribution, internally, of authority and duty. From inside and outside there was this remorseless moving-in of the armed gangs, with their titles of importance, their kingships and their baronies, to feed from other men's harvests. And the armed gangs became social and natural orders, blessed by their gods and their churches, with at the bottom of the pyramid, over a tale of centuries, the working cultivator, the human and natural man – sometimes finding a living space, a settled working area; as often deprived of it – but in any case breaking the land and himself to support this rising social estate, which can be seen to culminate in the medieval 'order' of the Norman and then the English kings: a more complete because more organized and more extended exploitation, under its banner 'Feed him ye must.'

There is only one real question. Where do we stand, with whom do we identify, as we read the complaints of disturbance, as this order in its turn broke up? Is it with the serfs, the bordars and cotters, the villeins; or with the abstracted order to which, through successive generations, many hundreds of thousands of men were never more than instrumental? And supposing we could make that choice rightly – though the historian who really places himself with the majority of men, and tries to see the world as they were experiencing it, is always improbable – where do we identify, as the order develops into new kinds of order?

It depends, in part, on how the break-up is described. Conventionally it is often dated from the Black Death, in which, within a generation, more than a million people died and many settlements were abandoned. Successive outbreaks of plague had been reducing the pressure of a rising population on an extending cultivated land, and the social relations between lords and tenants and labourers had been correspondingly altered. But there were forces within the order itself which were in any case leading to change. There was the growth of towns and of monasteries: often founded by feudal lords but developing new and complicated social and economic relations and concepts. There was the clearance of woodlands, for timber, for fuel and for pasture, and the drive for more pasture, in the growth of the wool trade, led to major enclosures, the destruction of many arable villages, and the rapid development of new kinds of capitalist landlord. It is not, taken as a whole, a story of decline from the medieval order, but of vigorous, often brutally vigorous, growth. The suppression of the monasteries released large new areas of land for the consolidation of new kinds of ownership. Down to the Civil War there was some official resistance to wholesale enclosure and the new kinds of ownership, but in the Restoration a government of the new kind of landlord was at last in control. This marked the decisive establishment of the new order which had been developing for at least two centuries: an order already physically present in the great pastoral estates and in the rebuilt houses, especially the 'country houses' which since the beginning of the sixteenth century had been replacing the castles and the fortified manors and which, as we have seen, were to be the visible centres of the new social system. A more settled and centralized order – a system of social and economic rather than directly military and physical control – was now fully in being, in a more prosperous and more populated country. Following the fortunes, through these centuries, of the dominant interests, it is a story of growth and achievement, but for the majority of men it was the substitution of one form of domination for another: the mystified feudal order replaced by a mystified agrarian capitalist order, with just enough continuity, in titles and in symbols of authority, in successive compositions of a 'natural order', to confuse and control.

But then the great problem of English rural history is the endless complication of intermediate classes: between the feudal lord and the serf; between the great landowner and the hired landless labourer. Any simple description, of feudalism itself or of the successive stages of capitalism, underestimates the importance of the intermediate groups: the freemen and some of the villeins; the freehold and large tenant farmers; the smaller landowners; the small farmers and cottagers with rights on the commons and in the common fields. The periods of disturbance include the emergence but also the suppression, the struggles, the internal divisions of these intermediate groups. Yet we have only to look at rural Britain even today to see how some of these intermediate classes survive: still, inevitably, under severe economic pressures. Many historians of rural England, many writers drawing on its experience, have identified throughout with the lords and the landowners. This is the common position of imaginative literature until at least the eighteenth century. But there have also been powerful spokesmen, in every period, for the intermediate classes: indeed many more than there have been for the real and permanent majority of the truly exploited and landless. These varying, sometimes unconscious, identifications matter, for it is in their light that we must examine both the reactions to disturbance and the recurrent myth of a happier and more natural past.

And the interesting fact then is that the myth of the happier past was used, though in different ways, from each of these identifying positions. We have seen it in the lord's service in Jonson and Carew: a mystification of the land and the estate into the poetic counters of a Golden Age and of Paradise. What was there being celebrated was of course not quite a feudality: the estate is taken as given; it has no apparent origins, as it has no apparent work. But Saxham was a product of the agrarian disturbance: engrossed around 1500, it passed to the Crofts family in 1531, and owed its importance at the time Carew visited it to a connection with the court; it was a favourite stopping-place on the way to and from the races at Newmarket, and masques were performed there, as part of the entertainment, and this brought the poets. A quiet precise set of social relationships is then mystified by the image of the paternal lord.

All that is left of Saxham now, to quote the historian of its village, is

a moat in the middle of a field, a monument or two in the church, and a very small charity.

He adds, reflecting on the two hundred years of that family:

They might have done more.

Penshurst of course still stands, and appears in brochures and advertisements, but it began its relevant existence –

rear'd with no man's ruine, no mans grone

– as a crown manor which had lapsed by execution and attainder and was then presented by Edward VI to William Sidney, tutor and chamberlain of the court, formerly steward of the household of Henry VIII. That is not quite a timeless order, half a century later when Jonson visited it. Like Saxham, it was a place where the arts were notably patronized, but as an estate it rested on the characteristic sixteenth-century situation in which the quickest means to profit was an association at court. The social image conceals, again, a quite precise and recent set of social relationships. The return of hospitality, to the royal source of the property, has its inner bonds as well as its formalities.

It is essential to remember the recent character of these 'traditional' settlements when we are asked to take up a position towards the more evidently new and speculating landowners. Penshurst and Saxham, now taken as symbols of the old natural order, were direct creations of the new order, as were all the 'country houses', whether idealized or not. But given the background of a consolidated and mystified profit, it was easy to complain, with an apparent humanity, against the crude grasping of the successive new men. By comparison with this nature, now, after the royal gift, apparently yielding of itself, it is easy to feel the harshness of the words Jonson gives to Volpone, on the evident capitalism of the time:

> I use no trade, no venture;
> I wound no earth with ploughshares, fat no beasts
> To feed the shambles; have no mills for iron,
> Oil, corn, or men, to grind them into powder:
> I blow no subtle glass, expose no ships
> To threat'nings of the furrow-faced sea.
> I turn no monies in the public bank,
> No usurer private.

This might, indeed, in its abnegation – its position above the wounding and grinding of the ordinary and visible pursuit of wealth – be a master of Penshurst speaking. Except that it is Volpone, the confidence man, the fox: an irony that repays reflection.

From the other extreme of the society, from the position of the landless and the exposed, the idea of a golden age seems harder to understand. But the functional difference is evident. What is marked in the lordly use is a preternatural presence: a magical and inherited island in a rising and pitiless sea. For the landless, understandably, the deprivation is more total. Indeed, it is seen from within the 'natural order' itself, and the reference to an earlier time is then more critical and absolute:

> When Adam delved and Eve span
> Who was then the gentleman?

It is on the long corruption, not the lucky exception, that the landless insist. Even the redemption by Christ has not reached them:

We are men formed in Christ's likeness, and we are kept like beasts.

That was the declaration of one of the most remarkable organizations of the poor peasants, the Great Society of the fourteenth century. It is not mystifying, but a challenge in terms of a supposedly shared religious belief. Behind much of the feeling of the landless, however, the idea of an earlier and uncorrupted age persisted, and was to find a bewildering variety of historical ascriptions as time and deprivation continued. In the justified hatred of any current race of landlords, and in a time of historical ignorance, there could be an endless retrospect to a time before they existed, before any landlords existed, and what name or period is given is then secondary and arbitrary. It is retrospect as aspiration, for such an idea is drawn not only from the Christian idea of the Garden of Eden – the simple, natural world before the Fall – but also from a version of the Golden Age which is more than that of a magically self-yielding nature. This version is based on the idea of a primitive community, a primitive communism. This is not in Hesiod, where the men of the Golden Age live like gods. Its origins seem to be Hellenistic, and it is explicit in Virgil:

no peasants subdued the fields; it was not lawful even to assign or divide the ground with landmarks: men sought the common gain, and the earth itself bore everything more generously at no one's bidding.
(*Georgics*, I)

This is a fusion of ideas of the self-yielding earth and a conscious community of property and purpose. It can be contrasted with Lucretius' view of primitive men as unable to see the common good. But the fusion persisted, in one tradition, and this must be distinguished from the asocial and mystified Golden Age of the lordly uses: the self-yielding earth ratified by its proprietor, its Lord. We find many traces of the communal idea in Renaissance literature. As Spenser puts it, in the mouth of another fox, in *Mother Hubbard's Tale*:

> Nor ought cald mine or thine; thrice happie then
> Was the condition of mortall men.
> That was the golden age of Saturne old.

Or Chapman:

> Mine, and Thine, were then unusde,
> All things common: Nought abusde,
> Farely earth her frutage bearing.

This persistent and particular version of the Golden Age, a myth functioning as a memory, could then be used, by the landless, as an aspiration. In the words of the Great Society:

> All things under Heaven ought to be common.

It was a claim that was to be continued through the seventeenth-century Diggers to the Land Chartists and the radical labourers of our own time. The happier past was almost desperately insisted upon, but as an impulse to change rather than to ratify the actual inheritance.

Yet the most interesting use of the idea of a lost innocence comes not from the lordly or the landless, but from the shifting intermediate groups. For these were men caught (as in the Virgilian *Eclogues*) in successive but temporary settlements: achieving a place in the altering social structure of the land but continually threatened with losing it: with being pushed down, as eventually many were, into the exposed anonymity of the landless poor. Such men, who had risen by change, were quick to be bitter about renewed or continuing change. What they said about the agents of a new historical phase was authentically angry, but what they also said about the men below them – about the 'idle labourers' – makes the anger double-edged. This can be seen in the qualified humanism of Thomas More, in his *Utopia*. His complaint against the new exploiters and rack-renters is strong and clear.

There is a great numbre of gentlemen, which can not be content to live idle themselves, lyke dorres, of that whiche other have laboured for: their tenauntes, I meane, whom they polle and shave to the quicke, by reisyng their rentes.

The social identification with the smaller tenants and against the rich owners is equally evident.

That one covetous and unsatiable cormaraunte and very plage of his natyve contrey maye compasse aboute and inclose many thousand akers of grounde together within one pale or hedge, the husbandmen be thruste owte of their owne . . . or by violent oppression they be put besydes it, or by wronges and injuries thei be so weried, that they be compelled to sell all . . . .

This is the driving-out of the small men, in the familiar process of engrossing and enclosing. But to the decay of small owner-ship, and the decline of hospitality, is joined another tendency, which is almost as bitterly denounced:

To this wretched beggerye and miserable povertie is joined great wantonnes, importunate superfluitie and excessive riote. For not only gentle mennes servauntes, but also handicrafe men: yea and almooste the ploughmen of the countrey, with al other sortes of people, use much straunge and proude newefanglenes in their apparell, and to muche prodigall riotte and sumptuous fare at their table.

This is the sour denunciation of the luxurious poor, which was heard in Langland at the time of the Statute of Labourers, and which has been heard, since then, in almost every generation: not only the recurrent and ludicrous part-song of the rich; but the sharper, more savage anxiety of the middle men, the insecure. The two grounds of complaint, against the speculative rich and the idle poor, are brought together by More in a rhetorical climax:

Suffer not these riche men to bie up al, to ingrosse and forstalle, and with their monopolie to kepe the market alone as please them. Let not so many be brought up in idelness, let husbandry and tillage be restored, let clotheworkinge be renewed, that ther may be honest labours for this idell sort to passe their tyme in profitablye.

Back to work, that is to say, on our terms and our conditions and in our ways, and meanwhile God give us protection from the unfair competition of the powerful monopolists. The natural ideal is then the recreation of a race of small owners, and this is projected in the island of Utopia. Once again the myth of a primitive happier state is drawn upon, with some suggestions from accounts of the primitive economies seen by Vespucci and others in the new world. But in the island paradise it is not quite to be all things in common. It is to be, rather, a small-owner republic, with laws to regulate and protect but also to compel labour.

The social experience behind this is clear. An upper peasantry, which had established itself in the break-up of the strict feudal order, and which had ideas and illusions about freedom and independence from the experience of a few generations, was being pressed and expropriated by the great landowners, the most successful of just these new men, in the changes of the market and of agricultural techniques brought about by the growth of the wool trade. A moral protest was then based on a temporary stability: as again and again in the subsequent history of rural complaint. It is authentic and moving yet it is in other ways unreal. Its idea of local paternal care, and of national legislation to protect certain recent forms of ownership and labour, seems to draw almost equally on a rejection of the arbitrariness of feudalism, a deeply felt rejection of the new arbitrariness of money, and an attempted stabilization of a transitory order, in which small men are to be protected against enclosures but also against the idleness of their labourers. Thus a moral order is abstracted from the feudal inheritance and break-up, and seeks to impose itself ideally on conditions which are inherently unstable. A sanctity of property has to co-exist with violently changing property relations, and an ideal of charity with the harshness of labour relations in both the new and the old modes. This is then the third source of the idea of an ordered and happier past set against the disturbance and disorder of the present. An idealization, based on a temporary situation and on a deep desire for stability, served to cover and to evade the actual and bitter contradictions of the time.

Yet the eventual structure of feeling is not based only on an idea of the happier past. It is based also on that other and associated idea of innocence: the rural innocence of the pastoral, neo-pastoral and reflective poems. The key to its analysis is the contrast of the country with the city and the court: here nature, there worldliness. This contrast depends, often, on just the suppression of work in the countryside, and of the property relations through which this work is organized, which we have already observed. But there are other elements in the contrast. The means of agricultural production – the fields, the woods, the growing crops, the animals – are attractive to the observer and, in many ways and in the good seasons, to the men working in and among them. They can then be effectively contrasted with the exchanges and counting-houses of mercantilism, or with the mines, quarries, mills and manufactories of industrial production. That contrast, in many ways, still holds in experience.

But there is also, throughout, an ideological separation between the processes of rural exploitation, which have been, in effect, dissolved into a landscape, and the register of that exploitation, in the law courts, the money markets, the political power and the conspicuous expenditure of the city.

The rhetorical contrast between town and country life is indeed traditional: Quintilian makes it his first example of a stock thesis, and conventional contrasts between greed and innocence, in these characteristic locations, are commonplace in later Greek and Latin literature. But it was especially in relation to Rome that the contrast crystallized, at the point where the city could be seen as an independent organism. In the savage satires of Juvenal we find the tone which is more than conventional: a sustained and explicit catalogue of corruption.

> What can I do in Rome? I never learnt how
> To lie.

This teeming life, of flattery and bribery, of organized seduction, of noise and traffic, with the streets unsafe because of robbers, with the crowded rickety houses and the constant dangers of fire, is the city as itself: going its own way. A retreat to country or coast, from this kind of hell, is then a different vision from the mere contrast of rural and urban ways of life. It is, of course, a rentier's vision: the cool country that is sought is not that of the working farmer but of the fortunate resident. The rural virtues are there but as a memory, as in Satire XIV:

> Old mountain peasants
> Used to tell their sons ...
> Be content with a humble cottage ...

In the city these virtues are often a lying nostalgia:

> That clique in Rome who affect
> Ancestral peasant virtues as a front for their lechery.

For the vision is specifically urban, even when it is negative.

> In those days, when the world
> Was young, and the sky bright-new still, men lived differently.

But this conventional reference back, in Satire VI, is to a time

> When draughty
> Caves were the only homes men had, hearthfire and household
> Gods, family and cattle all shut in darkness together

and when the women were 'shaggier than their acorn-belching husbands'. What is idealized is not the rural economy, past or present, but a purchased freehold house in the country, or 'a charming coastal retreat', or even 'a barren offshore island'. This is then not a rural but a suburban or dormitory dream. And it is in direct reaction to the internal corruption of the city: the rise of lawyer, merchant, general, pimp and procurer; the stink of place and of profit; the noise and danger of being crowded together. Indeed in Satire XV it is the urban ideal that is celebrated:

Sovereign reason, the impulse to aid one another,
To gather our scattered groups into peoples, to abandon
The woods and forests where once our ancestors made their homes;
To build houses in groups, to sleep sounder because of our
  neighbours'
Presence around us, to learn collective security ...

And then the exact note is added:

> But today even snakes agree better than men.

This powerful satire of a corrupt city life has had an extraordinary influence in subsequent literature; and it has been
re-experienced, without influence, in many places and generations. But what matters is the way in which it was incorporated
into the milder conventional contrast of town and country ways
of life. Rome, after all, was a special case: an imperial capital,
a metropolis. It could have been traced to its sources, in the
exploitation of a hundred peoples. But its particular and spectacular corruption becomes very different when it is incorporated
into a version of relationships between any urban and any rural
order, as a way of ratifying the latter. This, clearly, is the point
of ideological transition.

The social and economic reasons for the growth of towns, the
new urban movement of the late Middle Ages and the post-
feudal settlement, are still highly controversial. There is a case
for some independent growth, as in the extension of trade
(Pirenne). There was growth in relation to religious houses and
army barracks. There was a very important development of
independent craft production, with its own tendencies to concentration and urban forms of control. But directly or indirectly
most towns seem to have developed as an aspect of the agricultural order itself: at a simple level as markets; at a higher
level, reflecting the true social order, as centres of finance,
administration and secondary production. There was then every
kind of interaction and tension, and some towns developed a
certain autonomy. But in the period we are speaking of, in the
sixteenth and seventeenth centuries when the ideological transition occurred, the effective bases of the society were still property
in land and the consequent rural production, and the towns, even
the capital, were functionally related to this dominant order.

One of the new bases, in mercantile profit, was indeed disturbing to just this direct relation. Much of the conventional complaint is an articulation of this precise disturbance. But as we read the abstract comparisons of rural virtue and urban greed, we must not be tempted to forget the regular, necessary and functional links between the social and moral orders which were so easily and conventionally contrasted.

Thus in Jonson's poem to Wroth we can all feel the contrast between the country gentleman and the worldly men of the city. But what are the lawyers doing, much of the time, if not proving titles to land? A large part of what is being passed across the exchanges is the surplus value of the unregarded labourers at home and, as trade developed, abroad. And as the moneyed order of the city extends in importance, where does much of the new capital go, but back to the land, to intensify the exploiting process? The greed and calculation, so easily isolated and condemned in the city, run back, quite clearly, to the country houses, with the fields and their labourers around them. And this is a double process. The exploitation of man and of nature, which takes place in the country, is realized and concentrated in the city, But also, the profits of other kinds of exploitation – the accumulating wealth of the merchant, the lawyer, the court favourite – come to penetrate the country, as if, but only as if, they were a new social phenomenon. As was said in 1577, about the merchants:

They often change estates with gentlemen as gentlemen do with them; by mutual conversion of one into the other.

That mutual conversion is the whole point. There is a common way of seeing the social process of this period as a kind of infection from the city:

from which (as if it were from a certain rich and wealthy seedplot) courtiers, lawyers and merchants be continuously transplanted.

Well, certainly; Penshurst is just such a case. But a real conflict of interest, between those settled on the land and those settled in the city, which continually defined itself in the shifting economy of the time, could be made the basis of an ideology, in which an innocent and traditional order was being invaded and destroyed by a new and more ruthless order.

The complicated shifts in ownership, in the whole period of the dissolution of feudalism, are certainly evident. Merchants and lawyers were the most identifiable and the most isolable kinds of new men. In the mid sixteenth century Robert Crole criticized the process in an unusually precise reference to that feudal order in which each man was expected to stay in the vocation to which he was born:

> If Merchants would meddle
> With merchandise only,
> And leave farms to such men
> As must live thereby
> Then they were most worthy.

Yet this rigidity of estate and vocation had been disappearing for at least two centuries, as much on the land as elsewhere. It is a pleasant fancy, but in the end an illusion, to suppose that it was only merchants who, as Crole continues,

> take farms
> To let them out again,
> To such men as must have them,
> Though it be to their pain:
> And to levy great fines
> Or to over the rent.

This was happening everywhere. It needed no merchant to teach it to landowners, as we have already seen from Thomas More. Or again, as one of Jonson's characters puts it, in *The Devil is An Ass*:

> We see those changes daily: the fair lands
> That were the client's, are the lawyer's now;
> And those rich manors there of goodman Taylor's
> Had once more wood upon them, than the yard
> By which they were measured out for the last purchase.
> Nature hath these vicissitudes.

Estates were certainly lost by litigation, and lawyers were among those who profited. But it is a simple case of projection when the whole process of the transformation of ownership of the land is identified with the coming of this kind of 'outsider'. Such an identification depends, indeed, on a mystifying retrospect.

'Goodman Taylor' with his 'rich manors' is an attractive figure, but we need not suppose, any more than in the case of Penshurst, that his title began in Eden. This is where the idea of a 'traditional' order is most effectively misleading. For there is no innocence in the established proprietors, at any particular point in time, unless we ourselves choose to put it there. Very few titles to property could bear humane investigation, in the long process of conquest, theft, political intrigue, courtiership, extortion and the power of money. It is a deep and persistent illusion to suppose that time confers on these familiar processes of acquisition an innocence which can be contrasted with the ruthlessness of subsequent stages of the same essential drives. There is no need to deny the conflicts of interest between the settled owners and the newly ambitious, or between the holders of landed capital and new mercantile capital, and there was of course a political reflection of these conflicts in the formation of 'country', 'court' and 'city' parties. But it is hardly for the twentieth-century observer, or the ordinary humane man, to try to insert himself, as any kind of partisan, into the complicated jealousies and bitterness of that shifting and relative historical process. Whenever we encounter their proceedings in detail, the land-owners, old and new, seem adequately described in the words of a modern agricultural historian: 'a pitiless crew'. The 'ancient stocks', to which we are sentimentally referred, are ordinarily only those families who had been pressing and exploiting their neighbours rather longer. And the 'intruders', the new men, were entering and intensifying a system which was already established and which, by its internal pressures, was developing new forms of predation. If we have humanity to spare, it is better directed to the unregarded men who were making and working the land, in any event, under the old owners and the new.

That temporary contrast, then, between country and city is only indirectly important. But there is another dimension in the whole contrast which requires emphasis. Of course a city eats what its country neighbours have grown. It is able to do so by the services it provides, in political authority, law and trade, to those who are in charge of the rural exploitation, with whom, characteristically, it is organically linked in a mutual necessity of profit and power. But then, at marginal points, as the processes of the city become in some respects self-generating, and especially in the course of foreign conquest and trade, there is a new basis for the contrast between one 'order' and another. The agents of power and profit become, as it were, alienated, and in certain political situations can become dominant. Over and above the interlocking exploitation, there is what can be seen as a factual exploitation of the country as a whole by the city as a whole.

For just because the city ordinarily concentrates the real social and economic processes of the whole society, so a point can be reached where its order and magnificence but also its fraud and its luxury seem almost, as in Rome, to feed on themselves; to belong in the city, and to breed there, as if on their own. Thus parasites collect around the real services, as in the legal and social underworlds of seventeenth-century London. Around the engrossing lawyers collect the confidence-men and the professional sharpers. Around the profit-making merchants collect the hucksters, the puffers, the overtly fraudulent. Around the political authority collect the informers, the go-between men, the fixers and (in the court as often as anywhere) the prostitutes; some from, some on their way to, what was called an aristocracy.

There is another service which the city increasingly provided, as a result of changes in the laws of inheritance. It became a necessary marriage-market (what was later called 'the season') for the relatively scattered country landowners. Around this, again, collected the pimps and procurers as well as the professional escorts, the keepers of salons, the intermediary rakes and the whores. When these various underworlds were quite visibly established, it was easy to project an image of the simple man from the country, arriving with his rural innocence in such surprising company. There was, no doubt, even some reality in it. In Jacobean comedy – in Massinger's *New Way to Pay Old Debts* or Middleton's *A Trick to Catch the Old One* – the vitality of these underworlds is evident, and it is titles to property, mortgage papers, which are passed and schemed for. It is then easy to appreciate the grossness of an Overreach, a Lucre, a Hoard or a Witgood, and, picking up the action at a selected point, to identify with the 'rightful owners', the good and the innocent, who pick their way to their estates, their rural inheritance, through these corrupting alleys of city society. But this, at its ordinary level, is indeed an ideology, for what is never inquired into is the real past and present of that 'settled' and 'lawful' country order from which they come.

In Restoration comedy, the contrast between 'country' and 'town' is commonly made, but with some evident ambiguity. Written by and for the fashionable society of the town, the plays draw on evidently anxious feelings of rejection, or a necessary appearance of rejection, of the coarseness and clumsiness, or simply the dullness, of country life. Certain rural stereotypes are established: a Blackacre or a Hoyden or a Tunbelly Clumsey; as later a Lumpkin and the whole lineage of Mummerset and the village clodhopper. Such types are easily laughed at, in the small talk of fashionable society. Separated from the country houses by which many of them were still maintained, the members of town society composed the sourest kind of counter-pastoral that anyone could have imagined. What was seen now, from this particular position, was

a great rambling lone house that looks as if it were not inhabited, the family's so small. There you'll find my mother, an old lame aunt, and myself, sir, perched up on chairs at a distance in a large parlor, sitting moping like three or four melancholy birds in a spacious volary.

That dull settled life was still associated, however, with settled relationships. A committed love was seen, in the same mode, as

more dismal than the country! Emilia, pity me, who am going to that sad place. Methinks I hear the hateful noise of rooks already – Kaw, Kaw, Kaw!

But what the birds cry is what the world cries in the end: that the settlement has to be made, into an estate and into a marriage. And this is the root of the ambiguity of feeling. What was going on, through the parades and visits and intrigues of London society, was just this making of marriages which were also necessary property transactions. It was impossible not to be cynical about it, while the game was being played, but equally this cynicism never reached the point of renouncing the advantages which were being played for; that is why it is cynicism, rather than real opposition.

Young Fashion: So, here's our inheritance, Lory, if we can but get into possession. But methinks the seat of our family looks like Noah's ark, as if the chief part on't were designed for the fowls of the air and the beasts of the field.

Lory: Pray, sir, don't let your head run upon the orders of building here; get but the heiress, let the devil take the house.

Young Fashion: Get but the house, let the devil take the heiress, I say.

And then, not surprisingly, the overt cynicism of this preliminary 'courting' – aptly so called – is prolonged into the marriage, which when based on a property transaction is no more evidently moral than the advantageous sex of the town. For the point about the cynicism of these weary and greedy intrigues – the coarse having and getting which reduces its players to a mutuality of objects – is that it is only the scum on a deeper cynicism, which as a matter of settlement, of ordered society, has reduced men and women to physical, bargainable carriers of estates and incomes.

> The wise will find a difference on our fate;
> You wed a woman, I a good estate.

When marriage is like that, it is not properly available as a moral contrast to the intrigues of the whores and the fortune-hunters in residence. Any system which puts that kind of social advantage or convenience above any idea of personal love or fidelity must breed, in its visible centres, those habits and tones which are now, with facility, called the 'immorality' of Restoration drama. What this phrase directs us to, whether to be admired or despised, is only a petty and superficial immorality; an exhausted and brittle, a desperately fast and bright reaction to a sober realization of the actual priorities of the system.

There is then no simple contrast between wicked town and innocent country, for what happens in the town is generated by the needs of the dominant rural class. The moral ratification of this drama is not marriage against an intrigue or an affair (again, aptly so-called), nor is it wit against folly, or virtue against vice. It is the steering of the estate into the right hands:

> A deed of conveyance of the whole estate real of Arabella Languish, widow, in trust to Edward Mirabell.

For indeed, if you stop to listen to it, the bright conversation of the town never really strays far from its quite inward concern with property and income. Even the apparent exceptions to the mode – the innocent, the unassuming, and the faithful – usually reveal themselves, in the end, as endowed. Fidelia, at the end of *The Plain Dealer*, when the greedy tricks of the town have been exposed and denounced, makes offer not only of her innocence but

such a present as this, which I got by the loss of my father, a gentleman of the north, of no mean extraction, whose only child I was; therefore left me in the present possession of two thousand pounds a year . . .

This, in the most real sense, is the way of the world.

The transition in feeling from the Jacobean contrast – between a Wellborn and an Overreach – to the Restoration unity – a Tunbelly Clumsey and a Young Fashion – is then a gain in frankness as well as a loss in both real and apparent standards. Certainly a coldness of attitude to the real processes by which land was secured has increased. An ideal is falling away, as well as a mystification. But we need not, at any stage, accept this town-and-country contrast at its face value. For in the trans-actions that mattered, who was it, after all, who came from the country? It was not the labourer or the cottager; the hunger of their families kept them in the fields. It was the landowner and his endowed son, the landowner's wife and her prospecting daughter, who came on their necessary business. When they were gulled or cheated, or mocked because they were behind the fashion, and then raised, in reply, their standards of a plain and simple honesty back home, we may see and feel with the persons behind the forms, but the forms we must see, now that the bones are dust. What they brought with them, and what they came to promote, rested on the brief and aching lives of the permanently cheated: the field labourers whom we never by any chance see; the dispossessed and the evicted; all the men and women whose land and work paid their fares and provided their spending money. It was no moral case of 'God made the country and man made the town'. The English country, year by year, had been made and remade by men, and the English town was at once its image and its agent (honest or dishonest, as advantage served). If what was seen in the town could not be approved, because it made evident and repellent the decisive relations in which men actually lived, the remedy was never a visitor's morality of plain living and high thinking, or a babble of green fields. It was a change of social relationships and of essential morality. And it was precisely at this point that the 'town and country' fiction served: to promote superficial comparisons and to prevent real ones.

6   Their Destiny Their Choice

Yet the transition marked by the Civil War, the Commonwealth, the Restoration and the constitutional settlement of 1688 fundamentally altered the social character of England, and it is not surprising that in ideology, in mediation and in new creative work the literature of the country also changed. In the poems of rural retreat there is a marked transition from the ideal of contemplation to the ideal of simple productive virtue, and then to its complications, as we shall see in Thomson. But there is also an interesting transition in what must be seen as the most significant line: that of the country-house poems. If we look from Marvell's *Upon Appleton House* to Pope's *Epistle to Burlington* we can see this change clearly.

It is possible to assimilate *Upon Appleton House* to the world of *Penshurst* and *Saxham*, through certain obvious continuities. Here again is the exceptional house, as against the 'hollow Palaces', the 'unproportion'd dwellings' of other places and other men:

> But all things are composed here
> Like Nature, orderly and near.

And now the reference is historical and retrospective:

> In which we the Dimensions find
> Of that more sober Age and Mind
> When larger sized Men did stoop
> To enter at a narrow loop;
> As practising, in doors so strait,
> To strain themselves through *Heavens Gate*

Here again there are the marks of a 'moral economy':

A stately *Frontispiece* of *Poor*
Adorns without the open Door:
Nor less the Rooms within commends
Daily new *Furniture* of *Friends*.

But then the changes become evident. The origin of the house is no longer mystified, but is openly and wittily stated and justified. This new house built by Fairfax, the Parliamentary General and founder of the New Model Army, had been completed only a year or two before the poem was written. It replaced an earlier house, in the same family, built on lands which passed to the Fairfaxes from the dissolution of the Cistercian priory of Appleton; the ruins of that priory were still visible in the grounds. Thus an explicit transition, in which so much landed property had in fact been founded, is not only admitted but justified, in spite of the acknowledgement of an earlier 'more sober Age and Mind'. Like every expropriated religious house, this nunnery, it appears to its subsequent possessors, had been vicious. An incident in the Fairfax family at that time – 'The *Nuns* smooth tongue has suckt her in' – is used to present a picture of a greedy, hypocritical and grasping order, and the consequent moral is drawn:

'But sure those Buildings last not long.
Founded by Folly, kept by Wrong'.

The dispossession and change can then be wholly ratified:

At the demolishing, this Seat
To Fairfax fell as by Escheat.
And what both *Nuns* and *Founders* will'd
'Tis likely better thus fulfill'd.
For if the Virgin prov'd not theirs,
The *Cloyster* yet remained hers.
Though many a *Nun* there made her Vow,
'Twas no *Religious House* till now.

This advance in candour is accompanied, significantly, by an increased willingness and ability to look at the immediate environment. The house is founded on a military fortune, and its garden, laid out 'in the just Figure of a Fort', is seen as a mutation into peace, in the form of a lost paradise:

When Gardens only had their Towrs
And all the Garrisons were Flowrs.

73

Yet the most remarkable and beautiful part of the poem (and that it is a composition of different ways of seeing, different essential directions and interests, is itself significant) is the look and walk into the fields and woods beyond. The magical country, yielding of itself, is now seen as a working landscape filled with figures: the mowers and haymakers, the 'Villagers in common' coming to graze their cattle on the mown meadows, the winter flooding of the river pastures. All these are seen, but in a figure: the conscious look at a passing scene: the explicit detached view of landscape:

> They seem within the polisht Grass
> A Landskip drawn in Looking-Glass.

Indeed the cleared meadows are seen as a canvas for a painter:

> A levell'd space, as smooth and plain,
> As Clothes for *Lilly* stretcht to stain.

But still the figures are *seen*, within this perspective: the 'wholesome heat' of the harvest, the mowing and the dance, the 'Villagers in common'. And it is no less significant that the poet, having seen this populated landscape, goes beyond it into the wood, the true retreat into Nature as a way of escaping the world:

> How safe, methinks, and strong, behind
> These Trees have I incamp'd my Mind.

When he comes back the flood has receded and the fields are green again in the Spring.

The tension within this remarkable poem is then of a different order from anything that preceded it. The house and its basis in dispossession are justified, as a religious and natural order. But at the same time there is a movement beyond them, into a working landscape, and into the natural retreat of the untouched wood. The feeling moves this way and that, with only the voice of the poem as control. In the measured delight there is also a new sadness, an awareness of other experiences: the conventional celebration of the house as

> Heaven's Centre, Nature's Lap.
> And Paradise's only Map

occurs within a felt contrast with the precarious times:

> 'Tis not, which once it was, the World;
> But a rude heap together hurl'd;
> All negligently overthrown,
> Gulfes, Deserts, Precipices, Stone.

It was inevitable that this should be so, in the mind of a Marvell. But beyond even this, it is an unbearable irony to read the elaborate formal praise of the beauty and innocence of the daughter of the house, and to be directed forward to her marriage. She is the mistletoe on the Fairfax oak

> Whence, for some universal good
> The *Priest* shall cut the Sacred Bud;
> While her glad Parents most rejoice
> And make their *Destiny* their *Choice*.

The irony is not only the personal destiny that this marriage was to be to the appalling George Villiers, 2nd Duke of Buckingham, within a few years of the idealization in the poem. It is that the fruit of this new house was to be that kind of political deal in which property and title were reconstituted. It is a marriage between Villiers the Royalist and the daughter of the leading Parliamentary General. Some Villiers lands had passed to the Fairfaxes: the marriage was a settlement of a complicated political and propertied kind. The destiny of a once living virtue was indeed to be that exact kind of choice, and in landholding as much as in political power we have to acknowledge the justice of Marvell's other observation, often applied to politics but not also, as it should be, to this long process of family acquisition, the dispossessions and the deals, the founding of houses:

> The same *Arts* that did *gain*
> A Pow'r must it *maintain*.

What eventually emerged from these complicated settlements, was a very different structure of feeling. Marvell's poem is truly transitional: a complication of feeling between an old order and a new. We can see the critical folly of assimilating all country-house poems to a single tradition, as if their occupants were some kind of unbroken line. In its extreme forms this is a true reification of the houses themselves: the house, and then by derivation its occupants, being the evident sign of an order, even though this order was being continually reconstituted by the political and economic formation of a new aristocracy and then a new agrarian capitalism. By the time we get to Pope, not in the idealizing pastorals but in the Epistles, we have the altered, the more explicit, feelings of just this class. The epistles to both Bathurst and Burlington are of 'the use of Riches', and what is recommended, between the extreme vices of miserliness and profligacy, is the prudent productive investment, tempered by reasonable charity:

> The Sense to value Riches, with the Art
> T'enjoy them, and the Virtue to impart,
> Not meanly, nor ambitiously pursu'd,
> Not sunk by sloth, nor rais'd by servitude;
> To balance Fortune by a just expence,
> Join with Oeconomy, Magnificence;
> With splendour, charity; with plenty, health;
> Oh teach us, BATHURST! yet unspoil'd by wealth!
>
> *(Epistle to Bathurst, 219–226)*

> Who then shall grace, or who improve the Soil?
> Who plants like BATHURST, or who builds like BOYLE.
> 'Tis Use alone that sanctifies Expence,
> And Splendor borrows all her rays from Sense.
>   His Father's Acres who enjoys in peace,
> Or makes his neighbours glad, if he encrease;
> Whose chearful Tenants bless their yearly toil,
> Yet to their Lord owe more than to the soil;
> Whose ample Lawns are not asham'd to feed
> The milky heifer and deserving steed;
> Whose rising Forests, not for pride or show,
> But future Buildings, future Navies grow:
> Let his plantations stretch from down to down,
> First shade a Country, and then raise a Town.
>
> *(Epistle to Burlington, 177–90)*

The order is no longer received and natural, as in Jonson and Carew, nor achieved and precarious, as in Marvell; it is a matter for conscious moral teaching. The house is properly subsidiary to the uses of money and productive investment, the creation rather than the celebration of Nature: nature in man's works rather than in a received or fortunate paradise. The poetry has altered in just these ways, from the ratifying traditional images, the conscious fusion of symbol and observation, to the direct moral argument in contemporary terms.

> 'Tis Use alone that sanctifies Expence.

But this conscious bourgeois ethic is qualified by two considerations. The idea of charity and benevolence is powerfully re-asserted: derived from the ideal of a natural moral economy, and with some verbal continuity from it, but now argued as exemplary, as in the celebration of the Man of Ross, and explicitly contrasted with another product of the landowning order: ironically (in the *Epistle to Bathurst*) that same Villiers, 2nd Duke of Buckingham, husband of the virgin of Appleton House:

> Great Villiers lies – alas! how chang'd from him,
> That life of pleasure, and that soul of whim!
> . . . There, Victor of his health, of fortune, friends,
> And fame; this lord of useless thousands ends.

The neglect of charity is now not only a moral and theological example, it is a default of use.

The second qualifying consideration is part of the isolation of the house as object: a completion and transformation of the process that began with the moral celebration of houses. Much of the *Epistle to Burlington* is near the head of that important eighteenth-century tradition of house-building and landscape-gardening, in which, as the outward sign of the new morality of improvement, the country was reshaped and redesigned. It is a condemnation of useless show and hollow palaces, as Jonson or Marvell might have expressed it, but it is also a conscious recommendation of how to build, how to lay out a park or a garden; the improvement of Nature:

> In all, let Nature never be forgot.
> But treat the Goddess like a modest fair,
> Nor over-dress, nor leave her wholly bare.

In this persuasive recommendation a new structure of feeling has become explicit, as part of a new economy. And it is to the complications of this morality of improvement that we must now turn.

7   The Morality of Improvement

(i)

The true history of the English countryside has been centred throughout in the problems of property in land, and in the consequent social and working relationships. By the eighteenth century, nearly half of the cultivated land was owned by some five thousand families. As a central form of this predominance, four hundred families, in a population of some seven or eight million people, owned nearly a quarter of the cultivated land. Beneath this domination, there was no longer, in any classical sense, a peasantry, but an increasingly regular structure of tenant farmers and wage-labourers: the social relationships that we can properly call those of agrarian capitalism. The regulation of production was increasingly in terms of an organized market.

The transition from feudal and immediately post-feudal arrangements to this developing agrarian capitalism is of course immensely complicated. But its social implications are clear enough. It is true that the predominant landowning class was also, in political terms, an aristocracy, whose ancient or ancient-seeming titles and houses offered the illusion of a society determined by obligations and traditional relations between social orders. But the main activity of this class was of a radically different kind. They lived by a calculation of rents and returns on investments of capital, and it was the process of rack-renting, engrossing and enclosure which increased their hold on the land.

Yet there was never any simple confrontation between the four hundred families and a rural proletariat. On the contrary, between these poles of the economic process there was an increasingly stratified hierarchy of smaller landowners, large tenants, surviving small freeholders and copyholders, middle and small tenants, and cottagers and craftsmen with residual common rights. A process begun in the sixteenth century was still powerfully under way, with many of the smaller farms being suppressed, especially on improved arable land, while at the same time the area of cultivated land was itself steadily and at times dramatically increased. Even within the social relations of landowner, tenant, and labourer, there was a continual evolution of new attitudes. An estate passed from being regarded as an inheritance, carrying such and such income, to being calculated as an opportunity for investment, carrying greatly increased returns. In this development, an ideology of improvement – of a transformed and regulated land – became significant and directive. Social relations which stood in the way of this kind of modernization were then steadily and at times ruthlessly broken down.

The crisis of values which resulted from these changes is enacted in varying ways in eighteenth-century literature. In poetry, as we shall see, the idealization of the happy tenant, and of the rural retreat, gave way to a deep and melancholy consciousness of change and loss, which eventually established, in a new way, a conventional structure of retrospect.

But before this development, there was a lively engagement with the human consequences of the new institutions and emphases. Indeed it was in just this interest that the novel emerged as the most creative form of the time. The problems of love and marriage, in a society dominated by issues of property in land, were extended from the later Jacobean comedy and the Restoration comedy of manners, and from the moral epistles of Pope, to the novels of Richardson and Fielding, and in the mode of their extension were transformed. Allworthy and Squire Western, the neighbouring landowners in Fielding's *Tom Jones*, or Lovelace in Richardson's *Clarissa*, are in some ways lineal descendants of the world of Wellborn and Overreach, and then of Tunbelly Clumsey and Young Fashion. The plot of *Tom Jones* is based on the desire to link by marriage the two largest estates in Somersetshire: the proposed marriage of Sophia Western to Blifil is conceived for this end; her marriage to Tom Jones, when he is eventually revealed as Allworthy's true heir, achieves what had formerly, for personal reasons, been rejected. Similarly, Clarissa Harlowe's proposed marriage to Solmes is part of her family's calculation in concentrating their estates and increasing their rank; it is from this that she recoils to the destructive and cynical world of the established landowning aristocrat, Lovelace.

What is dramatized, under increasing pressure, in the actions of these novels, is the long process of choice between economic advantage and other ideas of value. Yet whereas, in the plays, we saw this from one particular standpoint – the social world of London in which the contracts were made and in which, by isolation and concentration, the tone of the protesting and then the cynical observer could be established and maintained – in the novels we move out to the families themselves, and see the action in its homes and in its private character. For all the differences between Richardson and Fielding, this change is something they have in common. Instead of the formal confrontation between representatives of different groups – the wellborn and the overreachers – and the amused observation of a distanced way of the world, the action becomes internal, and is experienced and dramatized as a problem of character.

The open ideology of improvement is in fact most apparent in Defoe, but in an abstraction which marks an essential difference from Richardson and Fielding. There is some irony in this fact, in that in his *Tour of England and Wales*, in the 1720s, Defoe was an incomparable observer of the detailed realities of country life, with his notes on methods of production, marketing and rents. It is from him that we learn the degree of specialization and market-production in early eighteenth-century agriculture, and its intricate involvement with the cities, the ports, and the early coal, iron and cloth industrial areas. It is a frankly commercial world, with hardly any pastoral tinge, and Defoe's combination of intense interest and matter-of-fact reporting is the true predecessor of the major eighteenth-century tradition of rural inquiry, which runs on through William Marshall, the *Country Reports*, Arthur Young and the Annals of Agriculture, to Cobbett and the nineteenth century. This emphasis is the real line of development of a working agriculture, and is in itself a major index of change. Yet, with rare exceptions, this emphasis was in its own way an abstraction from the social relationships and the human world through which the new methods of production worked. It is only at the end of this line, in the crisis at the turn of the century, that the social and economic inquiries are adequately brought together. It is then not surprising that Defoe, for all his close and specialized observation of what was happening in the fields and markets, did not, in his novels, consider their underlying social reality. Rather he projected, into other histories, the abstracted spirit of improvement and simple economic advantage – as most notably in *Robinson Crusoe* – and created a fictional world of isolated individuals to whom other people are basically transitory and functional – as again in *Crusoe* and in *Moll Flanders*. Consciously and unconsciously, this emphasis of a condition and of an ethic was prophetic and powerful; but it is an indication of its character that what Crusoe improves is a remote island, and that what Moll Flanders trades in is her own person. The important improvement and trading were at once nearer home and more general, but the simple practice and ethic of improvement could be more readily and more singlemindedly apprehended in deliberately isolated histories.

In the real life of the country, the commercial spirit had to interlock with, and be tested by, other institutions, considerations and modes. Neither Richardson nor Fielding knew as much as Defoe about what was happening in rural England, but their emphasis, in very different ways, was on human relationships in their more detailed course: not the spirit of the time, but its more immediate experience.

Yet we cannot, in turn, make an abstraction of these human relationships. When the marriage of Sophia and Blifil is proposed, as a way of uniting the neighbouring estates, the character of Blifil is shown in the true contemporary commercial spirit:

as to that entire and absolute possession of the heart of his mistress which romantic lovers require, the very idea of it never entered his head. Her fortune and her person were the sole objects of his wishes, of which he made no doubt soon to obtain the absolute property . . .

Squire Western of course, uses his daughter to unite the estates, as if it were the most natural thing in the world. And Allworthy –

not one of those men whose hearts flutter at any unexpected and sudden tidings of worldly profit

– is nevertheless recommended to us by his more sober and philosophical calculations:

Wisdom . . . only teaches us to extend a simple maxim universally known and followed even in the lowest life, a little farther than that life carries it. And this is, not to buy at too dear a price. Now, whoever takes this maxim abroad with him into the grand market of the world, and constantly applies it to honours, to riches, to pleasures, and to every other commodity which that market affords, is, I will venture to affirm, a wise man, and must be so acknowledged in the worldly sense of the word; for he makes the best of bargains, since in reality he purchases everything at the price only of a little trouble, and carries home all the good things I have mentioned, while he keeps his health, his innocence and his reputation, the common prices which are paid for them by others, entire and to himself.

This, indeed, is very much the position from which *Tom Jones* is written. It is the morality of a relatively consolidated, a more maturely calculating society. From such a position, the cold greed of a Blifil, the open coarseness of a Squire Western, can be noted and criticized; but calculation, and cost, are given a wider scheme of reference. Love, honour, physical pleasure, loyalty: these, too, have to be brought into the reckoning with incomes and acres. The humanity is of a resigned and settled kind: firm and open when faced by the meaner calculators, but still itself concerned to find the balance – the true market price – of happiness. Tom Jones learns from his apparent disregard of advantage, but it is not only that his more immediate satisfactions are tolerately underwritten; it is also that Fielding's management of the action is directed towards restoring the balance in which personal satisfaction and material advantage are reconciled, compatible, and even identical. The novel continually raises questions about the relations between material fortune and human need and impulse, but it resolves them by an adaptation in which, by an act of will, by a planned and fortunate disclosure, they come loosely and easily together. The famous irony is then the literary means by which this trick can be played, noticed, and still win. The tone of the settlement, when Jones is discovered as the rightful heir, and the estates can be united in what is also a love match, is of a deliberate – one might say a calculating – geniality –

in which, to our great pleasure, though contrary, perhaps, to thy expectation, Mr Jones appears to be the happiest of all humankind.

The settlements, the adjustments, the pensions are then neatly worked; and the 'condescension, indulgence and beneficence', of this finally happy pair is such as to make those below them, the tenants and servants, bless the marriage.

There was need, certainly, for this consolidated morality. The openly cynical scramble for land and for heiresses, which had been the predominant tone of an earlier period, was succeeded, in the more settled process of the first half of the eighteenth century, by just this wider, longer-sighted building of position. Humanity, family interest, personal need, must now, if at all possible, be included in any rational and improving settlement. If it was not possible, the main current of advantage took its way, leaving its human casualties.

It is significant that this darker view comes to us, in literature, through a particular fanaticism: the isolation, by Richardson, of virginity, as a single response to the whole struggle for human value. It is true that, in *Pamela*, virginity is treated as the term of a bargain: not a value in itself, but an asset which must not be surrendered without the necessary security of marriage. But in *Clarissa* the virginity is not negotiable, at any level or by any means; it is no longer simply a physical but a spiritual virginity: an integrity of the person and the soul. When the marriage to Solmes is proposed, as part of 'the darling view of *raising a family*' (that is, of consolidating and improving the family estates), Clarissa's answer –

'For the sake of this plan of my brother's, am I, Madam, to be given in marriage to a man I never can endure?'

– is, though quieter, in the same world as Sophia's, on the proposed marriage to Blifil –

'Oh! sir, such a marriage is worse than death. He is not even indifferent; I hate and detest him.'

But the emphasis, in *Clarissa*, is taken right through. The exposure to Lovelace has nothing to do with the lucky chances of the market, or with raising the price of the human person. It is a total exposure, to a cynically calculating world – significantly that of an earlier kind of landowner, the unmediated because established cavalier, the 'wellborn'. No marriage contract can ratify that exposure; even rape cannot destroy Clarissa's virginity. This is the reverse of consolidation, of the necessary settlement, the striking of a bargain between advantage and value. The integrity of the human person is fanatically preserved, by its refusal to compromise and then its accepted destruction.

In his single emphasis, Richardson moved away from any negotiable world, and of course succeeded in specializing a general crisis to a personal and (in its context) fashionable issue. *Clarissa* is an important sign of that separation of virtue from any practically available world which is a feature of the later phases of Puritanism and still later of Romanticism. Though it engages with the current acquisitiveness and ambition of the landowning families, it is in the end not a criticism of a period or structure of society, but of what can be abstracted as 'the world'. This degree of retreat must be noted, but it is in its own way an answer to the problems being raised by an increasingly confident capitalist society. The specialization of virginity, and the paradoxical isolation and even destruction of the individual as a means of survival, are connected with that specialization of pity and charity, and the retreat from society into a nature which teaches humanity, which we shall later trace as responses to the continuing crises of a basically ruthless order, to which there was not, as yet, any available and adequate social response.

(ii)

It must then seem a world away, from the desperate and private emphases of *Clarissa*, to the calmly practical, the inquiring everyday tone of the actual agents of improvement. The social crisis can only be seen, in any connected way, when it is worked through in this everyday and general mode. As we read the agricultural writers, it is easy to accept their emphasis on a better use of the land, even when this is so often explicitly connected with the calculation of rents (Lovelace, interestingly, would never rack-rent old tenants; his income, like his sexual liberty, was inherited rather than speculative). We learn so much from these improving writers, and their achievement (together with that of the experimenting farmers and the better-known experimenting landowners) in providing more food is so impressive that it is easy for anybody who loves the land to place himself on their side. What is hardest to understand, for them as for us, is the ultimate consequence of just these improvements which in immediate terms were so readily justifiable.

To read the life of Arthur Young is to catch at once the spirit of improvement and its real complications. He grew up on an estate which had been in his father's family for generations, but which was set into order only by capital from his mother's side: a Jewish family which had come from Holland in the late seventeenth century. The old house was rebuilt into a mansion, as so often in this period. This social ambition overreached the family's income. Arthur Young was apprenticed as a merchant; he had wanted, like his father, to be a clergyman. When his father died, he had little money, and began to support himself by writing pamphlets. Then he returned to farm a copyhold of twenty acres, on his mother's small estate. Chronically short of capital, he never succeeded in becoming a successful farmer himself, but as an agricultural writer, collecting and publicizing the techniques and spirit of improved production, he made a new kind of life. More than any other man, he made the case for the second great period of enclosures, in the late eighteenth and early nineteenth centuries. He travelled constantly, and in the forty-six volumes of his *Annals of Agriculture* provided the essential means of communication for the new experimental agriculture. The changes came from use of the land itself: in new crops (especially roots), in drainage and reclamation, in planned soil fertility, and in stock breeding. But Young emphasized the connections of the agricultural interest with the other new social forces of the time: with mercantile capital (as he had good reason, from his personal history, to know); with early industrial techniques (as in earth-moving, which was mechanized for harbour-building and quarrying before it was applied to farming land); with the physical sciences (as in his collaboration with Priestley in soil-chemistry); and with political power and organization (as in his propaganda to the King and Parliament, and in his eventual appointment as Secretary of the new Board of Agriculture).

Young touched, at every point, what we now see as the modernization of the land in his century; but what he continually stressed was the backwardness of agriculture, its insufficient rate of progress, its neglect of great areas of waste land, its lack of investment by comparison with overseas trade. And increasingly, towards the end of his life, he admitted his own social experience and the result of his social observations. Thus improvement of land required considerable capital, and therefore the leadership of the landowners. But this not only increased the predominance of the landed interest; it created, by enclosure and engrossing to make large and profitable units, a greater number of the landless and the disinherited, who could not survive or compete in the new conditions. The slowness of many farmers to adopt the new methods was itself related to the land-holding system: since improvement often led to an increase of rent, there was a built-in deterrent at the very point of production. It was only a rare landowner, like Coke, who kept a reasonable relation between the profits of the new production and the rents of his tenants. Thus the economic process, which could be so easily justified in its own limited terms, had social results which at times contradicted it, and at other times led to the disaster of families and communities. When Young saw the full social results of the changes he had fought for, he was not alone in second thoughts and in new kinds of questioning:

I had rather that all the commons of England were sunk in the sea, than that the poor should in future be treated on enclosing as they have been hitherto.

86

8 Nature's Threads

(i)

It is in Young's eighteenth century – in the changes and contradictions of that rural England which he both helped to promote and incomparably recorded – that we find not only the genial accommodation of Fielding, the desperate and specialized fears of Richardson, but also a new and more serious social version of the lost peace and virtue of country life. The poems to the happy tenant, the idealized and independent self of the reflective pastoral tradition, are succeeded by poems of loss, change, regret: that structure of feeling, at once moved and meditating, appalled and withdrawn, which is caught so exactly in Goldsmith's couplet:

> E'en now, methinks, as pondering here I stand
> I see the rural virtues leave the land.

In the first half of the century the older structure still holds, though in Thomson's *The Seasons*, written between the 1720s and 1740s, there is so wide a range of attitudes – many of them, indeed, attitudes rather than feelings – that an element of contradiction is already beginning to appear. Thus Thomson can rehearse the Golden Age in the most conventional terms –

> Spontaneous Harvests wav'd
> Still in a Sea of yellow Plenty round . . .
> . . . Th'uncultivated Thorn a ruddy shower
> Of fruitage shed, on such as sat below,
> In blooming Ease, and from brown Labour, free . . .

– yet go on to say:

> But now what-e'er those gaudy Fables meant,
> And the white Minutes that they shadow'd out,
> Are found no more amid these Iron Times.

He can rehearse the familiar idyll of retirement –

> Oh knew he but his happiness, of men
> The happiest he! who far from public rage,
> Deep in the vale, with a choice few retir'd,
> Drinks the pure pleasures of the rural life

– but is sufficiently and characteristically ambiguous about the city, denouncing its fashion and luxury but admiring its learning and politeness, that the idyll, as even here with the 'choice few', takes on a distinctly suburban air. This is caught exactly in a late version of *Winter*, in the lines:

> permit the Rural Muse,
> O Chesterfield, to grace with Thee her Song!
> Ere to the Shades again she humbly flies.

There is a further ambiguity, growing towards actual contradiction, in Thomson's simultaneous celebration of improvement and of romantic wastes. The former note is new and significant; other examples can be found in Dyer's *The Fleece* and Philips' *Cyder*, where industrial processes of rural origin are consciously celebrated. In Thomson's *Castle of Indolence* Sir Industry conquers the 'pleasing land of drowsy-head' in the authentic modernizing spirit. This adds a dimension to the idyll of retirement, as here:

> Nor from his deep retirement banish'd was
> The amusing cares of rural industry.
> Still as with graceful change the seasons pass
> New scenes arise, new landskips strike the eye . . .
> Dark frowning heaths grow bright with Ceres' store.

And this becomes, at times, actual exhortation to improvement:

> Ye generous Britons, cultivate the Plow . . .
> So with superior Boon may your rich Soil,
> Exuberant, Nature's better Blessings pour
> O'er every Land; the naked Nations cloath,
> And be th'exhaustless Granary of the World.

This is the open ideology of the improving landowners, and corresponds very closely to real developments in the increase of corn-growing and corn exports. Thomson's celebration seems single-minded:

> Happy Britannia.' . . .
> . . . thy Vallies float
> With golden Waves; and on thy Mountains Flocks
> Bleat, numberless, while, roving round their sides.
> Bellow the blackening Herds, in lusty Droves
> Beneath, thy Meadows flame, and rise unquelled,
> Against the Mower's Sythe. On every Hand,
> Thy Villas shine. Thy Country teems with Wealth;
> And Property assures it to the swain,
> Pleas'd, and unweary'd, in his certain Toil.

In a revised version, the 'certain' toil has become 'guarded', but it is in any case the existing social order which guarantees the 'scattering of Plenty'. It is not what any improving agriculturist ever reported, but it is what most wanted to happen. In this order, poetry has a central place; it is the treasure of mankind, without which 'unassisted man' would be a savage. Without poetry

> Nor moral Excellence, nor social Bliss,
> Nor Law were his; nor Property, nor Swain
> To turn the Furrow, nor mechanic Hand,
> Harden'd to Toil, nor Servant prompt, nor Trade.

We shall need to recall these lines when Goldsmith sees poetry being simultaneously evicted with the villagers of Auburn. Yet Thomson's flattery of a social order is so gross, the role of poetry in the maintenance of an unequal propertied society so explicit, that even he had second thoughts. Between 1727 and 1744 the lines were revised to:

> . . . Nor moral Excellence, or social Bliss
> Nor guardian Law were his; nor various Skill
> To turn the Furrow, or to guide the Tool
> Mechanic.

The arts have been abstracted from the actual social relationships, and this represents a certain nervousness. There is the scene of harvest, where

> Behind the master walks, builds up the shocks;
> And conscious, glancing oft this way and that
> His sated eye, feels his heart heave with joy.

But the pride of affluence must, as in Pope's moral essays, be mixed with charity:

> Think, oh! grateful think
> How good the God of harvest is to you;
> Who pours abúndance o'er your flowing fields;
> While these unhappy partners of your kind
> Wide-hover round you, like the fowls of heaven,
> And ask their humble dole.

These 'partners', the poor, had been the excluded element in the panegyric of order and plenty, and it is in a growing admission of their existence that the structure of feeling has changed. Thomson even goes on to reflect the relatively new recognition – it is basically an eighteenth-century 'discovery' by the educated upper classes – that 'the poor' are not simply a charitable burden, a weight on the economy, but the actual producers of wealth:

> Ye masters, then
> Be mindful of the rough laborious hand,
> That sinks you soft in elegance, and ease.

Thomson does not, of course, resolve this range of attitudes, or question their contradictions. But it is significant that at just this time, and most notably in Thomson himself, we hear the tone that is later to dominate country writing: a melancholy and thoughtful withdrawal.

It is a long way from the celebration of the improved countryside – open, clearing and productive – to the romantic strain, a long step beyond Marvell, of

> Still let me pierce into the midnight depth
> Of yonder Grove, of wildest largest Growth . . .
> . . . These are the Haunts of Meditation . . .

Or again:

> Thus solitary, and in pensive guise
> Oft let me wander o'er the russet mead,
> And thro' the sadden'd grove; where scarce is heard
> One dying strain, to chear the woodman's toil.

It is here, deep in the woods which so often would be on the programme for clearance, that waste and bleakness excite. Unexpectedly, in the response to unproductive late autumn,

> the desolated prospect thrills the soul.
> He comes! he comes! in every breeze the Power
> Of philosophic Melancholy comes.

This is a crucial moment, for all its fustian. Nature, represented hitherto as a social order, a triumph of law and plenty, is being seen, alternatively, as a substitute order; lonely, prophetic, bearing the love of humankind in just those places where men are not; in

> twilight groves, and visionary vales.

It will take half a century for this change to work itself fully through, but Thomson is especially interesting because, in *The Seasons*, both versions of Nature, both attitudes to the country and the land, are simultaneously present.

What is at issue, really, is a dialectic of change. A much later poem, Cowper's *Yardley Oak* (1791), is in the main a traditional and melancholy reflection on history and the mutability of fortune, in the sight of the centuries-old oak that has become hollow and rotten. But there is an intermediate reflection, which seems to catch the dialectic of just the change that was being widely experienced:

> Nature's threads,
> Fine, passing thought, e'en in her coarsest works,
> Delight in agitation, yet sustain
> The force that agitates, not unimpair'd,
> But, worn by frequent impulse, to the cause
> Of their best tone their dissolution owe.

This sense, of a dissolution within a lively and productive exercise, is exact.

(ii)

We have then to distinguish two phases of the transition from reflection to retrospect. There are the poems which celebrate what, to borrow their characteristic language, we must call humble and worthy characters, in a country setting, in a more or less conscious contrast with the wealth and ambition of the city and the court. And then there are those which develop this ethical contrast, in which the contrast of country and city is as it were an atmosphere or a determining climate, into an historical contrast, in which the virtues are seen as unmistakably past, in an earlier and lost period of country life.

The first kind, of course, has a long ancestry. But there is an observable social movement from, say, Jonson's poem to Wroth, in which the virtues are found in a country gentleman, to Shenstone's *The School Mistress* (1748) and Gray's *Elegy Written in a Country Churchyard* (1750). This is in one way only an extension of social sympathy, but it is interestingly marked by a radical change of tone. In the later poems, there is a sense of ineradicable melancholy, which we can show by contrast with the sense of settlement, even of satisfaction and self-satisfaction, in an earlier celebration of a humble condition, Herrick's *A Thanksgiving* (1647):

> Lord, Thou hast given me a cell
> Wherein to dwell,
> A little house, whose humble Roof
> Is weather-proof . . .
> . . . Low is my porch, as is my Fate,
> Both void of state;
> And yet the threshold of my doore
> Is worn by th' poore.

As it happens, I first read this poem, as a child, under a roof and a porch probably lower than Herrick's, and I could then neither get the lines out of my mind nor feel other than angry about them. My father had brought it home, in a book called *Hours with English Authors*, which was a set-book at an evening class he was attending in the village. He had been asked (it is how values are taught) to learn it by heart; he asked me to see if he could. I remember looking and wondering who the poor were, and why they wore this threshold, if the poet's condition was indeed so low. I understand that better now. The poverty is seen in an upward glance, by the goldsmith's nephew, the former court poet, the Royalist parson, deprived of his living in the Commonwealth. The poverty of the majority of men is in a different dimension, below the level of comparison. But this was not the source of the anger, which came from a sense of the play at abasement, putting himself even lower than the porch and being so pleased about it. As I repeat the lines now, I seem still to hear the whine –

A *little* house, whose *humble* roof

(he was lucky, after all that, that it was weatherproof); the whine of a kind of feeling which we used to hear, in a few families, generally despised in the village: a self-conscious lowering when there was charity or religion around. It passed straight in my mind, this poem, to

God bless the squire and his relations
And keep us in our proper stations.

And when I later read Herrick's *Hock-Cart*, with its open management of feeling for the Earl of Westmorland, I felt I had been right, even in an untutored reading (I was of course told later, in Cambridge, that the poem was an example of Christian virtue and settlement, which we couldn't easily appreciate in these degenerate progressive times).

I cannot say I now prefer the tone of Shenstone –

Ah me full sorely is my heart forlorn,
To think how modest worth neglected lies.

– but anyone can feel the change of tone. There is the unmistakable sense that the set of the time is against a decent independence; that goodness is pushed inevitably into 'the dreary shades of dull obscurity'.

Shenstone, of course, was an estate-owner, and spent most of his fortune on an early and beautiful example of landscape gardening, at the Leasowes on the borders of Shropshire and Worcestershire. This was his version of the preservation of simplicity, in the sentiment of his *Rural Elegance*:

Paternal acres please no more
Adieu the simple and sincere delight –
Th' habitual scene of hill and dale,
The rural herds, the vernal gale,
The tangled vetch's purple bloom,

> The fragrance of the bean's perfume,
> Be theirs alone who cultivate the soil,
> And drink the cup of thirst, and eat the bread of toil.

It is this sense of farewell to simplicity that is the ultimate element of the new structure of feeling. And it is here, in the description of his schoolmistress's garden, that the familiar historical outline briefly appears:

> And here trim Rosmarine, that whilom crown'd
> The daintiest garden of the proudest peer;
> Ere, driven from its envy'd site, it found
> A sacred shelter for its branches here;
> Where edg'd with gold its glitt'ring skirts appear.
> Oh wassel days; O customs meet and well!
> Ere this was banished from its lofty sphere:
> Simplicity then sought this humble cell,
> Nor ever would She more with thane and lordling dwell

The archaism of the imitation of Spenser of course qualifies this familiar feeling, which is in any case rather a lot for rosemary to carry. 'Oh wassel days', in its retrospect through a literary manner, is an exact expression of the curious coincidence of a rural and a poetic retrospect which is so common in this kind of verse, and which has since become explicit in the formal identification of a lost rural and a lost literary culture. But the positive stress is on a decent independence, in a remote country setting and with a lingering backward look. Gray's *Elegy*, with its churchyard setting, draws of course on a traditional common place –

> The paths of glory lead but to the grave

– but there is also a sustained and ambiguous celebration of 'the short and simple annals of the poor'. It is ambiguous because it at once ratifies this remote simplicity –

> Far from the madding crowd's ignoble strife,
> Their sober wishes never learn'd to stray;
> Along the cool sequester'd vale of life
> They kept the noiseless tenour of their way

– and admits, with an edge of protest, the social as opposed to the abstracted rural condition:

94

> But knowledge to their eyes her ample page
> Rich with the spoils of time did ne'er unroll;
> Chill Penury repress'd their noble rage,
> And froze the genial current of the soul.

It cannot really be had both ways: the luck of the 'cool sequester'd vale' and the acknowledged repression of 'chill Penury'. But in this structure of feeling, temporarily, the ambiguities of the appeal to simplicity were held and mediated.

This may then be the key to that baffling poem, Goldsmith's *The Deserted Village* (1769). At first reading, the sense of the poem seems clear. The portraits of village parson and schoolmaster continue directly (and perhaps consciously) from Shenstone. And they are set within a more developed but still familiar contrast of simple happiness and ambitious luxury. But what is then difficult is the apparent precision of the social contrast between the happy and the ruined village. I do not mean the occasional gesture, in the style of 'Oh wassel days'.

> A time there was, ere England's griefs began
> When every rood of ground maintain'd its man.

I mean the apparent description of a contemporary social process, which takes the poem beyond the relatively static contrast of simplicity and luxury.

> But times are alter'd; trade's unfeeling train
> Usurp the land and dispossess the swain.

This is again not unfamiliar; it could fit into a sixteenth- or early seventeenth-century complaint. What is novel in *The Deserted Village* is the sense of observation: of a precise and visible social location. It is to 'Sweet Auburn' – here and here – that the dispossession happens.

It is still very difficult to be certain what village, if any, Goldsmith had in mind. It is sometimes assumed that he is remembering his childhood in Ireland, but we have to set against this his own claim, in 1770 (after twelve years' residence in England) that

> I have taken all possible pains, in my country excursions, for these four or five years past, to be certain of what I allege.

Then there is the letter in *Lloyd's Evening Post* (1762), now generally assigned to him, in which

> Wherever the traveller turns, while he sees one part of the inhabitants of the country becoming immensely rich, he sees the other growing miserably poor, and the happy equality of condition now entirely removed ... In almost every part of the kingdom, the laborious husbandman has been reduced.

And for a more immediate reference, a correspondent in the *Public Advertiser* (29 September 1780) records an incident of which Goldsmith had told him, in which 'several cottages were destroyed' near the house of 'a great West Indian'; perhaps a local basis for the unfeeling incursion of trade.

The social process is in fact one of clearance, of eviction and evacuation, to make way for a mansion and its grounds. It is based on engrossing –

> One only master grasps the whole domain

– and has as its result that

> > the man of wealth and pride
> Takes up a space that many poor supplied;
> Space for his lake, his park's extended bounds,
> Space for his horses, equipage and hounds.

I have already referred to an earlier example of this – perhaps in the 'wassel days' – in the Herberts' country seat in Wiltshire, where *Arcadia* was written. There were notable eighteenth-century examples in Oxfordshire and Dorset, and many smaller and less recorded cases. Goldsmith follows the dispossessed people of the village to the possible alternatives: to another part of the country, but

> If to some common's fenceless limits stray'd
> He drives his flock to pick the scanty blade
> Those fenceless fields the sons of wealth divide
> And even the bare-worn common is denied

– the continuing process of enclosure; to the city, but

> If to the city sped – what waits him there?
> To see profusion that he must not share

– a sense of the exaggerated contrasts of wealth and misery in the very aggregation that the city represents; and finally to exile and emigration –

> Where half the convex world intrudes between.

In these ways, the perspective is wide, and a real history is seen.

Yet there is another question that we are forced to put. What is strangest in the poem is its combination of protest and nostalgia, and the way these emotions are related, consciously and unconsciously, to the practice of poetry. Take first the invocation of the formerly happy village:

> Sweet Auburn! loveliest village of the plain
> Where health and plenty cheered the labouring swain,
> Where smiling spring its earliest visit paid,
> And parting summer's lingering blooms delayed.

The interest of this is its reliance on pastoral common place, which is at a literary as well as an historical distance from its object.

> Dear lovely bowers of innocence and ease
> Seats of my youth, when every sport could please.

It is not only the amalgamation of the memory of childhood and the memory of the village: it is that, in this mode of remembering, the objects seem to dissolve, in what is really a self-regarding poetic exercise.

> How often have I paused on every charm,
> The shelter'd cot, the cultivated farm,
> The never-failing brook, the busy mill,
> The decent church that topt the neighbouring hill,
> The hawthorn bush, with seats beneath the shade,
> For talking age and whispering lovers made.

It is perhaps the hawthorn bush that does it. We have to choose between the unamended scale of a child's vision and the at once vague and mechanical rehearsal of a known literary method. The people who live in the village are seen, in this mode, as the lay figures of pastoral:

> And all the village train from labour free
> Led up their sports beneath the spreading tree:

Still, as in Thomson, under that hawthorn!

> These were thy charms, sweet village! sports like these,
> With sweet succession, taught e'en toil to please.

But the sweet succession is in fact a series of literary reminiscences: a dissolving of the lives and work of others into an image of the past.

This is then the unseen irony of the poem, and the explanation of the eviction of Poetry. For what is in question, in the actual movement of feeling, is not only the life of the village, but the independence of the poet, who had hoped to retire there, where (odd echo of Carew)

> No surly porter stands in guilty state,
> To spurn imploring famine from the gate.

It is not only the frustration of that understandable hope –

> my long vexations past,
> Here to return – and die at home at last.

It is that the social forces which are dispossessing the village are seen as simultaneously dispossessing poetry (one remembers, ironically, the central presence of poetry in Thomson's plentiful and propertied social order):

> And thou, sweet Poesy, thou loveliest Maid,
> Still first to fly where sensual joys invade;
> Unfit in these degenerate times of shame,
> To catch the heart, or strike for honest fame.
> Dear charming nymph, neglected and denied,
> My shame in crowds, my solitary pride,
> Thou source of all my bliss, and all my woe,
> That found'st me poor at first, and keep'st me so.

If it is only the social history of the village that is in question, this simultaneous eviction of poetry is undeniably curious. But what happens is that from the intense personal situation, in which the independence of the poet is insufficient to maintain his life, and in which all the humanity he claims to represent is crushed and driven out by the coarse and unfeeling order of the new rich, a landscape extends, which is that of the village suffering a similar ignominy. The rural dispossession is, as we have seen, incisively observed. Its facts are present, palpably, in their own right. Yet the dispossession is subject, also, to another process; what I have called elsewhere, in relation to Gissing and Orwell, a negative identification. That is to say, the exposure and suffering of the writer, in his own social situation, are identified with the facts of a social history that is beyond him. It is not that he cannot then see the real social history; he is often especially sensitive to it, as a present fact. But the identification between his own suffering and that of a social group beyond him is inevitably negative, in the end. The present is accurately and powerfully seen, but its real relations, to past and future, are inaccessible, because the governing development is that of the writer himself: a feeling about the past, an idea about the future, into which, by what is truly an intersection, an observed present is arranged. We need not doubt the warmth of Goldsmith's feelings about the men driven from their village: that connection is definite. The structure becomes ambiguous only when this shared feeling is extended to memory and imagination, for what takes them over then, in language and idea, is a different pressure: the social history of the writer. Thus the nostalgic portraits of parson and schoolmaster are of men independent and honoured in their own place, supported by a whole way of living in which independence and community are actual. Against this self-dependent power, which is also that of the poet, the encroachment of wealth and fashion is fatal. Yet to be a poet is, ironically, to be a pastoral poet: the social condition of poetry – it is as far as Goldsmith gets – is the idealized pastoral economy. The destruction of one is, or is made to stand for, the destruction of the other. And then the village itself becomes a pastoral and a poetic mode: its expropriation is assigned to the general vices of wealth and luxury. Thus it is very significant that the old village was both happy and productive, while the new condition is both unhappy and unproductive –

> One only master grasps the whole domain,
> And half a tillage stints thy smiling plain,
> No more thy glassy brook reflects the day,
> But choked with sedges, works its weedy way;
> Along thy glades, a solitary guest,
> The hollow sounding bittern guards its nest;
> Amidst thy desert walk the lapwing flies
> And tires their echoes with unvaried cries.

It would indeed be easy if the social process were really that. But the actual history, in which the destruction of old social relations was accompanied by an increased use and fertility of the land, is overridden by the imaginative process in which, when the pastoral order is destroyed, creation is 'stinted', the brook is 'choked', the cry of the bittern is 'hollow', the lapwing's cries 'unvaried'. This creation of a 'desert' landscape is an imaginative rather than a social process; it is what the new order does to the poet, not to the land. The memory of 'sweet Auburn' is of a kind of community, a kind of feeling, and a kind of verse, which are no longer able to survive, under the pressure of 'trade's unfeeling train', but which equally cannot be gone beyond, into new relationship and imagination; which can only go into exile and a desperate protest, beyond history –

> Still let thy voice, prevailing over time,
> Redress the rigours of th' inclement clime.

It is exiled poetry, at the end of *The Deserted Village*, which must teach, hopefully:

> That trade's proud empire hastes to swift decay,
> As oceans sweep the labour'd mole away;
> While self-dependent power can time defy,
> As rocks resist the billows and the sky.

Here, with unusal precision, what we can later call a Romantic structure of feeling – the assertion of nature against industry and of poetry against trade; the isolation of humanity and community into the idea of culture, against the real social pressures of the time – is projected. We can catch its echoes, exactly, in Blake, in Wordsworth, and in Shelley.

(iii)

A different reconstruction of a happier past, with a conscious appeal to morality in the present, comes in Langhorne's *The Country Justice* (1774–7). Here the ultimate reference is to the free Briton, before the incursion of Saxon, Dane and Norman: a variant on that idea of the Norman Yoke which interpreted the Conquest as the institution of feudal property, oppression and landlordism, and the pre-Conquest period – especially the Saxon kingdom of Alfred – as a free and equal rural community. In Langhorne (and there is as much – as little – case for the one as the other) the free forefathers are the Britons; themselves also invaders, but far enough back. Yet the idea of liberty they represent is not only 'historical'.

> Were thoughts like these the Dream of ancient Time?
> Peculiar only to some Age, or Clime?
> And does not Nature thoughts like these impart,
> Breathe in the Soul, and write upon the Heart?

Here the idea of a primitive freedom, and of the perpetual impulse and teaching of 'Nature', are combined as in Rousseau, to whom the poem makes an oblique reference through the Corsican revolt. But Langhorne finds a more particular carrier of this ideal: the country magistrate, the justice of the peace, from the reign of Edward III:

> In happier Days, with more auspicious Fate,
> The far-fam'd Edward heal'd his wounded State . . .
> . . . The social Laws from Insult to protect,
> To cherish Peace, to cultivate Respect;
> The rich from wanton Cruelty restrain,
> To smooth the bed of Penury and Pain . . .
> . . . For this the rural magistrate, of Yore,
> Thy honours, Edward, to his Mansion bore.

The poem then moves to an identification of this traditional justice with the old country-houses –

> the plain Precincts of the antient Hall.

And this is made the basis for an attack on the new ways:

> Nor lightly deem, ye Apes of modern Race,
> Ye Cits that sore bedizen Nature's Face,
> Of the more manly Structures here ye view;
> They rose from Greatness that ye never knew.

The plain old order is being invaded (as we have heard before) by wealthy citizens, who have made their money in trade, and by the new vices of fashion, for which Langhorne's contempt is equally evident:

> Ye royal Architects, whose antic Taste,
> Would lay the Realms of Sense and Nature waste.

The arrival in the old country of these new men and new feelings darkens traditional justice:

> O Edward, here thy fairest Laurels fade!
> And thy long glories darken into Shade.

Harshness to the vagrant ex-soldier and cruel imprisonment of the unmarried mother are signs of the decay. The old justice, and its honourable humanity, are contrasted with the coldness and rigour of the new times.

Langhorne then looks at a more particular example: the treatment of the aged poor, by those appointed to deal with them:

> But chief thy Notice shall One Monster claim,
> A Monster furnished with a human Frame,
> The Parish-Officer! – though VERSE disdain
> Terms that deform the Splendor of the Strain;
> It stoops to bid Thee bend the Brow severe
> On the sly, pilfering, cruel Overseer;
> The shuffling Farmer, faithful to no Trust,
> Ruthless as Rocks, insatiate as the Dust!
> When the poor Hind, with Length of Years decay'd,
> Leans feebly on his once subduing Spade,
> Forgot the service of his abler Days,
> His profitable Toil, and honest Praise,
> Shall this low Wretch abridge his scanty Bread,
> This Slave, whose Board his former Labours spread?
> When Harvest's burning Suns and sickening Air
> From Labour's unbrac'd Hand the grasp'd Hook tear,
> Where shall the helpless Family be fed
> That vainly languish for a Father's Bread?
> See the pale Mother, sunk with Grief and Care,
> To the proud Farmer fearfully repair;
> Soon to be sent with Insolence away,
> Referr'd to Vestries, and a distant Day!
> Referr'd – to perish! Is my verse severe?
> Unfriendly to the human Character?
> Ah! to this Sigh of sad Experience trust:
> The Truth is rigid, but the Tale is just.

There is no reason to doubt the accuracy of this account of the treatment of 'paupers'. Langhorne tells the story of a shepherd

and his wife, found dead on a bed of fern from starvation. And
this, he argues, is the present Justice's fault:

> When thy good Father held this wide Domain,
> The voice of Sorrow never mourn'd in vain ...
> He left their interest to no Parish-Care,
> No Bailiff urged his little Empire there.

This retrospect is generalized into a familiar recall of the old
days:

> O Days long lost to Man in each Degree!
> The golden Days of Hospitality ...
> When WEALTH was Virtue's Handmaid, and her Gate
> Gave a free Refuge from the Wrongs of Fate;
> The Poor at Hand their natural Patrons saw,
> And Lawgivers were Supplements of Law!
> Lost are those Days, and FASHION's boundless Sway
> Has borne the Guardian Magistrate away ...
> The Rural Patron is beheld no more.

Back, then, to Penshurst and Saxham. Their successors have all
gone to the city or to Brighton. And with the landlord gone,
who is left to be just and humane? Only the ruffian bailiff and
the creeping, hypocritical, hymn-singing church-warden.

Langhorne's anger is generous, but this social vision is strange.
After a life as a private tutor and a clergyman, he married into a
landowning family and became a country magistrate in Somerset. In his way of seeing, humanity is projected into a lost rural
tradition, and inhumanity on to the agents of a contemporary
process. Thus it is the bailiff, not the landlord, who seizes the
flock of the shepherd who died of hunger:

> led by the Lure of unaccounted Gold.

There were of course such bailiffs and such agents, but it is idle
to isolate them from the social process which they served, and
from the engrossing landowners who (as Langhorne recognized)
retained the responsibility for it. It is as if a humane man could
not bring himself to see the real origins of the misery of his time,
in the class to which he was directly linked. He must either
idealize their past, or explain the present by their absence and
the irruption of new men.

Absentee landlords, of course, existed; and they are a class who, whatever they say, have always known what is being done, through and for them. But neither they nor the transplanted merchants can be isolated as the source of the drive to engross and enclose with all its consequent social rigours. The real process of transforming rural England was firmly in the hands of the all too present and commercially active landowners. And the real origin of change was the developing system of agrarian capitalism, which, as has been characteristic of capitalism throughout its history, succeeded in transforming its environment in a dramatically productive way, by making both men and nature instrumental to a dominating purpose.

Capitalism has in this sense always been an ambiguous process: increasing real wealth but distributing it unevenly; enabling larger populations to grow and survive, but within them seeing men only as producers and consumers, with no substantial claim on society except in these abstract capacities. There was thus a continuing contrast between the extraordinary improvement of the land and the social consequences of just this process, in the dispossessed and the vagrants, and the old, the sick, the disabled, the nursing mothers, the children who, unable to work in these terms, were seen as merely negative, an unwanted burden. To see the paradox of successful production and these human consequences would be to penetrate the inner character of capitalism itself. It was easier, for men like Langhorne, to separate the consequences from the system, and then to ascribe to social decay what was actually the result of social and economic growth.

Of course to the extent that the new social system was itself becoming more successful, more pervasive and more confidently aggressive, there was always likely to be a local basis for some kind of retrospective regret. In this place and that, different ways, different times could be actually remembered. But under the pressure of the general contradictions of the system this realistic local observation grew to a general historical outline, and then to a myth. The English landowning class, which had changed itself in changing its world, was idealized and displaced into an historical contrast with its own real activities. In its actual inhumanity, it could be recognized only with difficulty by men linked to and dependent on it, and the great majority of the poor and oppressed were without a connecting voice to make clear the recognition which was their daily experience. Thus a humane instinct was separated from society; it became a sympathy and a pity, *after* the decisive social events. The real ruling class could not be put in question, so they were seen as temporarily absent, or as the good old people succeeded by the bad new people – themselves succeeding themselves. We have heard this sad song for many centuries now: a seductive song, turning protest into retrospect, until we die of time.

Langhorne's vision of the old justice, and its contrast with the new, is a major element in the whole way of seeing the rural past which has become characteristic. As we have seen, he puts the old justice first one generation and then many generations back. This sliding vagueness about periods is normal, in the whole subsequent debate.

But let us, for the moment, agree to go back. What has been called the paternalism of the Tudor poor laws was always linked to an offensive against what was called vagrancy. This double character of the legislation is characteristic of the emergence of rural capitalism as a social order. In the scarce medieval economy, poverty could be seen as the consequence of what seemed natural calamities: famine, sickness and plague. Thus the response to poverty was, at least in theory, a natural charity, in which all men were involved by their existence in nature: a duty to God included this general duty to men, in a predominantly religious perspective. Of course the reality was very different: a normal poverty was built into the expected order, and abnormal poverty had to take its chance in a gratuitous system. But it was in the development from a generally scarce economy, and in the break-up and mobility of the post-feudal society, that a new ideology decisively appeared. It at once organized the response to poverty, as in the new sixteenth-century ideas of a compulsory poor-rate, classification of types of poverty, and new administrative machinery to deal with them; and, on the other side of the coin, it linked poverty to labour in new ways, so that the harrying of what was called vagrancy, itself the result of a socially created disturbance and mobility, became, in its turn, a moral duty. The collectors and overseers

had, from the beginning, this double function: that they organized relief and that they drove the exposed and dispossessed to
work. The biggest problem of this system was always its treatment of an inevitable and natural mobility. Much of the actual
purpose of the laws against vagrancy was to force the landless
to work for wages, in the new organization of the economy.
But this was rationalized, through the organization of relief on a
parochial basis, as the duty of people to care for their own, for
their neighbours; but then only for their own. The idea of
settlement, and then of paternal care, was counterposed to the
ideas of mobility, of the wandering 'sturdy rogues', the free
labourers.

This contrast has persisted, in a long crisis of values. It is still
common to hear an idealization of settlement, of neighbourhood,
as if it were the only reality of community. In the middle of the
twentieth century, T. S. Eliot, defining an idea of a Christian
society, could say that 'on the whole it would appear to be for the
best that the great majority of human beings should go on living
in the place in which they were born'. ('The great majority',
of course excludes a man who moved not only from one place
but from one continent to another.)

Around the idea of settlement, nevertheless, a real structure of
values has grown. It draws on many deep and persistent feelings:
an identification with the people among whom we grew up; an
attachment to the place, the landscape, in which we first lived
and learned to see. I know these feelings at once, from my own
experience. The only landscape I ever see, in dreams, is the
Black Mountain village in which I was born. When I go back
to that country, I feel a recovery of a particular kind of life,
which appears, at times, as an inescapable identity, a more
positive connection than I have known elsewhere. Many other
men feel this, of their own native places, and the strength of the
idea of settlement, old and new, is then positive and unques-
tioned. But the problem has always been, for most people, how
to go on living where they are. I know this also personally: not
only because I had to move out for an education and to go on
with a particular kind of work; but because the whole region in
which I was born has been steadily and terribly losing its people,
who can no longer make a living there. When I hear the ideal-

ization of settlement, I do not need to borrow the first feelings; I know, in just that sense, what neighbourhood means, and what is involved in separation and leaving. But I know, also, why people have to move, why so many moved in my own family. So that I then see the idealization of settlement, in its ordinary literary-historical version, as an insolent indifference to most people's needs. In particular the idealization of the old kind of poor law, whether in Langhorne or in twentieth-century writers, seems to me so deep an error as to deny the humanity which it conventionally expresses. Yet I can see that it must be difficult for anyone who has not experienced conditions of monopoly or near-monopoly employment to penetrate the ideology of that self-regarding paternalism. Settlement is indeed easy, is positively welcome, for those who can settle in a reasonable independence. For those who cannot – and under the pressures of change from a new mode of production these became the majority – it can become a prison: a long disheartening and despair, under an imposed rigidity of conditions. And the point of the acts of settlement was to maintain this rigidity, this implacable hold on men. From the feudal grip on the serf to the more complicated machinery of the poor law, this control is evident. The consequences of what is idealized as a moral economy can then be plainly read. You fitted where you were; if you went out, you were harried. As it was put in 1662, in the preamble to a new Act:

by reason of some defect in the law, poor people are not restrained from going from one parish to another, and do therefore endeavour to settle themselves in those parishes where there is the best stock, the largest commons or wastes to build cottages, and the most woods for them to burn and destroy.

There had been so many previous attempts to restrain such men and women from seeking their living. There had been licence systems, since the fourteenth century, for any servant or labourer leaving his parish; certificates from employers, to show that they were really 'at liberty'; the controlling machinery of the Statute and Hiring Fairs. Through the varying phases of this control of men as labour, the relief of poverty, which included some natural and kindly feelings, was bitter compromise. For on the one hand there was a failure of wages to rise as they should have, from the mid seventeenth to the late eighteenth century, in a period in which the prosperity of agriculture quite remarkably increased. On the other hand, all those who fell through the network of this primary control – women with children, orphans, the illegitimate, the sick and the old – were dealt with by a system of relief, based on settlement, which, through its many local variations, was as a whole inevitably cruel. 'Aged, lame or impotent persons', of less than three years residence, could be physically removed from the village, or lawfully neglected. Orphans were directed to apprenticeships which bound them to the favour and conditions of a master. Unmarried mothers were sent to prison. Families with too many children would be moved on wherever possible; ironically, they were less vulnerable in the towns and in the early industrial areas than in the villages; they made, sometimes, an economic unit there, while in the villages what was most wanted was the abstract producer, the single able-bodied man, the indoor farm-servant. There were of course parishes where humanity prevailed. But the system was a vicious driving of the most exposed, from one parish to another, and then the institution of work-houses, where this human debris – the sick, the old, the deranged, the unfortunate, the runaways – could be concentrated and then more directly controlled. As Crabbe later described one of these mixed workhouses:

> There Children dwell who know no parents' care:
> Parents, who know no Children's love, dwell there;
> Heart-broken Matrons on their joyless bed,
> Forsaken Wives and Mothers never wed;
> Dejected Widows with unheeded tears,
> And crippled Age with more than childhood's fears;
> The Lame, the Blind, and, far the happiest they!
> The moping Idiot and the Madman gay.

Even those who could stay in their parishes were subject to pressures, when they came in need. After 1693, relief of the settled old – such men as Langhorne described – was made subject to the authority of a justice, their names entered in a book and annually reviewed. An Act of 1697 ordered these pensioned paupers to wear a red or blue letter 'P' on their coats; they were now a category and marked.

In the face of all this, we are not likely to accept Langhorne's history, though we can accept his observation. It was a long-established system that produced the cruelty which appalled him, and there was never any chance of elevating the country justice above the standards of the rural society and economy to which he belonged. The good man caught in the system (one of them was Henry Fielding, in a different environment) might temper it with mercy; might see ways of reform. But the limits were there, as part of a whole reality. Justice and overseer, landlord and bailiff, belonged in a common and dominant world. That tale was indeed rigid, and it had not replaced the 'rural patrons'. It was founded on them.

> No longer truth, though shown in verse, disdain
> But own the Village Life a life of pain.

Crabbe's insistence is now easier to understand. The observation is that of Goldsmith or Langhorne, but in a new structure of feeling, which can dispense with retrospect. What is seen, in a new convention, is an existing, active and social contrast. The energy of the new convention springs from a rejection of the old: a rejection of 'pastoral':

> I grant indeed that fields and flocks have charms
> For him that grazes or for him that farms;
> But when amid such pleasing scenes I trace
> The poor laborious natives of the place,
> And see the mid-day sun, with fervid ray,
> On their bare heads and dewy temples play;
> While some, with feebler heads and fainter hearts,
> Deplore their fortune, yet sustain their parts;
> Then shall I dare these real ills to hide
> In tinsel trappings of poetic pride?

This is an alteration of landscape, by an alteration of seeing. The inclusion of work, and so of working men, is a conscious shift of affiliation. We have only to remember the fields around Penshurst to realize its magnitude, or *The Hock-Cart* to recognize the conscious amendment of feeling.

In one part of his recognition Crabbe had been preceded. Half a century earlier, the same challenge to 'pastoral' had been powerfully made:

> No Fountains murmur here, no Lambkins play,
> No Linnets warble, and no Fields look gay;
> 'Tis all a gloomy, melancholy Scene,
> Fit only to provoke the Muse's Spleen.

When sooty Pease we thresh, you scarce can know
Our native Colour, as from Work we go:
The Sweat, the Dust, and suffocating Smoke
Make us so much like Ethiopians look.
We scare our Wives, when Ev'ning brings us home;
And frighted Infants think the Bugbear come.
Week after Week, we this dull Task pursue,
Unless when winn'wing Days produce a new;
A new, indeed, but frequently a worse!
The Threshal yields but to the Master's Curse.

There is a decisive shift, in these lines, in the particularity of the
work and above all in that determining pronoun:

When sooty Pease *we* thresh.

For this is Stephen Duck, still called with a lingering patronage
the 'thresher-poet'. We get his history, in every sense, from his
first title page:

Who was many Years a poor Thresher in a Barn, at Charleton
in the County of Wilts, at the Wages of four Shillings and Six-
pence per Week, 'till taken Notice of by Her late Majesty Queen
CAROLINE; who, on Account of his great Genius, gave him an
Apartment at Kew, near Richmond, in Surry, and a Salary of
Thirty Pounds per Annum; after which he studied the learned
Languages, took Orders, and is now a dignified Clergyman.

Nothing can now diminish the simple power of one of his
earliest poems, *The Thresher's Labour*:

Let those who feast at Ease on dainty Fare
Pity the Reapers, who their Feasts prepare:
For Toils scarce ever ceasing press us now;
Rest never does, but on the Sabbath, show:
And barely that our Masters will allow.
Think what a painful Life we daily lead;
Each morning early rise, go late to Bed;
Nor, when asleep, are we secure from Pain;
We then perform our Labours o'er again:
Our mimic Fancy every restless seems;
And what we act awake, she acts in Dreams . . .
. . . Thus, as the Year's revolving Course goes round,
No respite from our Labour can be found;
Like Sisyphus, our Work is never done;
Continually rolls back the restless Stone.
New growing Labours still succeed the past;
And growing always new, must always last.

This was written while he was still a thresher, when

he work'd all Day for his Master; and, after the Labour of the Day, set to his Books at Night.

It is easy to feel the strain of this labourer's voice as it adapts, slowly, to the available models in verse: the formal explanation, the anxious classical reference, the arranged subordinate clauses of that self-possessed literary manner. Yet the feeling drives through these, in its own way, and it is remarkable, reading this simple and obvious truth, that Duck's name still, in the twentieth century, carries its 'limiting' associations.

A better target for wit – and certainly for contempt – is the subsequent social absorption. What happened was probably inevitable:

Persons of Distinction began to send for him in different Ways.

Exposed already to a conventional ideology –

> Contented Poverty's no dismal Thing,
> Free from the Cares unwieldy Riches bring . . .
> . . . The poor Man's labour relishes his Meat;
> His Morsel's pleasant, and his Rest is sweet . . .
> . . . But let us state the Case another Way:
> Were Poverty so hideous as they say,
> 'Tis nobler cheerfully to bear our Fate,
> Than murmur and repine beneath its Weight

– he was shifted from this sustaining, defensive if compromised self-respect to a different tone. Soon after his translation, he wrote *Gratitude, a Pastoral*: those two words, together, are the essential history.

> O You, MENALCAS, know my abject Birth,
> Born in a Cot, and bred to till the Earth:
> On rigid Worldlings always doom'd to wait,
> Forc'd at their frugal Hands my bread to get:
> But when my Wants to CAROLINE were known,
> She bless'd me with a Pasture of my own.
> This makes new Pleasures in my Bosom glow;
> These joyful Looks I to her Bounty owe.

This is frank and understandable, and it is no real surprise, a year or two later, to hear:

> Of blissful Groves I sing, and flow'ry Plains:
> Ye Sylvan Nymphs, assist my rural strains.

This, characteristically, is *On Richmond Park, and Royal Gardens*, where 'pastoral', as a game, was perpetually available. William Kent had designed, for Queen Caroline, a pavilion called Merlin's Cave – 'a Palladian façade under a thatched roof' – and Duck was stationed inside it as a guide. What then did the guide say?

> No plund'ring Armies rob our fruitful Plain;
> But, bless'd with Peace and Plenty, smiles the Swain.
> Not so he smiles upon the foreign Shores;
> Poor Peasants with their rigid Burdens groan,
> And till the Glebe for Harvest not their own.

It is a short and dramatic transition from

> The Morning past, we sweat beneath the Sun;
> And but uneasily our Work goes on.
> Before us we perplexing Thistles find,
> And Corn blown adverse with the muffling Wind.
> Behind our Master waits; and if he spies
> One charitable Ear, he grudging cries,
> 'Ye scatter half your Wages o'er the Land'.
> Then scrapes the Stubble with his greedy Hand.

But it is not only a transition from a Wiltshire field to Richmond Park and Royal Gardens; it is, as a decisive literary transition, a shift from 'we' to 'the swain'. Within a few years Duck was writing, with the worst of them, his imitations from the classics, elevated and hollowed to the shapes of that fashionable culture which was not only a literary stance – the 'high' tradition – but, as always, a social ratification. We can most clearly represent the consequent deadening, and the unconscious irony, in one of his verses, imitated from Claudian, which has for other and unforeseeable reasons become ludicrous:

> How bless'd the Swain of Bethnal-Green,
> Who ne'er a Court beheld,
> Nor ever rov'd beyond the Scene,
> Of his paternal Field.

With this sad history behind him, Crabbe had, in a sense, to begin all over again. He makes the distinction between the pleasant country of 'him that grazes or . . . him that farms' and the reality of the 'poor laborious natives of the place'. This is already interesting, as a notation of social reality: the effective distinction between the owner 'farming' and 'grazing' and the labourers only labouring. As contractors or architects, now, are said to 'build', but labourers only to 'work on a building site' or, in another convention, to 'lay bricks', 'carpenter', 'mix concrete'; the parts but not the whole of the process, which has been appropriated to the owner and the employer and which, not being in the labourers' direction, is in a real sense not truly theirs. But the more immediately governing distinction is between 'him that farms' and the 'I' of the poet. That much separation has occurred, in the shift of convention: the writer is the independent observer and not (or not wholly; we shall see an instance later) the poet-guest of his landlord patron. At the same time, from this kind of independent position, it is characteristically the aged labourer whom Crabbe, like Langhorne, sees:

> For now he journeys to his grave in pain;
> The rich disdain him; nay the poor disdain;
> Alternate masters now their slave command,
> Urge the weak efforts of his feeble hand,
> And when his age attempts its task in vain,
> With ruthless taunts, of lazy poor complain.

This is a break from an ideology, through what is at first a humanitarian observation. But the break is extended. In his counter-pastoral, Crabbe's first general evidence is a stretch of bad land; the unproductive, weed-ridden soil then inland from Aldeburgh in Suffolk. And it is important to note this, for any study of the literature and history of rural England has always to be aware of region and of place. 'A smiling countryside', as we shall see in Cobbett's *Rural Rides*, could give way, within a morning's journey, to 'a length of burning sand'. Generalizations about rural England, in this period as to a lesser extent in our own time, have often to give way to this fact of uneven development. Arthur Young's Suffolk was only just such a journey away from Crabbe's, in the same years.

Yet Crabbe's vision is more than a response to the fact of bad land, which might always, as in Young's campaigns, be improved. He turns from the 'length of burning sand' and makes the next essential point:

> But these are scenes where Nature's niggard hand
> Gave a spare portion to the famish'd land;
> Hers is the fault, if here mankind complain
> Of fruitless toil and labour spent in vain;
> But yet in other scenes more fair in view,
> Where Plenty smiles – alas! she smiles for few –
> And those who taste not, yet behold her store,
> Are as the slaves that dig the golden ore, –
> The wealth around them makes them doubly poor.

This is precisely the condition –

> But starving walks thro' Nature's lavish Stores

– which Duck had noticed and then placed safely overseas. It is the special crisis of rural as of industrial capitalism. There are many places in England where we might now be –

> Where Plenty smiles – alas! she smiles for few

– but we are probably in Leicestershire, or the land of the dependent villages around Belvoir Castle, where Crabbe was domestic chaplain to the principal landowner, the Duke of Rutland. Some of these lands had been enclosed just before he was writing: for example Croxton, in 1766, by a combined scheme of the Duke and the local clergy. It is in this country, under such rule, that the labourer is poor in the midst of plenty. On the bad land, the fault was Nature's; but here, whose fault?

The question is raised, but it is not finally in the character or power of Crabbe's vision to answer it. *The Village* is truly a counter-pastoral, opposing its description of pain to the 'pastoral' descriptions of pleasure. In the same mode, it is a polemic against flattering accounts of a moral economy; the care that ought to be given is not being given. As Crabbe puts it, with a glance back at Goldsmith:

> And doth not he, the pious man, appear,
> The 'passing rich with forty pounds a year?'
> Ah! no; a shepherd of a different stock,
> And far unlike him, feeds this little flock.

Parson and doctor – Crabbe's own men; Crabbe himself – neglect and even outrage what should be a moral duty.

The ambiguity of this social and moral position – of the

humane and indignant observer, who is also domestic chaplain to the Duke of Rutland – is interestingly reflected in the structure and even the grammatical case of the poem. Crabbe announces a central question:

> What labour yields, and what, that labour past,
> Age, in its hour of langour, finds at last.

Yet the dimension of his answer indicates his real audience, and, therefore, his real question.

> Or will you deem them amply paid in health,
> Labour's fair child, that languishes with wealth?
> Go then and see them rising with the sun
> Through a long course of daily toil to run;
> See them beneath the dog-star's raging heat
> When the knees tremble and the temples beat;
> Behold them, leaning on the scythes, look o'er
> The labour past, and toils to come explore;
> See them alternate suns and showers engage
> And hoard up aches and anguish for their age;
> Through fens and marshy moors their steps pursue,
> When their warm pores imbibe the evening dew;
> Then own that labour may as fatal be
> To these thy slaves, as thine excess to thee.

The reader has to ask, at this point, who this 'you' and 'thou' may be. The 'you' of the poem is in general the pastoral poet and, by extension, his complacent readers:

> Ye gentle souls, who dream of rural ease.

Yet in these other lines, briefly, there is another personality: 'thy slaves'; 'thine excess'. Not the pastoral poet, but the wealthy landowner, is briefly arraigned, to see the suffering of his labourers. Yet the arraignment rests on what is in effect a pastoral assumption: health is the 'fair child' of labour; it 'languishes' with wealth. This is more than an observation of the simple dependence of health on exercise; it is slanted association of health with labour and then of sickness with wealth, that in any real world is naïve. Crabbe overthrows one part of the naïveté in a straightforward way: this kind of labour and exposure destroys people physically. But the counterpart of this observation never comes, for attention is switched from the landowners who direct and expose the labour to the easier figure of the excessive consumer. When Crabbe returns to direct address, towards the end of the first book, this implicit identification becomes explicit:

> Say ye, oppressed by some fantastic woes,
> Some jarring nerve that baffles your repose,
> Who press the downy couch, while slaves advance
> With timid eye, to read the distant glance;
> Who with sad prayers the weary doctor tease,
> To name the nameless ever-new disease;
> Who with mock patience dire complaints endure,
> Which real pain, and that alone, can cure;
> How would ye bear in real pain to lie,
> Despised, neglected, left alone to die?

This is done from the life, we can be certain: from Crabbe's time as a medical student. But the contempt for a class of glutted and neurotic consumers, and the powerful contrast with the condition of the labourers, make us forget what is involved in that crucial passage from 'thy slaves' to 'thine excess'. Attention is switched, as so often, from the active directors of the social process to its more isolable and passive beneficiaries: the luxurious people of the town. These too have their 'slaves', their domestic servants, but they are attacked not for their connection to the exploitation, and not only for their indifference; simply, for the harm they are doing themselves and those near them.

The structure of Crabbe's values is then essentially clear: it is eighteenth-century humanitarianism, with its passionate insistence on care and sympathy, based on an implied standard of plain, virtuous and responsible living. It is in this sense still a pastoral vision, of simplicity and independence, made bitter and desperate by scenes in which it is continually denied: the neglect of the poor, the excesses of the rich. What Crabbe asks is self-respect and charity: that the rich should learn these virtues; that the poor should benefit from them. It is a moving appeal, within a social vision which had been briefly dynamic –

> Where Plenty smiles – alas! she smiles for few

– but which is finally static: a moral as opposed to a social contrast of poverty and wealth.

Thus the independence Crabbe announced, as the uncommitted observer who will tell the truth against the lies of the pastoral conventions, is in the end, precisely, the independence of priest or doctor: of those who care for soul and body, within the consequences of a social system. The urgency of care is so great that indignation is centred on those who are indifferent or who avoid the need. When the labourer, after working all his life, is old and ill, he needs a proper doctor, as opposed to

> A potent quack, long versed in human ills,
> Who first insults the victim whom he kills;

or a proper parson, as opposed to

> A jovial youth, who thinks his Sunday's task
> As much as God or man can fairly ask.

This case and this protest are of course honourable. Yet, as in the whole tradition, they have their limits, and these appear in *The Village*. Jonson and Carew, guests and poets in the country-houses of their patrons, complimented their hosts with a vision of a moral economy which, however idealizing, finally ratified the social position of the landowner. Crabbe does not flatter, when he restores the facts of labour to the idyllic landscape; but he also, doctor and priest, domestic chaplain to an enclosing landowner, is not really independent. In the first book of *The Village* he cleared a space for independent observation and for moral appeal. Yet in the end the morality is separated from the social relationships which breed poverty and indifference. It is the cause of paupers, not the creation of pauperism, which holds the attention and the feeling.

In the second book a limited independence is for a while retained: the vices of the poor – slander, drunkenness, prostitution – are not theirs alone; are even, explicitly, vices caught from the rich:

> The peer's disease in turn attacks the clown.

The hypocrisy of a double moral standard – that of a class society – is seen in the courts, when the justice's whore, looking at a poor girl who has been seduced,

> thanks the stars that made her keeper great.

This moral indignation is again, temporarily, a social in-dependence. But then something breaks:

> Yet why, you ask, these humble crimes relate,
> Why make the poor as guilty as the great?
> To show the great, those mightier sons of pride,
> How near in vice the lowest are allied . . .
> . . . So shall the man of power and pleasure see
> In his own slave as vile a wretch as he;
> In his luxurious lord the servant find
> His own low pleasures and degenerate mind;
> And each in all the kindred vices trace,
> Of a poor, blind, bewilder'd, erring race;
> Who, a short time in varied fortune past
> Die and are equal in the dust at last.

It is sonorous enough, but it is the road back from those fields around the castle. The 'varied fortune' is now morally relative to the 'equality' of death. It is the 'race' that errs, the 'human condition'. We have been told this so often, in a familiar ideology which introduces itself as a higher truth, that Crabbe's pathetic retreat may come as no surprise. But the announcement of a morality independent of social conditions, 'above' the mere 'variety' of 'fortune', is here, as elsewhere, the prelude to a particular social ratification. It is not really surprising, though after the quality of the earlier observations it is depressing, to find Crabbe concluding:

> And you, ye poor, who still lament your fate,
> Forbear to envy those you call the great;
> And know, amid the blessings they possess,
> They are, like you, the victims of distress.

The case then actually cited – the death of a relative of the Duke of Rutland – is of course real. But in the structure of the poem –

> the real picture of the poor

– it is and must be rhetorical. The insight, the indignation, the caring, of the independent observer, pass by stages to an abstracted general morality and thence to a convenient and ratifying homily:

> forbear to envy . . . they are, like you . . .

And then this, in a new form, is that glozing indifference to the reality of 'varied fortune' against which, when it had appeared in conventional pastoral modes, the poem had set out to act.

We have considered several instances of the melancholy of eighteenth-century poems of country life, and we have seen, in Crabbe, their culmination in distress. It is worth emphasizing these predominant feelings of loss and pain as we move to that common outline of the history of rural England, in which the campaign of parliamentary enclosures is seen as the destroyer of a traditional and settled rural community.

We have already seen, in Arthur Young, a first estimate of what enclosure amounted to, in its contradictory social and economic consequences. Nobody who follows these through in detail would wish to underestimate them. Yet there is a sense in which the idea of the enclosures, localized to just that period in which the Industrial Revolution was beginning, can shift our attention from the real history and become an element of that very powerful myth of modern England in which the transition from a rural to an industrial society is seen as a kind of fall, the true cause and origin of our social suffering and disorder. It is difficult to overestimate the importance of this myth, in modern social thought. It is a main source for the structure of feeling which we began by examining: the perpetual retrospect to an 'organic' or 'natural' society. But it is also a main source for that last protecting illusion in the crisis of our own time: that it is not capitalism which is injuring us, but the more isolable, more evident system of urban industrialism. The questions involved are indeed very difficult, but for just this reason they require analysis, at each point and in each period in which an element of this structure can be seen in formation.

There is no reason to deny the critical importance of the period of parliamentary enclosures, from the second quarter of the eighteenth century to the first quarter of the nineteenth century. By nearly four thousand Acts, more than six million acres of land were appropriated, mainly by the politically dominant landowners: about a quarter of all cultivated acreage. But it is then necessary to see the essential continuity of this appropriation, both with earlier and with later phases. It is necessary to stress, for example, how much of the country had already been enclosed, before this change of method in the mid-eighteenth century to a parliamentary act. The process had been going on since at least the thirteenth century, and had reached a first peak in the fifteenth and sixteenth centuries. Indeed in history it is continuous from the long process of conquest and seizure: the land gained by killing, by repression, by political bargains.

Again, as the economy develops, enclosure can never really be isolated from the mainstream of land improvements, of changes in methods of production, of price-movements, and of those more general changes in property relationships which were all flowing in the same direction: an extension of cultivated land but also a concentration of ownership into the hands of a minority.

The parliamentary procedure for enclosure made this process at once more public and more recorded. In this sense it was directly related to the quickening pace of agricultural improvement in the late eighteenth and early nineteenth centuries. In this period the area mainly affected was a belt from Yorkshire to Dorset, across the midland counties, and extending eastwards to Norfolk. The same process occurred, a little later, in the Scottish Lowlands. But large tracts elsewhere were already effectively enclosed: Kent, parts of Surrey and Sussex, parts of Essex and Suffolk; Devon, Cornwall, Somerset and western Dorset; much of Wales and the border counties of Hereford, Shropshire, Staffordshire and Cheshire; the important cultivated areas of Lancashire, Cumberland, Westmorland, Northumberland and Durham. The social importance of enclosures is then not that they introduced a wholly new element in the social structure, but that in getting rid of the surviving open-field villages and common rights, in some of the most populous and prosperous parts of the country, they complemented and were indeed often caused by the general economic pressure on small owners and especially small tenants. No reliable figures are now available, but it can be reasonably argued that as many people were driven from the land, and from some independent status in relation to it, by the continuing processes of rack-renting and short-lease policies, and by the associated need for greater capital to survive in an increasingly competitive market, as by explicit enclosure.

The number of landless, before this period of enclosure, was in any event high: in 1690, five landless labourers to every three occupiers, as compared with a proportion of five to two in 1831. Most of the peasantry, in another sense – the classical sense of the small owner-occupiers under social and political obligations – had been bought and forced out in the period of the building of large estates in the late seventeenth and early eighteenth centuries. G. E. Mingay has concluded that those who survived this process hung on till the fall in product prices in the 1820s, and declined steadily through the nineteenth century, under general pressures:

on the whole it seems that the level of prices and the prosperity of farming had more impact on owner-occupiers than had enclosures.

The peasantry in yet another and very tenuous sense, the small tenant farmers, were of course already part of the system of agrarian capitalism. Their numbers were affected by the economics of scale, and by the aggregation of estates, but enclosure as such did not greatly affect them: in 1831 nearly half of all farms were small, by any ordinary standard. Thus there is no simple case, in the late eighteenth century, of the expropriation of a peasantry. What really happened was that in the economically dynamic areas a capitalist social system was pushed through to a position of dominance, by a form of legalized seizure enacted by representatives of the beneficiary class. This is crucially important, and in the acreage it affected – a quarter of all cultivated land – it can be said to be decisive. But it cannot be isolated from the long development of concentration of landholding, from the related stratification of owners and tenants, and from the increasing number of the landless, which were the general consequences of agrarian capitalism.

The links with the Industrial Revolution are again important, but not as the replacement of one 'order' by another. It is true that many of the landless became, often with little choice, the working class of the new industrial towns, thus continuing that movement of wage labourers to the towns which had long been evident. But the growth of the industrial working-class must be related also, and perhaps primarily, to the growth of population, itself spectacular, which though primarily related to changes in the birth and death rates in the general modernization of the society, is related also to the increase in agricultural production which was so marked in the eighteenth century: especially in corn, but also in meat; changes themselves related to enclosure and more efficient production. The crisis of poverty, which was so marked in towns and villages alike in the late eighteenth and early nineteenth centuries, was a result of this social and economic process as a whole, and cannot be explained as the fall of one order and the institution of another. The essential connections between town and country, which had been evident throughout, reached a new, more explicit and finally critical stage. It was characteristic of rural England, before and during the Industrial Revolution, that it was exposed to increasing penetration by capitalist social relations and the dominance of the market, just because these had been powerfully evolving within its own structures. By the late eighteenth century we can properly speak of an organized capitalist society, in which what happened to the market, anywhere, whether in industrial or agricultural production, worked its way through to town and country alike, as parts of a single crisis.

Within these developments, violent alterations of condition occurred, to many thousands of tenants and labourers, and to hundreds of village communities. The new tone we have seen in eighteenth-century country writing is then related to these changes of condition, but also, as we have again seen, to ways of interpreting them. We can find the sense of collapse in Langhorne, from a part of the country where enclosure was not a main issue but where the whole economic and social process was exerting its pressures, as much as in Goldsmith, Crabbe, Cowper, and later Clare and Cobbett, from counties where enclosure was the most visible social fact.

At a certain stage, though, enclosure came to be isolated as a main cause. Young's change of mind, his recognition of social realities, came in the early years of the nineteenth century: by most acts of enclosure the poor had been injured, often grossly, and he imagined the poor man saying:

All I know is, I had a cow and Parliament took it from me.

Cobbett, by the 1820s, was speaking of the 'madness of enclosures' and even denying, with many argued instances, that they had increased production. He pointed out, what was undeniable, that the increased investment and concentration of money in the land had

worked detriment to the labourer. It was out of his bones that the means came. It was the *deduction made from him by the rise of prices* and by the *not-rise of his wages* (Cobbett's italics).

Cobbett argued in solid terms of the economics of farming, but inevitably from observation of single instances, as when he calculated that the value of bees on a particular Hampshire common was alone greater than the value of that same common enclosed, to say nothing of the cows, pigs and poultry, the apples and cherries, also raised there. But this is the familiar case of a local contrast between a mixed farming economy and the economics of specialization and scale; in the long run, in trading terms, the latter of course prevailed.

An interesting element was then added to the argument by social observation of life on the old commons. For example Thomas Bewick the engraver, in his *Memoir* written in the 1820s, remembers a Northumberland common of the 1780s, and comments:

On this common – the poor man's heritage for ages past, where he kept a few sheep, or a Kyloe cow, perhaps a flock of geese, and mostly a stock of bee-hives – it was with infinite pleasure that I long beheld the beautiful wild scenery that was there exhibited, and it is with the opposite feeling that I now find all swept away. Here and there on this common were to be seen the cottage, or rather hovel, of some labouring man, built at his own expense, and mostly with his own hands; and to this he always added a garth and a garden, upon which great pains and labour were bestowed to make productive ... These various concerns excited the attention and industry of the hardy occupants, which enabled them to prosper, and made them despise being ever numbered with the parish poor. These men ... might truly be called –
    'A bold peasantry, their country's pride'.

It is an attractive and wholly credible account, and we can learn from Bewick as he goes on to describe the independence and originality of mind of many of these men:

> I think I see him yet, sitting on a mound, or seat, by the hedge of his garden, regardless of the cold, and intent upon viewing the heavenly bodies; pointing to them with his large hands, and eagerly imparting his knowledge;

or his description of Anthony Liddell –

> The whole cast of his character was formed by the Bible, which he had read with attention, through and through. Acts of Parliament which appeared to him to clash with the laws laid down in it, as the Word of God, he treated with contempt. He maintained that the fowls of the air and the fish of the sea were free for all men; consequently game-laws, or laws to protect the fisheries, had no weight with him;

or of Thomas Forster the beekeeper, who hid many of his hives in the whin, to keep away 'the over-inquisitive'.

From recollections like these, and from more conscious and extended accounts of pre-enclosure villages, a picture was built up which has still great emotional force: of independent and honourable men, living in a working rural democracy, who were coldly and 'legally' destroyed by the new enclosing order.

It is this picture as a whole that we have, even reluctantly, to question. The character given by independence needs little argument, though the character of Thomas Forster the beekeeper, who sold the honey of his home-hives to his neighbours and of his whin-hives at a distance, seems already well on the way to independence in another sense: that of the private entrepreneur who has at best an ambiguous relation to his community. The other kind of character, in which a man has time and spirit to observe, to think and to read, obviously flourished in the relative independence of the cottager, but is also part of the whole history – the glory and the tragedy – of working men everywhere. I do not know any social condition in which, against all the apparent odds, such characters have not emerged: whether it is that of Bewick's commoners, or of the field labourers like Stephen Duck, or of the Sussex shepherd-diarists, or of the amateur geologists and botanists of the Lancashire mill-towns, or of the working-men scholars of our own century, the etymologists, the economists, the local historians. It is part of the insult offered to intelligence by a class-society that this history of ordinary thought is ever found surprising. There were, of course, in all these conditions, men of great capacity who gave a shape to their lives by long effort and wisdom. The values which these men lived and represented are opposed, always and everywhere, by the greed and pride of money, power and, too often, established learning. In that general sense, the growth of a system which rationalized greed and pride destroyed and has continued to destroy. But what we have also to notice is how much on the defensive, in how small a space of cleared life, the independence of the cottagers was maintained. The question we have to put to this version of social history is not whether some men emerged and survived – they will always do so, under any pressures – but whether, taken as a whole, the way of life could sustain a general independence. That, after all, is the test of community, as opposed to occasional private independence. And then at once we notice, even in Bewick, that the 'parish poor' are already there, as a distinguishable class. We have to notice, what Bewick tells us, that the independent cottagers:

held the neighbouring gentry in the greatest estimation and respect; and these again, in return, did not overlook them, but were interested in knowing that they were happy and well.

What they have is then a relative and fortunate independence, in an interval of settlement which we can be glad lasted many men's lifetimes. But it is not necessarily an order that we can oppose to what succeeded it, when the same neighbouring gentry showed their interest in a different way and enclosed the commons. The rural class-system was already there, and men were living as they could, sometimes well, in its edges, its margins, its as yet ungrasped and undeveloped areas.

Most records of loss come from these marginal lands: the commons and heaths. But parliamentary enclosure did not only operate on them. Indeed we cannot understand the social consequences of enclosure unless we distinguish between two fundamentally different processes: the enclosure of 'wastes', which in the eighteenth and nineteenth centuries accounted for some two million acres, and the enclosure of open arable fields, already under cultivation, which accounted for some four million acres. It is obvious that the social effects of these two processes must be radically different. What was being suppressed on the wastes was a marginal independence, of cottagers, squatters, isolated settlers in mainly uncultivated land. What was being suppressed in the open-field villages must have been a very different kind of community: the close nucleated villages of an old arable economy. It is remarkable, as W. G. Hoskins has observed, that there is hardly anything in literature to record the passing of such villages, though the complaints of the loss of commons are very numerous. It is possible to read Goldsmith's *Deserted Village* as such a record, but characteristically it is indirect. Yet it is the alteration of the social and economic character of the open-field arable villages that ought most to engage us, if we are thinking of any pre-enclosure 'rural democracy'. Certainly it was the changes here which contributed most substantially to the newly prosperous and consolidated agrarian capitalism. But what kind of social order really existed, in the old open-field village? We must be careful not to confuse the techniques of production – the open-field strips – with what can easily be projected from it, an 'open' and relatively equal society. It is worth looking at the description by a modern rural historian, Fussell, of 'a typical open-field village' of the early eighteenth century. There are three hundred souls. Of these, nearly two hundred are cottagers and labourers and their families, indoor servants, and the unattached poor – widows, orphans, the aged. Some seventy are the copyhold tenant farmers and their families. Some twenty are the freehold farmers and their families. The ten or twelve others are the squire and his family and the parson and his family. It is an interesting distribution, but it is not, at first sight, so dissimilar from the ordinary social structure of mature rural capitalism as to suggest a radically different social order. There are, in effect, three classes: the gentry; the small entrepreneurs; the unpropertied poor. The inequalities of condition which the village contains and supports are profound, and nobody, by any exercise of sentiment, can convert it into a 'rural democracy' or, absurdly, a commune. The social structure that will be completed after enclosure is already basically outlined.

Yet there are qualifications, and it is these we must try to weigh. Among the cottagers and labourers, for example, some are craftsmen and tradesmen (blacksmith, carpenter, cobbler, carrier, publican), and these and others (though not all the others) have small rights of grazing and fuel on nearby common pastures and wastes. It is easy, in retrospect, for these rights to seem petty, but for at least some men they were an important protection against the exposure of total hire. Again and again, down to our own day, men living in villages have tried to create just this kind of margin: a rented patch or strip, an extended garden, a few hives or fruit trees. When I was a child my father had not only the garden that went with his cottage, but a strip for potatoes on a farm where he helped in the harvest, and two gardens which he rented from the railway company from which he drew his wages. Such marginal possibilities are important not only for their produce, but for their direct and immediate satisfactions and for the felt reality of an area of control of one's own immediate labour. Under the long pressures of a dominating wage-economy, these exceptional areas have been critically important: they still occur, even in towns, in some subsidiary small trade or employment. And there can be little doubt that the pre-enclosure village made such opportunities available for more men than any immediately alternative community. In that sense, a degree of loss is real. But only a degree: for by these methods, while they remained marginal, no whole community could be economically sustained, and stratification within it was still inevitable.

To what extent, then, was there ever a genuine community, in such villages, in spite of the economic and social inequalities? It is very difficult to say, for there were major factual variations (we still need many more local studies and examples), and an estimate of 'community', at this distance in time, will be always to some extent subjective. We can of course look at institutions. The manorial courts, in which the business of the village was transacted according to customary rights, are often cited as 'communal'. These were, though, steadily decaying before enclosure, and retained only a declining importance until they were superseded by the completed system of propertied rule. The processes of local law and government show the same evolution: a steady concentration of power in the hands of the landowners, and a more evident (if not a more severe) arbitrariness as these came increasingly to represent a conscious national system and interest, in the constitution of the landowners as a political class. The reality of community must then have varied enormously. The detailed record of the Warwickshire village of Tysoe, which we can study in M. K. Ashby's remarkable biography of her father (*Joseph Ashby of Tysoe*, 1961), is a relevant example.

Until the end of the eighteenth century, Tysoe, the registers showed, had been a village of yeomen, craftsmen, tradesmen and a few labourers – not separate classes, but intermarrying, interapprenticed sections of the community, unified by farming in cooperation and by as great mutual dependence in other ways . . . In earlier years the division between classes in Tysoe had been no more than function or custom called for or worldly perspicacity earned . . . After the years of wretchedness it was so deep a ditch that every foolish mind fell into it.

But what is then interesting is that this change, in 'the years of wretchedness', is not the result of enclosure, but had preceded it. The increasing poverty in the village became a system of pauperism, and for this

enclosure could not be blamed in Tysoe.

The scarlet letters for paupers were sewn in the 1740s. The entry of 'Pauper' in the burial register became more regular through the eighteenth century, and was eventually shortened to a crude 'P'. Unemployment was registered from the 1780s. The roundsman system was active from the 1760s. The smallpox came recurrently, and the consequences of its heavy toll of lives led to peaks of poor relief in the 1770s. This community, it is clear, was so involved in and exposed to the crises of a general system that its neighbourliness was, at best, relative. The friendly and comparatively informal relief of an earlier period gave way, under just this pressure, to the cold and harsh treatment of a separate class of 'the poor'. At the same time, again before enclosure though increasing after it, there was the more evident class-consciousness of the parsons, as in the new style of vicarage, hedged from 'their' parishioners, and of the more prosperous farmers, now called 'gentlemen-farmers'. Enclosure is then a factor within this complex of change, but not a single isolated cause.

Another thing we can learn is that community must not always be seen in retrospect. In Tysoe there was a revival of community, as the village came together in the nineteenth century, to fight for its rights of allotment in the Town Lands. In many parts of rural Britain, a new kind of community developed as an aspect of struggle, against the dominant landowners, or as in the labourers' revolts in the time of the Swing machine-smashing and rick-burning or in the labourers' unions from Tolpuddle to Joseph Arch, against the whole class-system of rural capitalism. In many villages, community only became a reality when economic and political rights were fought for and partially gained, in the recognition of unions, in the extension of the franchise, and in the possibility of entry into new representative and democratic institutions. In many thousands of cases, there is more community in the modern village, as a result of this process of new legal and democratic rights, than at any point in the recorded or imagined past.

That is active community, and it must be distinguished from another version, which is sometimes the mutuality of the oppressed, at other times the mutuality of people living at the edges or in the margins of a generally oppressive system. This comes out in many ways, overlapping with the community of struggle or persisting as local and traditional habit. One way of considering the survival of this traditional mutuality would be according to the distance of a village from its principal land-owner. We have heard so much of the civilizing effect of this landowning class, from its own mouth and from the mouths it has hired, that it is worth recording the coming of a more extreme class-consciousness – a systematic shaming of the labourers and the poor – from what were now so often the rebuilt country-houses, and often by way of their attendant and employed clergy. The break of so many poor families from the Church of England into the nonconformist sects is directly related to this experience of landlord-and-parson religion. The barn-chapels of remote rural Britain are still moving witnesses of this radical community response. But the remoteness itself is very often a factor, whether regional or local. It has always seemed to me, from some relevant family experience, that the distance or absence of one of those 'great houses' of the land-lords can be a critical factor in the survival of a traditional kind of community: that of tolerant neighbourliness. Matthew Arnold gave a clue to this when he wrote, in *Culture and Anarchy*:

> When I go through the country, and see this and that beautiful and imposing seat of theirs crowning the landscape, 'There,' I say to myself, 'is a great fortified post of the Barbarians.'

They had been there, indeed, from periods of direct military rule and occupation; but they had settled into a more social order. And it was in the eighteenth century, most visibly, that these strong points of a class spread in a close network over so much of Britain, with subsidiary effects, on attitudes to landscape and to nature, that we shall come to notice.

But consider, directly, their social effect. Some of them had been there for centuries, visible triumphs over the ruin and labour of others. But the extraordinary phase of extension, rebuilding and enlarging, which occurred in the eighteenth century, represents a spectacular increase in the rate of exploitation: a good deal of it, of course, the profit of trade and of colonial exploitation; much of it, however, the higher surplus value of a new and more efficient mode of production. It is fashionable to admire these extraordinarily numerous houses: the extended manors, the neo-classical mansions, that lie so close in rural Britain. People still pass from village to village, guidebook in hand, to see the next and yet the next example, to look at the stones and the furniture. But stand at any point and look at that land. Look at what those fields, those streams, those woods even today produce. Think it through as labour and see how long and systematic the exploitation and seizure must have been to rear that many houses, on that scale. See by contrast what any ancient isolated farm, in uncounted generations of labour, has managed to become, by the efforts of any single re ' family, however prolonged. And then turn and look at what these other 'families', these systematic owners, have accumulated and arrogantly declared. It isn't only that you know, looking at the land and then at the house, how much robbery and fraud there must have been, for so long to produce that degree of disparity, that barbarous disproportion of scale. The working farms and cottages are so small beside them: what men really raise, by their own efforts or by such portion as is left to them, in the ordinary scale of human achievement. What these 'great' houses do is to break the scale, by an act of will corresponding to their real and systematic exploitation of others. For look at the sites, the façades, the defining avenues and walls, the great iron gates and the guardian lodges. These were chosen for more than the effect from the inside out; where so many admirers, too many of them writers, have stood and shared the view, finding its prospect delightful. They were chosen, also, you now see, for the other effect, from the outside looking in: a visible stamping of power, of displayed wealth and command: a social disproportion which was meant to impress and overawe. Much of the real profit of a more modern agriculture went not into productive investment but into that explicit social declaration: a mutually competitive but still uniform exposition, at every turn, of an established and commanding class power.

To stand in that shadow, even today, is to know what many generations of countrymen bitterly learned and were consciously taught: that these were the families, this the shape of the society. And will you then think of community? You will see modern community only in the welcome signs of some partial reclamation: the houses returned to some general use, as a hospital or agricultural college. But you are just as likely to see the old kinds of power still declared: in the surviving exploiters and in their modern relations – the corporation country-house, the industrial seat, the ruling-class school. Physically they are there: the explicit forms of the long class-society.

But turn for a moment elsewhere: to the villages that escaped their immediate presence; to the edges, the old commons still preserved in place-names; to the hamlets where control was remote. It can make some difference, as you go about every day, to be out of sight of that explicit command. And this is so, I do not doubt, in many surviving, precarious communities, the dispersed settlements of the west or some of the close villages of the east and midlands, where no immediate house has so outgrown its neighbours that it has visibly altered the scale. It makes a real difference that in day-to-day relations those other people and their commanding statements in stone are absent or at least some welcome distance away.

In some places still, an effective community, of a local kind, can survive in older terms, where small freeholders, tenants, craftsmen and labourers can succeed in being neighbours first and social classes only second. This must never be idealized, for at the points of decision, now as then, the class realities usually show through. But in many intervals, many periods of settlement, there is a kindness, a mutuality that still manages to flow. It is a matter of degree, as it was in the villages before and after enclosure. When the pressure of a system is great and is increasing, it matters to find a breathing-space, a fortunate distance, from the immediate and visible controls. What was drastically reduced, by enclosures, was just such a breathing-space, a marginal day-to-day independence, for many thousands of people. It is right to mourn that loss but we must also look at it plainly. What happened was not so much 'enclosure' – the method – but the more visible establishment of a long-developing system, which had taken, and was to take, several other forms. The many miles of new fences and walls, the new paper rights, were the former declaration of where the power now lay. The economic system of landlord, tenant and labourer, which had been extending its hold since the sixteenth century, was now in explicit and assertive control. Community, to survive, had then to change its terms.

In this period of change, it mattered very much where you were looking from. Points of view, interpretations, selections of realities, can now be directly contrasted. In history it is a period of rural society. In literature it is a complex of different ways of seeing even the same local life.

Imagine a journey, for example, round a thirty-mile triangle of roads, in the turning years of the late eighteenth and early nineteenth centuries. It is on the borders of Hampshire and Surrey: six miles from Selborne to Chawton; ten miles from Chawton to Farnham; fourteen miles from Farnham back to Selborne. In 1793, in Selborne, Gilbert White died. In 1777, when White had been keeping his famous journal for nine years, a boy of fourteen, William Cobbett, ran away from his father's small farm at Farnham. Cobbett was to ride back through these villages, many times, and in the 1820s to write his *Rural Rides*. When Gilbert White died, Jane Austen, not far away, in another parsonage, was beginning to write her novels of country society. From 1809, in Chawton, she was beginning to publish and to write her mature works. In this small locality, overlapping within a generation, there were these three people, three writers, who could hardly be more different. Both the country seen and the idea of the country vary so much in their work that we are forced, as we read them, into a new kind of consciousness.

What Cobbett gives us is detailed social observation, from the point of view of the condition of the majority of men. He combined Arthur Young's attention to the detailed practice of a working agriculture with a more persistent social questioning and observation. Thus in 1821:

(West of Uphusband):

. . . a group of women labourers, who were attending the measurers to measure their reaping work, presented such an assemblage of rags as I never before saw even amongst the hoppers at Farnham, many of whom are common beggars. I never before saw *country* people, and reapers too, observe, so miserable in appearance as these. There were some very pretty girls, but ragged as colts and as pale as ashes.

(Near Cricklade):
... The labourers seem miserably poor. Their dwellings are little better than pig-beds, and their looks indicate that their food is not nearly equal to that of a pig. Their wretched hovels are stuck upon little bits of ground *on the road side*, where the space has been wider than the road demanded. In many places they have not two rods to a hovel. It seems as if they had been swept off the fields by a hurricane, and had found shelter under the banks on the road side! Yesterday morning was a sharp frost; and this had set the poor creatures to digging up their little plots of potatoes ... And this is '*prosperity*', is it?

labourers - Near Cricklade

The great merit of Cobbett's observation is its detail. This included the facts of local variation:

(Near Gloucester):
... The labourers' dwellings, as I came along, looked good, and the labourers themselves pretty well as to dress and healthiness. The girls at work in the fields (always my standard) are not in rags, with bits of shoes tied on their feet and rags tied round their ankles, as they had in Wiltshire.

This is a new voice, in radical shift of social viewpoint:

The landlords and the farmers can tell their own tale. They tell their own tale in remonstrances and prayers, addressed to the House. Nobody tells the tale of the labourer.

This consciousness of viewpoint, of a class viewpoint, marks the distance from most previous accounts; and where Cobbett had been preceded, as in part by Crabbe, the range of detail brings in a world that marks the essential preparation for transition from the sympathetic poem to the realistic novel.

We remember Crabbe as we see Cobbett considering the relations between poverty and the quality of land:

(In Kent):
What a difference between the wife of a labouring man here, and the wife of a labouring man in the forests and woodlands of Hampshire and Sussex! Invariably have I observed that the richer the soil, and the

more destitute of woods; that is to say, the more purely a corn country, the more miserable the labourers.

It was in the cornlands that capitalist farming was most developed. It is on this contrast of social conditions that Cobbett insists:

The labouring people look pretty well. They have pigs. They invariably do best in the *woodland* and *forest* and *wild* countries. Where the mighty grasper has *all under his eye*, they can get but little.

This was the social basis of his opposition to enclosures: not what happened to production, as a total figure, but what happened, in detail, to the people and the land. It was in this sense that he observed:

This place presents another proof of the truth of my old observation: *rich land* and *poor labourers*.

Or again, comparing the disadvantage of wage-labour with the old system of feeding and lodging (the farmers 'cannot keep their work-people *upon so little* as they give them in wages'), he insisted:

The land produces, on an average, what it always produced, but there is a new distribution of the produce.

What was happening meanwhile to the landowners, and to their social structure, as rural capitalism extended? Cobbett looked very carefully at this, and made a familiar distinction between

a resident *native* gentry, attached to the soil, known to every farmer and labourer from his childhood, frequently mixing with them in those pursuits where all artificial distinctions are lost, practising hospitality without ceremony, from habit and not on calculation; and a gentry, only now-and-then residing at all, having no relish for country-delights, foreign in their manners, distant and haughty in their behaviour, looking to the soil only for its rents, viewing it as a mere object of speculation, unacquainted with its cultivators, despising them and their pursuits, and relying, for influence, not upon the good will of the vicinage, but upon the dread of their power. The war and paper-system has brought in nabobs, negro-drivers, generals, admirals, governors, commissaries, contractors, pensioners sinecurists, commissioners, loan-jobbers, lottery-dealers, bankers, stock-jobbers; not to mention the long and *black list* in gowns and three-tailed wigs. You can see but few good houses not in possession of one or the other of these. These, with the parsons, are now the magistrates.

It is an impressive list and Cobbett gives several names as examples. The fact that there had been the same kind of invasion, from at least the sixteenth century, must qualify the account. What Cobbett does not ask is where the 'invaders' came from. Many of them, in fact, were the younger sons of that same 'resident native gentry', who had gone out to these new ways to wealth, and were now coming back, Yet, 'native' or 'invader', the pressure on rents, and so through the tenant-farmer on the labourer, was visibly and dramatically increasing. Cobbett shortens the real time-scale, but then sees what is happening, as agrarian capitalism extends. He identifies money – first silver and gold, and then paper – as the agent of change. At first:

its consequences came on by slow *degrees*; it made a transfer of property, but it made that transfer in so small a degree, and it left the property quiet in the hands of the new possessor for so long a time, that the effect was not violent, and was not, at any rate, such as to uproot possessors by whole districts, as the hurricane uproots the forests.

This is an under-estimate of change from the sixteenth to eighteenth centuries, but what Cobbett is intent to record is the visible disturbance of his own time:

the *small gentry*, to about the *third* rank upwards (considering there to be five ranks from the smallest gentry up to the greatest nobility) are *all gone*, nearly to a man, and the small farmers along with them. The Barings alone have, I should think, swallowed up thirty or forty of these small gentry without perceiving it. They, indeed, swallow up the biggest race of all; but innumerable small fry slip down unperceived, like caplins down the throats of the sharks, while these latter *feel* only the cod-fish.

As clearly as anyone in the whole record Cobbett raises the familiar complaint about the reduction of intermediate classes in the rural economy. But while he sees this happening, he simultaneously introduces a new criterion of judgement. Identifying with the labourer, making 'always my standard' the girls at work in the fields, Cobbett sees the ruin of the small owners and some tenant farmers, but then says of the small gentry, with a new harshness:

So that, while they have been the active, the zealous, the efficient instruments, in compelling the working classes to submit to half-starvation, they have at any rate been brought to the most abject ruin themselves: for which I most heartily thank God.

Or again, of the farmers:

Here is much more than enough to make me rejoice in the ruin of the farmers; and I do, with all my heart, thank God for it; seeing that it appears absolutely necessary, that the present race of them should be totally broken up, in Sussex at any rate, in order to put an end to this cruelty and insolence towards the labourers, who are by far the greater number.

This is the hard anger which Cobbett shared with many of the labourers of his time, against the nearest targets to hand. It is the mood of the Bread or Blood riots of East Anglia in 1816, or of the widespread revolt of the labourers – the campaigns of 'Captain Swing' – in 1830. Cobbett noticed, in this, that he might have 'laid on the lash without a due regard to many', and he reflected:

Born in a farm-house, bred up at the plough-tail, with a smockfrock on my back, taking great delight in all the pursuits of farmers, liking their society, and having amongst them my most esteemed friends, it is natural that I should feel, and I do feel, uncommonly anxious to prevent, as far as I am able, that total ruin which now menaces them. But the labourer, was I to have no feeling for him? Was he not my *countryman* too? And was I not to feel indignation against those farmers, who had had the hard-heartedness to put the bell round his neck, and thus wantonly insult and degrade the class to whose toils they owed their own ease?

This conflict of loyalties, and yet the final determination, marks a crucial stage. It was often the case in the forced food-levies, the riots for a minimum wage, the rick-burnings, that the immediate targets, the farmers, had little enough to give, under the pressure for rents of the more safely removed and protected landowners. It is significant indeed that, in these disturbances, dispossessed and ruined and hard-pressed farmers often joined the rioting labourers. But this was the characteristic of a developing capitalist order in the land. The riots indeed mark the last stage of the *local* confrontation, in immediate and personal terms. Such disturbances had necessarily to be succeeded by the organization of class against class, in trade unionism and in its associated political movements. The structure of feeling that had held in direct appeal and in internal moral discrimination – the moral case, the moral warning, of such verse as Goldsmith's or Crabbe's – was now necessarily transformed into a different order of thinking and feeling. The maturity of capitalism as a system was forcing systematic organization against it.

This development, so crucial in the social history of rural England, has its consequence in a new kind of country writing, of which Cobbett is the outrider: a change of convention, so that the interaction of classes, now the decisive history, can begin to be described: no longer in reflection, but in a newly typical action. This is the crucial bearing of the transformation of fiction into a new kind of novel, which was to become, from the 1830s, the dominant literary form. Cobbett described and campaigned, as a reporter and finally as a tribune. His change of viewpoint, and the changes to which he so vividly responded, are the first important signs of a new method in literature.

But this change in the novel did not happen in Cobbett's time. Through his middle years, while the social changes were happening, Jane Austen was writing from a very different point of view, from inside the houses that Cobbett was passing on the road. When he was writing about the disappearance of the small gentry he was riding through Hampshire, not far from Chawton. It was also in Hampshire that he made his list of the new owners of country-houses and estates, from nabobs to stock-jobbers. We can find ourselves thinking of Jane Austen's fictional world, as he goes on to observe:

The big, in order to save themselves from being '*swallowed up quick*' ... make use of their *voices* to get, through place, pension, or sinecure, something back from the taxes. Others of them *fall in love* with the *daughters* and *widows* of paper-money people, big brewers, and the like; and sometimes their daughters *fall in love* with the paper-money people's sons, or the fathers of those sons; and whether they be Jews, or not, seems to be little matter with this all-subduing passion of love. But the *small gentry* have no resource.

This is a very different tone from anything that Jane Austen wrote, but it forces us to ask, as it were from the other side of the park wall: what were the conditions and the pressures within which she brought to bear her no less sharp observation; what was the social substance of her precise and inquiring personal and moral emphases?

It is a truth universally acknowledged, that Jane Austen chose to ignore the decisive historical events of her time. Where, it is still asked, are the Napoleonic wars: the real current of history? But history has many currents, and the social history of the landed families, at that time in England, was among the most important. As we sense its real processes, we find that they are quite central and structural in Jane Austen's novels. All that prevents us from realizing this is that familiar kind of retrospect, taking in Penshurst and Saxham and Buck's Head and Mansfield Park and Norland and even Poynton, in which all country houses and their families are seen as belonging, effectively, to a single tradition: that of the cultivated rural gentry. The continual making and remaking of these houses and their families is suppressed, in this view, for an idealizing abstraction, and Jane Austen's world can then be taken for granted, even sometimes patronized as a rural backwater, as if it were a simple 'traditional' setting. And then if the social 'background' is in this sense 'settled', we can move to an emphasis on a fiction of purely personal relationships.

But such an emphasis is false, for it is not personal relationships, in the abstracted sense of an observed psychological process, that preoccupy Jane Austen. It is, rather, personal *conduct*: a testing and discovery of the standards which govern human behaviour in certain real situations. To the social considerations already implicit in the examination of conduct, with its strong sense and exploration of the adequacy of social norms, we must add, from the evidence of the novels, a direct preoccupation with estates, incomes and social position, which are seen as indispensable elements of all the relationships that are projected and formed. Nor is this a preoccupation within a settled 'traditional' world; indeed much of the interest, and many of the sources of the action, in Jane Austen's novels, lie in the changes of fortune – the facts of general change and of a certain mobility – which were affecting the landed families at this time.

Thus it would be easy to take Sir Thomas Bertram, in *Mansfield Park*, as an example of the old settled landed gentry, to be contrasted with the new 'London' ways of the Crawfords (this is a common reading), were it not for the fact that Bertram is explicitly presented as what Goldsmith would have called 'a great West Indian': a colonial proprietor in the sugar island of Antigua. The Crawfords may have London ways, but the income to support them is landed property in Norfolk, and they have been brought up by an uncle who is an admiral. Sir Walter Elliott, in *Persuasion*, belongs to a landed family which had moved from Cheshire to Somerset, and which had been raised to a baronetcy in the Restoration, but his income, at this time, will not support his position; his heir presumptive has 'purchased independence by uniting himself to a rich woman of inferior birth'; and the baronet is forced to let Kellynch Hall to an admiral, since, as his lawyer observes:

This peace will be turning all our rich naval officers ashore. They will be all wanting a home . . . Many a noble fortune has been made during the war.

The neighbouring Musgroves, the second landowning family, are, by contrast,

in a state of alteration, perhaps of improvement. The father and mother were in the old English style, and the young people in the new.

Darcy, in *Pride and Prejudice*, is a landowner established for 'many generations', but his friend Bingley has inherited £100,000 and is looking for an estate to purchase. Sir William Lucas has risen from trade to a knighthood; Mr Bennett has £2,000 a year, but an entailed estate, and has married the daughter of an attorney, whose brother is in trade. Knightley, in *Emma*, owns Donwell Abbey, and Martin one of the new gentlemen farmers, is his tenant. The Woodhouses have little land but Emma will inherit £30,000, 'from other sources'. Elton, the vicar, has some independent property, but must make his way as he could, 'without any alliances but in trade'. Mr Weston belongs to a 'respectable family which for the last two or three generations had been rising into gentility and property'; he marries, through the militia, the daughter of 'a great Yorkshire family', and when she dies enters trade and purchases 'a little estate'. Harriet, finally revealed as the daughter of 'a tradesman, rich enough', marries her gentleman-farmer with the reasonable 'hope of more, of security, stability, and improvement'. The Coles live quietly, on an income from trade, but when this improves become 'in fortune and style of living, second only to the Woodhouses, in the immediate neighbourhood'. In *Sense and Sensibility*, the Dashwoods are a settled landowning family, increasing their income by marriages, and enlarging the settlements of their daughters; they are also enclosing Norland Common, and buying up neighbouring farms; the necessary cashing of stocks for enclosure and engrossing affect the rate of the family's immediate improvement. In *Northanger Abbey*, Catherine Morland, the daughter of a clergyman with two good livings and a considerable independence, goes with a local landowning family, the Allens, to Bath, and in that sharply observed social exchange meets the son of the family which has owned the Abbey estates since the dissolution of the monasteries; his sister has married on the 'unexpected accession' of her lover 'to title and fortune'.

To abstract this social history is of course to describe only the world of the novels within which the more particular actions begin and end. Yet it must be clear that it is no single, settled society, it is an active, complicated, sharply speculative process. It is indeed that most difficult world to describe, in English social history: an acquisitive, high bourgeois society at the point of its most evident interlocking with an agrarian capitalism that is itself mediated by inherited titles and by the making of family names. Into the long and complicated interaction of landed and trading capital, the process that Cobbett observed – the arrival of 'the nabobs, negro-drivers, admirals, generals' and so on – is directly inserted, and is even taken for granted. The social confusions and contradictions of this complicated process are then the true source of many of the problems of human conduct and valuation, which the personal actions dramatize. An openly acquisitive society, which is concerned also with the transmission of wealth, is trying to judge itself at once by an inherited code and by the morality of improvement.

The paradox of Jane Austen is then the achievement of a unity of tone, of a settled and remarkably confident way of seeing and judging, in the chronicle of confusion and change. She is precise and candid, but in very particular ways. She is, for example, more exact about income, which is disposable, than about acres, which have to be worked. Yet at the same time she sees land in a way that she does not see 'other sources' of income. Her eyes for a house, for timber, for the details of improvement, is quick, accurate, monetary. Yet money of other kinds, from the trading houses, from the colonial plantations, has no visual equivalent; it has to be converted to these signs of order to be recognized at all. This way of seeing is especially representative. The land is seen primarily as an index of revenue and position; its visible order and control are a valued product, while the process of working it is hardly seen at all. Jane Austen then reminds us, yet again, of the two meanings of improvement, which were historically linked but in practice so often contradictory. There is the improvement of soil, stock, yields, in a working agriculture. And there is the improvement of houses, parks, artificial landscapes, which absorbed so much of the actually increasing wealth. Professor Habakkuk has observed that

English landowners as a whole were a class of consumers, and the greater parts of their borrowings were contracted for non-productive purposes, to provide dowries, to fund short-term debts contracted as a result of extravagant living, to build mansions; the borrowings for enclosures, for example, were usually a small part of total indebtedness.

This is not to deny the function of many landowners in agricultural improvement, but to set it in its actual social context. It is the essential commentary on what can be abstracted, technically, as the agricultural revolution: that it was no revolution, but the consolidation, the improvement, the expansion of an existing social class.

Cultivation has the same ambiguity as improvement: there is increased growth, and this is converted into rents; and then the rents are converted into what is seen as a cultivated society. What the 'revolution' is for, then, is this: this apparently attainable quality of life. Jane Austen could achieve her remarkable unity of tone – that cool and controlled observation which is the basis of her narrative method; that lightly distanced management of event and description and character which need not become either open manipulation or direct participation – because of an effective underlying and yet unseen formula: improvement is or ought to be improvement. The working improvement, which is not seen at all, is the means to social improvement, which is then so isolated that it is seen very clearly indeed.

It is not seen flatteringly. The conversion of good income into good conduct was no automatic process. Some of the conscious improvers are seen as they were: greedy and calculating materialists. But what is crucial is that the moral pretension is taken so seriously that it becomes a critique: never of the basis of the formula, but coolly and determinedly of its results, in character and action. She guides her heroines, steadily, to the right marriages. She makes settlements, alone, against all the odds, like some supernatural lawyer, in terms of that exact proportion to moral worth which could assure the continuity of the general formula. But within this conventional bearing, which is the source of her confidence, the moral discrimination is so insistent that it can be taken, in effect, as an independent value. It is often said, by literary historians, that she derives from Fielding and from Richardson, but Fielding's genial manipulative bluff and Richardson's isolating fanaticism are in fact far back, in another world. What happens in *Emma*, in *Persuasion*, in *Mansfield Park*, is the development of an everyday, uncompromising morality which is in the end separable from its social basis and which, in other hands, can be turned against it. It is in this sense that Jane Austen relates to the Victorian moralists, who had to learn to assume, with increasing unease from Coleridge to George Eliot and Matthew Arnold, that there was no necessary correspondence between class and morality; that the survival of discrimination depended on another kind of independence; that the two meanings of improvement had to be not merely distinguished but contrasted; or, as first in Coleridge, that cultivation, in its human sense, had to be brought to bear as a standard *against* the social process of civilization. In these hands, decisively, the formula broke down: improvement was not improvement; not only not necessarily, but at times in definite contradiction. Jane Austen, it is clear, never went so far; her novels would have been very different, involving new problems of structure and language, if she had. But she provided the emphasis which had only to be taken outside the park walls, into a different social experience, to become not a moral but a social criticism. It is this transformation, and its difficulties, that we shall meet in George Eliot.

We must here emphasize again the importance of Cobbett. What he names, riding past on the road, are classes. Jane Austen, from inside the houses, can never see that, for all the intricacy of her social description. All her discrimination is, understandably, internal and exclusive. She is concerned with the conduct of people who, in the complications of improvement, are repeatedly trying to make themselves into a class. But where only one class is seen, no classes are seen. Her people are selected though typical individuals, living well or badly within a close social dimension. Cobbett never, of course, saw them as closely or as finely; but what he saw was what they had in common: the underlying economic process. A moral view of that kind had to come from outside, and of course when it came the language was rougher and harder. The precise confidence of an established world gave way to disturbing, aggressive and conflicting voices.

It was not a new experience; it had been there all the time, but only rarely recorded:

We are men formed in Christ's likeness, and we are kept like beasts.

> For Toils scarce ever ceasing press us now;
> Rest never does, but on the Sabbath, show;
> And barely that our Masters will allow.

Here I am, between Earth and Sky – so help me God. I would sooner lose my life than go home as I am. Bread I want and Bread I will have.

What we have done now is Soar against our Will but your harts is so hard as the hart of Pharo . . . So now as for this fire you must not take it as a front, for if you hadent been Deserving it wee should not have dont.

The first voice is from the fourteenth century; the second from the early eighteenth; the third and fourth from the early nineteenth century, in a new general crisis. It is a radically different morality from that of Jane Austen, but it is insistently moral, in its own general language. It is the voice of men who have seen their children starving, and now within sight of the stately homes and the improved parks and the self-absorbed social patterns at the ends of the drives.

Cobbett and Jane Austen mark two ways of seeing, two contrasted viewpoints, within the same country. Each kind of observation, however, is social, in the widest sense. But as we make our imaginary journey, on that triangle of roads, we discover, in Gilbert White, a different kind of observation, yet one of no less significance in the development of country writing. Anyone who lives in the country can experience at times, or seem to experience, an unmediated nature: in a direct and physical awareness of trees, birds, the moving shapes of land. What is new in Gilbert White, or at least feels new in its sustained intensity, is a development from this; a single and dedicated observation, as if the only relationships of country living were to its physical facts. It is a new kind of record, not only of the facts, but of a way of looking at the facts: a way of looking that will come to be called scientific:

The next bird that I procured (on the 21st of May) was a male red-backed butcher-bird, *lanius collurio*. My neighbour, who shot it, says that it might easily have escaped his notice, had not the outcries and chattering of the white-throats and other small birds drawn his attention to the bush where it was: its craw was filled with the legs and wings of beetles . . .

. . . The ousel is larger than a blackbird, and feeds on haws; but last autumn (when there were no haws) it fed on yew-berries: in the spring it feeds on ivy-berries, which ripen only at that season, in March and April.

These descriptions are from the formal letters published in *The Natural History of Selborne*. In tone and attention, over a lifetime, they compose a new kind of writing. It is not that White lacked what can be called 'powers of description'. When a natural event included an emotional response, as in the fearful summer of 1783, he could write to its level:

The sun, at noon, looked as blank as a clouded moon, and shed a rust-coloured ferruginous light on the ground, and floors of rooms; but was particularly lurid and blood-coloured at rising and setting. All the time the heat was so intense that butchers' meat could hardly be eaten on the day after it was killed; and the flies swarmed so in the lanes and hedges that they rendered the horses half frantic, and riding irksome.

It is simply, as the reading of his *Journal* over twenty-five years from 1768 to 1793 will confirm, that his customary mode of attention was outward: observing, inquiring, annotating, classifying. The quality of his feeling for the life around him is unquestionable; it is the devoted and delighted attention of a lifetime, from which anybody living in the country can still learn. But it is not what can easily be confused with it from many earlier and some later observations, the working of particular social or personal experience into the intricacies of things seen. White may remind us at times of Arthur Young and the other contributors to the *Annals of Agriculture*, in the close and detailed precision of his notes and observations. But what he is observing is not a working agriculture, except incidentally; it is a natural order, in a new sense: a physical world of creatures and conditions. While Cobbett and Jane Austen, in their different ways, were absorbed in a human world, Gilbert White was watching the turn of the year and the myriad physical lives inside it: nature in a sense that could now be separated from man.

It is a complicated change, and we must try to see its relation to a whole set of other changes which, through the eighteenth century, and then again in the generation of Cobbett and Jane Austen but in quite different ways, were bringing about a transformation of attitudes and feelings towards observed nature: new kinds of interest in landscape, a new self-consciousness of the picturesque, and beyond these and interacting with the more social observations, the new language, the new poetry, of Wordsworth and Clare.

A working country is hardly ever a landscape. The very idea of landscape implies separation and observation. It is possible and useful to trace the internal histories of landscape painting, landscape writing, landscape gardening and landscape architecture, but in any final analysis we must relate these histories to the common history of a land and its society. And if we are to understand the changes in English attitudes to landscape, in the eighteenth and nineteenth centuries, this is especially necessary. We have many excellent internal histories, but in their implicit and sometimes explicit points of view they are ordinarily part of that social composition of the land – its distribution, its uses, and its control – which has been uncritically received and sustained, even into our own century, where the celebration of its achievements is characteristically part of an elegy for a lost way of life.

Significantly, also, the history of English landscape in the eighteenth century has been, in the standard accounts, foreshortened. Reading some of these histories you might almost believe – you are often enough told – that the eighteenth-century landlord, through the agency of his hired landscapers, and with poets and painters in support, invented natural beauty. And in a way, why not? In the same ideology he invented charity, land-improvement and politeness, just as when he and his kind went to other men's countries, such countries were 'discovered'.

But the real history is very much more complicated. It was an application, in special social and economic circumstances, of ideas which were in themselves very far from new. Yet as always, in such cases, the particular application, in a real social context, had new and particular effects.

'Pleasing prospects': the characteristic eighteenth-century

phrase has the necessary double meaning. For we must not suppose that the wonder, the significance and the pleasure of observed shapes and movements of land were invented by specialization to a prospect. As far back as we have literature these feelings are recorded, and we can be certain that many more men than writers have looked with intense interest at all the features and movements of the natural world: hills, rivers, trees, skies and stars. Many kinds of meaning, philosophical and practical, have been derived from these long generations of observing. But the moment came when a different kind of observer felt he must divide these observations into 'practical' and 'aesthetic', and if he did this with sufficient confidence he could deny to all his predecessors what he then described, in himself, as 'elevated sensibility'. The point is not so much that he made this division. It is that he needed and was in a position to do it, and that this need and position are parts of a social history, in the separation of production and consumption.

The self-conscious observer: the man who is not only looking at land but who is conscious that he is doing so, as an experience in itself, and who has prepared social models and analogies from elsewhere to support and justify the experience: this is the figure we need to seek: not a kind of nature but a kind of man. He has a long and intricate history. He is there, in his own context, in the bucolic poets and in the earliest eclogues. He is there, identifiably, in Petrarch, who, as Burckhardt told us, climbed Mont Ventoux in Provence to see the panorama but when he had got to the top remembered a conflicting model, in a passage from Augustine:

men go forth and admire lofty mountains and broad seas and roaring torrents and the ocean and the course of the stars, and forget their own selves while doing so.

He is there in Aeneas Sylvius, describing the view from the Alban Hills and setting up his court on Monte Amiata. Castles and fortified villages had long commanded 'prospects' of the country below them. It was in more settled times that what was explicitly looked for was not the movement of enemies or strangers but the view itself: the conscious scene. Yet we have to remember that we do not know, from the times of disturbance, what was seen, what appreciated, in the long hours of watching, by generations of men. Most of the men who did the watching have left no records.

What we can say with certainty is that, from very early in history, such views were arranged as well as incidentally or accidentally found. In Egypt, in Mesopotamia and in China landscapes were designed; in Babylon especially there were arranged parks, avenues, gardens and fountains. Characteristically these arrangements were related to centres of power, and they have a long formal succession, down to Versailles and its modern imitations. But there is also a less noticed succession, to the private villas and then the country-houses of less centralized, less specifically hierarchical civilizations. There is a significant social difference: the villas of Italy, in which much of the creation of neo-pastoral literature occurred, were built with their rural surroundings and prospects in direct relation to the cities, as alternative country homes; while in England, for example, they were more scattered territorial seats, though the money for their building was significantly often derived from profit at court. Parks, originally woodlands enclosed for preserving and hunting game, were made in England from at latest the tenth century, and there was a significant increase in their number, in direct relation to the new country palaces, in the sixteenth century. Much of the enclosing of land and the building of houses was done at the expense of whole villages and cornfields that were cleared. The English landlords of the eighteenth century, following the same procedures, had these generations of predecessors in imposition and theft.

But there is still a transition from the hunting woodland to the landscape park. It is not easy to date this. There are examples (Compton Wynyates and Audley End) from the sixteenth and seventeenth centuries, but the systematic transformation occurs mainly in the eighteenth century and after. It is possible, in analysis, to separate the deer park, the imposing setting and the landscaped view, but in many real cases these types were combined, though in the later centuries the main game preserves – again with great damage to other men's settlements and livelihoods – were moved further and further out. It is into this complex of territorial establishment that we must re-insert the self-conscious development of landscape and what is called the 'invention' of scenery.

The main argument is well known. Eighteenth-century landlords, going on the Grand Tour and collecting their pictures by Claude and Poussin, learned new ways of looking at landscape and came back to create such landscapes as prospects from their own houses: create, that is, in the sense of hiring Brown ('the peasant') or Kent or Repton. Certainly we have to notice a change of taste in the laying-out of decorative grounds: from the seventeenth-century formal gardens under French and Italian and Dutch influence to the park landscapes of the eighteenth-century improvers. But to call this the invention of 'landscape' or of 'scenery' is to confuse the whole development. It is an ironic insularity to suppose that eighteenth-century Englishmen consciously imitating seventeenth-century Italian painters were 'discovering' scenery. But in any case the whole movement was more general.

The English idea of landscape was taken directly from the Dutch, and it is worth noting that the first great artistic composition of landscape in a mode adaptable to the physical characteristics of English land was the Dutch school of the seventeenth century, of van Ruysdael and Hobbema. To the English improvers this art, with its close associations with bourgeois improvement and with scientific inquiry into nature and into modes of perception, was a close analogue. When men could produce their own nature, both by the physical means of improvement (earth-moving with new machines; draining and irrigation; pumping water to elevated sites) and by the understanding of the physical laws of light and thence of artificial viewpoints and perspectives, there was bound to be a change from the limited and conventionally symbolic and iconographic decoration of the land under immediate view.

Paradise, originally a Persian walled garden, is already in Milton:

> a happy rural seat of various view

and the flowers, 'worthy of Paradise',

> not nice Art
> In Beds and curious Knots, but Nature born
> Pourd forth profuse.

Marvell at Appleton House, where there was a formal symbolic garden, had said of the water-meadows:

> They seem within the polish Grass
> A Landskip drawn in Looking-Glass:

an interesting image not only because the meadows are seen as landscape but because the sense of artifice – the seventeenth-century uses of mirror and perspective to compose and embellish landscape – is consciously present. Pope, pioneering and recommending a new style of gardening, against the artificial symmetries represented by Timon's villa, was also perceptually conscious, in a mode derived as much from science as from art:

> You look thro' a sloping Arcade of Trees, and see the Sails on the River passing suddenly and vanishing, as thro' a Perspective Glass.

His 'Genius of the Place', an apparent standard for 'natural' fidelity, is on closer examination an invitation to arrange and rearrange nature according to a point of view:

> Let not each beauty ev'ry where be spy'd,
> Where half the skill is decently to hide.

For what was being done, by this new class, with new capital, new equipment and new skills to hire, was indeed a disposition of 'Nature' to their own point of view. If we ask, finally, who the genius of the place may be, we find that he is its owner, its proprietor, its improver. Charles Cotton, in 1687, had written of the beauties of the gardens at Chatsworth and said, in his climax:

> But that which crowns all this, and does impart
> A lustre far beyond the Power of Art,
> Is the great Owner. He, whose noble mind
> For such a Fortune only was designed.

The genius of the place was the making of a place: that socially resonant word which echoed through the eighteenth century and which Jane Austen picked up, ironically, in the improving talk of Henry Crawford in *Mansfield Park*:

> By such improvements as I have suggested . . . you may give it a higher character. You may raise it into *a place*.

The taste for Claude and Poussin, the earthworks and waterworks and tree-planting of Brown and Kent and Repton, the conscious creations of Stourhead and the Leasowes, are then parts of this wider movement: means and episodes within it. Looking from art to landscape we can see many conscious imitations of particular scenes: the bands of light and shade and water, as in the canvas compositions; the buildings and groves to give verticals and points of emphasis; the framing of views by dark foregrounds of trees, as in Claude and Poussin but also as in theatre scenery, where the proscenium frame and the movable flats were being simultaneously developed. It is right to note these similarities and correspondences, and the degree of conscious imitation tells us much about the cultural mediocrity of the class, at the level of real art and literature. But in their own real terms they were not dependent. Cotton had already observed at Chatsworth:

> The Groves whose curled brows shade ev'ry lake
> Do everywhere such waving Landskips make
> As Painter's baffled Art is far above
> Who waves and leaves could never yet make move

It was that kind of confidence, to make Nature move to an arranged design, that was the real invention of the landlords. And we cannot then separate their decorative from their productive arts; this new self-conscious observer was very specifically the self-conscious owner. The clearing of parks as 'Arcadian' prospects depended on the completed system of exploitation of the agricultural and genuinely pastoral lands beyond the park boundaries. There, too, an order was being imposed: social and economic but also physical. The mathematical grids of the enclosure awards, with their straight hedges and straight roads, are contemporary with the natural curves and scatterings of the park scenery. And yet they are related parts of the same process – superficially opposed in taste but only because in the one case the land is being organized for production, where tenants and labourers will work, while in the other case it is being organized for consumption – the view, the ordered proprietary repose, the prospect. Indeed it can be said of these eighteenth-century arranged landscapes not only, as is just, that this was

154

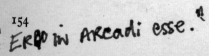
ERGO IN ARCADI esse.

the high point of agrarian bourgeois art, but that they succeeded in creating in the land below their windows and terraces
what Jonson at Penshurst had ideally imagined: a rural landscape emptied of rural labour and of labourers; a sylvan and
watery prospect, with a hundred analogies in neo-pastoral
painting and poetry, from which the facts of production had
been banished: the roads and approaches artfully concealed by
trees, so that the very fact of communication could be visually
suppressed: inconvenient barns and mills cleared away out of
sight (the bourgeois Sterling, in Colman and Garrick's *Clandestine Marriage*, had 'made a greenhouse out of the old laundry
and turned the brewhouse into a pinery'); avenues opening to
the distant hills, where no details disturbed the general view;
and this landscape seen from above, from the new elevated
sites; the large windows, the terraces, the lawns; the cleared
lines of vision; the expression of control and of command. It is
the social composition that Peacock, in *Headlong Hall*, satirically
observed:

a white, polished, angular building, reflected to a nicety in this wave-
less lake; and there you have Lord Littlebrain looking out of the
window.

But it is a commanding prospect that is at the same time a
triumph of 'unspoiled' nature: this is the achievement: an
effective and still imposing mystification. And we must insist
on this central character even while we also notice that caught
up and used and enjoyed within this social composition were
many real ways of seeing landscape which had different motives.
Dyer shared the improvers' ideology:

> Inclose, inclose, ye swains!
> Why will you joy in common field . . . .?
> . . . In fields
> Promiscuous held all culture languishes.

But when he looked from Grongar Hill he had an older
consciousness:

> And see the rivers, how they run
> Through woods and meads, in shade and sun;
> Sometimes swift, sometimes slow,

> Wave succeeding wave, they go
> A various journey to the deep
> Like human life to endless sleep.

This is not yet nature separated from the nature of man, but in the development of eighteenth-century landscape poetry the separated prospect eventually became commonplace. It was the moment that Thomson had described:

> Meantime you gain the height, from whose fair brow
> The bursting prospect spreads immense around.

It was the view for which Cowper seems to have invented our word 'scenery', and the consciousness of looking at the view is, within this convention, intrinsic:

> Here Ouse, slow winding through a level plain
> Of spacious meads with cattle sprinkled o'er,
> Conducts the eye along its sinuous course
> Delighted. There, fast rooted in their bank,
> Stand, never overlook'd, our favourite elms,
> That screen the herdsman's solitary hut;
> While far beyond, and overthwart the stream
> That, as with molten glass, inlays the vale,
> The sloping land recedes into the clouds;
> Displaying on its varied side the grace
> Of hedge-row beauties numberless, square tow'r,
> Tall spire, from which the sound of cheerful bells.
> Just undulates upon the list'ning ear.
> Groves, heaths, and smoking villages, remote.

It is in the act of observing that this landscape forms; the river 'conducts the eye'; the sloping land 'displays' its grace; the stream 'inlays' the vale. It is a beautiful picture, in the strict sense. Its sense of possession, from a separated vantage-point, is a genuinely abstract aesthetic, and there are hundreds of similar cases. The order was being projected while it was also being composed. At the centre of the society the conjunction was direct. In its marginal observers it became a poetic or pictorial convention.

And then, with apparent suddenness, a different question was put: by another poet, again looking out over the land, feeling its calm composition but finding the very fact of calm disturbing:

> 'Tis calm indeed! so calm, that it disturbs
> And vexes meditation with its strange
> And extreme silentness. Sea, hill and wood,
> This populous village! Sea, and hill, and wood,
> With all the numberless goings on of life
> Inaudible as dreams.

This disturbing meditation, by Coleridge, is a sign of a break in the conventional order. The real relations between man and nature, the real existence of the observer and of those whom he could see only dissolved into a landscape, returned as a problem: of identity, of perception and of nature itself.

There is the separation of possession: the control of a land and its prospects. But there is also a separation of spirit: a recognition of forces of which we are part but which we may always forget, and which we must learn from, not seek to control. In these two kinds of separation the idea of Nature was held and transformed.

'Why,' asked Addison, 'may not a whole Estate be thrown into a kind of garden by frequent Plantations. A man might make a pretty Landskip of his own Possessions.'

Wordsworth, almost a century later, took as the centre of his world not a possessive man but a wondering child:

> Frail creature as he is, helpless as frail,
> An inmate of this active universe:
> For feeling has to him imparted power
> That through the growing faculties of sense
> Doth like an agent of the one great Mind
> Create, creator and receiver both,
> Working but in alliance with the works
> Which it beholds.

Two principles of Nature can then be seen simultaneously. There is nature as a principle of order, of which the ordering mind is part, and which human activity, by regulating principles, may then rearrange and control. But there is also nature as a principle of creation, of which the creative mind is part, and from which we may learn the truths of our own sympathetic nature.

This active sympathy is the real change of mind, the new consciousness if only in a minority, in the very period in which the willed transformation of nature, not only of land and water but of its raw materials and its essential elements, was to enter a new phase, in the processes we now call industrial. The agrarian confidence of the eighteenth century had been counterpointed, throughout, by feelings of loss and melancholy and regret: from the ambivalence of Thomson to the despair of Goldsmith. Now, with Wordsworth, an alternative principle was to be powerfully asserted: a confidence in nature, in its own workings, which at least at the beginning was also a broader, a more humane confidence in men.

This movement is not, at first sight, very easy to distinguish from what, in the second half of the eighteenth century, is an evident alteration of taste. It is significant and understandable that in the course of a century of reclamation, drainage and clearing there should have developed, as a by-product, a feeling for unaltered nature, for wild land: the feeling that was known at the time as 'picturesque'. It is well known how dramatically the view of the Alps altered, from Evelyn's 'strange, horrid and fearful crags and tracts', in the mid 1640s, or Dennis's 'Ruins upon Ruins, in monstrous Heaps, and Heaven and Earth confounded' in 1688 to the characteristic awed praise of mid and later eighteenth-century and nineteenth- and twentieth-century travellers:

Not a precipice, not a torrent, not a cliff but is pregnant with religion and poetry.

(Gray, 1739)

Motionless torrents! silent cataracts!
Who made you glorious as the Gates of Heaven
Beneath the keen full moon?

(Coleridge, 1802)

In the course of the change, comparable districts in Britain – the Lake District, from the 1760s under the influence of Dalton and Brown; the Wye Valley and South Wales, the Scottish Highlands, North Wales, the New Forest, from the 1780s, under the direct influence of William Gilpin – became places of fashionable visiting and even of pilgrimage. Johnson's attitude to the Highlands –

the appearance is that of matter, incapable of form or usefulness, dismissed by nature from her care and left in its original elemental state

– seemed left far behind. That Nature was an improver; the new

Nature is an original. But we are bound to remember that most, though not all, of these tours to wild places were undertaken by people who were able to travel because 'nature' had not left their own lands in an 'original elemental state'. The picturesque journeys – and the topographical poems, journals, paintings and engravings which promoted and commemorated them – came from the profits of an improving agriculture and from trade. It is not, at this level, an alteration of sensibility; it is strictly an addition of taste. Like the landscaped parks, where every device was employed to produce a natural effect, the wild regions of mountain and forest were for the most part objects of conspicuous aesthetic consumption: to have been to the named places, to exchange and compare the travelling and gazing experiences, was a form of fashionable society. That in the course of the journeys some other experiences came we know well enough from Wordsworth and others; but it is Wordsworth who makes what for him is the vital distinction:

> even in pleasure pleased
> Unworthily, disliking here, and there
> Liking, by rules of mimic art transferred
> To things above all art; but more – for this,
> Although a strong infection of the age,
> Was never much my habit – giving way
> To a comparison of scene with scene,
> Bent overmuch on superficial things,
> Pampering myself with meagre novelties
> Of colour and proportion: to the moods
> Of time or season, to the moral power,
> The affections and the spirit of the place
> Insensible.

The conventional 'awe' of wild places, that Johnson in the Highlands had described as

terror without danger . . . one of the sports of fancy, a voluntary agitation of the mind, that is permitted no longer than it pleases

is something that Wordsworth had known, when he

> sought *that* beauty, which, as Milton sings,
> Hath terror in it.

But he had learned a more general perception:

> When every day brought with it some new sense
> Of exquisite regard for common things.
> And all the earth was budding with these gifts
> Of more refined humanity . . .
> . . . a spirit, there for me enshrined
> To penetrate the lofty and the low.

It is a complicated movement, including many feelings which were already familiar, but now united, even forced, into a principle of human respect and human community.

It is right to stress some continuity from Thomson and the eighteenth-century tradition. There is the use of the country, of 'nature', as a retreat and solace from human society and ordinary human consciousness:

> I well remember that those very plumes,
> Those weeds, and the high spear-grass on that wall,
> By mist and silent rain-drops silvered o'er,
> As once I passed, into my heart conveyed
> So still an image of tranquillity,
> So calm and still, and looked so beautiful
> Amid the uneasy thoughts which filled my mind,
> That what we feel of sorrow and despair
> From ruin and from change, and all the grief
> That passing shows of Being leave behind,
> Appeared an idle dream.

Characteristically, in this, it is the lonely observer who 'passes', and what he sees is a 'still life': an image against stress and change.

There is also continuity in a different dimension: the recognition, even the idealization, of 'humble' characters, in sympathy, in charity and in community. *Michael* is subtitled 'a pastoral poem', and it is so in the developed sense of the description of a rural independence – the shepherd and his family who are

> as a proverb in the vale
> For endless industry

– and its dissolution by misfortune, lack of capital, and final sale:

> The Cottage which was nam'd the Evening Star
> Is gone, the ploughshare has been through the ground
> On which it stood; final changes have been wrought
> In all the neighbourhood . . .

It is significant that Wordsworth links the 'gentle agency' of Nature with the fellow-feeling which binds him to such men as Michael: the link we observed in Thomson. Wordsworth often came closer to the actual men, but he saw them also as receding, moving away into a past which only a few surviving signs, and the spirit of poetry, could recall. In this sense the melancholy of loss and dissolution, which had been so marked in the late eighteenth-century country writing, is continued in familiar terms.

But there is also an important development in Wordsworth: a new emphasis, corresponding to just this view of history, on the dispossessed, the lonely wanderer, the vagrant. It is here that the social observation is linked to the perceptions of the lonely observer, who is also the poet. The old Cumberland beggar, in the poem of that title, is a later version of the old man whom Crabbe had observed, but the change of viewpoint is remarkable. He is not now evidence of the lack of community – of the village as a life of pain. On the contrary, more truly separated from its life in any direct way, he concentrates in himself, in his actual vagrancy, the community and charity which are the promptings of nature. It is in giving to him that fellow-feeling is kept alive. It is 'Nature's law' that none should exist divorced from:

> a spirit and pulse of good,
> A life and soul to every mode of being
> Inseparably link'd.

The beggar is the agent of this underlying, almost lost community:

> And while, in that vast solitude to which
> The tide of things has led him, he appears
> To breathe and live but for himself alone,
> Unblam'd, uninjur'd, let him bear about
> The good which the benignant law of heaven
> Has hung around him, and, while life is his,
> Still let him prompt the unletter'd Villagers
> To tender offices and pensive thoughts.

The spirit of community, that is to say, has been dispossessed and isolated to a wandering, challenging if passive, embodiment in the beggar. It is no longer from the practice of community, or from the spirit of protest at its inadequacy, but from that the instinct of fellow-feeling is derived. Thus an essential isolation and silence and loneliness have become the only carriers of nature and community against the rigours, the cold abstinence, the selfish ease of ordinary society.

It is a complex structure of feeling, but in its achievement a decisive phase of what must still be called country writing has been inaugurated. There is still the strong sense of observed nature as:

> a pastoral Tract
> Like one of these, where Fancy might run wild,
> Though under skies less generous and serene;
> Yet there, as for herself, had Nature fram'd
> A pleasure-ground.

But the decisive development is towards that landscape in which:

> The elements and seasons in their change
> Do find their dearest fellow-labourer there,
> The heart of man, a district on all sides
> The fragrance breathing of humanity,
> Man free, man working for himself, with choice
> Of time and place, and object.

These are the phrases of an actual rural independence, of the kind which had been directly observed in Cumberland, and then seen as threatened by change. But under the new stress there is a simultaneous affirmation and abstraction of 'Man', of 'Humanity':

> A solitary object and sublime
> Above all height . . . .
> . . . . Thus was Man
> Ennobled outwardly before mine eyes . . .
> . . . Remov'd, and at a distance that was fit.

The figure thus seen is at first the shepherd, moving and working in the mountains, but is then the idea of human nature –

> the impersonated thought,
> The idea or abstraction of the Kind

– which sustains the poet against 'the deformities of crowded life' and the distorted images of men in a pressing society. The labourer now merged with his landscape, a figure within the general figure of nature, is seen from a distance, in which the affirmation of Nature is intended as the essential affirmation of Man. It is in this spirit, at once separated and affirming a submerged general connection –

> Sea, hill and wood,
> This populous village! Sea and hill and wood
> With all the numberless goings on of life
> Inaudible as dreams

– that a new emphasis is placed on the act of poetry itself, the act of creation; as Wordsworth described it so often, or as Coleridge put it, from the disturbance within the apparent calm:

> And would we aught behold, of higher worth,
> Than that inanimate cold world allowed
> To the poor loveless ever-anxious crowd,
> Ah! from the soul itself must issue forth
> A light, a glory, a fair luminous cloud
> Enveloping the earth.

It is not now the will that is to transform nature; it is the lonely creative imagination; the man driven back from the cold world and in his own natural perception and language seeking to find and recreate man.

This is the 'green language' of the new poetry. The phrase is actually used by John Clare, in a poem called, significantly, *Pastoral Poesy*:

> A language that is ever green
> That feelings unto all impart,
> As hawthorn blossoms, soon as seen,
> Give May to every heart.

The conjunction is present also in Wordsworth's famous *Lines Written A Few Miles above Tintern Abbey*:

> Therefore am I still
> A lover of the meadows and the woods,
> And mountains; and of all that we behold
> From this green earth; of all the mighty world

> Of eye and ear, both what they half create
> And what perceive; well pleased to recognize
> In nature and the language of the sense,
> The anchor of my purest thoughts, the nurse,
> The guide, the guardian of my heart, and soul
> Of all my moral being.

This is, in a new sense, the 'green pastoral landscape':

> Here, if need be, struggling with storms, and there
> Strewing in peace life's humblest ground with herbs
> At every season green, sweet at all hours.

This is the philosophical conclusion; the climax, in *The Prelude*, of the formation of 'a Poet's mind'. But it was a new kind of poet, as it was a new kind of nature, that was now being formed.

John Clare, as a young labourer, had been excited beyond his capacity of explanation by some lines from Thomson's *Spring*:

> Come gentle Spring, ethereal mildness come,
> And from the bosom of yon dripping cloud,
> While music wakes around, veil'd in a shower
> Of shadowing roses, on our plains descend.

This can be read now as a theatrical invocation: a symbolic abstraction of the exalted movement of the seasons. But we can follow both a continuity and a transformation if we read, with it, some of Clare's developed verse:

> From dark green dumps among the dripping grain
> The lark with sudden impulse starts and sings
> And mid the smoking rain
> Quivers her russet wings.

The personified season has become the directly seen lark, but the movement is the same: the investment of nature with a quality of creation that is now, in its new form, internal; so that the more closely the object is described, the more directly, in a newly working language and rhythm, a feeling of the observer's life is seen and known, and the bird *is* the feeling, in the created poem.

Closer description of nature – of birds, trees, effects of weather and of light – is a very marked element in this new writing. Any anthology of natural descriptions would draw very heavily on verse and prose written since 1780. It is often a prolonged, rapt, exceptional description: an intricate working of particularity, as opposed to the more characteristic attribution of single identifying qualities in most earlier writing. This is clearly in part related to more intense observation, but we have only to compare it with the writing of men who were only (though remarkably) intent observers to realize what else is happening. Thus it would be easy to establish some kind of correlation between, say, Wordsworth and Clare on the one hand, and Gilbert White of Selborne on the other; an intense devotion to watching and describing nature is evident in all three men. Yet we have only to remember Gilbert White to see the essential differences:

The ousel is larger than a blackbird, and feeds on haws . . .

That close observation and description is of a separated object, another creature. It is at the opposite pole from the human separation of Wordsworth and Clare: a separation that is mediated by a projection of personal feeling into a subjectively particularized and objectively generalized Nature.

This movement is well known, as a fact of literary history. But Clare is in every way a deeply significant figure, for in him there is not only the literary change but directly, in his person and his history, the inwardness of the social transformation.

He was in no way the first of the labourer poets. Stephen Duck, as we saw, had written one fine poem before the court and the church and neo-classicism patronized and emasculated him. He had been followed by others, under a similar patronage: James Woodhouse the cobbler, who helped Shenstone lay out The Leasowes; Robert Dodsley the weaver; Robert Tatersal the bricklayer; Mary Collier the washer-woman; William Falconer the sailor; Ann Yearsley the milk-seller, who was encouraged to publish as Lactilla:

> No vallies blow, no waving grain uprears
> Its tender stalk to cheer my coming hour.

Robert Bloomfield ran away, at fourteen, from his work as a farmboy and became a cobbler in London, and in 1800 published *The Farmer's Boy*, with considerable effect, not excluding a description of him as 'our own more chaste Theocritus'. *The Farmer's Boy* is an honest imitation of Thomson's *Seasons*. Bloomfield was, he said, 'determined that what I said on Farming should be EXPERIMENTALLY true' but though his details have this accuracy of experience they are enclosed within a kind of external pointing and explanation, as in the general figure of Giles who has been projected from his own more immediate memories:

> Who could resist the call? that Giles had done
> Nor heard the birds, nor seen the rising sun,
> Had not Benevolence, with cheering ray,
> And Greatness stooped, indulgent to display
> Praise which does surely not to Giles belong
> But to the objects that inspired his song.

The creeping humility is an acquired taste. If it now provokes either anger or contempt we must not make the mistake of attacking Bloomfield but the men, the class, who reduced him and many thousands of others to this anxious obeisance. In a non-poetical manner he had his own very different feelings, as when he attacked a remark of Windham's:

the *common people* of his native country, are a rough set no doubt, but I dislike the doctrine of keeping them in their dirt, for though it holds good as to the preservation of potatoes, it would be no grateful reflection to good minds to know that a man's natural abilities had been smother'd for want of being able to read and write. How can we consistently praise the inestimable blessing of letters and not wish to extend it.

The smothering, indeed, was all too general and conscious.

To make the Society Happy and People Easy under the meanest Circumstances, it is requisite that great numbers of them should be Ignorant as well as Poor,

as Mandeville had expressed it, in a dominant attitude that lasted well into the nineteenth century. The taking-up for patronage may seem to contradict the smothering, but it was only another form of it. What was imposed on the labourer-poets was a definition of learning and cultivation, and more critically a definition of poetry, which, as it happened, was as mediocre as it was arrogant. Bloomfield could hardly get at his real experience because an external attitude had been consciously interposed –

> Live, trifling incidents, and grace my song,
> That to the humblest menial belong

– and even at his best he is constrained within a verse convention that is syntactically that of an observer rather than a participant: the third-person abstraction and personification of other men who labour; the ratification by literary allusion; the required periphrastic gesture:

> Dried fuel hoarded is his richest store
> And circling smoke obscures his little door:
> Whence creeping forth, to duty's call he yields,
> And strolls the Crusoe of his lonely fields.
> On whitethorns towering, and the leafless rose
> A frost-nipped feast in bright vermilion glows;
> Where clust'ring sloes in glossy order rise,
> He crops the loaded branch – a cumbrous prize.

Moreover the possibilities of development were conditioned by the fact of patronage; the extravagant praise was so regularly followed by neglect, at a time when a decent independence was no easier in literature than on the land itself. Bloomfield turned to *Rural Tales*, in the simpler style of the ballads, and Clare thought his *Richard and Kate* made him 'the first of Rural Bards in this country'. Also, for money, he turned to topographical tourist poems: as it happens going to my own native country, looking at mountains I have known all my life. What he makes of that landscape, in formal description, is not important; it is a catalogue of picturesque epithets. But he could say, with more feeling:

> Must scenes like these expand,
> Scenes so magnificently grand,
> And millions breathe, and pass away
> Unblessed, throughout their little day,
> With one short glimpse? By place confined,
> Shall many an anxious ardent mind,
> Sworn to the Muses, cower its pride,
> Doomed but to sing with pinions tied?

It is his own observation of a real experience, and it is not surprising that he moves at once to a contrast with Burns, in a different culture. It is as he touches his own limitations, in a whole social experience, that the strength he had tamed shows through.

John Clare's life must be seen in the same context. It is more tragic but also more urgent: more tragic because more urgent. We can properly see it, up to a certain point, in the context of rural change: the familiar association of Clare with the loss by enclosures. But to see it fully, we shall have to go beyond this, to the experience and the poetic development which he shared with Wordsworth, in a much wider social change.

We can of course find in Clare, in an explicit way, strongly felt responses to the visible aspects of recent rural change. For example in the 'May' of the *Shepherd's Calendar*:

> Old may day where's thy glorys gone
> All fled and left thee every one
> Thou comst to thy old haunts and homes
> Unnoticed as a stranger comes . . .
> . . . While the new thing that took thy place
> Wears faded smiles upon its face
> And where enclosure has its birth
> It spreads a mildew oer her mirth.

In 'October' the surviving gipsies are observed:

> On commons where no farmers claims appear
> Nor tyrant justice rides to interfere.

Or again, in more conscious argument, in *The Village Minstrel*:

> There once were lanes in nature's freedom dropt,
> There once were paths that every valley wound –
> Inclosure came, and every path was stopt;
> Each tyrant fix'd his sign where paths were found,
> To hint a trespass now who cross'd the ground:
> Justice is made to speak as they command;
> The high road now must be each stinted bound:
> – Inclosure, thou'rt a curse upon the land,
> And tasteless was the wretch who thy existence plann'd . . .
>
> O England! boasted land of liberty,
> With strangers still thou mayst thy title own,
> But thy poor slaves the alteration see,
> With many a loss to them the truth is known:

Like emigrating bird thy freedom's flown,
While mongrel clowns, low as their rooting plough,
Disdain they laws to put in force their own;
And every village owns its tyrants now,
And parish-slaves must live as parish kings allow

. . . Ye fields, ye scenes so dear to Lubin's eye,
Ye meadow-blooms, ye pasture-flowers, farewell!
Ye banish'd trees, ye make me deeply sigh,
Inclosure came, and all your glories fell,

There is an interesting edge of anger in the description of the
enclosing gentry as 'mongrel clowns', but also, of course, a
familiar displacement: the ancient liberty of England is being
suppressed, not by the visible and active landowners, but by
'low' and, as it would seem, alien 'tyrants'. It is how Goldsmith
had seen an earlier phase of the change; rural England then was

a picture of Italy just before its conquest by Theodoric the Ostro-
goth.

In the actual scale of the regulated conquest of land which
enclosure, among other procedures, represented, this persistent
image of invading barbarians is understandable. But the harder
fact, that these barbarians were well-born Englishmen, is
characteristically displaced. And then it is very much to the
point that the first general word chosen to describe the instigators
of the 'curse' of enclosure is 'tasteless'. This connects with that
structure of feeling which was beginning to form, from Goldsmith to the poets of the Romantic movement, and which is
particularly visible in Clare: the loss of the 'old country' is a
loss of poetry; the cultivation of natural feeling is dispossessed by
the consequences of improved cultivation of the land; wealth is
not only hard and cruel but tasteless.

Clare was very young when he wrote, in *Helpstone*, a familiar
rural elegy and retrospect. Its terms are especially interesting,
since it is 'industry' (in its earlier meaning of work) which
belongs to the old world, and 'wealth' to the new:

Sweet rest and peace! ye dear, departed charms,
Which industry once cherishe'd in her arms;
When ease and plenty, known but now to few,
Were known to all, and labour had its due,

We need not ask when, for the point of the memory is the contrast:

> Accursed Wealth! o'er-bounding human laws,
> Of every evil thou remains't the cause:
> Victims of want, those wretches such as me,
> Too truly lay their wretchedness to thee:
> Thou art the bar that keeps from being fed,
> And thine our loss of labour and of bread.

As a way of seeing the dispossession of labour by capital, this is exact. But it is set in a structure of feeling in which what wealth is most visibly destroying is 'Nature': that complex of the land as it was, in the past and in childhood, which both ageing and alteration destroy. There are the scenes of what is really an older agriculture –

> Thou far fled pasture, long evanish'd scene!
> Where nature's freedom spread the flow'ry green . . .
> . . . Where lowing oxen roam'd to feed at large,
> And bleeting there the Shepherd's woolly charge . . .

– alongside the more primitive land which is being directly altered: the brooks diverted, the willows felled, in drainage and clearance.

Over a century and a half I can recognize what Clare is describing: particular trees, and a particular brook, by which I played as a child, have gone in just this way, in the last few years, in an improved use of marginal land. And then what one has to consider is the extension of this observation – one kind of loss against one kind of gain – into a loss of 'Nature'. It is not only the loss of what can be called – sometimes justly, sometimes affectedly – a piece of 'unspoiled' country. It is also, for any particular man, the loss of a specifically human and historical landscape, in which the source of feeling is not really that it is 'natural' but that it is 'native':

> Dear native spot! which length of time endears . . .
> Nay e'en a post, old standard, or a stone
> Moss'd o'er by age, and branded as her own
> Would in my mind a strong attachment gain,
> A fond desire that they might there remain;
> And all old favourites, fond taste approves,
> Griev'd me at heart to witness their removes.

And then what is most urgently being mourned – the 'old favourites' approved by 'fond taste' – is a loss of childhood through a loss of its immediate landscape:

> But now, alas! those scenes exist no more;
> The pride of life with thee, like mine, is o'er.

It is wholly understandable that this was written at the age of sixteen. A way of seeing has been connected with a lost phase of living, and the association of happiness with childhood has been developed into a whole convention, in which not only innocence and security but peace and plenty have been imprinted, indelibly, first on a particular landscape, and then, in a powerful extension, on a particular period of the rural past, which is now connected with a lost identity, lost relations and lost certainties, in the memory of what is called, against a present consciousness, Nature. The first feeling is so urgent that it inevitably connects widely with other experience:

> His native scenes! O sweet endearing sound!
> Sure never beats a heart, howe'er forlorn,
> But the warm'd breast has soft emotions found
> To cherish the dear spot where he was born:
> E'en the poor hedger, in the early morn
> Chopping the pattering bushes hung with dew,
> Scarce lays his mitten on a branching thorn,
> But painful memory's banish'd thoughts in view
> Remind him, when 'twas young, what happy days he knew.

And the transition is then almost unnoticed, as in *Joys of Childhood*:

> Dull is that memory, vacant is that mind,
> Where no sweet vision of the past appears.

Living in this connecting feeling, Clare recognized, even while he created, the conversion of particular memories into the generalizing 'sweet vision of the past'. His most crucial recognition, relating quite centrally to the tradition we have been examining, comes in another verse of the same poem:

> Fancy spreads Edens wheresoe'er they be;
> The world breaks on them like an opening flower,
> Green joys and cloudless skies are all they see;
> The hour of childhood is a rose's hour . . .

The natural images of this Eden of childhood seem to compel a particular connection, at the very moment of their widest generality. Nature, the past and childhood are temporarily but powerfully fused:

> In nature's quiet sleep as on a mother's breast.

The plough that disturbs this nature connects with the hardest emotions of maturity: dispossession, the ache of labour, the coldness of the available world: a complex of feeling and imagery in the experience of this man and of everyone; of each personal generation and of this generation in history. But what is then achieved, against this experience of pain, is a way of feeling which is also a way of writing:

> A language that is ever green

– the language of what Clare now recreates as 'pastoral poesy', in the title of the poem from which the line comes. This is a radical development of language and of the idea of literature; its strength in its connecting feelings of human warmth and community, in a time of real dispossession, eviction and social division; its paradoxical weakness in the making of this connection through withdrawal into 'nature', into the 'Eden' of the heart, and into a lonely, resigned and contemplative love of men:

> Unruffled quietness hath made
> A peace in every place,
> And woods are resting in their shade
> Of social loneliness.

It is wholly understandable, this development of responses to a disturbing history and an altering landscape: the real scenes of both at once dissolved and recreated in images which carry the meanings and yet compose a way of seeing that suppresses them. As so often in romantic poetry, it is the survival of human feeling in a factual dispossession:

> While threshing in the dusty barn
> Or squashing in the ditch to earn
> A pittance that would scarce allow
> One joy to smooth my sweating brow
> Where drop by drop would chase and fall
> Thy presence triumphed over all.

The presence is poetry, speaking to and for the humanity of the hedger, the thresher, the man actually altering the landscape in the service and for the gain of others; but distorted by its very loneliness into an opposition to that noise of the world, the noise of actual exploitation and, ironically, of direct response to it:

> Bred in a village full of strife and noise,
> Old senseless gossips, and blackguarding boys,
> Ploughmen and threshers, whose discourses led
> To nothing more than labour's rude employs,
> 'Bout work being slack, and rise and fall of bread
> And who were like to die, and who were like to wed.

It is from this actual village, where a community lives under pressure, that the poet withdraws to the quiet of nature, where he can speak for his own and others' humanity, through re-membered ballads and contemplated scenes; a speaking silence from which he is torn, bitterly and desperately, to put what he has written back into the noise of the market: profit, malice, envy; a fashionable contempt for his simplicity; and then again, but now virtually breaking the mind, into the speaking silence of the neglected poet, the man alone with nature and with poverty, recreating a world in his green language:

> I am, but what I am
> Who cares or knows?

It was as far as the mind could go, within that structure. Any new direction required an alteration of structure and of essential convention. Clare marks the end of pastoral poetry, in the very shock of its collision with actual country experience. He could not accept Lamb's characteristic advice, which had tamed so many: 'transplant Arcadia to Helpstone. The true rustic style, the Arcadian English, I think is to be found in Shenstone.' He is, rather, the culmination, in broken genius, of the movement which we can trace from a century before him: the separation of Nature from the facts of the labour that is creating it, and then the breaking of Nature, in altered and now intolerable relations between men. What we find in Clare is not Jonson's idealization of a landscape yielding of itself, nor Thom-son's idealization of a productive order that is scattering and guarding plenty. There was a conscious reaction to this, in Goldsmith, in Langhorne, and in Crabbe. But there was also an unconscious reaction, to a country from which any acceptable social order had been decisively removed. Clare goes beyond the external observation of the poems of protest and of melancholy retrospect. What happens in him is that the loss is internal. It is to survive at all, as a thinking and feeling man, that he needs the green language of the new Nature.

But there is a wider reason for the stress of the change. Men accustomed to seeing their immediate environment through received intellectual and literary forms had by the eighteenth century to notice another dramatic alteration of landscape: the rapidly expanding and changing city. It is characteristic that a minor poet, Charles Jenner (1736–74) should attempt a series of 'Town' or 'London' *Eclogues*; but now the absence of pastoral images had a different bearing:

> I spy no verdant glade, no gushing rill,
> No fountain gushing from the rocky hill.

He was walking on the outskirts of expanding London:

> Where'er around I cast my wand'ring eyes
> Long burning rows of fetid bricks arise,
> And nauseous dunghills swell in mould'ring heaps
> While the fat sow beneath their covert sleeps.

His conclusion is a simple negation:

> Since then no images adorn the plain
> But what are found as well in Gray's Inn Lane
> Since dust and noise inspire no thought serene
> And three-horse stages little mend the scene
> I'll stray no more to seek the vagrant muse
> But ev'n go write at home and save my shoes.

It is fortunate that this was an exceptional response. As London grew, dramatically, in the eighteenth century, it was being intensely observed, as a new kind of landscape, a new kind of society.

Yet it was at first difficult to separate what was new from traditional images of the city. In Thomson, for example, there is an interesting combination of new and old attitudes. There is the conventional contrast with the innocence of the country, as here in *Autumn*:

> This is the life which those who fret in guilt
> And guilty cities never knew – the life
> Led by primeval ages uncorrupt.

Connecting with this, but developing more specific complaints:

> The city swarms intense. The public haunt,
> Full of each theme and warm with mixed discourse,
> Hums indistinct. The sons of riot flow
> Down the loose stream of false enchanted joy
> To swift destruction.
>
> (*Winter*)

But this moral view, of waste and profligacy, allows room for the contrast not only with innocent nature but also with civilized industry. The celebration of production, which had embraced the land, now extends to the city:

> Full are thy cities with the sons of art;
> And trade and joy, in every busy street,
> Mingling are heard; even Drudgery himself
> As at the car he sweats, or, dusty, hews
> The palace stone, looks gay.
>
> (*Summer*)

And Thomson could extend this celebration of industry to a full positive view of the city:

> Hence every form of cultivated life
> In order set, protected, and inspired
> Into perfection wrought. Uniting all,
> Society grew numerous, high, polite,
> And happy. Nurse of art, the city reared
> In beauteous pride her tower-encircled head;
> And stretching street on street, by thousands drew,
> From twining woody haunts, or the tough yew
> To bows strong-straining, her aspiring sons.
>   Then commerce brought into the public walk
> The busy merchant; the big warehouse built;
> Raised the strong crane; choked up the loaded street
> With foreign plenty; and thy stream, O Thames,
> Large, gentle, deep, majestic king of floods!
> Chose for his grand resort.
>
> (*Autumn*)

This celebration combines a bourgeois sense of achieved production and trade with an Augustan sense of civilized order. And because it does so, it can be turned, very quickly, into one of the newly emphasized fears of the city: the fear of the mob joining the older fear of the city's avarice:

> Let this through cities work his eager way
> By legal outrage and established guile,
> The social sense extinct; and that ferment
> Mad into tumult the seditious herd,
> Or melt them down to slavery.

The legal and financial superstructure of the celebrated trade and industry is then seen as of a piece with riot and sedition, in an activity that has turned into a ferment.

It was within this difficult complex that eighteenth-century observers developed their views of the city, and especially, for it was the leading city of the world, of London. Voltaire saw the pursuit of industry and urbane pleasure as the marks of the city and thence of civilization itself. The golden age and the Garden of Eden, lacking industry and pleasure, were not virtuous but ignorant: the city, and especially London, was the symbol of progress and enlightenment, its social mobility the school of civilization and liberty:

> Rival of Athens, London, blest indeed
> That with thy tyrants had the wit to chase
> The prejudices civil factions breed.
> Men speak their thoughts and worth can win its place . . .
> In London, who has talent, he is great.

Adam Smith, rather differently, saw the city as securing and extending the industry of the country: a centre of freedom and order but in its very dependence as a market and manufacturing centre liable to breed a volatile and insecure people. This came nearer to the real contradictions of London. On the one hand, in polite literature, there was a new urbanity, including even the conventional rural gestures, in the world of Pope and Johnson and Swift. But theirs was an isolated London, though Johnson, in his imitation of Juvenal, could see the city through other eyes. On the other hand, in Hogarth and Fielding, Gay and Defoe, there was a darker reality. Hogarth's *Gin Lane* brings us

nearer to mid eighteenth-century London than any urbane formulation; and whether it is the moral contrast of his *Industry
and Idleness* and of Lillo's *The London Merchant*, or the ambivalent
low-life vigour of Gay's *Beggar's Opera* or Defoe's *Moll Flanders*,
the sense of the actuality of London is at the opposite pole from
the ideal of civilized order. The 'insolent rabble', 'the insolence
of the mob', the 'idle, profligate and debauched' workmen are
commonplaces of middle-class observation. The thieving-shops,
the stews and the rookeries, the fetid cellars and the dangerous
tenements, formed a large part of the visitor's or middle-class
observer's sense of this 'rival of Athens'.

What is then compounded in this view is a contradictory
reality: of vice and protest, of crime and victimization, of despair
and independence. The contrasts of wealth and poverty were
not different in kind from those of the rural order, but were more
intense, more general, more evidently problematic, in their very
concentration into the feverishly expanding city. The 'mob' was
often violent, unpredictable, capable of being used for reaction,
but it was also a name that overlaid, as George Rudé has
shown, 'movements of social protest in which the underlying
conflict of poor against rich' was clearly visible. In the time of
Wilkes, for example, these popular protests were on the side of
liberty where the civilized order of London was against it.

At the same time this complexity had acquired, in the city, a
physical embodiment. As Fielding observed in 1751:

whoever considers the Cities of London and Westminster, with the
late vast increases of their suburbs, the great irregularity of their
buildings, the immense numbers of lanes, alleys, courts and bye-
places, must think that had they been intended for the very purpose
of concealment, they could not have been better contrived.

It is then ironic to reflect that much of the physical squalor and
complexity of eighteenth-century London was a consequence
not simply of rapid expansion but of attempts to control that
expansion. For complex reasons, ranging from fear of the
plague to fear of social disorder – itself a transference and
concentration in London of the disturbances of the rural
economy – there had been repeated attempts to limit the city's
growth. From the first phase of its rapid expansion, in the late
sixteenth century, when a proclamation of 1580 came out against

new buildings, through the seventeenth-century controls on trade and further proclamations against building, to as late as 1709, when a Bill against new houses was attempted, there was a prolonged struggle, by ruling-class interests, to restrain the growth of London, and in particular to prevent the poor settling there. Under the statutes and proclamations there was usually an explicit exception for houses 'fit for inhabitants of the better sort'. Poor people and vagrants, the casualties of a changing rural economy, or the hard-pressed or ambitious seeing in London some escape from their subordinate destiny, were the explicit objects of exclusion from the developing city. Yet the general changes were of an order which made exclusion impossible. Not only the retinues of servants but many thousands of others flooded in, and the main consequence of the limitations was a long-continued wave of overcrowded and insecure speculative building and adaptation within the legal limits: forced labyrinths and alleys of the poor. And this was happening as part of the same process as the building of town mansions, the laying out of squares and fashionable terraces: the 'Georgian' London now so often abstracted. As indeed so often, a ruling class wanted the benefits of a change it was itself promoting, but the control or suppression of its less welcome but inseparable consequences. Much of the complaint against London (and much of the praise) has to be read in this double sense.

This is true of the image of the 'Great Wen', which can be found well before Cobbett's more famous description:

London, the Metropolis of Great Britain, has been complained of for ages as a kind of monster, with a head enormously large, and out of all proportion to its body. And yet, at the juncture when this complaint was first made (about 200 years ago) the buildings of London hardly advanced beyond the City bounds ... If therefore the increase of buildings, begun at such an early period, was looked upon to be no better than a wen or excrescence upon the body-politic, what must we think of those numberless streets and squares which have been added since!

That is Tucker in 1783. The image of the 'monster', of the diseased 'wen', was to be used again and again as London continued to expand. But the real implications of the image were not always seen as clearly as Cobbett saw them. What the expansion of London actually indicated was the true condition and development of the country as a whole. If it was seen as monstrous, or as a diseased growth, this had logically to be traced back to the whole social order. But of course it was easier to denounce the consequences and ignore, or go on idealizing, the general condition.

London was already a city of half a million inhabitants in 1660, at a time when the next largest city was Bristol with some thirty thousand. Between 1700 and 1820 it rose to a million and a quarter. The centralization of political power; the replacement of feudalism by an agrarian aristocracy and then an agrarian bourgeoisie, with all its effects in modernization of the land; the immense development of a mercantile trade: these outstanding developments had acquired, over the generations, an unstoppable momentum: a concentration and a demand which then fed on itself. The nineteenth-century city, in Britain and elsewhere, was to be the creation of industrial capitalism. Eighteenth-century London was the astonishing creation of an agrarian and mercantile capitalism, within an aristocratic political order. At each stage it drew in much of the rest of the country: the drovers bringing their cattle from Wales or Scotland for its meat; gangs of girls walking from North Wales to pick its strawberries; and more fundamentally, beyond those organized if extraordinary journeys, thousands in search of work or of a place to hide; refugees from a disturbance or a no less tolerable rigidity. What induced them, Arthur Young asked, to 'quit their healthy clean fields for a region of dirt, stink and noise?' He could have found part of his answer in the condition of the villages, and in the expulsion of population which the 'improving' social order had enforced. He saw another part of the answer in the course of his question:

> Young men and women in the country fix their eye on London as the last stage of their hope ... The number of young women that fly there is incredible.

An unequal interaction between country and city was now far advanced and pervasive. There was the recourse to law, to the capital market and to the marriage market, in the consolidation and extension of the landlords. There was the promotion of distilling, as a remedy for what Defoe, in 1713, called the 'disaster' of the overproduction of corn. Gin Lane, in this way, ran back to the country-houses ('the distilling of corn is one of the most essential things to support the landed interest', *Review*, 9 May 1713). All around London itself, the country was transformed to supply the city: grain for the people and hay for the horses; pigs on the waste lands (as Jenner saw in his *Eclogue*); fruit and vegetables and milk. It was not the later case of an industrial centre being fed by its rural hinterland. It was a case of a capital city drawing the character of an economy and a society into its extraordinary centre: order and chaos both.

For London was not, in the later sense, an industrial city. It was a capital centre of trades and of distribution: of skilled craftsmen in metals and in print; of clothing and furniture and fashion; of all the work connected with shipping and the market. All these trades developed in its expansion, though there were many local changes. A significant characteristic of the eighteenth-century development was an expansion of what was noted in 1749 as the 'gainful branches of agency, factorage, brokerage, negotiation and insurance for the other parts of the kingdom'. There were 'agents, factors, brokers, insurers, bankers, negotiators, discounters, subscribers, contractors, remitters, ticket-mongers, stock-jobbers and . . . a great variety of other dealers in money, the names of whose employments were wholly unknown to our forefathers'. A 'Computation of the Increase of London', in 1719, noted the importance of the growth of Public Funds as leading to 'new offices and societies', bringing 'great numbers of other people to live in and about London'. By comparison with the established trades and crafts, themselves responsive to the increases in wealth and trade and display, this financial business was that of a minority. But it underlines the specific significance which, allied to its concentration of political power, the capital was acquiring. The new industrial city, when it came in the North, would be a creation of one or two kinds of work, and in its physical characteristics would reflect this singular emphasis. London, quite apart from its historical variety, was plural and various: not only in the sense of its hundreds of trades but in the sense that it was managing and directing so much of other people's business. A dominant part of the life of the nation was reflected but also created within it. As its population grew it went into deficit, not only in food but in the balance of material production; but this was much more than compensated by the fact of its social production: it was producing and reproducing, to a dominant degree, the social reality of the nation as a whole.

It was in this still eighteenth-century sense that Blake, himself a craftsman and a Londoner, saw the capital city:

> I wander thro' each charter'd street,
> Near where the charter'd Thames does flow . . .

He had originally written 'dirty' street and 'dirty' Thames, and these would have been evident enough; but what he adds is the perception of 'chartering': the organization of a city in terms of trade. Suddenly, within this, he sees the capital in a new way: not the riot, the noise or the monstrous wen of earlier and contemporary observation; but an organization, a systematic state of mind:

> . . . And mark in every face I meet
> Marks of weakness, marks of woe.
>
> In every cry of every Man
> In every Infant's cry of fear,
> In every voice, in every ban,
> The mind-forg'd manacles I hear.

The cries, the fears and the bans would all have been evident, but Blake now generalizes them to an imposed and yet self-imposed organized repression: 'the mind-forg'd manacles'. What he then sees, dramatically, are the submerged connections of this capital system:

> How the Chimney-sweeper's cry
> Every black'ning Church appalls;
> And the hapless Soldier's sigh
> Runs in blood down Palace walls.
>
> But most thro' midnight streets I hear
> How the youthful Harlot's curse
> Blasts the new born Infant's tear
> And blights with plagues the Marriage hearse.

This is very far from the traditional way of seeing innocence in the country, vice in the city. The innocence and the vice are in and of the city, in its factual and spiritual relations. The palace which impressively symbolizes power has to be seen as running with blood: the real but suppressed relationship is made visible, as also in the conventions of church and marriage against the reality of those who suffered and were despised and outcast. It is not just an observation of, say, the chimney-sweepers; before Blake wrote there had been vigorous and partly successful campaigns against the appalling conditions of the chimney-sweeping children. It is a making of new connections, in the whole order of the city and of the human system it concentrates and embodies. This forcing into consciousness of the suppressed connections is then a new way of seeing the human and social order as a whole. It is, as it happens, a precise prevision of the essential literary methods and purposes of Dickens.

It is worth stressing this in Blake, since although he inherits many eighteenth-century pastoral images, in his whole work he transforms them to elements of a general condition. The simplifying contrast between country and city is then decisively transcended. It is significant that one of his best-remembered phrases is 'England's green and pleasant land', but this is not the language of rural retrospect or retreat. The whole purpose of his struggle is, as he says, to build 'Jerusalem/In England's green and pleasant land': to build the holy as against the unholy city.

There are then interesting connections and contrasts with Wordsworth, whose seventh book of *The Prelude*, 'Residence in London', is one of the major early records of new ways of seeing the city. Wordsworth's narrative includes experiences more various than Blake's visions, but there are two more immediate differences. Wordsworth sees the city with his country experience behind him and shaping his vision; he then sees it in ways that relate to Blake, but with the specific character of the city, as an exceptional kind of social organization, dominant.

Wordsworth begins with the ordinary attitude of those who have lived at a distance from London: 'of wonder and obscure delight' in its history and its marvels. Even then, he tells us, he wondered

> how men lived
> Even next-door neighbours, as we say, yet still
> Strangers, nor knowing each the other's name.

But the sense of wonder and attraction was dominant, and he recalls his moment of arrival, when 'having thridded the long labyrinth of the suburban villages' he entered its 'vast dominion' and, amazed that anything 'external to the living mind should have such mighty sway', felt a 'weight of ages', 'power growing under weight'. This was

> the vast metropolis
> Fount of my country's destiny and the world's;
> That great emporium, chronicle at once
> And burial-place of passions, and their home
> Imperial, their chief living residence.

This an authentic way of seeing not just a city but the capital city, embodying and directing the whole country. But Wordsworth also sees the city in older ways. Love does not easily thrive:

> Among the close and overcrowded haunts
> Of cities, where the human heart is sick

and while 'the roar continues' in the streets

> Escaped as from an enemy, we turn
> Abruptly into some sequestered nook;

as Thomson had recommended, for the country against the city, hearing:

> At distance safe, the human tempest roar.

But these feelings are not at the centre of Wordsworth's experience of London. In quite new ways he tries to describe the city as a form of society; the

> endless stream of men and moving things! . . .
> . . . the quick dance,
> Of colours, lights and forms; the deafening din;
> The comers and the goers face to face.
> Face after face.

This is direct observation of a new set of physical and sense relationships: a new way of seeing men in what is experienced as a new kind of society. It is in this sense, of a new kind of alienation, that he reflects in ways that compare with but are different from Blake:

> O Friend! one feeling was there which belonged
> To this great city, by exclusive right;
> How often, in the overflowing streets,
> Have I gone forwards with the crowd, and said
> Unto myself, 'The face of every one
> That passes by me is a mystery!'
> Thus have I looked, nor ceased to look, oppressed
> By thoughts of what and whither, when and how,
> Until the shapes before my eyes became
> A second-sight procession, such as glides
> Over still mountains, or appears in dreams.
> And all the ballast of familiar life,
> The present, and the past; hope, fear; all stays,
> All laws of acting, thinking, speaking man
> Went from me, neither knowing me, nor known.

These important lines are, I believe, the first expression of what has since become a dominant experience of the city. Blake saw a common condition of 'weakness and woe'. Wordsworth saw strangeness, a loss of connection, not at first in social but in perceptual ways: a failure of identity in the crowd of others which worked back to a loss of identity in the self, and then, in these ways, a loss of society itself, its overcoming and replacement by a procession of images: the 'dance of colours, lights and forms', 'face after face' and there are no other laws. No experience has been more central in the subsequent literature of the city.

But it can go either way, from this perceptual confusion, this confession of mystery. Wordsworth immediately extended it to a received idea: the mystery of all human life, as in the identity label around the neck of the blind beggar, which he saw as a 'type' of the limits of human knowledge. This is less interesting than the original dissolution, but it is a characteristic factor of this kind of experience that it cannot easily be sustained. Every kind of philosophical and social attitude is poised to enter the very vacuum it has created. Wordsworth followed his own sense of mystery with the kind of denunciation of the 'crowd', the 'masses', which has become so familiar. The unnatural confusion is:

> what the mighty City is itself
> To all except a straggler here and there,
> To the whole swarm of its inhabitants;
> An undistinguishable world to men,
> The slaves unrespited of low pursuits,
> Living amid the same perpetual flow
> Of trivial objects, melted and reduced
> To one identity, by differences
> That have no law, no meaning and no end.

In the 1850 version he softened but did not essentially change this contemptuous blocking; its stereotype is one dominant way in which the social and perceptual confusion has gone. But there is another way, which has also remained important. Looking back on the experience, he proposed a different way of seeing, which historically has been crucial:

> . . . that among the multitudes
> Of that huge city, oftentimes was seen
> Affectingly set forth, more than elsewhere
> Is possible, the unity of men,
> One spirit over ignorance and vice
> Predominant, in good and evil hearts
> One sense for moral judgements, as one eye
> For the sun's light.

This historically liberating insight, of new kinds of possible order, new kinds of human unity, in the transforming experience of the city, appeared, significantly, in the same shock of recognition of a new dimension which had produced the more familiar subjective recoil. The objectively uniting and liberating forces were seen in the same activity as the forces of threat, confusion and loss of identity. And this was how, through the next century and a half, the increasingly dominant fact of the city was to be both paradoxically and alternatively interpreted.

For the transformation was on the point of becoming general. The special case of London, though it would remain of outstanding significance, was about to be joined by many other cases, in ways that both connect and confuse. London was a capital, a centre of civilization in the oldest sense, as Wordsworth himself had seen it:

> This City now doth like a garment wear
> The beauty of the morning; silent, bare,
> Ships, towers, domes, theatres and temples lie
> Open unto the fields and to the sky –
> All bright and glittering in the smokeless air.

As I said earlier, this is the city before the noise of the working day, and also before the smoke of its later development. But it is a permanent way of seeing any historical city: its public buildings and its defining centres of culture and learning. Paris, still half the size of London, was about to enter a period of major growth; Naples, Vienna, Berlin, Rome, St Petersburg, Budapest, Moscow were to follow. The cities of civilization, in this capital sense, were moving into a significantly renewed expansion and cultural importance. But other kinds of city were expanding even more rapidly. In England, in the course of the Industrial Revolution, even London's continuing and rapid growth must be compared with the still more rapid, the explosive growth of the new industrial cities of the North. London between 1821 and 1841 grew by twenty per cent; Manchester, Birmingham, Leeds and Sheffield by more than forty per cent; Bradford by sixty-five per cent. Ways of seeing the city, in its historical and capital senses, had been, as we have noted, various. The sheer scale of London, when it stood almost alone, had provoked the sense of a new human dimension, a new kind of society. But the industrial cities were something different again. Though still in their early stages they announced, even more decisively than the growth of capitals, the new character of the city and the new relations between city and country.

Dickens's city was London, and London, as we have seen, though it dominated both national and urban development, was in many ways specific: ways which have much to do with Dickens's particular creative achievement. When he looked at the other and even newer kind of city – the industrial concentration of Coketown (Preston) in *Hard Times* – he made a simpler, more rhetorical emphasis. Coketown was a 'triumph of fact'; you saw nothing in it 'but what was severely workful'. It was

a town of red brick, or of brick that would have been red if the smoke and ashes had allowed it; but as matters stood it was a town of un-natural red and black like the painted face of a savage.

In its human as in its physical landscape it was, in this view, uniform:

It contained several large streets all very like one another, and many small streets still more like one another, inhabited by people equally like one another, who all went in and out at the same hours, with the same sound upon the same pavements, to do the same work, and to whom every day was the same as yesterday and tomorrow, and every year the counterpart of the last and the next.

But whatever the adequacy of this uniform view as an image of a new and unnatural industrial order, it implicitly contradicted Dickens's own characteristic way of seeing people and their actions. Indeed it is tacitly dropped at every other point even in *Hard Times*, where the people, quite clearly, are not 'equally like one another'; where indeed their emphatic differences and contrasts are in the end the decisive organization of the novel.

This contradiction reminds us of the confusion which pre-vailed, in Dickens's time and beyond, between the idea of the city and the idea of industry. The identification between them, which had its social base in the new industrial towns, was in some important ways misleading, both generally and specifically for any understanding of Dickens. He could turn aside and denounce a Coketown, but his engagement with city experience, in the full sense, was an engagement with the very different fact of London, and it was to this that his real interests and his genius corresponded.

For a city like London, as we have seen, could not easily be described in a rhetorical gesture of repressive uniformity. On the contrary, its miscellaneity, its crowded variety, its randomness of movement, were the most apparent things about it, especially when seen from inside.

It is true that this miscellaneity and randomness in the end embodied a system: a negative system of indifference; a positive system of differentiation, in law, power and financial control. But the characteristic of London – capital city of a complex national and overseas economy and society – was that this was not, in any simple way, physically apparent. The order and the system of Coketown, even after we have allowed for the rhetoric of the description, were indeed quite visible and on the surface. The streets and houses, built in a short period of rapid expansion around what had been until recently a village or small market-town, were systematic and uniform in a way that most streets in London, in Dickens's time, quite evidently were not. The new industrial towns were organized around their decisive places of work – usually a single kind of work – in ways that London never had been or would be. So that while Dickens was affected by general images of the city as a new kind of social order, and in the case of Coketown and in other minor instances elsewhere could directly project these, his central response to the new experience of the city was more various and, I would say, more penetrating. He belongs much more, in this, to the vision of Blake or of Wordsworth, than to the later, more totalizing visions of the period after 1870. But what he saw, and what in a new kind of novel he learned to embody, went to the heart of the problem. For what London had to show, more fundamentally, even to modern experience, than the uniform cities of the early Industrial Revolution, was a contradiction, a paradox: the coexistence of variation and apparent randomness with what had in the end to be seen as a determining system: the visible individual facts but beyond them, often hidden, the common condition and destiny.

Dickens's creation of a new kind of novel – a creative achievement which had many false starts, many lapses, but in the end was decisive – can be directly related to what we must see as this double condition: the random and the systematic, the visible and the obscured, which is the true significance of the city, and especially at this period of the capital city, as a dominant social form.

Dickens's ultimate vision of London is then not to be illustrated by topography or local instance. It lies in the form of his novels: in their kind of narrative, in their method of characterization, in their genius for typification. It does not matter which way we put it: the experience of the city is the fictional method; or the fictional method is the experience of the city. What matters is that the vision – no single vision either, but a continual dramatization – is the form of the writing.

We can show this first in one decisive way. As we stand and look back at a Dickens novel the general movement we remember – the characteristic movement – is a hurrying seemingly random passing of men and women, each heard in some fixed phrase, seen in some fixed expression: a way of seeing men and women that belongs to the street. There is at first an absence of ordinary connection and development. These men and women do not so much relate as pass each other and then sometimes collide. Nor often in the ordinary way do they speak to each other. They speak at or past each other, each intent above all on defining through his words his own identity and reality; in fixed self-descriptions, in voices raised emphatically to be heard through and past other similar voices. But then as the action develops, unknown and unacknowledged relationships, profound and decisive connections, definite and committing recognitions and avowals are as it were forced into consciousness. These are the real and inevitable relationships and connections, the necessary recognitions and avowals of any human society. But they are of a kind that are obscured, complicated, mystified, by the sheer rush and noise and miscellaneity of this new and complex social order.

This creation of consciousness – of recognitions and relationships – can then be seen as the purpose of Dickens's developed fiction. The need for it is at the centre of his social and personal vision:

Oh for a good spirit who would take the housetops off, with a more potent and benignant hand than the lame demon in the tale, and show a Christian people what dark shapes issue from amidst their homes, to swell the retinue of the Destroying Angel as he moves forth among them. For only one night's view of the pale phantoms rising from the scenes of our too long neglect; and from the thick and sullen air where Vice and Fever propagate together, raining the tremendous social retributions which are ever pouring down, and ever coming thicker. Bright and blest the morning that should rise on such a night; for men, delayed no more by stumbling-blocks of their own making, which are but specks of dust on the path between them and eternity, would then apply themselves, like creatures of one common origin, owing one duty to the Father of one family, and tending to one common end, to make the world a better place. Not the less bright and blest would that day be for rousing some who have never looked out upon the world of human life around them, to a knowledge of their own relation to it, and for making them acquainted with a perversion of nature in their own contracted sympathies and estimates; as great, and yet as natural in its development, when once begun, as the lowest degradation known. But no such day had ever dawned for Mr Dombey, or his wife; and the course of each was taken.

That potent and benignant hand, which takes off the housetops and shows the shapes and phantoms which arise from neglect and indifference; which clears the air so that people can see and acknowledge each other, overcoming that contraction of sympathy which is against nature: that hand is the hand of the novelist; it is Dickens seeing himself. And it is significant that this comes in a description of the city, in this same forty-seventh chapter of *Dombey and Son*. He is describing, in the image of a dense black cloud hanging over the city, the human and moral consequences of an indifferent and 'unnatural' society. It is an image to which he often returns: the obscurity, the darkness, the fog that keep us from seeing each other clearly and from seeing the relation between ourselves and our actions, ourselves and others.

For this is the other aspect of Dickens's originality. He is able to dramatize those social institutions and consequences which are not accessible to ordinary physical observation. He takes them and presents them as if they were persons or natural phenomena. Sometimes as the black cloud or as the fog through which people are groping and looking for each other. Sometimes as the Circumlocution Office, or Bleeding Heart Yard, where a way of life takes on physical shape. Sometimes as if they were human characters, like Shares in *Our Mutual Friend*, and of course the Great Expectations. The law, the civil service, the stock exchange, the finance houses, the trading houses, come through, in these ways, as the 'impersonal' forces – the alienated human forces – that they are.

This way of seeing connects with his moral naming of characters: Gradgrind, McChoakumchild, Merdle. But it connects also in a less obvious way with a kind of observation which again belongs to the city: a perception, one might say, that the most evident inhabitants of cities are buildings, and that there is at once a connection and a confusion between the shapes and appearances of buildings and the real shapes and appearances of the people who live in them.

As in this passage from *Little Dorrit*:

Upon that establishment of state, the Merdle establishment in Harley Street, Cavendish Square, there was the shadow of no more common wall than the fronts of other establishments of state on the opposite side of the street. Like unexceptionable society, the opposing rows of houses in Harley Street were very grim with one another. Indeed, the mansions and their inhabitants were so much alike in that respect, that the people were often to be found drawn up on opposite sides of dinner-tables, in the shade of their own loftiness, staring at the other side of the way with the dullness of the houses.

Everybody knows how like the street, the two dinner-rows of people who take their stand by the street will be. The expressionless uniform twenty houses, all to be knocked at and rung at in the same form, all approachable by the same dull steps, all fended off by the same pattern of railing, all with the same impracticable fire-escapes, the same inconvenient fixtures in their heads, and everything without exception to be taken at a high valuation – who has not dined with these? The house so drearily out of repair, the occasional bow-window, the stuccoed house, the newly-fronted house, the corner house with nothing but angular rooms, the house with the blinds always down, the house with the hatchment always up, the house where the collector has called for one quarter of an idea, and found nobody at home – who has not dined with these?

The house that nobody will take, and is to be had a bargain – who does not know her? The showy house that was taken for life by the disappointed gentleman, and which does not suit him at all – who is unacquainted with that haunted habitation?

This is a formal description which takes the analogy of houses and people right through, and in the end playfully. But it recurs in more local insights, where the house and the life being lived in it are indistinguishable (this is again from *Little Dorrit*):

The debilitated old house in the city, wrapped in its mantle of soot, and leaning heavily on the crutches that had partaken of its decay and worn out with it, never knew a healthy or a cheerful interval, let what would betide. You should alike find rain, hail, frost and thaw lingering in that dismal enclosure, when they had vanished from other places; and as to snow, you should see it there for weeks, long after it had changed from yellow to black, slowly weeping away its grimy life. The place had no other adherents. As to street noises, the rumbling of which in the lane merely rushed in at the gateway in going past, and rushed out again: making the listening mistress Affery feel as if she were deaf, and recovered the sense of hearing by instantaneous flashes. So with whistling, singing, talking, laughing and all pleasant human sounds, they leaped the gap in a moment, and went upon their way.

Or again:

It was now summertime; a grey, hot, dusty evening. They rode to the top of Oxford Street, and there alighting, dived in among the great streets of melancholy stateliness, and the little streets that try to be as stately and succeed in being more melancholy, of which there is a labyrinth near Park Lane. Wildernesses of corner houses, with barbarous old porticoes and appurtenances, horrors that came into existence under some wrong-headed person in some wrong-headed time, still demanding the blind admiration of all ensuing generations and determined to do so until they tumbled down; frowned upon the twilight. Parasite little tenements, with the cramp in their whole frame, from the dwarf-hills in the mews, made the evening doleful. Rickety dwellings of undoubted fashion, but of a capacity to hold nothing comfortable except a dismal smell, looked like the last result of the great mansions breeding in-and-in; and, where their little supplementary bows and balconies were supported on thin iron columns, seemed to be scrofulously resting upon crutches. Here and there a Hatchment, with the whole science of Heraldry in it, loomed down upon the street, like an Archbishop discoursing on Vanity. The shops, few in number, made no show, for popular opinion was as nothing to them.

This method is very remarkable. It has its basis, of course, in certain properties of the language: perceptions of relations between persons and things. But in Dickens it is critical. It is a conscious way of seeing and showing. The city is shown as at once a social fact and a human landscape. What is dramatized in it is a very complex structure of feeling. Thus he can respond warmly to the miscellaneous bustle and colour of a mobile commercial life:

> Mr Dombey's offices were in a court where there was an old-established stall of choice fruit at the corner: where perambulating merchants, of both sexes, offered for sale at any time between the hours of ten and five, slippers, pocket-books, sponges, dogs' collars, Windsor soap, and sometimes a pointer or an oil-painting.
> The pointer always came that way, with a view to the Stock Exchange, where a sporting taste (originating generally in bets of new hats) is much in vogue.

It is characteristic that when Mr Dombey arrives none of these passing commodities is offered to him. His kind of trade, reflected in his house – his 'Home-Department' – has established itself in colder, more settled, more remote ways; and then another aspect of the city is evident:

> Mr Dombey's house was a large one, on the shady side of a tall, dark, dreadfully genteel street in the region between Portland Place and Bryanstone Square. It was a corner house, with great wide areas containing cellars frowned upon by barred windows, and leered at by crooked-eyed doors leading to dust-bins. It was a house of dismal state, with a circular back to it, containing a whole suite of drawing-rooms looking up a gravelled yard, where two gaunt trees, with blackened trunks and branches, rattled rather than rustled, their leaves were so smoke-dried. The summer sun was never on the street, but in the morning about breakfast time, when it came with the water-carts and the old-clothes men, and the people with geraniums, and the umbrella-mender, and the man who trilled the little bell of the Dutch clock as he went along. It was soon gone again to return no more that day; and the bands of music and the straggling Punch's shows going after it, left it a prey to the most dismal of organs, and white mice; with now and then a porcupine, to vary the entertainments; until the butlers whose families were dining out, began to stand at the house-doors in the twilight, and the lamp-lighter made his nightly failure in attempting to brighten up the street with gas. It was as blank a house inside as outside.

The contrast between the dismal establishment and the strolling variety of the streets is very clearly made. Again, the characteristics of houses and of people are consciously exchanged:

cellars frowned upon by barred windows, and leered at by crooked-eyed doors.

This transposition of detail can then be extended, again with some traditional support, to a way of seeing the city as a destructive animal, a monster, utterly beyond the individual human scale:

She often looked with compassion, at such a time, upon the stragglers who came wandering into London, by the great highway hard by, and who, footsore and weary, and gazing fearfully at the huge town before them, as if foreboding that their misery there would be but as a drop of water in the sea, or as a grain of sea-sand on the shore, went shrinking on, cowering before the angry weather, and looking as if the very elements rejected them. Day after day, such travellers crept past, but always, as she thought, in one direction – always towards the town. Swallowed up in one phase or other of its immensity, towards which they seemed impelled by a desperate fascination, they never returned. Food for the hospitals, the churchyards, the prisons, the rivers, fever, madness, vice, and death - they passed on to the monster, roaring in the distance, and were lost.

That is one way of seeing it: the rhetorical totalizing view from outside. But Dickens moves with still greater certainty into the streets themselves: into that experience of the streets – the crowd of strangers – which many of us now have got used to but which in Blake and Wordsworth was seen as strange and threatening. Dickens recreates and extends this experience, in a new range of feeling, when Florence Dombey runs away from her father's dark house:

The cheerful vista of the long street, burnished by the morning light, the sight of the blue sky and airy clouds, the vigorous freshness of the day, so flushed and rosy in its conquest of the night, awakened no responsive feelings in her so hurt bosom. Somewhere, anywhere, to hide her head! somewhere, anywhere, for refuge, never more to look upon the place from which she fled!
But there were people going to and fro; there were opening shops and servants at the doors of houses; there was the rising clash and roar of the day's struggle. Florence saw surprise and curiosity in the faces flitting past her; saw long shadows coming back upon the pavement; and heard voices that were strange to her asking her where she went,

and what the matter was; and though these frightened her the more at first, and made her hurry on the faster, they did her the good service of recalling her in some degree to herself, and reminding her of the necessity of greater composure.

Where to go? Still somewhere, anywhere! still going on; but where! She thought of the only other time she had been lost in the wide wilderness of London – though not lost as now – and went that way.

This street of the city is seen in very particular ways. It is a place of everyday business, not frightening in itself but amounting in its combined effect to a 'wide wilderness'. It is a place as difficult to relate to as her 'shut-up house'. But another note is struck: a physical effect which is also a social fact sharply seen: the same social fact against which Dickens's effort at recognition and kindness is consistently made:

the rising clash and roar of the day's struggle.

The only companion she finds is her dog, and she goes on with him:

With this last adherent, Florence hurried away in the advancing morning, and the strengthening sunshine, to the City. The roar soon grew more loud, the passengers more numerous, the shops more busy, until she was carried onward in a stream of life setting that way, and flowing, indifferently, past marts and mansions, prisons, churches, market-places, wealth, poverty, good, and evil, like the broad river side by side with it, awakened from its dreams of rushes, willows, and green moss, and rolling on, turbid and troubled, among the works and cares of men, to the deep sea.

What is emphatic here is not only the noise and the everyday business; not only the miscellaneity – 'prisons, churches'; but through all this the indifference, in an unwilled general sense:

a stream of life setting that way, and flowing, indifferently.

It is again not a matter of particular acts or characters. It is a general phenomenon – a stream, a way of life. It is what Arthur Clennam and his wife go down into, in *Little Dorrit*, having learned, painfully, a precarious but still inviolable human connection:

They went quietly down into the roaring streets, inseparable and blessed; and as they passed along in sunshine and in shade, the noisy and the eager and the arrogant and the froward and the vain, fretted, and chafed, and made their usual uproar.

The individual moral qualities, still sharply seen, are heard as it were collectively, in the 'roaring streets'. This is an advance in consciousness which comes through, directly, as a change of fictional method.

For we have to relate this view not simply to description – animated description – but to the power of dramatizing a social and moral world in physical terms. The physical world is never in Dickens unconnected with man. It is of his making, his manufacture, his interpretation. That is why it matters so much what shape he has given it.

Dickens's methods, in this, relates very precisely to his historical period. It was in just this capacity to remake the world, in the process we summarize as the Industrial Revolution, that men reached this crisis of choice; of the human shape that should underlie the physical creation. At one extreme Dickens can see this as comic:

The earth was made for Dombey and Son to trade in, and the sun and moon were made to give them light. Rivers and seas were formed to float their ships; rainbows gave them promise of fair weather; winds blew for or against their enterprises; stars and planets circled in their orbits, to preserve inviolate a system of which they were the centre.

This is a mocking of a familiar commercial confidence but not at all in the name of an undisturbed nature. Rather it is a way of seeing the kind of system that is imposed, that is *made* central. It is qualified, precisely, by the other kinds of physical life and confidence in which men are making their own worlds, carrying them about with them through the noise and the crowding. It is not only that power is ambiguous – the power to create new worlds. There is also a choice: a choice of the human shape of the new social and physical environment. Or there can be a choice – we *can* be in a position to choose – if we see, physically and morally, what is happening to people in this time of unprecedented change:

The first shock of a great earthquake had, just at that period, rent the whole neighbourhood to its centre. Traces of its course were visible on every side. Houses were knocked down; streets broken through and stopped; deep pits and trenches dug in the ground; enormous heaps of earth and clay thrown up; buildings that were undermined and shaking, propped by great beams of wood. Here, a chaos of carts, over-thrown and jumbled together, lay topsy-turvy at the bottom of a steep unnatural hill; there, confused treasures of iron soaked and rusted in something that had accidentally become a pond. Everywhere were bridges that led nowhere; thoroughfares that were wholly impassable; Babel towers of chimneys, wanting half their height; temporary wooden houses and enclosures, in the most unlikely situations; carcasses of ragged tenements, and fragments of unfinished walls and arches, and piles of scaffolding, and wildernesses of bricks, and giant forms of cranes, and tripods straddling above nothing. There were a hundred thousand shapes and substances of incompleteness, wildly mingled out of their places, upside down, burrowing in the earth, aspiring in the air, mouldering in the water and unintelligible as any dream. Hot springs and fiery eruptions, the usual attendants upon earthquakes, lent their contributions of confusion to the scene. Boiling water hissed and heaved within dilapidated walls; whence also, the glare and roar of flames came issuing forth; and mounds of ashes blocked up rights of way, and wholly changed the law and custom of the neighbourhood.

In short, the yet unfinished and unopened railroad was in progress; and from the very core of all this dire disorder, trailed smoothly away, upon its mighty course of civilization and improvement.

This is the apprehension of direct disturbance, but Dickens goes on to see what in the end matters more: not the disorder of change, but the kind of new order that is made to emerge from it:

The miserable waste ground, where the refuse-matter had been heaped of yore, was swallowed up and gone; and in its frowsy stead were tiers of warehouses, crammed with rich goods and costly mer-chandise. The old by-streets now swarmed with passengers and vehicles of every kind; the new streets that had stopped disheartened in the mud and waggon-ruts, formed towns within themselves, originating wholesome comforts and conveniences belonging to them-selves, and never tried nor thought of until they sprung into existence. Bridges that had led to nothing, led to villas, gardens, churches, healthy public walks. The carcasses of houses, and beginnings of new thoroughfares, had started off upon the line at steam's own speed, and shot away into the country in a monster train.

As to the neighbourhood which has hesitated to acknowledge the railroad in its straggling days, that had grown wise and penitent, as any Christian might in such a case, and now boasted of its powerful and prosperous relation. There were railway patterns in its drapers' shops, and railway journals in the windows of its newsmen. There were rail-way hotels, office-houses, lodging-houses, boarding-houses, railway plans, maps, views, wrappers, bottles, sandwich-boxes, and time-tables; railway hackney-coach and cabstands; railway omnibuses, railway streets and buildings, railway hangers-on and parasites, and flatterers out of all calculation. There was even railway time observed in clocks, as if the sun itself had given in. Among the vanquished was the master chimney-sweeper, whilom incredulous at Staggs's Gardens, who now lived in a stuccoed house three storeys high, and gave himself out, with flourishes upon a varnished board, as contractor for the cleansing of railway chimneys by machinery.

To and from the heart of this great change, all day and night, throbbing currents rushed and returned, incessantly like its life's blood. Crowds of people and mountains of goods, departing and arriving scores upon scores of times in every four-and-twenty hours, produced a fermentation in the place that was always in action. The very houses seemed disposed to pack up and take trips. Wonderful Members of Parliament, who, little more than twenty years before, had made themselves merry with the wild railroad theories of engineers, and given them the liveliest rubs in cross-examination, went down into the north with their watches in their hands, and sent on messages before by the electric telegraph, to say that they were coming. Night and day the conquering engines rumbled at their distant work, or, advancing smoothly to their journey's end, and gliding like tame dragons into the allotted corners grooved out to the inch for their reception, stood bubbling and trembling there, making the walls quake, as if they were dilating with the secret knowledge of great powers yet unsuspected in them, and strong purposes not yet achieved.

The complexity of this feeling is a true complexity of insight. All the pride of power – the new power of the Industrial Revolution – is felt in the language: the circulation by railway is the 'life's blood'. But there is also the recognition of this power over-riding all other human habits and purposes. It is the recognition confirmed, later, in

the power that forced itself upon its iron way – its own – defiant of all paths and roads, piercing through the heart of every obstacle, and dragging living creatures of all classes, ages and degrees behind it.

The railway is at once the 'life's blood' and 'the triumphant monster, Death'. And in this dramatic enactment Dickens is responding to the real contradictions – the power for life or death; for disintegration, order and false order – of the new social and economic forces of his time. His concern is always to keep human recognition and human kindness alive, through these unprecedented changes and within this unrecognizably altered landscape.

The very houses seemed disposed to pack up and take trips.

That is the mobility, the critical mobility, which was altering the novel. It is also the altered, the critically altered relationships between men and things, of which the city was the most evident social and visual embodiment. In seeing the city, as he here sees the railways, as at once the exciting and the threatening consequence of a new mobility, as not only an alien and indifferent system but as the unknown, perhaps unknowable, sum of so many lives, jostling, colliding, disrupting, adjusting, recognizing, settling, moving again to new spaces. Dickens went to the centre, the dynamic centre, of this transforming social experience.

Most novels are in some sense knowable communities. It is part of a traditional method – an underlying stance and approach – that the novelist offers to show people and their relationships in essentially knowable and communicable ways. The full extent of Dickens's genius can then only be realized when we see that for him, in the experience of the city, so much that was important, and even decisive, could not be simply known or simply communicated, but had, as I have said, to be revealed, to be forced into consciousness. And it would then be possible to set up a contrast between the fiction of the city and the fiction of the country. In the city kind, experience and community would be essentially opaque; in the country kind, essentially transparent. As a first way of thinking, there is some use in this contrast. There can be no doubt, for example, that identity and community became more problematic, as a matter of perception and as a matter of valuation, as the scale and complexity of the characteristic social organization increased. Up to that point, the transition from country to city – from a predominantly rural to a predominantly urban society – is transforming and significant. The growth of towns and especially of cities and a metropolis; the increasing division and complexity of labour; the altered and critical relations between and within social classes: in changes like these any assumption of a knowable community – a whole community, wholly knowable – became harder and harder to sustain. But this is not the whole story, and once again, in realizing the new fact of the city, we must be careful not to idealize the old and new facts of the country. For what is knowable is not only a function of objects – of what is there to be known. It is also a function of subjects, of observers – of what is desired and what needs to be known. And what we have then to see, as throughout, in the country writing, is not only the reality of the rural community; it is the observer's position in and towards it; a position which is part of the community being known.

Thus it is still often said, under the pressure of urban and metropolitan experience, and as a direct and even conventional contrast, that a country community, most typically a village, is an epitome of direct relationships: of face-to-face contacts within which we can find and value the real substance of personal relationships. Certainly this immediate aspect of its difference from the city or the suburb is important; it is smaller in scale; people are more easily identified and connected within it; the structure of the community is in many ways more visible. But a knowable community, within country life as anywhere else, is still a matter of consciousness, and of continuing as well as day-to-day experience. In the village as in the city there is division of labour, there is the contrast of social position, and then necessarily there are alternative points of view. It is to these points of view, in the nineteenth-century country novel, that we must now turn, for while the contrast between country and city is dramatic and important, the intricate developments within country life and country writing are also inescapable and significant.

Look back, for a moment, at the knowable community of Jane Austen. It is outstandingly face-to-face; its crises, physically and spiritually, are in just these terms: a look, a gesture, a stare, a confrontation; and behind these, all the time, the novelist is watching, observing, physically recording and reflecting. That is the whole stance – the grammar of her morality. Yet while it is a community wholly known, within the essential terms of the novel, it is as an actual community very precisely selective. Neighbours in Jane Austen are not the people actually living nearby; they are the people living a little less nearby who, in social recognition, can be visited. What she sees across the land is a network of propertied houses and families, and through the holes of this tightly drawn mesh most actual people are simply not seen. To be face-to-face in this world is already to belong to a class. No other community, in physical presence or in social reality, is by any means knowable. And it is not only most of the people who have disappeared, in a stylized convention as precise as Ben Jonson's. It is also most of the country, which becomes real only as it relates to the houses which are the real nodes; for the rest the country is weather or a place for a walk.

It is proper to trace the continuity of moral analysis from Jane Austen to George Eliot, but we can do this intelligently only if we recognize what else is happening in this literary development: a recognition of other kinds of people, other kinds of country, other kinds of action on which a moral emphasis must be brought to bear. For just as the difference between Jonson and Crabbe is not the historical arrival of the 'poor laborious natives' but a change in literary bearings which allows them suddenly to be seen, so the difference between Jane Austen and George Eliot, and between both and Thomas Hardy, is not the sudden disintegration of a traditional rural order but a change in literary bearings which brings into focus a persistent rural disturbance that had previously been excluded or blurred.

Thus *Adam Bede* is set by George Eliot in Jane Austen's period: at the turn of the eighteenth into the nineteenth century. What she sees is of course very different: not primarily because the country has changed, but because she has available to her a different social tradition.

The germ of *Adam Bede* was an anecdote told me by my Methodist Aunt Samuel ... an anecdote from her own experience ... I afterwards began to think of blending this and some other recollections of my aunt in one story, with some points in my father's early life and character.

Thus the propertied house is still there, in the possession of the Donnithornes. But they are now seen at work on their income, dealing with their tenants:

'What a fine old kitchen this is!' said Mr Donnithorne, looking round admiringly. He always spoke in the same deliberate, well-chiselled, polite way, whether his words were sugary or venomous, 'And you keep it so exquisitely clean, Mrs Poyser. I like these premises, do you know, beyond any on the estate.'

We have encountered this 'deliberate, well-chiselled, polite' way of speaking before, but it is not now among relative equals, just as the old Squire's way of looking is not now simply an aspect of character but of character in a precise and dominating social relationship. As Mrs Poyser says, it seems 'as if you was an insect, and he was going to dab his finger-nail on you'.

The proposition that is put, through the politeness, is in fact a reorganization of the tenancy, for the estate's convenience, which will take away the Poysers' corn land; it is accompanied by a threat that the proposed new neighbour, 'who is a man of some capital, would be glad to take both the farms, as they could be worked so well together. But I don't want to part with an old tenant like you.'

It is not a particularly dramatic event, but it is a crucial admission of everyday experience which had been there all the time, and which is now seen from an altered point of view. The politeness of improvement is then necessarily counterpointed by the crude facts of economic power, and a different moral emphasis has become inevitable. This is then extended. The young squire is anxious to improve the estate – as the tenants saw it, 'there was to be a millennial abundance of new gates, allowances of lime, and returns of ten per cent' – and he takes up Adam Bede as the manager of his woods. But in what is essentially the same spirit he takes up Hetty Sorrel as his girl and succeeds in ruining her. A way of using people for convenience is an aspect of personal character – this emphasis is not relaxed – but it is also an aspect of particular social and economic relationships. And then, as George Eliot observes ironically:

It would be ridiculous to be prying and analytic in such cases, as if one was inquiring into the character of a confidential clerk. We use round, general, gentlemanly epithets about a young man of birth and fortune.

Jane Austen, precisely, had been prying and analytic, but into a limited group of people in their relations with each other. The analysis is now brought to bear without the class limitation; the social and economic relationships, necessarily, are seen as elements, often determining elements, of conduct.

It is more important to stress this aspect of George Eliot's development of the novel than her inclusion of new social experience in a documentary sense. Certainly it is good to see the farmers and the craftsmen, and almost the labourers, as people present in the action in their own right. But there are difficulties here of a significant kind. It is often said about the Poysers in *Adam Bede*, as about the Gleggs and the Dodsons in *The Mill on the Floss*, that they are marvellously (or warmly, richly, charmingly) done. But what this points to is a recurring problem in the social consciousness of the writer. George Eliot's connections with the farmers and craftsmen – her connections as Mary Ann Evans – can be heard again and again in their language. Characteristically, she presents them mainly through speech. But while they are present audibly as a community, they have only to emerge in significant action to change in quality. What Adam or Dinah or Hetty say, when they are acting as individuals, is not particularly convincing. Into a novel still predicated on the analysis of individual conduct, the farmers and craftsmen can be included as 'country people' but much less significantly as the active bearers of personal experience. When Adam and Dinah and Hetty talk in what is supposed to be personal crisis – or later, in a more glaring case, when Felix Holt talks – we are shifted to the level of generalized attitudes or of declamation. Another way of putting this would be to say that though George Eliot restores the real inhabitants of rural England to their places in what had been a socially selective landscape, she does not get much further than restoring them *as a landscape*. They begin to talk, as it were collectively, in what middle-class critics still foolishly call a kind of chorus, a 'ballad-element'. But as themselves they are still only socially present, and can emerge into personal consciousness only through externally formulated attitudes and ideas.

I would not make this point bitterly, for the difficulty is acute. It is a contradiction in the form of the novel, as George Eliot received and developed it, that the moral emphasis on conduct – and therefore the technical strategy of unified narrative and analytic tones – must be at odds with any society – the 'knowable community' of the novel – in which moral bearings have been extended to substantial and conflicting social relationships. One would not willingly lose the Poysers, the Gleggs, and the Dodsons, but it is significant that we can talk of them in this way in the plural, while the emotional direction of the novel is towards separated individuals. A knowable community can be, as in Jane Austen, socially selected; what it then lacks in full social reference it gains in an available unity of language in all its main uses. But we have only to read a George Eliot novel to see the difficulty of the coexistence, within one form, of an analytically conscious observer of conduct with a developed analytic vocabularly, and of people represented as living and speaking in mainly customary ways; for it is not the precision of detailed observation but the inclusive, socially appealing, loose and repetitive manner that predominates. There is a new kind of break in the texture of the novel, an evident failure of continuity between the necessary language of the novelist and the recorded language of many of the characters.

This is not, it must be emphasized, a problem of fact. The consciousness of actual farmers and tradesmen was as strong and developed as that of the established and manoeuvring proprietors of Jane Austen's world; these people also are, and are shown as, inclusive, socially appealing, loose and repetitive; it is a common way of talking at any time. But whereas the idiom of the novelist, in Jane Austen, is connected with the idiom of her characters, in George Eliot a disconnection is the most evident fact and the novelist herself is most acutely aware of this. Speech and narrative and analysis, in Jane Austen, are connected by a *literary* convention. While the 'deliberate, well-chiselled, polite' idiom is the product of a particular education and of the leisured, dominating relationships which the education served, it is also idealized, conventionalized; the novelist's powers of effect and precision are given without hesitation to her characters, because, for all the individual moral discrimination, they are felt to belong in the same world. At points of emotional crisis and confrontation this is especially so, and it is the novelist who articulates a personal experience, in a way for the sake of her group, and to give it an idiom. But then it is clear that George Eliot is not *with* anyone in quite this way: the very recognition of conflict, of the existence of classes, of divisions and contrasts of feeling and speaking, makes a unity of idiom impossible. George Eliot gives her own consciousness, often disguised as a personal dialect, to the characters with whom she does really feel: but the strain of the impersonation is usually evident – in Adam, Daniel, Maggie, or Felix Holt. For the rest she gives out a kind of generalizing affection which can be extended to a generalizing sharpness (compare the Poysers with the Gleggs and Dodsons), but which cannot extend to a recognition of lives individually made from a common source; rather, as is said in that foolish mode of praise, the characters are 'done'. For there is a point often reached in George Eliot when the novelist is conscious that the characters she is describing are 'different' from her probable readers; she then offers to know them, and to make them 'knowable', in a deeply inauthentic but socially successful way. Taking the tip from her own difficulty, she works the formula which has been so complacently powerful in English novel-writing: the 'fine old', 'dear old', quaint-talking, honest-living country characters. Observing very promptly the patronage of economic power – 'deliberate, well-chiselled, polite' in the exercise of its crude controls – she still slips against her will into another patronage: since the people she respects in general (and of course for good reasons) she cannot respect enough in particular unless she gives them, by surrogate, parts of her own consciousness. There are then three idioms uneasily combined: the full analytic, often ironic power; the compromise between this and either disturbed intense feelings or a position of moral strength; and the self-consciously generalizing, honest rustic background.

I can feel enough connection with the problems George Eliot was facing to believe I could make these points in her presence; that I am, in a sense, making them in her presence, since her particular intelligence, in a particular structure of feeling, persists and connects. Some years ago a British Council critic described George Eliot, Hardy, and Lawrence as 'our three great autodidacts'. It was one of the sharp revealing moments of English cultural history. For all three writers were actively interested in learning, and while they read a good deal for themselves were not without formal education. Their fathers were a bailiff, a builder, and a miner. George Eliot was at school till sixteen and left only because her mother died. Hardy was at Dorchester High School till the same age and then completed his professional training as an architect. Lawrence went into the sixth form at Nottingham High School and after a gap went on to Nottingham University College. It is not only that by their contemporary standards these levels of formal education are high; it is also that they are higher, absolutely, than those of four out of five people in contemporary Britain.

So the flat patronage of 'autodidact' can be related to only one fact: that none of the three was in the pattern of boarding school and Oxbridge which by the end of the century was being regarded not simply as a kind of education but as education itself: to have missed that circuit was to have missed being 'educated' at all. In other words, a 'standard' education was that received by one or two per cent of the population; all the rest were seen as 'uneducated' or as 'autodidacts'; seen also, of course, as either comically ignorant or, when they pretended to learning, as awkward, over-earnest, fanatical. The effects of this on the English imagination have been deep.

But to many of us now, George Eliot, Hardy and Lawrence are important because they connect directly with our own kind of upbringing and education. They belong to a cultural tradition much older and more central in Britain than the comparatively modern and deliberate exclusive circuit of what are called the public schools. And the point is that they continue to connect in this way into a later period in which some of us have gone to Oxford or Cambridge; to myself, for instance, who went to Cambridge and now teach there. For it is not the education, the developed intelligence, that is really in question; how many people, if it came to it, on the British Council or anywhere else, could survive a strictly intellectual comparison with George Eliot? It is a question of the relation between education – not the marks or degrees but the substance of a developed intelligence – and the actual lives of a continuing majority of our people: people who are not, by any formula, objects of record or study or concern, but who are specifically, literally, our own families. George Eliot is the first major novelist in whom this question is active. That is why we speak of her now with a connecting respect, and with a hardness – a sort of family plainness – that we have learned from our own and common experience.

The problem of the knowable community is then, in a new way, a problem of language.

In writing the history of unfashionable families, one is apt to fall into a tone of emphasis which is very far from being the tone of good society, where principles and beliefs are not only of an extremely moderate kind, but are always presupposed, no subjects being eligible but such as can be touched with a light and graceful irony. But then, good society has its claret and its velvet carpets, its dinner-engagements six weeks deep, its opera and its fairy ballrooms; rides off its *ennui* on thoroughbred horses, lounges at the club, has to keep clear of crinoline vortices, gets its science done by Faraday, and its religion by the superior clergy who are to be met in the best houses: how should it have time or need for belief and emphasis? But good society, floated on gossamer wings of light irony, is of very expensive production; requiring nothing less than a wide and arduous national life condensed in unfragrant, deafening factories, cramping itself in mines, sweating at furnaces, grinding, hammering, weaving under more or less oppression of carbonic acid – or else, spread over sheepwalks, and scattered in lonely houses and huts on the clayey or chalky corn-lands, where the rainy days look dreary. This wide national life is based entirely on emphasis – the emphasis of want, which urges it into all the activities necessary for the maintenance of good society and light irony . . .

This striking paragraph from *The Mill on the Floss* is at once the problem and the response. The emphasis of want is undoubtedly central in George Eliot, and she sees work here as it is, without any sentimental contrast between the town and the village labourer. Emphasis as a class feeling: this is what she acknowledges and accepts. But then it has to be noticed that she writes of it with her own brand of irony; she is defensive and self-conscious in the very demonstration of emphasis, so that in this structure of communication the very poor become the 'unfashionable'. Her central seriousness, and yet her acute consciousness of other and often congenial tones, is at once a paradox of language and of community. We find this again in two characteristic passages in *Adam Bede*:

Paint us an angel, if you can, with a flowing violet robe, and a face paled by the celestial light; paint us yet oftener a Madonna, turning her mild face upward and opening her arms to welcome the divine glory; but do not impose on us any aesthetic rules which shall banish from the region of Art those old women scraping carrots with their work-worn hands, those heavy clowns taking holiday in a dingy pot-house, those rounded backs and stupid weather-beaten faces that have bent over the spade and done the rough work of the world – those homes with their tin pans, their brown pitchers, their rough curs, and their clusters of onions. In this world there are so many of these common coarse people, who have no picturesque sentimental wretchedness. It is so needful we should remember their existence . . .

I am not ashamed of commemorating old Kester: you and I are indebted to the hard hands of such men – hands that have long ago mingled with the soil they tilled so faithfully, thriftily making the best they could of the earth's fruits, and receiving the smallest share as their own wages.

The declaration is again serious, but who is being spoken to in the anxious plea: 'do not impose on us any aesthetic rules which shall banish . . .'? Who made the compact of 'you and I', who must be shown as indebted? Who, finally, provoked the consciousness which requires the acknowledgement 'I am not ashamed' and its associated language of 'clowns' and 'stupid weather-beaten faces', mixing as it so strangely does with the warmth of memory of the kitchens and with the truth about wages, the firm rejection of 'picturesque sentimental wretchedness'?

In passages like these, and in the novels from which they are taken, George Eliot has gone further than Crabbe in *The Village*, and yet is more self-conscious, more uneasily placating and appealing to what seems a dominant image of a particular kind of reader. The knowable community is this common life which she is glad to record with a necessary emphasis; but the known community is something else again – an uneasy contract, in language, with another interest and another sensibility.

What is true of language will be true of action. George Eliot extends the plots of her novels to include the farmers and the craftsmen, and also the disinherited. But just as she finds it difficult to individuate working people – falling back on a choral mode, a generalizing description, or an endowment with her own awkwardly translated consciousness – so she finds it difficult to conceive whole actions which spring from the substance of these lives and which can be worked through in relation to their interests. *Adam Bede* is the nearest to this, but it is overriden, finally, by an external interest: Hetty is a subject to that last moment on the road before she abandons her baby; but after that moment she is an object of confession and conversion – of *attitudes* to suffering. This is the essential difference from Hardy's *Tess of the D'Urbervilles*, which has the strength to keep to the subject to the end. Adam Bede and Dinah Morris – as one might say the dignity of self-respecting labour and religious enthusiasm – are more important, finally. Even the changed, repentant Arthur is more important than the girl whom the novelist abandons in a moral action more decisive than Hetty's own confused and desperate leaving of her child.

Yet still the history she is writing is active: a finding of continuity in the stress of learned feelings. *The Mill on the Floss* is the crisis of just this development and tension. It is an action written from within the emphasis of want: but now of want not as leading to ordinary work but as human deprivation; in the guarded, unattractive rituals of survival of the small farmers, the Dodsons; in the rash independence of Tulliver, broken by the complications of law and economic pressure that he does not understand. In neither of these ways, as George Eliot sees them, can any fullness of life be achieved, but there is no other way through; only the imagined escapes, the reading and the history, and then the unwilled, temporary escape of the trip on the river: a fantasy of comfort. All that can then finally happen is a return to childhood and the river; a return which releases feeling, but as death, not life. From the social history, which had been seen as determining but as narrowly determining, there is a contraction of sympathy to the exposed and separated individual, in whom the only action of value, of any full human feeling, is located. And then what in *The Mill on the Floss* is an active, desperate isolation becomes, in a new way of seeing, a sad resignation.

For in the subsequent works, for all their evidence of growing maturity and control – a control, precisely, based on sad resignation; a maturity construed as that exact feeling – the actions become more external to that common world in which the emphasis of want had been seen as decisive. As if overcome by the dead weight of the interests of a separated and propertied class, the formal plots of the later works are in a different social world. *Felix Holt* is made to turn on the inheritance of an estate, and this is a crucial surrender to that typical interest which preoccupied the nineteenth-century middle-class imagination. Of course Esther rejects the inheritance in the end; George Eliot's moral emphasis is too genuinely of an improving kind, of a self-making and self-made life, to permit Esther to accept the inheritance and find the fashionable way out. The corruption of that inheriting world, in which the price of security is intrigue, is powerfully shown in Mrs Transome and Jermyn. But the emphasis of want is now specialized to Felix Holt: to the exposed, separated, potentially mobile individual. It is part of a crucial history in the development of the novel, in which the knowable community – the extended and emphatic world of an actual rural and then industrial England – comes to be known primarily as a problem of ambivalent relationship: of how the separated individual, with a divided consciousness of belonging and not belonging, makes his own moral history.

This is the source of the disturbance, the unease, the divided construction of the later George Eliot novels (the exception is *Middlemarch*, significantly a novel of a single community again; a small town just before the decisive historical changes). Yet we have only to compare George Eliot with her contemporary, Anthony Trollope, to see the significance of this disturbance. Trollope, in his Barsetshire novels, is at ease with schemes of inheritance, with the interaction of classes and interests, with the lucky discovery and the successful propertied marriage. His interest is all in how it happens, how it is done. An even, easy narrative tone, with a minimum of searching analysis, can then achieve all that is asked of it: a recorded observation, an explanation at that level of social mechanics. To read *Doctor Thorne* beside *Felix Holt* is not only to find ease in Trollope where there is disturbance in George Eliot; to find a level of interest corresponding with the plot instead of struggling to break free of a dutifully sustained external complication; to find the conventional happy ending where property and happiness can coexist and be celebrated instead of an awkward, stubborn, unappeased resignation. It is also, quite evidently, to see the source of these differences in a real social history.

Near the beginning of *Doctor Thorne*, Trollope announces with characteristic confidence the state of his rural England:

Its green pastures, its waving wheat, its deep and shady and – let us add – dirty lanes, its paths and stiles, its tawny-coloured, well-built rural churches, its avenues of beeches, and frequent Tudor manions, its constant county hunt, its social graces, and the air of clanship which pervades it, has made it to its own inhabitants a favoured land of Goshen. It is purely agricultural: agricultural in its produce, agricultural in its poor, and agricultural in its pleasures.

Here the extent of realism is the mannered concession that the lanes are dirty. For the rest, what is seen is a social structure with pastoral trimmings. The agricultural poor are placed easily between the produce and the pleasures. And while this easy relationship holds, there is no moral problem of any consequence to disturb the smooth and recommending construction.

England is not yet a commercial country in the sense in which that epithet is used for her; and let us hope that she will not soon become so. She might surely as well be called feudal England, or chivalrous England. If in western civilized Europe there does exist a nation among whom there are high signors, and with whom the owners of the land are the true aristocracy, the aristocracy that is trusted as being best and fitted to rule, that nation is the English.

As a description of mid nineteenth-century England this is ludicrous; but as a way of seeing it without extended question it is perfect. It takes the values for granted, and can then study with a persistent accuracy the internal difficulties of the class, and especially the problem of the relation between the inheriting landed families and the connected and rising cadet and professional people. Trollope shares an interest in getting into that class, which is what the inheritance plot had always mainly served, and he can describe its processes without further illusion, once the basic illusion of describing the landowners as an aristocracy has been accepted. George Eliot, by contrast, questioning in a profoundly moral way the real and assumed relations between property and human quality, accepts the emphasis of inheritance as the central action, and then has to make it external, contradictory, and finally irrelevant, as her real interest transfers to the separated and exposed individual, who becomes sadly resigned or must go away. What happens to the Transomes' land in *Felix Holt*, or to Grandcourt's in *Daniel Deronda*, is no longer decisive; yet around the complications of that kind of interest a substantial part of each novel is built. In this sense, George Eliot's novels are transitional between the form which had ended in a series of settlements, in which the social and economic solutions and the personal achievements were in a single dimension, and the form which, extending and complicating and then finally collapsing this dimension, ends with a single person going away on his own, having achieved his moral growth through distancing or extrication. It is a divided consciousness of belonging and not belonging; for the social solutions are still taken seriously up to the last point of personal crisis, and then what is achieved as a personal moral development has to express itself in some kind of physical or spiritual renewal – an emigration, at once resigned and hopeful, from what had been offered as a decisive social world.

The complications of the inheritance plot, with its underlying assumption of a definite relation between property and human quality, had in fact been used in one remarkable novel, significantly based on a whole action rather than on individual analysis. Emily Brontë's *Wuthering Heights* is remarkable because it takes the crisis of inheritance at its full human value, without displacement to the external and representative attitudes of disembodied classes. There is a formal contrast of values between the exposed and working Heights and the sheltered and renting Grange, and the complicated relations between their families are consistently determined by the power and endurance of the Heights. Yet the creation is so total that the social mechanism of inheritance is transcended. It is class and property that divide Heathcliff and Cathy, and it is in the positive alteration of these relationships that a resolution is arrived at in the second generation. But it is not in social alteration that the human solution is at any point conceived. What is created and held to is a kind of human intensity and connection which is the ground of continuing life. Unaffected by settlements, it survives them and, in a familiar tragic emphasis, survives and is learned again through death. This tragic separation between human intensity and any available social settlement is accepted from the beginning in the whole design and idiom of the novel. The complication of the plot is then sustained by a single feeling, which is the act of transcendence. George Eliot, by contrast, working in a more critically realist world, conceives and yet cannot sustain acceptable social solutions; it is then not transcendence but a sad resignation on which she finally comes to rest. As a creative history, each of these solutions has a decisive importance, for each is reworked by the significant successors of George Eliot and Emily Brontë: Thomas Hardy and D. H. Lawrence.

The country action of George Eliot's *Daniel Deronda* takes

place in Wessex. But whereas the Loamshire and Stonyshire of *Felix Holt* had been George Eliot's England, the Wessex of *Daniel Deronda* might be Jane Austen's Hampshire or Derbyshire: the great and the less great houses, and the selected 'knowable community', as it is to be found again later in Henry James and in other 'country-house novels' of our own century. *Daniel Deronda* was finished in 1876, but by that time there was a new Wessex in the novel: the country of Hardy. To move from one to the other is to repeat, ironically, the movement from the world around Chawton to the world of *Adam Bede*: a reappearance, a remaking of the general life, with its known community and its hard emphasis of want.

For George Eliot, in writing her only novel set in her own time, had moved significantly away from the full and known world of her earlier works. She had her own clear reasons for this. If the decisive history was that of character and of the frustration of human impulse by an unacceptable and yet inevitable world, she needed to create no more than the conditions for this kind of moral, intellectual and ideal history. The social conditions for a more generally valuing history were in every real sense behind her.

And this is the right away, I believe, to introduce the question of George Eliot's important attitudes to the past, especially the rural past. In *Adam Bede*, for example, she had looked back with a generalizing affection to the first years of the nineteenth century, 'those old leisurely times', and concluded:

Leisure is gone – gone where the spinning wheels are gone, and the pack-horses, and the slow waggons, and the pedlars, who brought bargains to the door on sunny afternoons. Ingenious philosophers tell you, perhaps, that the great work of the steam-engine is to create leisure for mankind. Do not believe them: it only creates a vacuum for eager thoughts to rush in. Even idleness is eager now – eager for amusement: prone to excursion-trains, art-museums, periodical literature, and exciting novels: prone even to scientific theorizing, and cursory peeps through microscopes. Old Leisure was quite a different personage: he only read one newspaper, innocent of leaders, and was free from that periodicity of sensations which we call post-time. He was a contemplative, rather stout gentleman, of excellent digestion – of quiet perception, undiseased by hypothesis: happy in his inability to know the causes of things, preferring the things themselves. He lived chiefly in the country, among pleasant seats and homesteads, and was fond of sauntering by the fruit-tree wall, and scenting the apricots when they were warmed by the morning sunshine, or of sheltering himself under the orchard boughs at noon, when the summer pears were falling. He knew nothing of weekday services, and thought none the worse of the Sunday sermon if it allowed him to sleep from the text to the blessing – liking the afternoon service best because the prayers were the shortest, and not ashamed to say so; for he had an easy, jolly conscience, broad-backed like himself, and able to carry a great deal of beer and port-wine – not being made squeamish by doubts and qualms and lofty aspirations. Life was not a task to him, but a sinecure; he fingered the guineas in his pocket, and ate his dinners, and slept the sleep of the irresponsible; for had he not kept up his charter by going to church on the Sunday afternoons!

Fine old Leisure! Do not be severe upon him, and judge him by our modern standard; he never went to Exeter Hall, or heard a popular preacher, or read *Tracts for the Times* or *Sartor Resartus*.

It is lightly enough written, an ironic rumination on the past which has been extended into a kind of history; a personification, using the simplest devices of fiction, which is significantly very different from the active personifications of Dickens: the shaping contemporary forces. Old Leisure is history, is a time and a period; but with his apricots and his orchard, his single news-paper, his port-wine and his guineas in his pocket, he is a class figure who can afford to saunter, who has leisure precisely in the sweat of other men's work. This foreshortening, this selec-tion, this special indulgence are all characteristic of what has become a main form of the modern rural retrospect.

Yet in being lightly done, conveying a clear picture yet always ready to qualify, to smile, to move on, it seems protected against the very feelings, including the emphasis of want, which it effectively mediates and suppresses. For it was not *Tracts for the Times* or *Sartor Resartus* or the newspapers or science which disturbed Old Leisure as he fingered his guineas. It was – but can one say it, while the smiling reminiscence continues? – men who in just those years were being broken by endless work and by the want of bread; Old Leisure the roundsman, Old Leisure with the pauper's letter on his back, Old Leisure in the work-house as a reward for fifty years in the fields. Yet there is another leisure, a quiet, of some childhood days, and of a father asleep on a Sunday afternoon, which can suddenly, in inattention, become a whole past and an historical scheme.

George Eliot's most extended rural retrospect – important because it is not given as a dream by the fire but as conscious historical interpretation – is the introduction to *Felix Holt*. It is more persuasive and more substantial than the dream of Old Leisure, but in its whole organization shows even more clearly the structure of feeling which was being laid over the country. The description of the meadows and the hedgerows has the warmth of observation and of memory; it is the green language of Clare. But the passenger on the box of the stage-coach, through whose eyes we are directed to look is more than a nature poet; he has, as it were naturally, combined with these perceptions a quite solid set of social presuppositions. When he sees the shepherd 'with a slow and slouching walk', he knows by some alchemy that the shepherd feels 'not bitterness except in the matter of pauper labourers and the bad luck that sent contrarious seasons and the sheep rot'.

What bitterness about the 'pauper labourers'? That he might become one of them, which was always possible and even likely? Or that they troubled the ratepayers? In this moment of watching, when the quiet landscape has 'an unchanging still- ness, as if Time itself were pausing', and when 'it was easy for the traveller to conceive that town and country had no pulse in common', there is a sudden conflation, a stereotyping, of 'rural Englishmen' whose 'notion of Reform was a confused com- bination of rick-burners, trades-unions, Nottingham riots, and in general whatever required the calling-out of the yeomanry'.

Who then, the traveller might ask as Time pauses, were the yeomanry called out to face? Who, always somewhere else, was burning the ricks or combining under the threat of transporta- tion? These others by the conflation of 'rural Englishmen' are effectively abolished.

The passenger on the box could see that this was the district of protuberant optimists, sure that old England was the best of all possible countries, and that if there were any facts which had not fallen under their own observation, they were facts not worth observ- ing: the district of clean little market-towns without manufactures, of fat livings, an aristocratic clergy, and low poor-rates.

And this is then not the known but the knowable community: a selected society in a selected point of view. The low poor-rates –

that index of the emphasis of want: are they an irony or a comfort? For when the poor are suddenly present it is not as people but as 'a brawny and many-breeding pauperism' – that word, 'breeding', that George Eliot so often uses where the poor are in question, as if they were animals; in any case not men but a condition, an 'ism'. And 'brawny'? – getting strong and fat, no doubt, on the poor-rates.

The point of this willing illusion is then suddenly seen: it is manufacturing and the railways which destroy this old England. The full modern myth comes quite sharply into focus.

The breath of the manufacturing town, which made a cloudy day and a red gloom by night on the horizon, diffused itself over all the surrounding country, filling the air with eager unrest. Here was a population not convinced that old England was as good as possible.

The unrest, that is to say, is a product of industrialization; in being placed in that way, after the country idyll, it can itself be placed and on the whole rejected. What is then being bought from this view on the box-seat is a political comfort: a position which admits one set of causes for radicalism but in a comfortable contrast with the settled content of the old rural order. The social position of the observer is then quite clear: a whole reality is admitted in the industrial districts; a selected reality in the rural.

After the coach had rattled over the pavement of a manufacturing town, the scene of riots and trades-union meetings, it would take him in another ten minutes into a rural region, where the neighbourhood of the town was only felt in the advantages of a near market for corn, cheese, and hay, and where men with a considerable banking account were accustomed to say that 'they never meddled with politics themselves'.

Of course; because the visible unrest of the town, in a whole action, is compared not with the whole knowable community of the rural region, but with the condition and point of view of 'men with a considerable banking account'. A willing, lulling illusion of old country life has now paid its political dividends. A natural country ease is contrasted with an unnatural urban unrest. The 'modern world', both in its suffering and, crucially, in its protest against suffering, is mediated by reference to a lost condition which is better than both and which can place both: a condition imagined out of a landscape and a selective observation and memory.

This is then the structure on which we must fix our attention, for it connects crucially with George Eliot's development. A valuing society, the common condition of a knowable community, belongs ideally in the past. It can be recreated there for a widely ranging moral action. But the real step that has been taken is withdrawal from any full response to an existing society. Value is in the past, as a general retrospective condition, and is in the present only as a particular and private sensibility, the individual moral action.

The combination of these two conclusions has been very powerful; it has shaped and trained a whole literary tradition. And this is the meaning of George Eliot's Wessex, in the only novel set in her own actual period: a narrowing of people and situations to those capable, in traditional terms, of limitation to an individual moral action; the fading-out of all others, as most country people had been faded out in that view from the box-seat; the recreation, after all the earlier emphasis of want, of a country-house England, a class England in which only certain histories matter, and to which the sensibility – the bitter and frank sensibility – of the isolated moral observer can be made appropriate. She is able, conscientiously, to narrow her range because the wide-ranging community, the daily emphasis of want, is supposed past and gone with old England. All that is left is a set of personal relationships and of intellectual and moral insights, in a history that for all valuing purposes has, disastrously, ended.

We can then see why Mr Leavis, who is the most distinguished modern exponent of just this structure of feeling, should go on, in outlining the great tradition, from George Eliot to Henry James. It is an obvious transition from that country-house England of *Daniel Deronda* (of course with Continental extensions and with ideas, like Deronda's Zionism, about everywhere) to the country-house England of James. But the development that matters in the English novel is not to James; it is within that same Wessex, in the return of a general and inescapable history, to the novels of Hardy.

Looking back at the real rural England of the early nineteenth
century, it is indeed easy to see an old way of life overshadowed
by the tumultuous development of the new industrial system.
The decisive forces, in the national economy, were the general
industrial and financial development and the crises of trade.
Rural England, in some ways, was the place where the final
shocks were taken, the final costs paid. But this was not because
agriculture, as an isolable activity, was declining. As late as the
1830s, with the national population rapidly expanding, well over
ninety per cent of the demand for grain was met from home
growing, and food production in general continued the long
upward rise from the eighteenth-century improvements. Yet
what happened in the villages to the labourers and the poor was,
after 1815, as bad as anything in the long centuries of exploitation and degradation. To most contemporary observers it
seemed worse than anything they had known.

The fundamental causes of this apparent paradox are indeed
very difficult to decide. Basically, the poverty and suffering
which reached a critical level after 1815 were the consequence of
the establishment of a capitalist order in farming: that long
transformation which was already decisively established by the
mid eighteenth century. We have had enough experience, since,
of the economics of capitalism to know that it is no paradox,
within its terms and its order, to have rising production coexist-
ent with widespread unemployment and substantial pauper-
ization. For in subjecting an economy to the disciplines of
wage-labour and the market, it exposes men to new kinds of hazard, as its crises of credit and of prices work through. Yet there
was always a contradiction in English agrarian capitalism: its
economics were those of a market order; its politics were those of

a self-styled aristocracy and squirearchy, exerting quite different and 'traditional' disciplines and controls. This contradiction has been seen (by Hobsbawm and Rudé) as the most convincing explanation of the notorious Speenhamland system and its effects. This system, beginning in 1795, was a last and as it turned out disastrous attempt to preserve the social order of the villages, by subsidizing low wages out of the rates, on a scale calculated by the price of bread and the number of children. It was a political reflex in terms of an older kind of society – the 'right to live' by the mere fact of existence and of membership, however subordinate, of a local community. In impulse it has much to its credit, when compared, for example, with the specifically capitalist Poor Law of the 1830s. But it was a moral reflex after the decisive immoral event: an attempted guarantee to all those labourers and poor who by the long and repeated actions of the same owning class, driving up their production, their landholdings and their rents, had been unsettled and exposed. We need not idealize the labourer's earlier condition to see how dearly he now paid for the confusion of his masters. In all previous settlements he had been bearing the real cost of expansion and improvement; but now he bore it, with increasing emphasis, as a pauper, an object of charity: a fate that was foreshadowed in this place and that, this period and that, through many earlier generations, but that now, in the widening crisis, grew to something like a system. And all the time the landless labourers, the displaced cottagers, were being joined by smaller farmers being forced out of tenancies by the long processes of engrossment, concentration of ownership and rising rents. During the high prices of the Napoleonic wars, many of these smaller farms had survived. In the postwar depression they failed in their thousands, and the numbers of the landless and of the despairing emigrants very rapidly increased.

To make many men poor and dependent, and then to offer them charitable relief, can perhaps be seen as humane. But the landowning class required dependence, in social and political quite as much as in directly economic terms. Slowly, through this period, there began, in many villages, a direct political struggle. The provision and control of pauper relief went alongside the intensified importance and prosecution of the Game Laws. The figure of what is still called the 'poacher' becomes characteristic. A last property in nature, in its old wild life but now its 'preservation' of wild life as 'game', was directly and repeatedly challenged by men living and finding their living in their own places, their own country, but now, by the arbitrariness of law, made over into criminals, into rogues, into marginal men.

The history of the game laws, and of the men who defied them, is a central feature of the class struggle in nineteenth-century rural society. In orthodox accounts the morality and the aesthetic of the so-called owners, who developed in just this period their leisurely rituals of shooting and hunting, have been widely publicized, and very much later – when it didn't so much matter – there was a minor cult of the 'poacher' as a 'character'; the attractive and vagrant rogue. But there was always a different morality, which I remember hearing in the talk of small farmers and labourers. The immense presumption of this lordly ownership of rabbits and fish and birds –

And every beast did thither bring
Himself to be an offering

– was at once savagely asserted and skilfully challenged. I have heard my grandfather talk of the 'labourer's supper' with what seemed to me then as now an understandable pride: a rabbit knocked off behind the hedge, a swede knocked off at the edge of the path: a meal for eight children. If there are any now ready to mourn the loss of a country way of life, let them mourn the 'poachers' who were caught and savagely punished, until a different and urban conscience exerted some controls. Or if there are any who wish to attack those who destroyed country customs, let them attack the thieves who made the finding of food into theft.

It is a hard thing to say, but for all the talk of degeneration of the labourer (and the objective conditions then imposed on him were beyond any question what are now called 'dehumanizing'), what I mainly notice, from this terrible period, is a development of spirit and of skill. It is often said of the whole process of industrialization and urbanism that all the able people went off to the factories and the towns, or decided to emigrate, leaving only the slow, the feckless and the ignorant. Even radical

223

historians speak of the 'bold peasantry' of the eighteenth century and of the 'dispirited rural proletariat' of the nineteenth. Broken and dispirited men there were, in their many thousands. They had their predecessors, through the long generations. But where in the eighteenth century can we find men of the strength and character of those who organized the Swing campaign of rick-burnings, the bread-or-blood confrontations, the breakings of threshing-machines or the Tolpuddle union?

Nineteenth-century rural history has been seen too often in a liberal and patronizing perspective: the only apparent alternative to the reactionary perspective which idealizes country against city. But though the suffering and poverty were deep and long, there was more spirit, more self-organization and in the end more achievement among the rural labourers than among most of their apparently preferred predecessors. I suppose it is the rick-burning that causes the trouble. Desperate acts of desperate and ignorant men! I doubt that. They were on starvation wages. They saw plenty of wealth around them, and the law protecting its gross inequalities. They wanted enough to live on, 'and by fair means or foul we will have it'. What impresses me most, because it is a creative spirit, is their courage and their willingness to act, their findings of actions which would have some effect, in a cause of relieving extreme poverty and hunger which anyone now (but now does not count; their children were hungry then) would support.

You have not such damned flats [submissive people] to deal with as you had before.

That is a wheelwright talking to magistrates in 1830. He is the voice of many, and he has to be respected. Violence solves nothing? Submission solved nothing either. Lord Littlebrain nodded at the deference and added a wing to his house.

If we had never had any fires our wages would not have been more than ten shillings a week; now they are eleven shillings.

That is the conclusion of Norfolk labourers. A Kent curate reported a common saying in his village:

Them there riots and burnings did the poor a terrible deal of good.

Some good indeed but not nearly enough, when the whole history is reckoned. Swing and the bread-or-blood riots were only the beginning of what had, necessarily, to be a long campaign, against the greed of the owners and against the apparently objective conditions of an agricultural system in recurrent crisis. At the time of Swing, the majority of men who worked on the land were already landless labourers: five to every two occupiers of land. Population had increased in the rural counties: doubling between 1750 and 1830; increasing most rapidly in the crisis years up to 1830. The failures and confusions of rural society had created widespread unemployment, and in this period the rate of emigration was much below the rate of natural increase. Of the 686,000 families of agricultural labourers, some 300,000 people, in the 1830s, were on poor-relief. For those in employment, wages were highly variable, often, ironically, according to the distance of their villages from the new kinds of urban and industrial work: ranging from fourteen shillings a week on farms in the industrial West Riding to as low as seven shillings a week – rarely as much as nine – in the still wholly or largely agricultural counties of the south and west.

These were the real conditions of the majority of families in 'old England'. Above them, the social structure of agrarian capitalism continued to develop. Work in agriculture was still expanding, though in a falling proportion within a dramatically increasing total population. As to holdings, there was a general but slow trend towards larger farms. Half the farmers still worked their land with their families only. Farms above 300 acres by 1851, occupied more than a third of the cultivated land, while farms below 100 acres occupied only about a fifth. At the same time, there was the familiar gradation of intermediate rural classes: small farmers (under 100 acres), 134,000 families; medium farmers (100 to 300 acres), 64,000 families; large farmers (over 300 acres) 17,000 families. Of all these, owner-occupiers held about twenty per cent of the land at the beginning of the nineteenth century; by the end of the century, about twelve per cent.

At the apex of this structure were the large landowners. In the eighteenth century, about half the cultivated land was owned by five thousand families, and nearly a quarter by only four hundred families. In 1873, the same kind of predominance was evident: half of the country was owned by some seven thousand people, in a rural population of around ten millions. In the course of the nineteenth century, through electoral reform, the political power of the landowners was diminished, though not decisively until the 1870s. At the same time, however, the social structure of rural England could no longer be isolated from the social structure of the country as a whole. This is true in the simple sense that, following the Industrial Revolution, agriculture, though not in itself diminished, formed a much smaller part of the total economy. At the beginning of the nineteenth century it provided forty per cent of the national product; in mid-century twenty per cent; by the end of the century, less than ten per cent. At the beginning of the century, a third of all workers were employed in agriculture; in mid-century, a fifth; by the end of the century, less than a tenth; though again the numbers actually employed did not greatly change (the figures for 1801 and 1881 – 1,700,000 – are identical). But within this process, we cannot distinguish wholly separate industrial and landowning classes in the developing capitalist system. Eighteenth-century landowners were already involved in early extracting and manufacturing industries. In the course of the nineteenth century, the income of landowners from other sources –

government and bank stocks, canal and railway shares, urban ground rents, and the profits and royalties of harbour facilities and mines of various kinds, quarries, ironworks, brickworks and other ventures.

– became more and more important. Nor were these landowners an exclusive class. As since the sixteenth century, there was a constant interchange between landed property and other kinds of property and income. The historian of English landed society in the nineteenth century, F. M. L. Thompson, has observed that the absorption into the landed interest of other kinds of men and property

must be accounted a prime reason for the failure of the cleavage between capitalists and landowners to become so deep as to be unbridgeable.

The complications of this interaction, as revealed for example in the controversy over the Corn Laws, make it impossible for us to conceive a simple 'rural England' set over against a simple 'industrial England'. On the contrary, just because of the nature of its own development into an agrarian capitalism, agriculture, while retaining many specific interests as against other kinds of production, and of course while including conflicting specific interests within itself (as between pasture and corn) offered no basis for the contrast of one whole way of life with another whole way. The social crisis of nineteenth-century England had its specific colouring, and its particular issues, in the countryside, but it was still a general crisis, because of the intricate inter-connections of urban and rural property, industrial and agricultural production, and industrial and agricultural labour and settlement. The crisis of nineteenth-century rural England took many forms: the long struggle over rents and leases, between owners and tenants; the long struggle over prices, and the relation of home production to exports, in a developing free-trade economy; the long struggle between employers and workers, on wages and the right to form unions; the long struggle between the demand for cheap labour and the rights of men, women and children, and specifically the right to education. Each of these was fought out in the social structures of rural England, but it is not only that each was fought in the context and pressure of the society and the economy as a whole; it is also that each struggle was a form of a specifically capitalist society and economy, and was increasingly seen in these terms.

The whole situation was then profoundly affected by the diminishing importance of agriculture as a proportion of the economy, which we have already noted. But the key relationship, in the consequent interaction between urban and rural and industrial and agricultural England, was undoubtedly the market. A point was reached, late in the century, when the development of industrial production and the consequent changes of national economic policy led to a pattern in which manufactured goods were exported against imports of cheap foreign food. This never, of course, became a total pattern. As late as 1868, some eighty per cent of food was still grown at home. Imports rose steeply from the 1870s, but within a still expanding market, both in overall population, and in the increased demand for meat and dairy produce, as compared with bread, which was the result of a rising general standard of living. This process had important general effects on agriculture, and accelerated its relative decline. But it was not a simple process. The effects were more marked in grain (affected by the opening of the prairies, and by the steamships and the railways) than in meat and dairy produce, where the demand was rising and where home prices fell much less. There were then crucial regional variations in the effects of these market alterations: the corn-growing counties of the south and east were in a very different position from the pasture counties of the north and west; and there was also, under the market pressure, a general movement away from grain and towards stock. The great depression of the 1870s to the 1890s, of which so much has been made in the conventional histories, was a very complicated phenomenon, in which, to speak generally, the producers of grain lost their advantage, and the producers of livestock (in part from the expanding market; in part from the fall in cost of feed, due to the very loss of the grain producers) gained. What happened within this change in the market was a redirection of agricultural production, and this in turn took its place within the existing social and economic crisis of a rural society within a capitalist England.

Rises and falls on the market, that is to say, which differentially affected agriculture as a mode of capitalist production, worked their final effect through a whole social and economic structure in which the classical problems of rural England – ownership of the land, the means of production, the possession and function of capital for investment, and the persistent problems of wages, housing and education – were also the predominant problems of the society as a whole. There is an important sense in which certain rural social structures, of an established kind, prevented the realization of the community of these problems between rural and urban workers. But connection of a kind was eventually made. From the 1850s to the 1890s, emigration from the villages to the towns, especially in certain parts of the country, became heavy. This was not, in the strict sense, a rural depopulation, though a few counties suffered permanent absolute losses. More generally what happened was that the rural population failed to grow, while the urban population continued to grow dramatically, in a general population increase, and while emigration to other lands notably increased.

It is significant that the families who left the villages in this period were, first, the landless labourers, and, second, many of the older craftsmen, who were being displaced by forms of industrial production. The existing structure of land ownership, that is to say, showed itself, in one main respect, in the character of the emigration. What came out, dramatically, in leaving the land, was how the land itself had hitherto been distributed.

Yet at the end of the nineteenth century more people were living in the rural districts than in the whole nation only a century earlier. And for all the changes they were still living within a capitalist rural order: the few proprietors, the many tenant farmers and landless labourers. That system was there in the 'golden age' from the 1850s to the early 1870s; it was there in the 'great depression' of the 1870s and 1880s. Advantageous trade or disastrous trade were filtered alike through this dominant system. Eventually, and it is something to celebrate in a mild way, many of the landlords got out, but not until the twentieth century: the biggest transfer of ownership into the hands of farmers took place after 1914: in thirteen years one quarter of the land of England and Wales went from landlords to owner-occupiers. But at a price, of course; what was called a realization of capital for more profitable investment elsewhere.

And all the time, within this changing history, the labourers were there: a much smaller proportion of the whole working population, as industrial and urban employment increased, but still as many in number, at the end of the nineteenth century, as they had been at the beginning. These were the men and women who emerged in literature as 'Hodge'.

We can hear some of them talking in Alexander Somerville's *Whistler at the Plough* (1862). Somerville was the son of a Scottish labourer: barnman, barrowman, part of a family of small farmers, labourers, craftsmen; the women working beside them. His account of his early days in *Autobiography of a Working Man* (1848) is a classic: not only in its details – his parents owning a small pane of glass and carrying it round as a window from 'house' to 'house', hovel to shed – but in its description of that shifting world of hard marginal labour. Somerville's own destiny was extraordinary: after years of labouring and poaching he took the shilling as a soldier, to escape unemployment, and after he had enlisted he wrote a letter to a newspaper saying that the troops would not turn out against a demonstration in support of the Reform Bill. He was discovered and viciously flogged. He became a hero in radical circles but continued to drift and eventually became an informer. *Whistler at the Plough* was written in the agency of the Anti-Corn Law League. Later he emigrated to Canada.

This is, in itself, a significant history, and it reminds us of the ambiguity of some of the articulate observers of working rural life. Like the 'peasant poets', their way to print and employment lay through patronage; Somerville's one wholly independent expression of opinion was savagely punished. Yet what he and others record, in spite of the difficulties, is part of the essential record that breaks up, into its real hard details, 'Old Leisure' or 'Old England'. The fact of fear, in a shameful dependence, can never be forgotten. It is there in his account of a labourer speaking in Wiltshire:

Perry appeared to me about 35 years of age. He was of middling stature, wore a straw hat, red neckerchief, and a fustian coat . . . He was rather agitated at first, and hesitated so much as to make some of his neighbours call 'Don't be afeared to speak, William'. It was to this that he alluded in saying that he had no reason to be afraid to speak . . .
. . . He had five children, the eldest ten years of age, the others of the age of 8, 6, 4 and 3. He had 7s a week to maintain his family . . . This day he had walked three miles and a half to his work. He took a bit of bread with him, and had a drink of water; and had a little when he got home. ('We all know that's true.' A voice: 'What makes you tremble so?') If, said Perry, I had been home to a good supper and a quart of good ale, I should not tremble.

Another neighbouring labourer was sorry the local estate did not yet have game preservation; if it had, 'they would not be so hard run up for victuals then'.

'But the gaol', said I; 'you might be caught and sent to gaol?'
'Well', they replied, 'the gaol itself ben't so bad as the workhouse; and better do anything than starve.'

When Somerville later visited Perry, he found that the farmer who employed him had come to his wife and told her that in spite of her having so many young children she must go out to work in the fields; 'he needed hands for the hay'. The farmer added that:

'he wished he could only find out which of his men it was that spoke first at the meeting; he would find means to make them regret it'.

Yet Perry did not oppose Somerville publishing his account.

They thought they were as bad as they could be.

This is an account not only of conditions, which need to be remembered, but of the hard mustering of spirit among many ordinary men. I have heard by word of mouth so many such stories, down to my father's generation, that I believe it to be centrally true. We should certainly emphasize the suffering of the labourers and their families, but we do them an extraordinary injustice if we suppose, with the orthodoxy, that they were broken and ignorant men. I knew my father's father well. When he was evicted from his cottage, before 1914, he spoke about it at a village meeting, and my father has told me how he listened to his hard, strong father and was astonished when while speaking he broke down and cried. The line through William Perry is very long.

Think of Joseph Arch, born in 1826; his father often unemployed, his mother, as so often, a former servant, raising a family by taking in washing, cutting slices of barley bread for her children. No fresh meat, except by poaching: 'it is hardly an exaggeration to say that every other man you meet was a poacher', and Arch defends them. In 1872 Arch and others started the Union:

I stood on my pig-stool and spoke out straight and strong for Union.

In the end he got into Parliament, by the votes of the Norfolk labourers after the last male extension of the franchise. Much of his early spirit was in the end patronized and incorporated, as happened similarly with most of the urban labourers' representatives. But to read, in his *Autobiography*, of his speaking and organizing and the way he stood up to threats, is to touch an extraordinary strength.

Or think of Joseph Ashby of Tysoe, who has been so remarkably recorded by his daughter M. K. Ashby. Born in 1859, the illegitimate son of a servant, he worked in his village and his district not only with strength and courage but with remarkable intelligence and an impressive self-teaching. His collection of local history is a part of this shadowed culture; his democratic skills are just as impressive. In the village as in the industrial towns there were many men like Ashby: intelligent, self-taught, strong and honourable. Working all their lives at a hard and ill-paid employment, they worked second lives for their own people.

We need to remember them as we come to read Richard Jefferies, who in a quite different way entered the literary tradition. When Joseph Arch was starting the Union, and there was widespread national controversy, three letters were published in *The Times* from Richard Jefferies, Coate Farm, Swindon, and the paper celebrated them in a leading article. What did the letters say?

Never once in all my observation have I heard a labouring man or woman make a grateful remark; and yet I can confidently say that there is no class of persons in England who receive so many attentions and benefits from their superiors as the agricultural labourers.

That was the tune to play against Arch. But who had written it?

Jefferies was born in 1848 at Coate, near Swindon. His great-grandfather was a miller and baker in Swindon and in 1800 bought some forty acres of land two or three miles out of town. Richard's grandfather took over the Swindon business in 1816, moving there from London. In 1822 a house was built at Coate and for some years remained empty. As Richard's father wrote later:

I was the first that lived in it, after leaving school at 14 – my Eldest Sister as Housekeeper and Dairy Maid managed it for Father.

Commenting later on Richard's description of Coate, his father said:

How he could think of describing Coate as such a pleasant place and deceive so I could not imagine, in fact nothing scarcely he mentions is in Coate proper only the proper one was not a pleasant one Snodshill was the name of my Waggon and cart, he styled it Coate Farm it was not worthy of the name of Farm it was not Forty Acres of Land.

Fourteen acres of this land had to go in the late 1860s, and in 1878, a few months before Jefferies was beginning *Hodge and his Masters*, his father sold up and moved to Bath, where he became an odd-job gardener.

When Richard was four, he was sent to live with an aunt in Sydenham. He stayed there until he was nine, revisiting Coate for a month's annual holiday. Back with his parents, he was sent to small private schools in Swindon. At sixteen, with a cousin, he ran away from home, got to France for a week, and was eventually caught by the police in Liverpool and sent back to Swindon. His first job was as a reporter on the *North Wiltshire Herald*, a new Conservative paper in Swindon, irregularly from 1866 to 1868, and he worked later on the *Wiltshire and Gloucestershire Standard*, irregularly until 1873. In 1874 he married the daughter of a farming neighbour, and moved into Swindon, His letters to *The Times* brought him wide opportunities as a writer of articles on farming and country life, and for most of 1875 he lived in Surbiton with the aunt with whom he had spent his early childhood. He moved his own family to Swindon in 1877, and it was from there that *Hodge and his Masters* was written. In the seventies, in addition to many articles, he published three novels, *The Scarlet Shawl*, *Restless Human Hearts*, and *World's End*, and three country books, *The Gamekeeper at Home*, *Wild Life in a Southern County*, and *The Amateur Poacher*. The writing of *Hodge* came at a time when he was becoming reasonably established as a writer, after years of poverty and uncertainty. In the eighties, he continued writing articles, and published many books: *Wood Magic* and *Bevis*; *Nature near London*, *The Life of the Fields*, *The Open Air*; *Greene Ferne Farm*, *The Dewy Morn*, *After London*, *Amaryllis at the Fair*, *The Story of My Heart*. But his youth had been interrupted by illness, and from the early 1880s this was increasingly serious. He moved to Sussex and died at Goring on 14 August 1887. The cause of death was recorded as 'chronic fibroid phthisis – exhaustion'. He was thirty-eight.

It is worth recalling this social and personal history as we try to understand the character and development of his work. He is a major contributor to the social history of rural England. Yet it is social history which is both avowedly and unavowedly a work of art; written, as has significantly often been the case, by a man whose relationships to his material are in some ways marginal and paradoxical. There is a myth of Jefferies, which the books themselves do something to create: the lifelong countryman, son of generations of yeomen farmers, steeped in what is called 'the moral importance of the underlying, ageless, agricultural pattern'. The reality is different and more interesting. The suburban writer and journalist, recreating the country of his adolescence on the struggling smallholding; the sick man, perhaps the most brilliant imaginative observer of trees and animals and flowers and weather in his century, going on looking and writing until he said at the end: 'nothing for man in nature ... unless he has the Beyond', or, in his last essay, 'perhaps in course of time I shall find out also, when I pass away, physically, that as a matter of fact there never was any earth'; the ambitious, hardworking young man, writing in the interest of landed proprietors and employers, who found, in his letters to *The Times*, 'the statements made by "The Son of a Wiltshire Labourer" ... such as I feel bound to resent on the part of the farmers of this county', from 'Coate Farm', Swindon.

The social reality is equally significant. This is the countryside of North Wiltshire and South Gloucestershire, where a portable threshing-machine had been invented and where rioting labourers, soon after Jefferies' father moved to Coate, had fought pitched battles with the local Yeomanry; where at Swindon, just down the road, a railway workshop was being built, and the town expanded rapidly as a junction and repair centre; where, in Jefferies' time as a young reporter, the long depression of agriculture was beginning. As he himself wrote:

The changes which have been crowded into the last half-century have been so numerous and so important that it would be almost reasonable to suppose the limit had been reached for the present, and that the next few generations would be sufficiently occupied in assimilating themselves to the new conditions of existence. But so far from this being the case, all the facts of the hour point irresistibly to the conclusion that the era of development has but just commenced.

The greater part of the material of *Hodge and his Masters* was absorbed when Jefferies was a young reporter on the *Wiltshire and Gloucestershire Standard* in the early 1870s: the 'old newspaper', in chapter three of the second volume is, that one, just as 'Fleeceborough' is Cirencester and 'The Juke's Country' around Badminton. He was not considered a particularly good reporter, but then he was observing on his own account, following his own interests. He ranged from the precise observation of an effect of light on landscape, as in the brilliant description near the beginning of 'Hodge's Fields', through such incidents as taking the milk to the train in 'Haymaking' or the description of a country station in 'Mademoiselle, the Governess', on through such collected observations, establishing the pattern of an institution, as in 'The Solicitor' or 'The Bank', to a kind of composed observation, moving between characters and a way of life, as in 'Leaving his Farm', 'Going Downhill', 'An Ambitious Squire', or 'Hodge's Last Masters'. In each of these kinds his genius is evident, and in the last, particularly, he is working essentially as a novelist. It is characteristic that he was prepared to have his *Amaryllis at the Fair* published either as 'a novel' or as 'scenes of country life'. Those elements which, in his explicit fiction, he added to the imaginative strength, the deeply perceived connections between character and society and physical environment, of his essays and sketches, bear witness as much to the weakness of the form of the novel of his day, as to a personal weakness, in a certain proneness to a weak, late, pre-Raphaelite idealization and romanticism. On the other hand, as we read the first sentence of *Hodge and his Masters*, at the doorway of 'the Jason Inn at Woodbury', it is to the strengths of the tradition of the realist novel that we feel we are being introduced.

The limits appear, in our subsequent reading, and one of them, especially, needs definition. For all his claims of a 'fair and impartial spirit', Jefferies was no neutral observer. He was at times the committed writer, who had known in depth the whole crisis of this rural civilization and whose attachments were firm and clear. But he was also at times the class reporter or even the party hack, from the unpleasant whimsical fawning of the last pages of 'Fleeceborough' to the sour rant at the end of

'A Winter's Morning' or the correspondence-column stereotypes of 'The Cottage Girls'. At times, clearly, he wrote what his readers wanted to hear, during a social crisis, just as his *Times* letters had been an intervention against Arch and the Agricultural Labourers' Union. What his readers saw, and what at times he saw himself, was not men and women, marked (as he stressed of farmers) by 'individuality of character', but the gross figure, the abstraction, of Labour or Hodge.

To understand this process, the evident and sometimes pathetic illusions, the contradictory yet often powerful sympathies, we have to see Jefferies in the full ambiguity of his social position: son of a struggling smallholder who at last sold up and became a day-labourer; that insecurity of position which so often produces the upward fawning and the downward massing and blackening which in towns would be called petty-bourgeois. But we must see also, as in Lawrence, the gifted young man who was writing his way out of this whole situation, necessarily through readers who were placed socially above him, and on whom the complex pressures were severe and lasting.

For Jefferies did not end where he began. In his late essays (and the same development is evident in Lawrence) there is a different position.

Is money earned with such expenditure of force worth the having? Look at the arm of a woman labouring in the harvest field – thin, muscular, sinewy, black almost, it tells of continued strain. After much of this she becomes pulled out of shape, the neck loses its roundness and shows the sinews, the chest flattens . . . There is so much in the wheat, there are books of meditation in it, it is dear to the heart. Behind these beautiful aspects comes the reality of human labour – hours upon hours of heat and strain; there comes the reality of a rude life, and in the end little enough of gain. The wheat is beautiful, but human life is labour.

To this humane recognition he added – and it is not surprising that it has been so little emphasized – a hardening economic and political perspective. In *Thoughts on the Labour Question*, and especially in the second section, 'The Divine Right of Capital', he pushed beyond observation of the hardness of work.

'But they are paid to do it', says Comfortable Respectability . . . Go down into the pit yourself . . . Why do they do it? Because Hunger and Thirst drive them: these are the fearful scourges, the whips

236

worse than the knout, which lie at the back of Capital and give it its power.

Seeing the political changes of the extension of the franchise, he looked back at the old system and the labourers' opinion of it:

Plainly put, the rule of parson and squire, tenant and guardian, is repellent to them in these days. They would rather go away.

He argued for the development of rural democracy:

The total absence of any authority, any common centre, tends to foster what appears an utter indifference.

But a

sense of independence can only arise when the village governs itself by its own council, irrespective of parson, squire, tenant or guardian.

A parish council, a reading-room, a gymnasium, council cottages, a women's institute: these were some of the means to a new rural independence.

It is a crucial recognition. It connects with my own feeling, which I learned in a family that had lived through this experience, that there is more real community in the modern village than at any period in the remembered past. The changes that came, through democratic development and through economic struggle, sweetened and purified an older order. Yet to hold to this reality is to recognize an extending connection, for it is not, in the strict sense, a rural vision at all. Or at least it does not seem so when it is set against that structure of feeling which in a way derives from the earlier Jefferies.

I have had to trace this in my mind, in a kind of self-analysis, and Jefferies, more than anyone, is a way of touching it. There is the intensity, a lonely intensity, of his feelings for the physical world: the green language that connects him with Clare and with Lawrence. But the working rural world, where the physical experiences are most commonly found, is decisively altering. The labourers' options are very firmly for change. A fault can then occur, in the whole ordering of a mind. Defence of a 'vanishing countryside' – 'the open air', 'the life of the fields' – can become deeply confused with that defence of the old rural order which is in any case being expressed by the landlords, the rentiers, and their literary sympathizers. A physical hatred of the noise and rush of the city can be converted, as in Jefferies' *After London*, to a powerful but acrid vision of the metropolis reclaimed by the swamp and the reappearance of a woodland feudal society (the 'rural' equivalent of William Morris's 'medievalism'). Thus in a strange relation to an active delight in trees and flowers and birds there is a virtually unconscious extension to the values and attachments of an unjust and arbitrary society. 'The hedgerows have gone, the squires have gone': I have actually heard that said, as if it were a single process. The roots of this confusion are still, today, very tangled and stubborn.

Jefferies did not live to resolve the full difficulty. It can be felt in all its contemporary strength, remembering the ordinary social structure of contemporary 'defences of the countryside', as we read his late essay *Primrose Gold in Our Villages*, in which he describes, bitterly, the new Tory political formations in rural England: the heirs to those who had resisted the labourers' vote now moving in, so skilfully, to organize that vote. 'Primrose Gold': the phrase is so exact. The simple flower as a badge of political manoeuvre; the yellow of the flower and of the money that is the real source of power; the natural innocence, the political dominance: it is all there.

Flowers and privilege; factory smoke and democracy. This imagery was being formed, in a shadowed country, under the growth of industry and the cities. It is a persistent imagery, but there was always another tradition: Cobbett, Arch, Ashby; late Jefferies; Thomas Hardy.

Thomas Hardy was born a few miles from Tolpuddle, a few years after the deportation of the farm labourers who had come together to form a trade union. This fact alone should remind us that Hardy was born into a changing and struggling rural society, rather than the timeless backwater to which he is so often deported. It reminds us also that he wrote in a period in which, while there were still local communities, there was also a visible and powerful network of the society as a whole: the law and the economy; the railways, newspapers and the penny post; a new kind of education and a new kind of politics.

The Hardy country is of course Wessex: that is to say mainly Dorset and its neighbouring counties. But the real Hardy country, we soon come to see, is that border country so many of us have been living in: between custom and education, between work and ideas, between love of place and an experience of change. There can be no doubt at all of Hardy's commitment to his own country, and in a natural way to its past, as we can see in his naming of Wessex. But his novels, increasingly, are concerned with change. They are set within the period from just before his own birth to the actual time when he was writing: the last and deepest novels, *Tess* and *Jude the Obscure*, are significantly the most contemporary. There is always a great deal in them of an old rural world: old in custom and in memory, but old also in a sense that belongs to the new times of conscious education, the oldness of history and indeed of prehistory: the educated consciousness of the facts of change. Within the major novels, in several different ways, the experiences of change and of the difficulty of choice are central and even decisive.

It is this centrality of change, and of the complications of change, that we miss when we see him as a regional novelist:

the incomparable chronicler of his Wessex, the last voice of an old rural civilization. That acknowledgement, even that warm tribute, goes with a sense that the substance of his work is getting further and further away from us: that he is not a man of our world or the nineteenth-century world, but simply the last representative of old rural England or of the peasantry.

The very complicated feelings and ideas in Hardy's novels, including the complicated feelings and ideas about country life and people, belong very much in a continuing world. He writes more consistently and more deeply than any of our novelists about something that is still very close to us wherever we may be living: something that can be put, in abstraction, as the problem of the relation between customary and educated life; between customary and educated feeling and thought. This is the problem we saw in George Eliot and that we shall see again in Lawrence. It is the ground of their significant connection.

Most of us, before we get any kind of literary education, get to know and to value – also to feel the tensions of – a customary life. We see and learn from the ways our families live and get their living; a world of work and of place, and of beliefs so deeply dissolved into everyday actions that we don't at first even know they are beliefs, subject to change and challenge. Our education, quite often, gives us a way of looking at that life which can see other values beyond it: as Jude saw them when he looked across the land to the towers of Christminster. Often we know in ourselves, very deeply, how much those educated values, those intellectual pursuits, are needed urgently where custom is stagnation or where old illusions are still repeated as timeless truths. We know especially how much they are needed to understand change – change in the heart of the places where we have lived and worked and grown up.

The ideas, the values, the educated methods are of course made available to us if we get to a place like Christminster: if we are let in as Jude was not. But with the offer, again and again, comes another idea: that the world of everyday work and of ordinary families is inferior, distant; that now we know this world of the mind we can have no respect – and of course no affection – for that other and still familiar world. If we retain an affection, Christminster has a name for it: nostalgia. If we retain respect, Christminster has another name: politics or the even more dreaded 'sociology'.

But it is more than a matter of picking up terms and tones. It is what happens to us, really happens to us, as we try to mediate those contrasted worlds: as we stand with Jude but a Jude who has been let in; or as we go back to our own places, our own families, and know what is meant, in idea and in feeling, by the return of the native. This has a special importance to a particular generation, who have gone to the university from ordinary families and have to discover, through a life, what that experience means. But it has also a much more general importance; for in Britain generally this is what has been happening: a moving out from old ways and places and ideas and feelings; a discovery in the new of certain unlooked-for problems, unexpected and very sharp crises, conflicts of desire and possibility.

In this characteristic world, rooted and mobile, familiar yet newly conscious and self-conscious, the figure of Hardy stands like a landmark. It is not from an old rural world or from a remote region that Hardy now speaks to us; but from the heart of a still active experience, of the familiar and the changing, which we can know as an idea but which is important finally in what come through as personal pressures – the making and failing of relationships, the crises of physical and mental personality – which Hardy as a novelist at once describes and enacts.

But of course we miss all this, or finding it we do not know how to speak of it and value it, if we have picked up, here and there, the tone of belittling Hardy. It is now very common.

When the ladies retired to the drawing-room I found myself sitting next to Thomas Hardy. I remember a little man with an earthy face. In his evening clothes, with his boiled shirt and high collar, he had still a strange look of the soil.

This is Somerset Maugham, with one of his characteristic tales after dinner. It is a world, one may think, Hardy should never have got near; never have let himself be exposed to. But the tone and the response are significant, all the way from that dinner-table and that drawing-room to the 'look of the soil', in the rural distance. All the way, for some of us, to the land, the work, that comes up in silver as vegetables, or to the labour that enters that company – the customary civilized company – with what is seen as an earthy face. It is there again when Henry James speaks of 'the good little Thomas Hardy' or when F. R. Leavis says that *Jude the Obscure* is impressive 'in its clumsy way'.

A tone of social patronage, supported by crude and direct suppositions about origin, connects interestingly with a tone of literary patronage and in ways meant to be damaging with a strong and directing supposition about the substance of Hardy's fiction. If he was a countryman, a peasant, a man with the look of the soil, then this is the point of view, the essential literary standpoint, of the novels. That is to say the fiction is not only about Wessex peasants, it is by one of them who of course had managed to get a little (though hardly enough) education. Some discriminations of tone and fact have then to be made.

First, we had better drop 'peasants' altogether. Where Hardy lived and worked, as in most other parts of England, there were, as we have seen, virtually no peasants, although 'peasantry' as a generic word for country people was still used by writers. The actual country people were landowners, tenant farmers, dealers, craftsmen and labourers, and that social structure – the actual material, in a social sense, of the novels – is radically different, in its variety, its shading, and many of its basic human attitudes from the structure of a peasantry. Secondly, Hardy is none of these people. Outside his writing he was one of the many professional men who worked within this structure, often with uncertainty about where they really belonged in it. A slow gradation of classes is characteristic of capitalism anywhere, and of rural capitalism very clearly. Hardy's father was a builder who employed six or seven workmen. Hardy did not like to hear their house referred to as a cottage, because he was aware of this employing situation. The house is indeed quite small but there is a little window at the back through which the men were paid, and the cottages down the lane are certainly smaller. At the same time, on his way to school, he would see the mansion of Kingston Maurward (now fortunately an agricultural college) on which his father did some of the estate work, and this showed a sudden difference of degree which made the other distinction comparatively small though still not unimportant. In becoming an architect and a friend of the family of a vicar (the kind of family, also, from which his wife came) Hardy moved to a different point in the social structure, with connections to the educated but not the owning class, and yet also with connections through his family to that shifting body of small employers, dealers, craftsmen and cottagers who were themselves never wholly distinct, in family, from the labourers.

Within his writing his position is similar. He is neither owner nor tenant, dealer nor labourer, but an observer and chronicler, often again with uncertainty about his actual relation. Moreover he was not writing for them, but about them, to a mainly metropolitan and unconnected literary public. The effect of these two points is to return attention to where it properly belongs, which is Hardy's attempt to describe and value a way of life with which he was closely yet uncertainly connected, and the literary methods which follow from the nature of this attempt. As so often when the current social stereotypes are removed the critical problem becomes clear in a new way.

It is the critical problem of so much of English fiction, since the actual yet incomplete and ambiguous social mobility of the nineteenth century. And it is a question of substance as much as of method. It is common to reduce Hardy's fiction to the impact of an urban alien on the 'timeless pattern' of English rural life. Yet though this is sometimes there the more common pattern is the relation between the changing nature of country living, determined as much by its own pressures as by pressures from 'outside', and one or more characters who have become in some degree separated from it yet who remain by some tie of family inescapably involved. It is here that the social values are dramatized in a very complex way and it is here that most of the problems of Hardy's actual writing seem to arise.

One small and one larger point may illustrate this argument, in a preliminary way. Nearly everyone seems to treat Tess as simply the passionate peasant girl seduced from outside, and it is then surprising to read quite early in the novel one of the clearest statements of what has become a classical experience of mobility:

Mrs Durbeyfield habitually spoke the dialect; her daughter, who had passed the Sixth Standard in the National School under a London-trained mistress, spoke two languages: the dialect at home, more or less; ordinary English abroad and to persons of quality.

Grace in *The Woodlanders*, Clym in *The Return of the Native*, represent this experience more completely, but it is in any case a continuing theme, at a level much more important than the trivialities of accent. And when we see this we need not be tempted, as so often and so significantly in recent criticism, to detach *Jude the Obscure* as a quite separate kind of novel.

A more remarkable example of what this kind of separation means and involves is a description of Clym in *The Return of the Native* which belongs in a quite central way to the argument I traced in *Culture and Society*:

> Yeobright loved his kind. He had a conviction that the want of most men was knowledge of a sort which brings wisdom rather than affluence. He wished to raise the class at the expense of individuals rather than individuals at the expense of the class. What was more, he was ready at once to be the first unit sacrificed.

The idea of sacrifice relates in the whole action to the familiar theme of a vocation thwarted or damaged by a mistaken marriage, and we shall have to look again at this characteristic Hardy deadlock. But it relates also the general action of change which is a persistent social theme. As in all major realist fiction the quality and destiny of persons and the quality and destiny of a whole way of life are seen in the same dimension and not as separable issues. It is Hardy the observer who sets this context for personal failure:

> In passing from the bucolic to the intellectual life the intermediate stages are usually two at least, frequently many more; and one of these stages is sure to be worldly advance. We can hardly imagine bucolic placidity quickening to intellectual aims without imagining social aims as the transitional phase. Yeobright's local peculiarity was that in striving at high thinking he still cleaved to plain living – nay, wild and meagre living in many respects, and brotherliness with clowns. He was a John the Baptist who took ennoblement rather than repentance for his text. Mentally he was in a provincial future, that is, he was in many points abreast with the central town thinkers of his date ... In consequence of this relatively advanced position, Yeobright might have been called unfortunate. The rural world was not ripe for him. A man should be only partially before his time; to be completely to the vanward in aspirations is fatal to fame ... A man who advocates aesthetic effort and deprecates social effort is only likely to be understood by a class to which social effort has become a stale matter. To argue upon the possibility of culture before luxury to

the bucolic world may be to argue truly, but it is an attempt to disturb a sequence to which humanity has been long accustomed.

The subtlety and intelligence of this argument from the late 1870s come from a mind accustomed to relative and historical thinking, not merely in the abstract, as he learned from Mill or from Darwin, but in the process of observing a personal experience of mobility. This is not country against town, or even in any simple way custom against conscious intelligence. It is the more complicated and more urgent historical process in which education is tied to social advancement within a class society, so that it is difficult, except by a bizarre personal demonstration, to hold both to education and to social solidarity ('he wished to raise the class'). It is the process also in which culture and affluence come to be recognized as alternative aims, at whatever cost to both, and the wry recognition that the latter will always be the first choice, in any real history.

The relation between the migrant and his former group is then exceptionally complicated. His loyalty drives him to actions which the group can see no sense in, its overt values supporting the association of education with personal advancement which his new group has already made but which for that very reason he cannot accept.

'I am astonished, Clym. How can you want to do better than you've been doing?'

'But I hate that business of mine . . . I want to do some worthy things before I die.'

'After all the trouble that has been taken to give you a start, and when there is nothing to do but keep straight on towards affluence, you say you . . . it disturbs me, Clym, to find you have come home with such thoughts . . . I hadn't the least idea you meant to go backward in the world by your own free choice . . .'

'I cannot help it,' said Clym, in a troubled tone.

'Why can't you do . . . as well as others?'

'I don't know, except that there are many things other people care for which I don't . . .'

'And yet you might have been a wealthy man if you had only persevered . . . I suppose you will be like your father. Like him, you are getting weary of doing well.'

'Mother, what is doing well?'

The question is familiar but still after all these years no question is more relevant or more radical. Within these complex pressures the return of the native has a certain inevitable nullity, and his only possible overt actions can come to seem merely perverse. Thus the need for social identification with the labourers produces Clym's characteristic negative identification with them; becoming a labourer himself and making his original enterprise that much more difficult: 'the monotony of his occupation soothed him, and was in itself a pleasure'.

All this is understood and controlled by Hardy but the pressure has further and less conscious effects. Levin's choice of physical labour, in *Anna Karenina*, includes some similar motives but in the end is a choosing of people rather than of an abstract Nature – a choice of men to work with rather than a natural force in which to get lost. Yet this crucial distinction is obscured by the ordinary discussion of Hardy's attachment to country life, which would run together the 'timeless' heaths or woods and the men working on them. The original humanist impulse – 'he loved his kind' – can indeed become anti-human: men can be seen as creatures crawling on this timeless expanse, as the imagery of the heath and Clym's work on it so powerfully suggests. It is a very common transition in the literature of that period but Hardy is never very comfortable with it, and the original impulse, as in *Jude the Obscure*, keeps coming back and making more precise identifications.

At the same time the separation of the returned native is not only a separation from the standards of the educated and affluent world 'outside'. It is also, to some degree inevitably, a separation from the people who have not made his journey; or more often a separation which can mask itself as a romantic attachment to a way of life in which the people are merely instrumental: figures in a landscape or, when the literary tone fails, in a ballad. It is then easy, in an apparently warm-hearted way, to observe for the benefit of others the crudity and limitations but also the picturesqueness, the rough humour, the smocked innocence of 'the bucolic'. The complexity of Hardy's fiction shows in nothing more than this: that he runs the whole gamut from an external observation of customs and quaintness, modulated by a distinctly patronizing affection (as in *Under the Greenwood Tree*), through a very positive identification of intuitions of nature and the values of shared work with human depth and fidelity (as in *The Woodlanders*), to the much more impressive but also much more difficult humane perception of limitations, which cannot be resolved by nostalgia or charm or the simple mysticism of nature, but which are lived through by all the characters, in the real life to which all belong, the limitations of the educated and the affluent bearing an organic relation to the limitations of the ignorant and the poor (as in parts of *Return of the Native* and in *Tess* and *Jude*). But to make these distinctions and to see the variations of response with the necessary clarity we have to get beyond the stereotypes of the autodidact and the countryman and see Hardy in his real identity: both the educated observer and the passionate participant, in a period of general and radical change.

Hardy's writing, or what in abstraction can be called his style, is obviously affected by the crisis – the return of the native – which I have been describing. We know that he was worried about his prose and was reduced by the ordinary educated assumptions of his period to studying Defoe, Fielding, Addison, Scott and *The Times*, as if they could have helped him. His complex position as an author, writing about country living to people who almost inevitably saw the country as empty nature or as the working-place of their inferiors, was in any case critical in this matter of language. What have been seen as his strengths – the ballad form of narrative, the prolonged literary imitation of traditional forms of speech – seem to me mainly weaknesses. This sort of thing is what his readers were ready for: a 'tradition' rather than human beings. The devices could not in any case serve his major fiction where it was precisely disturbance rather than continuity which had to be communicated. It would be easy to relate Hardy's problem of style to the two languages of Tess: the consciously educated and the unconsciously customary. But this comparison, though suggestive, is inadequate, for the truth is that to communicate Hardy's experience neither language would serve, since neither in the end was sufficiently articulate: the educated dumb in intensity and limited in humanity; the customary thwarted by ignorance and complacent in habit. The marks of a surrender to each mode are certainly present in Hardy but the main body of his mature writing is a more difficult and complicated experiment. For example:

> The season developed and matured. Another year's instalment of flowers, leaves, nightingales, thrushes, finches, and such ephemeral creatures, took up their positions where only a year ago others had stood in their place when these were nothing more than germs and inorganic particles. Rays from the sunrise drew forth the buds and stretched them into long stalks, lifted up sap in noiseless streams, opened petals, and sucked out scents in invisible jets and breathings.
>
> Dairyman Crick's household of maids and men lived on comfortably, placidly, even merrily. Their position was perhaps the happiest of all positions in the social scale, being above the line at which neediness ends, and below the line at which the *convenances* began to cramp natural feeling, and the stress of threadbare modishness makes too little of enough.
>
> Thus passed the leafy time when arborescence seems to be the one thing aimed at out of doors. Tess and Clare unconsciously studied each other, ever balanced on the edge of a passion, yet apparently keeping out of it. All the while they were converging, under an irresistible law, as surely as two streams in one vale.

This passage is neither the best nor the worst of Hardy. Rather it shows the many complicated pressures working within what had to seem a single intention. 'The leafy time when arborescence' is an example of inflation to an 'educated' style, but the use of '*convenances*', which might appear merely fashionable, carries a precise feeling. 'Instalment' and 'ephemeral' are also uses of a precise kind, within a sentence which shows mainly the strength of what must be called an educated point of view. The consciousness of the natural process, in 'germs and inorganic particles' (he had of course learned it from Darwin who with Mill was his main intellectual influence) is a necessary accompaniment, for Hardy's purpose, of the more direct and more enjoyed sights and scents of spring. It is loss not gain when Hardy reverts to the simpler and cruder abstraction of 'Dairyman Crick's household of maids and men', which might be superficially supposed to be the countryman speaking but is actually the voice of the detached observer at a low level of interest. The more fully Hardy uses the resources of the whole language, as a precise observer, the more adequate the writing is. There is more strength in 'unconsciously studied each other', which is at once educated and engaged, than in the 'two streams in one vale', which shared with the gesture of 'irresistible law' a synthetic quality, here as of a man playing the countryman novelist.

Hardy's mature style is threatened in one direction by a willed 'Latinism' of diction or construction, of which very many particular instances can be collected (and we have all done it, having taken our education hard), but in the other direction by this much less noticed element of artifice which is too easily accepted, within the patronage we have discussed, as the countryman speaking (sometimes indeed it is literally the countryman speaking, in a contrived picturesqueness which is now the novelist's patronage of his rural characters). The mature style itself is unambiguously an educated style, in which the extension of vocabulary and the complication of construction are necessary to the intensity and precision of the observation which is Hardy's essential position and attribute.

The grey tones of daybreak are not the grey half-tones of the day's close, though the degree of their shade may be the same. In the twilight of the morning, light seems active, darkness passive; in the twilight of evening, it is the darkness which is active and crescent, and the light which is the drowsy reverse.

This is the educated observer, still deeply involved with the world he is watching, and the local quality of this writing is the decisive tone of the major fiction.

The complication is that this is a very difficult and exposed position for Hardy to maintain. Without the insights of consciously learned history and of the educated understanding of nature and behaviour he cannot really observe at all, at a level of extended human respect. Even the sense of what is now called the 'timeless' – in fact the sense of history, of the barrows, the Roman remains, the rise and fall of families, the tablets and monuments in the churches – is, as I have said, a function of education. That real perception of tradition is available only to the man who has read about it, though what he then sees through it is his native country, to which he is already deeply bound by memory and experience of another kind: a family and a childhood; an intense association of people and places, which has been his own history. To see tradition in both ways is indeed Hardy's special gift: the native place and experience but also the education, the conscious inquiry. Yet then to see living people, within this complicated sense of past and present, is another problem again. He sees as a participant who is also an observer; this is the source of the strain. For the process which allows him to observe is very clearly in Hardy's time one which includes, in its attachment to class feelings and class separations, a decisive alienation.

If these two noticed Angel's growing social ineptness, he noticed their growing mental limitations. Felix seemed to him all Church; Cuthbert all College. His Diocesan Synod and Visitations were the mainsprings of the world to the one; Cambridge to the other. Each brother candidly recognized that there were a few unimportant scores of millions of outsiders in civilized society, persons who were neither University men nor Churchmen; but they were to be tolerated rather than reckoned with and respected.

This is what is sometimes called Hardy's bitterness, but in fact it is only sober and just observation. What Hardy sees and feels about the educated world of his day, locked in its deep social prejudices and in its consequent human alienation, is so clearly true that the only surprise is that critics now should still feel sufficiently identified with that world – the world which coarsely and coldly dismissed Jude and millions of other men – to be willing to perform the literary equivalent of that stalest of political tactics: the transfer of bitterness, of a merely class way of thinking, from those who exclude to those who protest. But the isolation which can follow, while the observer holds to educated procedures but is unable to feel with the existing educated class, is severe. It is not the countryman awkward in his town clothes but the more significant tension – of course with its awkwardness and its spurts of bitterness and nostalgia – of the man caught by his personal history in the general crisis of the relations between education and class, relations which in practice are between intelligence and fellow-feeling. As he observes of the Clare brothers:

Perhaps, as with many men, their opportunities of observation were not so good as their opportunities of expression.

That after all is the nullity, in a time in which education is used to train members of a class and to divide them from other men as surely as from their own passions (for the two processes are deeply connected). Hardy can see it as a process in others, in a class, but the real history of his writing is that he knew, in himself, the experience of separation: a paradoxical separation, for a more common experience was still close and real.

It is with this complex pressure in mind that we must look at the country which Hardy was describing. He could respond so closely because his own mobility was in a mobile and changing society. It is how he saw others, in his fine essay on the *Dorsetshire Labourer* (which can be compared with Jefferies' on the *Wiltshire Labourer*):

They are losing their individuality, but they are widening the range of their ideas, and gaining in freedom. It is too much to expect them to remain stagnant and old-fashioned for the pleasure of romantic spectators.

This double movement, of loss and liberation, of exposure and of advantage, is the characteristic he shares with his actual rural world.

A modern Wessex of railways, the penny post, mowing and reaping machines, union workhouses, lucifer matches, labourers who could read and write, and National school children.

The point is not only Hardy's recognition of this modernity, but the fact that virtually every feature of it that he lists preceded his own life (the railway came to Dorchester when he was a child of seven). The effects of the changes of course continued, and the complex effects of the movement of the general economy with its contrasting effects on different areas and sections of a rural society from which there was still a general movement to the towns, worked their slow way through. The country was not timeless but it was not static either; indeed, it is because the change was long (and Hardy knew it was long) that the crisis took its particular forms. It was with a fine detail, seeing the general effects from the society as a whole but also the internal processes and their complicated effects on the rural social structure, that Hardy recorded and explained this process, as here in *Tess*:

All the mutations so increasingly discernible in village life did not originate entirely in the agricultural unrest. A depopulation was also going on. The village had formerly contained, side by side with the agricultural labourers, an interesting and better-informed class, ranking distinctly above the former – the class to which Tess's father and mother had belonged – and including the carpenter, the smith, the shoemaker, the huckster, together with nondescript workers other than farm-labourers; a set of people who owed a certain stability of aim and conduct to the fact of their being life-holders like Tess's father, or copy-holders, or, occasionally, small freeholders. But as the long holdings fell in they were seldom again let to similar tenants, and were mostly pulled down, if not absolutely required by the farmer for his hands. Cottagers who were not directly employed on the land were looked upon with disfavour, and the banishment of some starved the trade of others, who were thus obliged to follow. These families, who had formed the backbone of the village life in the past, who were the depositaries of the village traditions, had to seek refuge in the larger centres; the process, humorously designated by statisticians as 'the tendency of the rural population towards the large towns' being really the tendency of water to flow uphill when forced by machinery.

Here there is something much more than the crude and sentimental version of the rape of the country by the town. The originating pressures within rural society itself are accurately seen, and are given a human and social rather than a mechanical dimension.

Indeed we miss almost all of what Hardy has to show us if we impose on the actual relationships he describes, a neo-pastoral convention of the countryman as an age-old figure, or a vision of a prospering countryside being disintegrated by Corn Law repeal or the railways or agricultural machinery. It is not only, for example, that Corn Law repeal and the cheap imports of grain made less difference to Dorset: a county mainly of grazing and mixed farming in which the coming of the railway gave a direct commercial advantage in the supply of milk to London: the economic process described with Hardy's characteristic accuracy in *Tess*:

They reached the feeble light, which came from the smoky lamp of a little railway station; a poor enough terrestrial star, yet in one sense of more importance to Talbothays Dairy and mankind than the celestial ones to which it stood in such humiliating contrast. The cans of new milk were unladen in the rain, Tess getting a little shelter from a neighbouring holly tree . . .
 . . . 'Londoners will drink it at their breakfasts tomorrow, won't they?' she asked. 'Strange people that we have never seen? . . . who

don't know anything of us, and where it comes from, or think how we two drove miles across the moor tonight in the rain that it might reach 'em in time?'

The new real connection, and yet within it the discontinuities of knowledge and of condition, are the specific forms of this modern rural world. What happened now in the economy as a whole, in an increasingly organized urban and industrial market, had its partly blind effects – a new demand here, collapse and falling prices elsewhere – on an essentially subordinated and now only partial domestic rural economy. But the market forces which moved and worked at a distance were also deeply based in the rural economy itself: in the system of rent and trade; in the hazards of ownership and tenancy; in the differing conditions of labour on good and bad land, or in socially different villages (as in the contrast between Talbothays and Flintcomb Ash); and in what happened to people and to families in the interaction between general forces and personal histories – that complex area of ruin or survival, exposure or continuity. This was Hardy's actual society, and we cannot suppress it in favour of a seamless abstracted 'country way of life'.

It is true that there were continuities beyond this dominant social situation, in the lives of particular communities (though two or three generations, in a still partly oral culture, could often sustain an illusion of timelessness). It is also obvious that in most rural landscapes there are very old and often unaltered physical features, which sustain a quite different time-scale. Hardy gave great importance to these, and this is not really surprising when we consider his whole structure of feeling. But all these elements were overridden, as for his kind of novelist they must be, by the immediate and actual relationships between people, which occurred within existing contemporary pressures and were at most modulated and interpreted by the available continuities.

The pressures to which Hardy's characters are subjected are then pressures from within a system of living, itself now thoroughly part of a wider system. There is no simple case of an internal ruralism and an external urbanism. It is not urbanism but the hazard of small-capital farming that changes Gabriel Oak from an independent farmer to a hired labourer and then a bailiff. Henchard is not destroyed by a new and alien kind of dealing but by a development of his own trade which he has himself invited. It is Henchard in Casterbridge who speculates in grain as he had speculated in people; he is in every sense, within an observed way of life, a dealer and a destructive one; his strength compromised by that. Grace Melbury is not a country girl 'lured' by the fashionable world but the daughter of a successful timber merchant whose own social expectations, at this point of his success, include a fashionable education for his daughter. Tess is not a peasant girl seduced by the squire; she is the daughter of a lifeholder and a small dealer who is seduced by the son of a retired manufacturer. The latter buys his way into a country-house and an old name. Tess's father and, under pressure, Tess herself, are damaged by a similar process, in which an old name and pride are one side of the coin and the exposure of those subject to them the other. That one family fell and one rose is the common and damaging history of what had been happening, for centuries, to ownership, and to its conse-quences in those subject to it. The Lady Day migrations, the hiring fairs, the intellectually arrogant parson, the casual gentle-man farmer, the landowner spending her substance elsewhere: all these are as much parts of the 'country way of life' as the dedicated craftsman, the group of labourers and the dances on the green. It is not only that Hardy sees the realities of labouring work, as in Marty South's hands on the spars and Tess in the swede field. It is also that he sees the harshness of economic processes, in inheritance, capital, rent and trade, within the continuity of the natural processes and persistently cutting across them. The social process created in this interaction is one of class and separation, as well as of chronic insecurity, as this capitalist farming and dealing takes its course. The profound disturbances that Hardy records cannot then be seen in the sentimental terms of neo-pastoral: the contrast between country and town. The exposed and separated individuals, whom Hardy puts at the centre of his fiction, are only the most developed cases of a general exposure and separation. Yet they are never merely illustrations of this change in a way of life. Each has a dominant personal history, which in psychological terms bears a direct relation to the social character of the change.

One of the most immediate effects of mobility, within a structure itself changing, is the difficult nature of the marriage choice. This situation keeps recurring in terms which are at once personal and social: Bathsheba choosing between Boldwood and Oak; Grace between Giles and Fitzpiers; Jude between Arabella and Sue. The specific class element, and the effects upon this of an insecure economy, are parts of the personal choice which is after all a choice primarily of a way to live, of an identity in the identification with this or that other person. And here significantly the false marriage (with which Hardy is so regularly and deeply concerned) can take place either way: to the educated coldness of Fitzpiers or to the coarseness of Arabella. Here most dramatically the condition of the internal migrant is profoundly known. The social alienation enters the personality and destroys its capacity for any loving fulfilment. The marriage of Oak and Bathsheba is a case of eventual stability, after so much disturbance, but even that has an air of inevitable resignation and lateness. It is true that Hardy, under pressure, sometimes came to generalize and project these very specific failures into a fatalism for which in the decadent thought of his time the phrases were all too ready. In the same way, seeing the closeness of man and the land being broken by the problems of working the land, he sometimes projected his insistence on closeness and continuity into the finally negative images of an empty nature and the tribal past of Stonehenge and the barrows, where the single observer, at least, could feel a direct flow of knowledge. Even these, however, in their deliberate hardness – the uncultivable heath, the bare stone relics – confirm the human negatives, in what looks like a deliberate reversal of pastoral. In them the general alienation has its characteristic monuments, though very distant in time and space from the controlling immediate disturbance.

But the most significant thing about Hardy, in and through these difficulties, is that more than any other major novelist since this difficult mobility began he succeeded, against every pressure, in centring his major novels in the ordinary processes of life and work. It is this that is missed when in the service of an alienating total view – an abstraction of rural against urban forces – what he deliberately connected is deliberately taken apart. The best-known case is the famous description, in *Tess*, of the threshing-machine, which has often been abstracted to argue that the essential movement of the fiction is alien industrialism against rural humanity:

Close under the eaves of the stack, and as yet barely visible, was the red tyrant that the women had come to serve – a timber-framed construction, with straps and wheels appertaining – the threshing machine which, whilst it was going, kept up a despotic demand upon the endurance of their muscles and nerves.

A little way off there was another indiscreet figure; this one black, with a sustained hiss that spoke of strength very much in reserve. The long chimney running up beside an ash-tree, and the warmth which radiated from the spot, explained without the necessity of much daylight that here was the engine which was to act as the primum mobile of this little world. By the engine stood a dark motionless being, a sooty and grimy embodiment of tallness, in a sort of trance, with a heap of coals by his side: it was the engineman. The isolation of his manner and colour lent him the appearance of a creature from Tophet, who had strayed into the pellucid smokelessness of this region of yellow grain and pale soil, with which he had nothing in common, to amaze and to discompose its aborigines.

But this powerful vision of an alien machine must not blind us to the fact that this is also an action in a story – the action of a real threshing-machine. It stands in that field and works those hours because it has been hired, not by industrialism but by a farmer. And there are whole human beings trying to keep up with it and with him:

Thus the afternoon dragged on. The wheat-rick shrank lower, and the straw-rick grew higher, and the corn-sacks were carted away.

At six o'clock the wheat-rick was about shoulder-high from the ground. But the unthreshed sheaves remaining untouched seemed countless still, notwithstanding the enormous numbers which had been gulped down by the insatiable swallower, fed by the man and Tess, through whose two young hands the greater part of them had passed . . .

. . . A panting ache ran through the rick. The man who fed was weary, and Tess could see that the red nape of his neck was encrusted with dirt and husks. She still stood at her post, her flushed and perspiring face coated with the corn-dust, and her white bonnet embrowned by it. She was the only woman whose place was upon the machine so as to be shaken bodily by its spinning, and the decrease of the stack now separated her from Marian and Izz, and prevented their changing duties with her as they had done. The incessant quivering, in which every fibre of her frame participated, had thrown her into a stupefied reverie in which her arms worked on independently of her consciousness.

We can see here the relation to Crabbe, in the attention to the faces and the bodies of labourers, but also the development from him: the decisive development to an individuation which yet does not exclude the common condition. For this is Tess the girl and the worker: the break between her consciousness and her actions is as much a part of her emotional as of her working life. It is while she is working, here and elsewhere, that her critical emotional decisions are taken; it is through the ache and dust of the threshing-machine that she again sees Alec. Hardy thus achieves a fullness which is quite new, at this depth, in all country writing: the love and the work, the aches of labour and of choice, are in a single dimension.

Nor is this only an emphasis of pressure or of pain. Hardy often sees labour, with a fine insight, as a central kind of learning and relationship:

They had planted together, and together they had felled; together they had, with the run of the years, mentally collected those remoter signs and symbols which seen in few are of runic obscurity, but all together made an alphabet. From the light lashing of the twigs upon their faces when brushing through them in the dark, they could pronounce upon the species of tree whence they stretched; from the quality of the wind's murmur through a bough, they could in like manner name its sort afar off.

This, from *The Woodlanders*, is the language of the immediate apprehension of 'nature', but it is also more specifically the language of shared work, in 'the run of the years'. Feeling very acutely the long crisis of separation, and in the end coming to more tragically isolated catastrophes than any others within this tradition, he yet created continually the strength and the warmth of people living together: in work and in love; in the phsyical reality of a place.

To stand working slowly in a field, and feel the creep of rainwater, first in legs and shoulders, then on hips and head, then at back, front, and sides, and yet to work on till the leaden light diminishes and marks that the sun is down, demands a distinct modicum of stoicism, even of valour. Yet they did not feel the wetness so much as might be supposed. They were both young, and they were talking of the time when they lived and loved together at Talbothays Dairy, that happy green tract of land where summer had been liberal in her gifts: in substance to all, emotionally to these.

The general structure of feeling in Hardy would be much less convincing if there were only the alienation, the frustration, the separation and isolation, the final catastrophes. What is defeated but not destroyed at the end of *The Woodlanders* or the end of *Tess* or the end of *Jude* is a warmth, a seriousness, an endurance in love and work that are the necessary definition of what Hardy knows and mourns as loss. Vitally – and it is his difference from Lawrence, as we shall see; a difference of generation and of history but also of character – Hardy does not celebrate isolation and separation. He mourns them, and yet always with the courage to look them steadily in the face. The losses are real and heartbreaking because the desires were real, the shared work was real, the unsatisfied impulses were real. Work and desire are very deeply connected in his whole imagination. The passion of Marty or of Tess or of Jude is a positive force coming out of a working and relating world; seeking in different ways its living fulfilment. That all are frustrated is the essential action: frustrated by very complicated processes of division, separation and rejection. People choose wrongly but under terrible pressures: under the confusions of class, under its misunderstandings, under the calculated rejections of a divided separating world.

It is important enough that Hardy keeps to an ordinary world, as the basis of his major fiction. The pressures to move away from it, to enter a more negotiable because less struggling and less divided life, were of course very strong. And it is even more important, as an act of pure affirmation, that he stays, centrally, with his central figures; indeed moves closer to them in his actual development, so that the affirmation of Tess and of Jude – an affirmation in and through the defeats he traces and mourns – is the strongest in all his work.

'Slighted and enduring': not the story of man as he was, distant, limited, picturesque; but slighted in a struggle to grow – to love, to work with meaning, to learn and to teach; enduring in the community of this impulse, which pushes through and beyond particular separations and defeats. It is the continuity not only of a country but of a history and a people.

London, Hardy wrote, in 1887:

> appears not to *see itself*. Each individual is conscious of *himself*, but nobody conscious of themselves collectively, except perhaps some poor gaper who stares round with a half-idiotic aspect.

This way of seeing London has a clear continuity from Wordsworth in *The Prelude*, though it has become more emphatic. Moreover, in the contrasting idea of a 'collective consciousness', it has been altered and extended by the democratic and industrial experience and language of the nineteenth century. Yet there is still the sense of paradox: that in the great city itself, the very place and agency – or so it would seem – of collective consciousness, it is an absence of common feeling, an excessive subjectivity, that seems to be characteristic.

Nor is the feeling particular to Hardy. A sharper and altered social criticism, again with a lineage to Wordsworth, had begun in Carlyle. In Coleridge and in Southey the urban and industrial revolution had been seen as an agency of social atomism. Carlyle, in 1831, had written of London:

> How men are hurried here; how they are hunted and terrifically chased into double-quick speed; so that in self-defence they *must not* stay to look at one another!

And he had gone on to diagnose the separateness of people in the city, a separateness within what was now, characteristically, called 'aggregation':

> There in their little cells, divided by partitions of brick or board, they sit strangers . . . It is a huge aggregate of little systems, each of which is again a small anarchy, the members of which do not *work* together, but *scramble* against each other.

Or if this is too quickly diagnosed, in an ordinary tradition, as romantic anti-urbanism, it is relevant to notice its direct continuation in Engels, in *The Condition of the Working Class in England in 1844*:

The very turmoil of the streets has something repulsive, something against which human nature rebels. The hundreds of thousands of all classes and all ranks crowding past each other, are they not all human beings with the same qualities and powers, and with the same interest in being happy? And have they not, in the end, to seek happiness in the same way, by the same means? And still they crowd by one another as though they had nothing in common, nothing to do with one another, and their only agreement is the tacit one, that each keep to his own side of the pavement, so as not to delay the opposing streams of the crowd, while it occurs to no man to honour another with so much as a glance. The brutal indifference, the unfeeling isolation of each in his private interest becomes the more repellent and offensive, the more these individuals are crowded together, within a limited space. And, however much one may be aware that this isolation of the individual, this narrow self-seeking is the fundamental principle of our society everywhere, it is nowhere so shamelessly barefaced, so self-conscious as just here in the crowding of the great city. The dissolution of mankind into monads, of which each one has a separate principle, the world of atoms, is here carried out to its utmost extremes.

This is a new kind of argument. The perceptual confusion and ambivalence which Wordsworth made explicit has been simplified and developed to an image of the human condition within urban and industrial capitalism. Dickens, observing the condition, had worked to reveal a practical underlying connection, in human love and sympathy. Engels and Marx, as they went on looking, worked to reveal a different underlying condition: a new collective proletarian consciousness and self-consciousness, which would transform the society from its bases in industry and the cities. Still what was commonly seen, in immediate experience, was a social dissolution in the very process of aggregation.

Older ways of seeing the city of course persisted. Hardy saw London as a 'monster whose body had four million heads and eight million eyes', and he wrote this memorable description of a crowd, at the Lord Mayor's Show of 1879:

As the crowd grows denser it loses its character of an aggregate of countless units, and becomes an organic whole, a molluscous black creature having nothing in common with humanity, that takes the shape of the streets along which it has lain itself, and throws out horrid excrescences and limbs into neighbouring alleys; a creature whose voice exudes from its scaly coat and who has an eye in every pore of its body. The balconies, stands and railway-bridge are occupied by small detached shapes of the same tissue, but of gentler motion, as if they were the spawn of the monster in their midst.

The distance of the observer, now no longer in the streets but physically or spiritually above them, is a new element, but the evident fear of crowds, with the persistence of an imagery of the inhuman and the monstrous, connects with and continues that response to the mob which had been evident for so many centuries and which the vast development of the city so acutely sharpened. As late as the early twentieth century, one main response to the city – as evident, though in varying tones, even in a Dickens or a Hardy as in the most reactionary politician or magistrate – identified the crowding of cities as a source of social danger: from the loss of customary human feelings to the building up of a massive, irrational, explosive force.

By the middle of the nineteenth century the urban population of England exceeded the rural population: the first time in human history that this had ever been so, anywhere. As a mark of the change to a new kind of civilization the date has unforgettable significance. By the end of the nineteenth century, the urban population was three-quarters of the whole. Moreover, this was not only an internal shift. The population as a whole was dramatically increasing. The nine millions of 1801 had doubled by 1851, and doubled again by 1911. Yet to understand this whole process more closely we have to push beyond the general classification of 'urbanization'. This is particularly important if we are to understand the significance of the city. Even as late as 1871 more than half the population lived in villages or in towns of less than twenty thousand people. Only just over a quarter lived in cities, and the mark for the city, in that computation, is a hundred thousand people: in terms of later developments still comparatively small. When as early as the 1840s writers began to speak of the period as 'an age of great cities' (the title of a book by Robert Vaughan in 1843), it was more in terms of their significant novelty and their economic dominance than in any absolute sense. City life, until our own century, even in a highly industrial society, was still a minority experience, but it was widely and accurately seen as a decisive experience, with much more than proportionate effects on the character of the society as a whole.

At the same time the real stages of the process of urbanization have to be kept in mind, as we look at the development of nineteenth-century literature. Much of it was still of the country and the small town (Hardy observed of George Eliot: 'she had never touched the life of the fields: her country-people having seemed to him, too, more like small townsfolk than rustics'). The persistence of rural and small-town settings is wholly understandable, if we remember the real process, though something must be allowed for a formal and traditional persistence. But then alongside this, in some real proportion to the growth of large cities, a new kind of literature was also rapidly developing.

Early nineteenth-century writing about London was emphatic about its variety: the sheer miscellaneity and peripatetic enjoyment of Pierce Egan's *Life in London* (1821), for example. There is the intense interest in oddities of occupation and in eccentric characters, which continued the chapbook tradition and found its organized urban equivalent in the new Sunday newspapers. In the same dimension there is an interest in crime: the 'Newgate' tradition, as in Jerrold's *St Giles and St James's*. It is easy to see how many of these popular elements were among Dickens's raw material: his creative development is essentially their transformation. But their influence is wider. There is a direct relation, for example, between Egan's kind of light-hearted observation and Henry Mayhew's observation of many thousands of London workers, in *London Labour and the London Poor* (1861) and his other *Morning Chronicle* articles. But in Mayhew as in Dickens the mode is both received and transformed: the workers and the poor become more than 'lively coves'; though speaking for themselves in Mayhew's incomparable records of conversations they still jump from the page with an extraordinary liveliness:

When I've bought 3d of cresses, I ties 'em up into as many little bundles as I can. They must look biggish or the people won't buy them, some puffs them out as much as they'll go. All my money I earns I puts in a club and draws out to buy clothes with. It's better than spending it in sweet-stuff, for them as has a living to earn. Besides it's like a child to care for sugar-sticks, and not like one who's got a living and vittals to earn. I ain't a child, and I shan't be a woman till I'm twenty, but I'm past eight, I am.

The houses we clean out, all says it's far the best plan, ours is. 'Never no more nightmen,' they say. You see, sir, our plan's far less trouble to the people in the house, and there's no smell – least I never found no smell, and it's cheap too. In time the nightmen'll disappear; in course they must, there's so many new dodges comes up, always some one of the working classes is a being ruined. If it ain't steam, it's something else as knocks the bread out of their mouths quite as quick.

It is not only the convincing talk. It is Mayhew's range and care, about the details of so many kinds of work, about money and spending and ways of life. It is also his clear understanding that:

morality on £5000 a year in Belgrave Square is a very different thing to morality on slop wages in Bethnal Green.

Yet it was really only Dickens who could take this experience into the novel. Mayhew's brother Augustus wrote several novels of London life – *Kitty Lamere* (1855), *Paved with Gold* (1858), *The Finest Girl in Bloomsbury* (1861), and Henry collaborated with him in *The Greatest Plague of Life* (a lady's search for a servant, 1847) and *Living for Appearances* (1855). But though the accuracy of the reporting is often there, the transition to theme – in detail to plot and to sustained characterization – is limited by earlier models and structures. Kingsley's *Alton Locke* (1850) is a different case. It is an indignant and powerful exposure of the tailoring sweatshops, and in its general views of backstreet London it is repelled and apocalyptic, in the manner of Dickens seeing Coketown. This is the rhetorical and external mode of Disraeli's *Coningsby* or *Sybil*, painting the industrial towns of the north; a generalized social scene with representative characters whose destiny is determined by an abstract political morality. Dickens is nearest to this mode, significantly, in *Hard Times*. In the London novels, as we saw, his vision is closer and more complicated: the elements of rejection depend, fundamentally, on the elements of acceptance; and this is as true of the people as of the more general scenes of the streets and the city.

The only novelist of the mid-nineteenth century who comes as close as Dickens to the intricacies and paradoxes of city experience is Elizabeth Gaskell. Yet her achievement is different because her city is different – Manchester is at the centre of explicit industrial conflicts in ways that London was not. This does not mean, of course, that industrial conflict was absent from London, but in the variety of trade and in the functions of the capital in government and law and finance there was a different, less isolating perspective. Dickens's accounts of work, which he is sometimes said to have neglected, belong to this complex. Elizabeth Gaskell writes in a city in which industrial production and a dominant market are the determining features, and in which, in quite different ways from London, there is the new hard language of class against class. *Mary Barton* (1848) enacts at a very deep if confused level the full human consequences of a class struggle. It is a story less of the poor and the outcast than of starving working men and their families who are beginning to realize their common condition and to unite to amend it. It is significant that the creator of John Barton, '*the* person with whom all my sympathies went', drew back, under pressure from her publishers and in her own understandable uncertainties, from full imaginative identification with the act of conscious violence against an oppressor: the explicit and untypical expression of the power of new working-class organization. But that she can enter as far as she does into a world of necessary class-consciousness, while never losing touch with the individual people who are forced by systematic exploitation to learn this new way of thinking, is profoundly impressive and is a true mark of radical change.

For that, in this period, is the visible difference between London and the new industrial cities. London had a long history of political radicalism, significantly based mainly in the skilled craftsmen and the artisans: the older kind of working class. Industrial radicalism, of a class-conscious kind, belonged much more to the cities which were being built to a more single and visible pattern, and in the first half of the century these were the dominant trend. The rates of population increase in Manchester, Leeds, Bradford, Birmingham, Liverpool and Sheffield, especially between 1820 and 1850, were in the strict sense phenomenal (some increased in a decade by more than forty per cent). But it was not just a matter of numbers: these were cities built as places of work: physically in their domination by the mills and engines, with the smoke blackening the buildings and effluents blackening the rivers; socially in their organization of homes – 'housing' – around the places of work, so that the dominant relation was always there. It is no surprise that so many investigators and visitors reported 'no mutual confidence, no bond of attachment . . . between the upper and lower classes of society', and that the employers, perhaps even before the 'operatives', thought of themselves, in their common and competitive employment, as a class. There were slums in London that were as bad as anything in Manchester, but the social relations of London were more complex, more mystified, and so not only less accessible to general observation but liable always to be interpreted in the older terms of 'rich' and 'poor' rather than 'employers' and 'employed'.

This difference is critically important in the development of nineteenth-century literature. To see the Industrial Revolution and its consequences, which as a matter of fact were already changing London, writers went, understandably, to the northern industrial cities. It was only later – in Dickens as late as *Our Mutual Friend* and in most other writers nearer the end of the century – that more was seen than the phenomena of industrial production and its immediate social and physical consequences. The true reflection in London – the growth of the great dock areas and their associated large-scale industries, the expansion of banking, the new financial importance of the Stock Exchange – was less dramatically visible, in a connected way. Cobbett had seen it as a political system, in his first denunciation of the 'Wen'. Dickens saw it as a financial system, in his growing understanding of the impersonal forces of money and shares. But it was only late in the century that a physical contrast, which had been long developing, became generally available as an interpretative image. By the 1880s everyone, it seemed, could see the East End and the West End, and in the contrast between them see the dramatic shape of the new society that had been quite nationally and generally created.

Yet it is as early as the seventeenth century that we hear of this significant internal division of London. Petty, in 1662, explained London's westward growth as a means of escape, by grace of the prevailing westerly winds, from the 'fumes, steams and stinks of the whole easterly pyle'. An observer of 1780, Archenholz, noted that:

there has been within the space of twenty years truly a migration from the east end of London to the west . . . where fertile fields and the most agreeable gardens are daily metamorphosed into houses and streets.

In these western areas the pattern of land ownership – of large aristocratic estates – was different from the limited and miscellaneous holdings of the east, and the physical consequences, in relative space, were always apparent. But in the nineteenth century there was also a marked shift of industry to the east. East London, became, in effect, an industrial city, quite apart from the transforming development of the docks between 1800 and 1850, with their associated canals and railways. A social division between East End and West End, which had been noted by some observers from early in the century, deepened and became more inescapably visible. Conditions in the East End were being described as 'unknown' and 'unexplored' (that is by those with access to print) in the middle of the century, and by the 1880s and 1890s 'Darkest London' was a conventional epithet. John Hollingshead's *Ragged London in 1861*, James Greenwood's *A Night in a Workhouse* (1866) and *The Wilds of London* (1874), were succeeded by George Sims's *How the Poor Live* (1883), Walter Besant's *Children of Gibeon* (1886) and Arthur Morrison's *Tales of Mean Streets* (1894). The researches of the Social Democratic Federation (published in the *Pall Mall Gazette* in 1885) were followed by the extensive studies of Charles Booth, beginning with the first volume of *Life and Labour of the People in London* in 1889 (a statistically-based survey undertaken originally because he doubted the earlier radical reports), and by the work of the Salvation Army, described in William Booth's *In Darkest England* (1890). A predominant image of the darkness and poverty of the city, with East London as its symbolic example, became quite central in literature and social thought.

It was an overwhelming and memorable recognition. But it is important, just because it was so, to see the very different ways in which it was mediated in literature. There is already a striking change between, say, Mayhew's *London Labour and the London Poor*, in mid-century, and Charles Booth's *Life and Labour of the People of London*. Mayhew is often now preferred, and he is indeed more readable and more accessible. His studies were based on direct contacts with people, telling their own stories in their own words, and though he set out to cover the whole range systematically, and often checked his findings with those he was writing about, his mode of vision belonged to an earlier world, before the scale of the problem and the sustained consideration of systematic remedies had altered social vision. Booth's deliberate impersonality – mapping and grading before visiting; systematic tabulation – is less readable and less attractive, but it belongs to a way of seeing which the new society itself was producing: that empirical version of the sociological imagination which was to be developed by Rowntree, by the Webbs and by the social investigators of our own time. It is deficient in many respects: in its intrinsic reduction of the poor to objects of study; in its depersonalization by classification and grading; in its lack of general ideas about the character of society. But it has two corresponding strengths. It is a mode which belongs with the substitution of social services for random charity: the services themselves (administered then as now in the spirit of the investigations, but administered and extended none the less) are a response of a new kind to the problems of the city. Moreover the statistical mode itself, which to Dickens and other early Victorian humanists had seemed destructive and hateful, was a necessary response to a civilization of this scale and complexity. It is hardly surprising that the statistical mode in modern social investigation began effectively in Manchester, in the 1830s: it is part of that version of the world. But without it, nevertheless, much that needed to be seen, in a complicated, often opaque and generally divided society, could not, as a basis for common experience and response, be seen at all.

For the sense of the great city was now, in many minds, so overwhelming, that its people were often seen in a single way: as a crowd, as 'masses' or as a 'workforce'. The image could be coloured either way, for sympathy or for contempt, but its undifferentiating character was persistent and powerful. George Gissing, in *Demos* (1886) and *The Nether World* (1889), saw in the great majority of people this single quality or condition, and under the stress of this experience the problem of the individual and society acquired, as we shall see, a new and bitter dimension. The individual was the person who must escape, or try to escape, from this repulsive and degrading mass. Gissing looked back to Dickens and recognized that 'he taught English people a certain way of regarding the huge city', but in Gissing himself, and perhaps in London by the 1880s, the paradoxical Dickensian movement of indignation and recognition had separated out into a simpler structure: indignant or repelled observation of men in general; exceptional and self-conscious recognition of a few individuals. Within this structure, Gissing saw very powerfully, as here in his observation of the more evident organization of work:

It was the hour of the unyoking of men. In the highways and byways of Clerkenwell there was a thronging of released toilers, of young and old, of male and female. Forth they streamed from factories and workrooms, anxious to make the most of the few hours during which they might live for themselves. Great numbers were still bent over their labour, and would be for hours to come, but the majority had leave to wend stablewards. Along the main thoroughfares the wheel-track was dangerous; every omnibus that clattered by was heavily laden with passengers; tarpaulins gleamed over the knees of those who sat outside. This way and that the lights were blurred into a misty radiance; overhead was mere blackness, whence descended the lashing rain. There was a ceaseless scattering of mud; there were blocks in the traffic, attended with rough jest or angry curse; there was jostling on the crowded pavement. Public-houses began to brighten up, to bestir themselves for the evening's business. Streets that had been hives of activity since early morning were being abandoned to silence and darkness and the sweeping wind.

But this is not the crowd of earlier observations. A predictable movement, however jostling and chaotic, has replaced the sense of randomness and variety. And the people are then seen through their general condition: 'the majority had leave to wend stablewards' is an ironic denunciation but also a way of seeing a hopeless, overbearing general movement.

The physical city is also differently seen: not the variety of earlier London, but an oppressive and utilitarian uniformity.

What terrible barracks, those Farrington Road Buildings! Vast sheer walls, unbroken by even an attempt at ornament; row above row of windows in the mud-coloured surface, upwards, upwards, lifeless eyes, mirky openings that tell of bareness, disorder, comfortlessness within ... Acres of these edifices, the tinge of grime declaring the relative dates of their erection; millions of tons of brute brick and mortar, crushing the spirit as you gaze. Barracks, in truth; housing for the army of industrialism, an army fighting with itself, rank against rank, man against man, that the survivors may have whereon to feed.

This systematic observation and interpretation of the relatively new industrial London is at so great a distance from the earlier chaos and variety that Gissing even observes, in the middle of its description, of an older type of building:

One is tempted to say that Shooter's Gardens are a preferable abode. An inner courtyard, asphalted, swept clean ...

Yet even that has been brought within the system:

... looking up to the sky as from a prison.

Even as he recognizes Dickens's power of seeing the city he changes the general effect:

... London as a place of squalid mystery and terror, of the grimly grotesque, of labyrinthine obscurity and lurid fascination.

That is more, say, Reynolds or Augustus Mayhew than Dickens, but it is in any case the old London, including 'mystery' and 'obscurity'. Gissing's own view, even when he is describing Dickens, is more single and more organized:

a great gloomy city, webbed and meshed, as it were, by the spinnings of a huge poisonous spider;

or, in a different mood, 'murky, swarming, rotting London'. Even variations of condition illustrate the general hopelessness rather than positive differences:

On the south is Hoxton, a region of malodorous market streets, of factories, timber-yards, grimy warehouses, of alleys swarming with small trades and crafts, of filthy courts and passages leading into pestilential gloom; everywhere toil in its most degrading forms; the thoroughfares thundering with high-laden waggons, the pavements trodden by working folk of the coarsest type, the corners and lurking holes showing destitution at its ugliest. Walking northwards, the explorer finds himself in freer air, amid broader ways, in a district of dwellinghouses only; the roads seem abandoned to milkmen, cat's meat vendors, and costermongers. Here will be found streets in which every window has its card advertising lodgings; others claim a higher respectability, the houses retreating behind patches of garden-ground, and occasionally showing plastered pillars and a balcony. The change is from undignified struggle for subsistence to mean and spirit-broken leisure; hither retreat the better-paid of the great slave-army when they are free to eat and sleep.

The one fate is different from, but no better than, the other. The only way out is for the exceptional individual, but his fate is a scrambling and ambiguous mobility, in which more often than not he will either go under, after years of effort (Reardon or Biffen in *New Grub Street*), or prosper but deteriorate morally (Mortimer in *Demos*, Milvain in *New Grub Street*), since from the destructive general condition the only forms available, for a successful career, lead to an exploitation of labour or of the minds of others, and this exploitation is itself only possible because of the stupidity, indifference or brutality of the exploited.

It is a bitter and sombre way of seeing, softened only towards the end by glimpses of older kinds of intellectual life and of the country, which are explicitly forms of retreat and of salvation. Gissing wrote the history of the internal migrant as powerfully but even more bitterly than Hardy. Mortimer in *Demos* can be compared with Clym Yeobright in *Return of the Native*, but there is a distance of time and spirit which is in part the real distance between the city and the country, in this rapidly changing society; a distance which appears again as Jude moves from Marygreen to Christminster. More is at issue and more is at stake in the city; its handholds are more precarious and more dangerous; its brief resting-points less discernible; its forms of success and failure of new and more problematic kinds. In *Born in Exile* and *The Unclassed* Gissing wrote, from the inside, classic accounts of that internal migration which has since become so widely significant. The problem which had been raised in Dickens and George Eliot – in Dickens as part of a general condition; in George Eliot as an inescapable moral challenge – was now, in a generation, harsher and more confused. We can see its range from the bitterness of Gissing and the greyness of Mark Rutherford to the tragedy of Hardy and the challenging jaunty confidence of Wells. All these moods, formed in this time of settlement, of limited mobility and of transformation, were to be directly inherited, in our own century.

It is awareness of the problems of mobility, and thence, if often indirectly, of the problems of the observer, which distinguishes Gissing from those other writers about London in the 1880s and 1890s, who have been called, characteristically, the Cockney School:

> Billy Chope, slouching in the opposite direction, lurched across the pavement as they met, and taking the nearer hand from his pocket, caught and twisted her arm, bumping her against the wall.
> 'Garn,' said Lizerunt, greatly pleased: 'le' go.' For she knew that this was love.
> 'Where yer auf to, Lizer?'

This is a new sound of the city. It has a briskness, a narrative directness, which in the novels and especially the short-stories of the nineties became characteristic. The conscious or self-conscious narrator, in any of his modes from Jane Austen to George Eliot and from Dickens to Gissing, has gone and has been replaced by what becomes a quite standard professional storytelling. Elizabeth Hunt becomes not only Liza Hunt but Lizerunt, in this mode of sharp memorability. She 'knew' that the twist of the arm and the bump against the wall 'was love' because she was available for knowing, as exactly this kind of projected and sharply-named character. The mode of speech is not qualified or parenthetically mocked (as sometimes in Gissing); it has emerged in what can be called its own right, but a right that depends on the new general convention of storytelling distance.

The careful orthographic simulation is an important mark of the change. The relation between English spelling and the many native varieties of English pronunciation has always and even notoriously been problematical. Examples of deliberately varied orthography can be collected from as early as the Elizabethans: Shakespeare himself did it for Welsh and French speakers, and versions of a 'rural' dialect – a conflation of regions – also became commonplace. Dickens picked up some of the variations of London speech. But the systematic convention of class modes of speech belongs, effectively, to the late nineteenth century, in a period of obviously increasing class consciousness which was extending to just these parts of behaviour. Some orthographic reconstruction was affectionately done, as in William Barnes's Dorset poems. But it is significant that Hardy decided against this practice, on any systematic basis, and gave as his reason its falsely distancing effect, its reduction of persons to types. In this exact sense the carefully rendered 'Cockney dialect' of Arthur Morrison, who wrote *Lizerunt* in 1893, or of Kipling in *The Record of Badalia Herodsfoot* (1890) and his soldier-ballads, became conventional. A reduction is present also in Gissing – for reasons that belong to just the mode of observation and relationship which Hardy opposed. Its readers learned to trace its details, with what they believed to be affectionate respect, and what they also believed to be distance.

'Where yer auf to, Lizer?' But the 'where' is the standard conventional spelling, unlike almost any pronunciation; the 'yer' and the 'Lizer' pick up a general speech-habit; the 'auf' remains doubtful to this day, with its variant as 'orf', since the long 'o', with its possibility of an 'r' sound, has been widespread in speech modes as variant as the 'Cockney' and the upper-middle-class. None of the details can ever be settled; the underlying relations between spelling and any mode of English pronunication are too complex. But it is a significant mark of a way of seeing which has been praised for its naturalism and for its apparent exclusion of self-conscious authorial commentary. The real point is that the 'commentary' is now completely incorporated; it is part of a whole way of seeing, at a 'sociological' distance. The confident, winning ways of these late Victorian and Edwardian storytellers depend, in the very course of their often real success, on that descriptive, representative, carefully-observed naturalism, from which the problems of consciousness and the problems of explicit and controversial ideas have been set aside. There they are, the people: pathetic or enduring; the violent and their victims: available pieces of life: the famous naturalist 'slice'.

It is a tone which belongs to the new city experience, but which, when critically seen, is also a direct form of interpretation. In Henry Nevinson's *The St George of Rochester* (1894) or in Edwin Pugh's *A Small Talk Exchange* (1895) there is more continuity with the listening records and observations of Mayhew; but in Kipling and in Morrison this has evolved to presentation, with marked differences of effect, and in other writers such as Adcock and Rook there is a mixture of the modes: now recording, now presenting the people of the city. It is significant that Morrison, who shared so much, at the beginning, with Gissing, in his general observations, should have given so much attention, in *A Child of the Jago* and *The Hole in the Wall*, to criminality and violence. This was very widely present, in the new as in the old city, but it was, characteristically, more presentable, more of a story, than the full and more varied texture. This selection of violence in urban fiction can be traced back, in one dimension to the long tradition of 'roguery'; but in its growingly dominant prevalence it is better seen as a mode of experiencing urban life which catches in its isolated areas and incidents not only an understandable kind of respectable interest (fascination and horror, in a single mode of distance) but also the most explicit and isolable form of action, when not a society but a population is being observed and described.

In its persistent attention, however, Morrison's fiction has a substance which is ultimately very different from that of Kipling the myth-maker; or, to take a significant and contemporary comparison within London, from that of Conan Doyle. London in the Sherlock Holmes stories becomes again the city of 'labyrinthine obscurity and lurid fascination'. Indeed the urban detective, prefigured in a minor way in Dickens and Wilkie Collins, now begins to emerge as a significant and ratifying figure: the man who can find his way through the fog, who can penetrate the intricacies of the streets. The opaque complexity of modern city life is represented by crime; the explorer of a society is reduced to the discoverer of single causes, the isolable agent and above all his means, his technique. Conan Doyle's London has acquired, with time, a romantic atmosphere which some look back to with a nostalgia as evident and systematic as any rural retrospect: the fog, the gaslight, the hansom cabs, the street urchins, and through them all, this eccentric sharp mind, this almost disembodied but locally furnished intelligence, which can unravel complexity, determine local agency, and then, because there the inquiry stops, hand the matter over to the police and the courts: the clear abstract system beyond all the bustle and fog.

It was a way of seeing which had a sharp local power. As in Gissing and Morrison and the others it has left many memorable images of that particular city. But there are other images, as there is another history. The city of darkness, of oppression, of crime and squalor, of a reduced humanity, was of course also differently experienced: not only in the liveliness of stories like Rook's *Billy the Snide* (1899), but very notably in Wells, who in this and other ways belongs to a history which the more simply memorable images reduce or exclude.

For the city could still be seen as a city of light. It was so in the simplest physical sense. As early as 1780 Archenholz had written:

> The lamps, which have two or four branches, are enclosed in crystal globes and fixed on posts at a little distance from each other. They are lighted at sunset in winter as well as in summer whether the moon shines or not. In Oxford Road alone there are more lamps than in all the city of Paris. Even the great roads for seven or eight miles round are crowded with them which makes the effect exceedingly grand.

Gas-lighting, from the beginning of the nineteenth century, had been used for effect and display as much as for utility, and many residents and visitors shared the mid-century impression of Hans Christian Andersen:

> the great world metropolis mapped out in fire below me.

At the end of the century, Le Gallienne was writing:

> London, London, our delight,
> Great flower that opens but at night.
> Great city of the midnight sun,
> Whose day begins when day is done.
>
> Lamp after lamp against the sky
> Opens a sudden beaming eye,
> Leaping a light on either hand
> The iron lilies of the Strand.

This light was an obvious image for the impressive civilization of the capital, visibly growing in wealth and in conscious public effect. Whatever was happening in the East End, and often in conscious relation to it, the West End was being newly designed and improved: Trafalgar Square, a new palace, new Houses of Parliament, new parks and highways. An American visitor, Colman, stressed the visible contrasts:

> In the midst of the most extraordinary abundance, here are men, women and children dying of starvation; and running alongside of the splendid chariot, with its gilded equipages, its silken linings, and the liveried footman, are poor, forlorn, friendless, almost naked wretches, looking like the mere fragments of humanity.

The emphatic display and magnificence of the eighteenth-century country-houses, that superimposition on the evident poverty of the subjected majority, was being re-enacted, on a much greater scale, in this wealthy and class-divided city. As a centre of trade and political influence the capital was attracting, also, in familiar ways, every kind of talent, from many parts of the world. The perception of 'darkest London', in the largely separated East End, was a consequence of the blaze of light in that part of the city which was a national and international capital. It is characteristic that Conan Doyle, who had created in Sherlock Holmes a version of pure intelligence penetrating the obscurity which baffled ordinary men, should have collected statistical evidence of the intellectual pre-eminence of London, both native and as a result of the centralization of the 'brightest intellects in every walk of life'. This version of a glittering and dominant metropolitan culture had enough reality to support a traditional idea of the city, as a centre of light and learning, but now on an unprecedented scale. The cultural centralization of England was already at this time more marked, at every level, than in any comparable society. Even to oppose and reject the city, men came to the city; there was no other ready way.

But this, though important, was a comparatively superficial effect. Metropolitan culture often confuses its pre-eminence as an agent or consumer of human gifts with their often different and more varied real sources. What can be said more seriously, as the new urban civilization is weighed, is that distinctive new kinds of social thought and social organization were being created within it, whether as a response to its chaos or as a heightening of faculties from its more evident stimulus. Hardy had deplored the absence, in London, of any 'collective consciousness', but it was from the cities of England – the industrial cities quite as much as the capital – that new democratic forms and ideas were decisively extending. We can see one aspect of this in Wells. He was as appalled as anyone by the social conditions of the cities, and especially by the housing, that 'sustained disaster ... massacre, degeneration and disablement of lives'. In the mood of Gissing he saw the:

pavements that had always a thin veneer of greasy, slippery mud, under grey skies that showed no gleam of hope of anything for (a limitless crowd of dingy people) but dinginess until they died.

He saw the East End as a 'sordid-looking wilderness', in which the people had 'a white dull skin that looked degenerate and ominous to a West-end eye'. It was not a tragic but a feeble, anxious, deprived population. Escape from this shabby and limited life, in the East End or in the more respectable and more anxious suburbs, was seen often in terms of the rural retreat or the idealized jolly refuge. But also, as most clearly in *Tono-Bungay*, Wells saw the real order of rural England: the country-house England which he described in Bladesover:

The great house, the church, the village, and the labourers and the servants in their stations and degrees ... a closed and complete social system. About us were other villages and great estates, and from house to house, interlacing, correlated, the Gentry, the fine Olympians, came and went.

Whatever the changes of the industrial and urban revolutions, this predominant social system had survived. Real changes were no more than an intrusion or a gloss upon it. In the centre of London its essential features were still as marked as in the villages. It had prevented all real growth. What had then happened in the city was indeed an outgrowth, a projection, of that simpler order. As such it was a cancer:

the unorganized, abundant substance of some tumorous growth-process, a process which indeed bursts all the outlines of the affected carcass.

This is the diseased shape of a city and a civilization. But the monster is now less satanic; it has a more human shape. It is:

like some fat, proud flunkey, like pride, like indolence, like all that is darkening and heavy and obstructive in life. It is matter and darkness, it is the anti-soul, it is the ruling power of this land, Stupidity.

To see the city like this is to make a very different emphasis. Wells, more clearly than anyone before him, saw the connection between the ruling power of the city and the ruling power of the country-houses. And if the common factors of this power were pride, indolence and stupidity, they could be differently opposed: not by retrospective innocence, but by conscious progress: through education, science and socialism.

Wells thus gathers up and unites what had been, through the century, very different and even alternative traditions. If the ugliness and meanness of industrialism and urbanism were the cancerous results of an outgrown but still rigid and stupid system, there was a new way of opposing the city which not only did not depend on an idealized version of a rural order but saw just that order as part of the disease. Moreover, if this were so, there were available and active real forces to fight it: forces released by new civilizing energies but held back by a false social order.

This Wellsian view, which cannot be reduced to a simple proposal of unlimited and mindless technology (though that was always latent, and in the real social difficulties could at times be abstracted) connects with the socialist view which had been steadily developing. For it was not only the achievements of science and of material production which gave promise of a new civilization. It was the growth, within the cities, of new kinds of social organization. This had indeed been widely overlooked, in many of the more general denunciations. There was indeed much aggregation, much atomism, as Carlyle and the others had suggested. But this was never the whole story. There was the struggle to create new forms of local government: a response to overcrowding and chaos but emerging as something far better than the old local arbitrariness of landowners – the only previous system. There was the struggle for the vote and for the reform of parliament, again centred in the cities. There was the fight for education, led from the cities and in the end imposed only with difficulty on rural areas still governed by landlords and their dependants who had a vested interest in ignorance. There was the active growth of municipal as well as metropolitan culture: the struggle for new amenities – the libraries and the institutes – in the new needs of the towns. And there was something else, in a different dimension from this impressive liberal improvement. There was the growing organization of the working-class itself: the great civilizing response to industrial tyranny and anarchy: the creation of the unions out of the network of urban friendly and benefit societies, and beyond this expression of a new and active neighbourliness the vision of mutuality as a new kind of society: the cooperatives, the socialism, again of the new cities. Growing against all opposition, through the course of the century, this movement had reached, by the 1880s, even the East End of London: that symbolic wasteland which Gissing and others had described. For Engels it was changing:

> That immense haunt of misery is no longer the stagnant pool it was six years ago. It has shaken off its torpid despair, has returned to life, and has become the home of what is called the 'New Unionism'; that is to say, of the organization of the great mass of 'unskilled' workers.

These were the days of the organization of the gasworkers, of the matchgirls' strike, of the great dock strike of 1889. And, as Engels argued, these new unions and struggles were in a different dimension from the craft unionism of an earlier period:

> Faith in the eternity of the wages system was seriously shaken; their founders and promoters were Socialists either consciously or in feeling.

Out of the very chaos and misery of the new metropolis, and spreading from it to rejuvenate a national feeling, the civilizing force of a new vision of society had been created in struggle, had gathered up the suffering and the hopes of generations of the oppressed and exploited, and in this unexpected and challenging form was the city's human reply to the long inhumanity of city and country alike.

Wordsworth had glimpsed in the city, in its dissolving and transforming conditions, a new possibility of 'the unity of man'.

In many ways, this sense of higher kinds of social organization and cooperation had been kept alive and had found new forms in the very cities in which exploitation and inhumanity had been most concentrated and most evident. Subject to many failures and losses of hope, it had yet persisted and grown: education, cooperation, democracy, socialism: ideas and institutions slowly gathering strength. Gissing, who knew this process, and at first supported it, came to believe, as anyone might, that it would be overborne and corrupted by the sheer mass of ignorance and deformity which the cities were also multiplying. He saw 'those brute forces of society which fill with wreck the abyss of the nether world'. Into this abyss would disappear, also, the dreams of change. *Demos*, that 'story of English Socialism', disproves, with a classic sourness, the possibility of socialist idealism. It is this second stage of misery, not only the raw suffering but the collapse of that kind of hope, which leads him back to the dream of 'reading Homer under a cottage roof'. Wells, more vigorous and more confident, saw this and other dangers: the triumph of a commercial demagogy, in the world of *Tono-Bungay*, as Gissing had seen the triumph of a commercial press and literature in *New Grub Street*. The new freedoms and the new education could be corrupted or incorporated, and the city would breed their degraded substitutes on an unimaginable scale. Even the new social and political movements, the bearers of civilization, could be confused, corrupted, incorporated: the cancerous growth could overwhelm them.

But in Wells at least, as in the new socialism, there was still the sense of possibility: that history could go either way: that the only alternative to a new social order was an increasing chaos, the cities smashing themselves to pieces. Nearly a century later, this is an unfinished struggle. It must be looked at again. But as the new century came, Hardy's words can be remembered, yet in an altered sense. The new organizations of the labour movement, the new institutions of education and democracy, were the ways in which London and the other cities, and the nation which they now dominated, were beginning to see themselves: to be conscious of themselves and in this very consciousness – a collective consciousness – to see the shapes of a different society.

Yet perception of the new qualities of the modern city had been associated, from the beginning, with a man walking, as if alone, in its streets. It is there at the start in Blake:

> I wander thro' each charter'd street
> Near where the charter'd Thames does flow.

And in Wordsworth:

> How often in the overflowing Streets
> Have I gone forward with the Crowd, and said
> Unto myself, the face of everyone
> That passes by me is a mystery ...
> ... Until the shapes before my eyes became
> A second-sight procession, such as glides
> Over still mountains, or appears in dreams.

In the urban novelists, this experience was often recreated in a character, as in Dickens's Florence Dombey:

> ... the rising clash and roar of the day's struggle ... surprise and curiosity in the faces flitting past her ... long shadows coming back upon the pavement ... voices that were strange to her asking her where she went ... Where to go? Still somewhere, anywhere! Still going on; but where! She thought of the only other time she had been lost in the wide wilderness of London ...

In Elizabeth Gaskell the isolation is related to a social contrast:

> It is a pretty sight to walk through a street with lighted shops; the gas is so brilliant, the display of goods so much more vividly shown than by day, and of all shops the druggist's looks the most like the tales of our childhood, from Aladdin's garden of enchanted fruits to the charming Rosamund with her purple jar.
> No such associations had Barton; yet he felt the contrast between the well-filled, well-lighted shops and the dim gloomy cellar, and it

made him moody that such contrasts should exist. They are the mysterious problem of life to more than him. He wondered if any in all the hurrying crowd had come from such a house of mourning. He thought they all looked joyous, and he was angry with them. But he could not, you cannot, read the lot of those who daily pass you by in the street.

This is the mood of Dickens though less complex and less dramatic: an insistence on human sympathy just because the obstacles, the contradictions, the mysteries, are so clearly seen. This is usually true also of those frequent episodes, from Dickens to Wells, in which a character enters a sleeping city and is overwhelmed by the thought of all the hidden lives so close to him. Yet this experience, clearly, could go either way: into an affirmation of common humanity, past the barriers of crowded strangeness; or into an emphasis of isolation, of mystery – an ordinary feeling that can become a terror. Words-worth explored both kinds of response, and nineteenth-century literature expanded this exploration, in both directions.

In world literature, in Balzac, in Baudelaire and in a different way in Dostoievsky, the image of the city grew into a kind of dominance. Balzac had shown the social intricacy of the city, and its constant mobility; since his purpose was to describe this, the consequent image, though complex, is clear. Dostoievsky, on the other hand, emphasized the elements of mystery and strangeness and the loss of connection; comparably with Dickens but drawing on different ultimate responses, he then worked to create recognitions. His difference from Dickens is that the source of the recognition is not in a smothered sense of society but in a spiritual acknowledgement, on the far side of isolated despair. Baudelaire, meanwhile, reversed both these values. Isolation and loss of connection were the conditions of a new and lively perception:

Multitude and solitude: terms that an active and fertile poet can make equal and interchangeable.

The city was a 'spree of vitality', an instantaneous and transitory world of 'feverish joys'. It taught the soul to:

give itself utterly, with all its poetry and charity, to the unexpectedly emergent, to the passing unknown.

There was a new kind of pleasure, a new enlargement of identity, in what he called bathing oneself in the crowd.

Into the twentieth century, this was to become a major response. This social character of the city – its transitoriness, its unexpectedness, its essential and exciting isolation and process- ion of men and events – was seen as the reality of all human life. It was not often Baudelaire's joyful acceptance; but in a late religious fatalism, in an aesthetic detachment, or in more everyday senses of the pleasure of variety and the instantaneous, this vision spread and even came to predominate in much Western literature. There might still be a contrast of the city with the country, drawing on the older senses of rural settlement and innocence. But the contrast would work the other way: of consciousness with ignorance; of vitality with routine; of the present and actual with the past or the lost. City experience was now becoming so widespread, and writers, disproportionately, were so deeply involved in it, that there seemed little reality in any other mode of life; all sources of perception seemed to begin and end in the city, and if there was anything beyond it, it was also beyond life.

It is important to trace the very different strands of this response. In Gissing, as I have said, the lonely figure walking the streets is overwhelmed by the crowds and the ugliness. As he observed, more accurately of himself than of Dickens, his nominal source:

Murky, swarming, rotting London, a marvellous rendering of the impression received by any imaginative person who, in low spirits, has had occasion to wander about London's streets.

In the passage I quoted earlier, when Gissing was describing London, I omitted this isolating emphasis, so that it might now be seen more clearly. After the journey through Hoxton to the north:

To walk about a neighbourhood such as this is the dreariest exercise to which man can betake himself; the heart is crushed by uniformity of decent squalor; one remembers that each of these dead-faced houses, often each separate blind window, represents a 'home', and the associations of the word whisper blank despair.

Or of the Farringdon Road barracks:

> Pass by in the night, and strain imagination to picture the weltering mass of human weariness, of bestiality, of unmerited dolour, of hopeless hope, of crushed surrender, tumbled together within those forbidding walls.

Yet Gissing, like the more confident Wells, was still directly involved in social observation of an actual city. Before he had written, however, a comparable despair had found a different literary mode: that of the city as symbol.

The city had long had a symbolic dimension, most powerfully in the religious image of the Holy City, the City of God. In a variant of this mode, William Blake saw London and England and wanted to build Jerusalem. But there was now a sharp alteration. It comes most clearly in English with James Thomson's poems: *The Doom of a City*, written in 1857, and *The City of Dreadful Night*, written between 1870 and 1873. As we read these remarkable poems, we can see substantial connections with some of the other literature we have discussed. We are often reminded of Dickens, and we can be reminded, also, of Richard Jefferies's better-known and subsequent vision of the destruction of a city in *After London* (1885). In distinguishable ways, in these very different writers, a common structure of feeling was being formed. But what is distinct in Thomson, when all the connections have been noted, is that his city is projected and is significantly total: it is a symbolic vision of the city as the condition of human life.

The City of Dreadful Night is the better known, but there is an impressive strength in *The Doom of a City*, written when he was only twenty-three. More consciously, there, he moves from an actual city to a visionary city, the City of the Dead. He leaves the house which was his cage, where:

> The mighty City in vast silence slept,
> Dreaming away its tumult, toil and strife;
> But sleep, and sleep's rich dreams were not for me,
> For me, accurst, whom terror and the pain
> Of baffled longings, and starved misery ...
> ... Drove forth as one possest.

It is a new kind of lonely walking, through the streets of the city:

I passed through desert streets, beneath the gleam
Of lamps that lit my tumbling life alone . . .
. . . Within a buried City's maze of stone;
Whose peopling corpses, while they ever dream
Of birth and death – of complicated life
   Whose days and months and years
Are wild with laughter, groans and tears,
As with themselves and Doom
They wage, with loss or gain, incessant strife,
Indeed, lie motionless within their tomb.

He crosses the 'desert sea', 'ignorant of chart and star', and
arrives at a city which is that vision realized; a restless and evil
city which has been transformed into stone:

Stone statues all throughout the streets and squares,
Grouped as in social converse or alone;
Dim stony merchants holding out rich wares
To catch the choice of purchasers of stone.

This is the silent city, which he has been forced to find:

In my old common world, well fenced about
With myriad lives that followed well my own,
Terror and deadly anguish found me out
And drove me forth to seek the dread Unknown.

It is the 'wide and populous solitude' of Death's kingdom, but a
death that is an arrest of a turbulent life:

The whole vast sea of life around me lay,
The passionate, heaving, restless, sounding life . . .
. . . Arrested in full tumult of its strife.

This, at last, is COSMOPOLIS. A man arrives there by isolation:

The cords of sympathy which should have bound me
In sweet communication with earth's brotherhood
I drew in tight and tighter still around me,
Strangling my lost existence for a mood.

This is 'Solitude in midst of a great City', where every 'deed and
word and glance and gesture' spread through the myriads of
inhabitants, affecting every other creature; but the mysterious
union has been broken and the consequence is the city of death.

What he then sees is the destruction of the city, by fire and storm and by the arrival of the beasts. The stone people who are all its inhabitants are broken with the buildings with which they have blended:

> Of the City's vast palatial pride
> Of all the works of man on every side ...
> ... Remained no vestige.

When he returns to his own city

> Its awfulness of life oppressed my soul;
> The very air appeared no longer free,
> But dense and sultry in the close control
> Of such a mighty cloud of human breath,
> The shapeless houses and the monstrous ships
> Were brooding thunderclouds that could eclipse
> The burning sun of day.

The storm will come here also. The City sings that it is 'rich and strong ... wise and good and free', but its evil is as evident as its power, its guilt as its wealth. Its heritage is vast and rich, but its

> Chief social laws seem strictly framed to secure
> That one be corruptingly rich, another bitterly poor,
> And another just starving to death; thy fanes and
> mansions proud
> Are beleaguered with filthy hovels wherein poor wretches
> crowd ...

Its

> flaring streets each night affront the patient skies
> With a holocaust of woes, sins, lusts and blasphemies.

So this city, this London, is doomed, unless it repents. In *The City of Dreadful Night* the projection is more complete.

> The City is of Night, but not of Sleep;
> There sweet sleep is not for the weary brain;
> The pitiless hours like years and ages creep,
> A night seems termless hell. This dreadful strain
> Of thought and consciousness which never ceases,
> Or which some moment's stupor but increases,
> This, worse than woe, makes wretches there insane.

It is a projected city in which a particular mode of being, specifically the 'dreadful strain of thought and consciousness', has been actualized.

> How he arrives there none can clearly know ...
> ... But being there one feels a citizen ...
> Poor wretch, who once hath paced that dolent city
> Shall pace it often, doomed beyond all pity.

It is now a common condition of the inhabitants of this City of Night that

> They are most rational and yet insane
> An outward madness not to be controlled;
> A perfect reason in the central brain
> Which has no power, but sitteth wan and cold,
> And sees the madness, and foresees as plainly
> The ruin in its path, and trieth vainly
> To cheat itself refusing to behold.

They are, rich and poor:

> The saddest and the weariest men on earth.

But might 'our isolated units' be brought 'to act together for some common end?' A long procession comes to the cathedral, for every kind of human activity, and there they are given a new sense of life which is a perception of delusion:

> O melancholy Brothers, dark, dark, dark!
> ... It was the dark delusion of a dream ...
> ... This little life is all we must endure ...
> ... We bow down to the universal laws
> Which never had for man a special clause.

A loss of belief in the false dreams of God or immortality, or of any convincing living purpose, is now the condition of the city and the condition of man. Yet the loss of purpose occurs within an unprecedented human closeness:

> Wherever men are gathered, all the air
>   Is charged with human feeling, human thought;
> Each shout and cry and laugh, each curse and prayer,
>   Are into its vibrations surely wrought;
> Unspoken passion, wordless meditation,
> Are breathed into it with our respiration;
>   It is with our life fraught and overfraught.

So that no man there breathes earth's simple breath,
　　As if alone on mountains or wide seas;
But nourishes warm life or hastens death
　　With joys and sorrows, health and foul disease,
Wisdom and folly, good and evil labours,
Incessant of his multitudinous neighbours;
　　He in his turn affecting all of these.

That City's atmosphere is dark and dense,
　　Although not many exiles wander there,
With many a potent evil influence,
　　Each adding poison to the poisoned air;
Infections of unutterable sadness,
Infections of incalculable madness,
　　Infections of incurable despair.

This powerful vision brings together, in an immensely influential though not often acknowledged structure, the fact of the city and of the new anguished consciousness. Struggle, indifference, loss of purpose, loss of meaning – features of nineteenth-century social experience and of a common interpretation of the new scientific world-view – have found, in the City, a habitation and a name. For the city is not only, in this vision, a form of modern life; it is the physical embodiment of a decisive modern consciousness.

This can be traced in many ways in twentieth-century literature, and directly to T. S. Eliot.

Unreal City,
Under the brown fog of a winter dawn,
A crowd flowed over London Bridge, so many,
I had not thought death had undone so many.
Sighs, short and infrequent, were exhaled,
And each man fixed his eyes before his feet.
Flowed up the hill and down King William Street,
To where Saint Mary Woolnoth kept the hours
With a dead sound on the final stroke of nine.

This is the city of death in life, as Thomson had seen it. It is the modern wasteland, and through it a powerful convention of urban imagery became almost commonplace. Eliot's early images are more particularized and more isolated, but the continuity is evident:

The burnt-out ends of smoky days.
And now a gusty shower wraps
The grimy scraps
Of withered leaves about your feet
And newspapers from vacant lots . . .
. . . The morning comes to consciousness
Of faint stale smells of beer
From the sawdust-trampled street
With all its muddy feet that press
To early coffee-stands.
With the other masquerades
That time resumes,
One thinks of all the hands
That are raising dingy shades
In a thousand furnished rooms.

In the end this is as relentless and as conventional as pastoral. Indeed it is in effect neo-urban imagery, of the same literary kind as the isolated neo-pastoral. A selected urban landscape mediates a general despair in the isolated observer. Significantly it also mediates a social contempt which is even sourer than that of Gissing:

They are rattling breakfast plates in basement kitchens,
And along the trampled edges of the street
I am aware of the damp souls of housemaids
Sprouting despondently at area gates.

In his later verse, Eliot related loss of meaning in the city to the loss of God. By implication, or by direct statement, the human settlements of the past are given a different significance, and the rural settlements – isolated and remote, visited from the city – acquire, if only by default, a traditional significance. This regular association of rural living with the past and with tradition, and then by symbolic rather than historical association with religious faith, became commonplace. The city it seemed, was what man had made without God.

Can you keep the City that the LORD keeps not with you?
A thousand policemen directing the traffic
Cannot tell you why you come or where you go . . .
. . . Where there is no temple there shall be no homes,
Though you have shelters and institutions,
Precarious lodgings while the rent is paid,
Subsiding basements where the rat breeds

Or sanitary dwellings with numbered doors
Or a house a little better than your neighbour's;
When the Stranger says: 'What is the meaning of this city?
Do you huddle close together because you love each other?'
What will you answer? 'We all dwell together
To make money from each other?' or 'This is a community'?
And the Stranger will depart and return to the desert.

The Stranger is from Thomson, but the ideology is now more developed. The Stranger's question is never put, for example, to the village of Crabbe. The 'timekept City' is implicitly contrasted with the natural rhythms of blood, day and night, and the seasons; a rural past is conflated with faith or with innocence: a new version of pastoral, by the emphasis of urban negations. The experience of the streets, of the uncertain stranger, is then developed from its original social and perceptual confusions to an analogue of purgatory:

In the uncertain hour before the morning
    Near the ending of interminable night
    At the recurrent end of the unending
After the dark dove with the flickering tongue
    Had passed below the horizon of his homing
    While the dead leaves still rattled on like tin
Over the asphalt where no other sound was
    Between three districts where the smoke arose
    I met one walking, loitering and hurried
As if blown towards me like the metal leaves
    Before the urban dawn wind unresisting.
    And as I fixed upon the down-turned face
That pointed scrutiny with which we challenge
    The first-met stranger in the waning dusk
    I caught the sudden look of some dead master
Whom I had known, forgotten, half recalled
    Both one and many; in the brown baked features
    The eyes of a familiar compound ghost
Both intimate and unidentifiable.
    So I assumed a double part, and cried
    And heard another's voice cry: 'What! are *you* here?'
Although we were not. I was still the same,
    Knowing myself yet being someone other –
    And he a face still forming; yet the words sufficed
To compel the recognition they preceded.
    And so, compliant to the common wind,
    Too strange to each other for misunderstanding,

In concord at this intersection time
Of meeting nowhere, no before and after,
We trod the pavement in a dead patrol.

The sceptical pessimism of Thomson, the social pessimism of Gissing, the religious pessimism of Eliot: each found a landscape in the city. But the characteristic imagery of the urban pre-occupation developed in other ways also. In Virginia Woolf the discontinuity, the atomism, of the city were aesthetically experienced, as a problem of perception which raised problems of identity – and which was characteristically resolved on arrival in the country:

The Old Kent Road was very crowded on Thursday, the eleventh of October, 1928. People spilt off the pavement. There were women with shopping-bags. Children ran out. There were sales at drapers' shops. Streets widened and narrowed. Long vistas steadily shrunk together. Here was a market. Here a funeral. Here a procession with banners upon which was written 'Ra-Un', but what else? Meat was very red. Butchers stood at the door. Women almost had their heels sliced off. Amor Vin – that was over a porch. A woman looked out of a bedroom window, profoundly contemplative, and very still. Apple-john and Applebed, Undert—. Nothing could be seen whole or read from start to finish. What was seen begun – like two friends starting to meet each other across the street – was never seen ended. After twenty minutes the body and mind were like scraps of torn paper tumbling from a sack and, indeed, the process of motoring fast out of London so much resembles the chopping up small of identity which precedes unconsciousness and perhaps death itself that it is an open question in what sense Orlando can be said to have existed at the present moment. Indeed we should have given her over for a person entirely disassembled were it not that here, at last, one green screen was held out on the right, against which the little bits of paper fell more slowly; and then another was held out on the left so that one could see the separate scraps now turning over by themselves in the air; and then green screens were held continuously on either side, so that her mind regained the illusion of holding things within itself and she saw a cottage, a farmyard and four cows, all precisely life-size.

This fragmentary experience – now accelerated by 'motoring fast' – has remained a perceptual condition. It is deeply related to several characteristic forms of modern imagery, most evident in painting and especially in film which as a medium contains much of its intrinsic movement. There is indeed a direct relation between the motion picture, especially in its development in cutting and montage, and the characteristic movement of an observer in the close and miscellaneous environment of the streets. But this should remind us that the perceptual experience itself does not necessarily imply any particular mood, let alone an ideology. This experience of urban movement has been used, at all levels of seriousness and of play, to express a gamut of feelings from despair to delight. The single vision of Eliot's characteristic imagery, of smoke, scraps, grime, dinginess, has been very powerful but not overwhelming. We can see this most clearly if we look at Joyce's *Ulysses*, which is the most extended and memorable realization in our literature of these fundamentally altered modes of perception and identity.

Wordsworth, near the beginning, had lost his familiar bearings:

> All laws of acting, thinking, speaking man
> Went from me, neither knowing me nor known.

But as the experience was prolonged it became clear that for 'laws' we must read 'conventions'. Generations of men and women learned to see in new ways, though it needed the genius of Joyce to take these new ways into the deep substance of literary method itself. In Joyce, the laws and the conventions of traditional observation and communication have apparently disappeared. The consequent awareness is intense and fragmentary, subjective primarily, yet in the very form of its subjectivity including others who are now with the buildings, the noises, the sights and smells of the city, parts of this single and racing consciousness. We can participate in just this experience as Bloom walks through Dublin:

He crossed to the bright side, avoiding the loose cellarflap of number seventyfive. The sun was nearing the steeple of George's church. Be a warm day I fancy. Specially in these black clothes feel it more. Black conducts, reflects (refracts is it?) the heat. But I couldn't go in that light suit. Make a picnic of it. His eyelids sank quietly often as he walked in happy warmth. Boland's breadvan delivering with trays our daily but she prefers yesterday's loaves turnovers crisp crowns hot. Makes you feel young. Somewhere in the east: early morning: set off at dawn, travel round in front of the sun, steal a day's march on him. Keep it up for ever never grow a day older technically. Walk along a strand, strange land, come to a city gate, sentry there, old ranker too, old Tweedy's big moustaches leaning on a long kind of a spear. Wander through awned streets. Turbaned faces going by. Dark caves of carpet shops, big man, Turko the terrible, seated crosslegged smoking a coiled pipe. Cries of sellers in the streets. Drink water scented with fennel, sherbet. Wander along all day. Might meet a robber or two. Well, meet him. Getting on to sundown. The shadows of the mosques along the pillars: priest with a scroll rolled up. A shiver of the trees, signal, the evening wind. I pass on. Fading gold sky. A mother watches from her doorway. She calls her children home in their dark language. High wall: beyond strings twanged. Night sky moon, violet, colour of Molly's new garters. Strings. Listen. A girl playing one of those instruments what do you call them: dulcimers. I pass.

Here the fantasy of the Oriental city begins from the smell of bread in Boland's van, but each sight or sound or smell is a trigger to Bloom's private preoccupations. Under the pressure of his needs, the one city as it passes is as real as the other.

This is the profound alteration. The forces of the action have become internal and in a way there is no longer a city, there is only a man walking through it. Elizabeth Gaskell, we remember, went from the window of the druggist to 'Aladdin's garden of enchanted fruits', but within a rigidly controlled objective frame: 'the tales of our childhood' – writer and reader can share this memory; 'no such associations had Barton' – the objectively seen character, separate in situation and in culture, is made sharply distinct. In *Ulysses* the relation between action and consciousness, but also the relation between narrator and character, has been modulated until the whole shape of the language has changed:

He approached Larry O'Rourke's. From the cellar grating floated up the flabby gush of porter. Through the open doorway the bar squirted out whiffs of ginger, teadust, biscuitmush. Good house, however: just the end of the city traffic. For instance M'Auley's down there: n.g. as position. Of course if they ran a tramline along the North Circular from the cattle market to the quays value would go up like a shot.

Bald head over the blind. Cute old codger. No use canvassing him for an ad. Still he knows his own business best. There he is, sure enough, my bold Larry, leaning against the sugarbin in his shirtsleeves watching the aproned curate swab up with mop and bucket. Simon Dedalus takes him off to a tee with his eyes screwed up. Do you know what I'm going to tell you? What's that Mr O'Rourke? Do you know what? The Russians, they'd only be an eight o'clock breakfast for the Japanese.

Stop and say a word: about the funeral perhaps. Sad thing about poor Dignam, Mr O'Rourke.

Turning into Dorset Street he said freshly in greeting through the doorway:

– Good day Mr O'Rourke.

– Good day to you.

– Lovely weather, sir.

– 'Tis all that.

Here the contrast of dimensions is direct: the substance of Bloom's observations, speculations and memories – on a thread of narrative action – is an active exchange, even an active community, within the imagined speech of thought, whereas what is actually said when he reaches O'Rourke is flat and external: what the received conventions have become. The substantial reality, the living variety of the city, is in the walker's mind:

He walked along the curbstone. Stream of life . . .

. . . Cityful passing away, other cityful coming, passing away too: other coming on, passing on. Houses, lines of houses, streets, miles of pavements, piledup bricks, stones. Changing hands. This owner, that. Landlord never dies they say. Other steps into his shoes when he gets his notice to quit. They buy the place up with gold and still they have all the gold. Swindle in it somewhere. Piled up in cities, worn away age after age. Pyramids in sand. Built on bread and onions. Slaves. Chinese wall. Babylon. Big stones left. Round towers. Rest rubble, sprawling suburbs, jerrybuilt, Kerwan's mushroom houses, built of breeze. Shelter for the night.

No one is anything.

Joyce's originality in these parts of his work is remarkable. It is a necessary innovation if this way of seeing – fragmentary, miscellaneous, isolated – is to be actualized on the senses in a new structure of language.

The genius of *Ulysses* is that it dramatizes three forms of consciousness (and in this sense three characters) – Bloom, Stephen and Molly. Their interaction but also their lack of connection is the tension of composition of the city itself. For what each enacts for the other is a symbolic role, and the reality to which they may ultimately relate is no longer a place and a time, for all the anxious dating of that day in Dublin. It is an abstracted or more strictly an immanent pattern of man and woman, father and son; a family but not a family, out of touch and searching for each other through a myth and a history. The history is not in this city but in the loss of a city, the loss of relationships. The only knowable community is in the need, the desire, of the racing and separated forms of consciousness.

Yet what must also be said, as we see this new structure, is that the most deeply known human community is language itself. It is a paradox that in *Ulysses*, through its patterns of loss and frustration, there is not only search but discovery: of an ordinary language, heard more clearly than anywhere in the realist novel before it; a positive flow of that wider human speech which had been screened and strained by the prevailing social conventions: conventions of separation and reduction, in the actual history. The greatness of *Ulysses* is this community of speech. That is its difference from *Finnegans Wake* in which a single voice – a voice offering to speak for everyone and everything. 'Here Comes Everybody' – carries the dissolution to a change of quality in which the strains already evident in the later sections of *Ulysses* (before the last monologue) have increased so greatly that the interchange of voices – public and private, the voices of a city heard and overheard – has given way to a surrogate, a universal isolated language. Where *Ulysses* was the climax, *Finnegans Wake* is the crisis of the development we have been tracing: of the novel and the city; the novel of 'acting, thinking, speaking' man.

But this development has another significance. It takes us back to Hardy's observation of London, where

each individual is conscious of *himself*, but nobody conscious of themselves collectively.

The intense self-consciousness, the perceptual subjectivity, was, as we have seen, very powerfully developed, as a literary mode. It relates, directly, not only to what is called 'stream of consciousness' or 'internal monologue', but also to that modernist version of 'symbolism' in which the isolation and projection of significant objects is a consequence of the separated subjectivity of the observer. These processes compose a powerful response to what is known, even conventionally, as city experience, but even when they are held at what appear directly aesthetic levels they are profoundly related to underlying models of life and society;

quite as clearly, in the end, as when they explicitly overlap with ideological versions of an essential isolation, alienation, loss of community. It is then ironic that most modern versions of the rural past have been conventional and subsidiary elements of just these methods and ideologies: rhetorical projections of connection or community or belief.

Yet there is another kind of development, which relates more to Joyce. Given the facts of isolation, of an apparently impassable subjectivity, a 'collective consciousness' reappears, but in an altered form. This is the 'collective consciousness' of the myth, the archetype; the 'collective unconscious' of Jung. In and through the intense subjectivities a metaphysical or psychological 'community' is assumed, and characteristically, if only in abstract structures, it is universal; the middle terms of actual societies are excluded as ephemeral, superficial, or at best contingent and secondary. Thus a loss of social recognition and consciousness is in a way made into a virtue: as a condition of understanding and insight. A direct connection is then forged between intense subjectivity and a timeless reality: one is a means to the other and alternative terms are no more than distractions. The historically variable problem of 'the individual and society' acquires a sharp and particular definition, in that 'society' becomes an abstraction, and the collective flows only through the most inward channels. Not only the ordinary experiences of apparent isolation, but a whole range of techniques of self-isolation, are then gathered to sustain the paradoxical experience of an ultimate collectivity which is beyond and above community. Social versions of community are seen as variants of the 'myth' – the encoded meaning – which in one or other of its forms is the only accessible collective consciousness. There is a language of the mind – often, more strictly, of the body – and there is this assumed universal language. Between them, as things, as signs, as material, as agents, are cities, towns, villages: actual human societies.

In the twentieth century there has been a deep and confused and unfinished conflict between this reappearance of the collective, in its metaphysical and psychological forms, and that other response, also within the cities, which in new institutions and in new social ideas and movements offered to create what Hardy and others had seen as lacking: a collective consciousness which could see not only individuals but also their altered and altering relationships, and in seeing the relationships and their social causes find social means of change.

Out of the cities, in fact, came these two great and transforming modern ideas: myth, in its variable forms; revolution, in its variable forms. Each, under pressure, offers to convert the other to its own terms. But they are better seen as alternative responses, for in a thousand cities, if in confused forms, they are in sharp, direct and necessary conflict.

Rural Britain was subsidiary, and knew that it was subsidiary, from the late nineteenth century. But so much of the past of the country, its feelings and its literature, was involved with rural experience and so many of its ideas of how to live well, from the style of the country-house to the simplicity of the cottage, persisted and even were strengthened, that there is almost an inverse proportion, in the twentieth century, between the relative importance of the working rural economy and the cultural importance of rural ideas. This has had its effect on the ways in which the ideas have been expressed and developed, but it is a complex effect, with both positive and negative results.

Three main lines can be traced, and each of them is complex. There is an important persistence and development of what came to be called the 'regional' novel, with some of its roots in George Eliot and Hardy but with a significant limitation of scope. This is complicated, as we shall see, by a persistence and degeneration of the 'country-house novel'. Then there is a development, perhaps originating in Meredith, of feelings about the earth and about natural growth, which in one mode continues forms of landscape description and nature poetry, in the green language of Clare, but in another mode is an imagery of human relationships and especially of love and desire. Third, and overlapping with natural description, there is an important development of memoirs, observations, accounts of rural life: many of them pervaded by a sense of the vanishing past and in this sense developing towards the collection of lore, even folklore; but others centred on the uses and abuses of land, on relations with a threatened natural world, and on the conditions of a human environment. No simple judgements are possible, along any of these lines. Indeed many of the problems arise from the fact that true and false feelings, true and false ideas, true and false histories, lie so closely together, often within the same work.

One unambiguously decadent form can be described at once. It is already clear in the country-house world of *Daniel Deronda* that a new and weak form is emerging: the country-house not of land but of capital. To put it this way is not to idealize the earlier country-houses; we have seen too much of their reality for that. But there is an obvious change in, for example, the country-houses of Henry James, which have become the house-parties of a metropolitan and international social round, the stage-settings of a more general social drama. And it is not James who forces the difference; the life he saw, often critically, was there. Its determining dimension is now not land but money; houses, parks and furniture are explicitly objects of consumption and exchange. People bargain, exploit and use each other, with these houses as the shells of their ambition and intrigue. Money from elsewhere is an explicit and dominant theme. Social cultivation, still linked in Jane Austen with the general process of improvement, is now a complicated process that flows from a wider society. Detached capital, detached income, detached consumption, detached social intercourse inhabit and vacate, visit and leave, these incidentally surviving and converted houses. An internal capitalization, consumption, and indifference to real neighbours has become external and mobile, accentuating all its inherent vices. The houses are places where events prepared elsewhere, continued elsewhere, transiently and intricately occur.

It has been said that James did not know or understand the best country-house England, but it seems to me that he knew it all too well. For the shell, the façade, of a quite different way of living, was now the reality. It was possible, of course, to seal off the shell, to concentrate, meticulously, on its internal involutions, as in Ivy Compton-Burnett and some other successors. But more commonly the façade has been presented with an increasing grossness, and James's moral anxieties have been reduced to a mechanical transience and intricacy. Anyone who wanted to isolate human relationships now had this conventionally isolating and theatrical scene in which to perform. There have been some ludicrous examples, in novels offering themselves as serious, into our own generation. There have also been a few consciously reactionary idealizations of this supposed class and its way of life, as in Evelyn Waugh.

But the true fate of the country-house novel was its evolution into the middle-class detective story. It was in its very quality of abstraction, and yet of superficially impressive survival, that the country-house could be made the place of isolated assembly of a group of people whose immediate and transient relations were decipherable by an abstract mode of detection rather than by the full and connected analysis of any more general understanding. Sometimes the formula is merely instrumental, as in Agatha Christie and others. Sometimes, as in Dorothy Sayers, it is combined with middle-class fantasies about the human nature of the traditional inhabitants. But tradition, elsewhere, is reduced to old architecture, old trees and the occasional ghost. It seems to me very fitting that a mode of analysis of human relationships which came out of Baker Street, out of the fogs of the transient city, should find a temporary resting-place in this façade way of life, before it returned eventually to its true place in the streets. For the country-house, while it retained its emotional hold, was indeed a proper setting for an opaqueness that can be penetrated in only a single dimension: all real questions of social and personal relationship left aside except in their capacity to instigate an instrumental deciphering. In very recent times it had been leased again as a centre for criminal planning or espionage or the secret police. But the point is that the country-house, in the twentieth century, has just this quality of abstract disposability and indifference of function. The real houses can be anything from schools and colleges and hospitals to business retreats, estate offices and subsidized museums. In the same way, emotionally, they can be the centres of isolated power, graft or intrigue, or what are called the 'status symbols' – meaning the abstractions – of success, power and money which are founded elsewhere but left conveniently out of sight. It is not a sad end; it is a fitting end. The essential features were always there, and much of the history that changed them came out of them, in their original and continuing domination and alienation.

Meredith's country-houses are already precarious: the traditional image interacting with a growing admission of confusion and guilt. Meredith's genuine radicalism started and stopped within that dimension. But on its edges there developed a more interesting phenomenon: a version of the virtues of the 'common people'. This was from the beginning ambiguous, as it had been in parts of George Eliot. Meredith was much influenced by one of the worst things she wrote: an essay of 1856 called *The Natural History of German Life*, which has been significantly revived in some recent description of 'the peasant' which has had an interesting progeny.

> Custom with him holds the place of sentiment, of theory, and in many cases of affection . . . The peasant never questions the obligation of family ties – he questions no custom – but tender affection, as it exists among the refined part of mankind, is almost as foreign to him as white hands and filbert-shaped nails.

Her uncritical transition from Germany to England, where there were no 'peasants', is notable enough. But what is more important is that within the fastidious phrases a stock figure can be seen as emerging, and we have been hearing his grunts ever since. Honest grunts though; that is usually the point. He is not the simple natural figure of Wordsworth; he is something that is about to be called elemental. Rough land, rough grappling with nature, rough feelings, rough honesty. He can still be looked down the nose at, as Maugham looked at Hardy: 'an earthy face . . . a strange look of the soil'. But he has, whether he knows it or not, a romantic destiny. What are white hands and filbert-shaped nails against these strong sunburned arms, this lean weatherbeaten face, this intimate acquaintance with the streams of passionate growth in bulls and in wheat?

Meredith in his novels sticks mainly to the limitations; the countryman is hard, stubborn, enduring, confined. But the virtues of Earth, in the new fertile sense, were about to break through. If you read *Rhoda Fleming* you can already see the outlines of many later novels, but if you read the poems you can hear the new rhythm itself:

> Teach me to feel myself the tree
> And not the withered leaf.
> Fixed am I and await the dark-to-be.

And O, green bounteous Earth!
Bacchante Mother! stern to those
Who live not in thy heart of mirth;
Death shall I shrink from, loving thee? . . .
. . . Earth knows no desolation
She smells regeneration
In the moist breath of decay.

That is *Ode to the Spirit of Earth in Autumn*. It can be traced,
like so much else, to Wordsworth and the early Romantic
movement, yet it is becoming a new and more suggestive action,
as significantly in *Modern Love*:

But in the largeness of the evening earth
Our spirits grew as we went side by side.
The hour became her husband and my bride.

Or in his collection *A Reading of Earth*:

She winnows, winnows roughly; sifts
To dip her chosen in her source.

We can see what Charles Sorley meant when he said, looking
back from 1912:

Tennyson is most pre-eminently paltry and superficial when he
sings about nature and earth. He was not long in hedging her in with
the shapely corsets of alliterative verbiage. Meredith was the first to
break through this barrier and discover her in her truth.

This now conscious intercourse with the Earth became, in its
fusion of agricultural and sexual imagery (see Lawrence's
descriptions of ploughing and milking in the first chapter of
The Rainbow) a dominant mode; dominant also in the special
sense that the imagery is male, to the female Earth. The emotional basis for the rough peasant lover, the deep passions of this
life of the soil, is to be found here but is only one of its figures.

For there was also a projection into observed country figures,
and this was sharpened by a received contrast with the frenzied
materialism of the cities. It is a long way from the simplicity of
Wordsworth's observed pastoral figures to Meredith's:

A revelation came on Jane,
The widow of a labouring swain:
And first her body trembled sharp,
Then all the woman was a harp

301

> With winds along the strings; she heard
> Though there was neither tone nor word.

But this silent physicality, a release of 'elemental' energy against the frustrations of a mechanical civilization, touched a deep chord in a confused imagination. There was the simple physical act, the pulsing life of the earth, and then, equally available, there was the naked relapse, the soothing merging:

> Imbedded in a land of greed,
> Of Mammon-quakings dire as Earth's,
> My care was but to soothe my need;
> At peace among the littleworths.

A working country, that is to say, was becoming, yet again but in a new way, a place of physical and spiritual regeneration. It was now the teeming life of an isolated nature, or the seasonal rhythm of the fundamental life processes. Neither of these feelings was new in itself. What was new was their fusion into a structure of feeling in which the earth and its creatures – animals and peasants almost alike – were an affirmation of vitality and of the possibility of rest in conscious contrast with the mechanical order, the artificial routines, of the cities. At its strongest this was a socially adapted pantheism. At its strangest it was a displacement of sexual feeling, in the awkward course of the Victorian liberation: a transitional imagery, in which sex was ploughing, a bed of bluebells was a breast: neither activity quite stated, neither feature quite seen; the intensity part of their confused secret. Yet if you turned to doubt, there was the cold sick nerve of money and the city; property and repression and ugliness; the frustration of worldly conventions and routines.

What came to be called the regional novel is not only this, though there is a significant and persistent undercurrent of the rural-sexual metaphor: in Lawrence, evidently; in T. F. Powys, though his fables belong to a more ironically observing dimension; in a whole series of novels of passions submerged in landscapes; and in a lively tradition of anecdotes of rural bawdy. Lawrence and Powys had wider interests, but in the more obvious forms there is in effect a dissolution and then an exploitation of a nineteenth-century achievement. Some of the more vulnerable examples came to the obvious parody of *Cold*

Comfort Farm, but what has to be said about that odd work is not easy. The excessive gestures of some of the regional novels led straight to this kind of satire, but what is also drawn on, in it, is a suburban uneasiness, a tension of attraction and repulsion, a brittle wit which is a kind of evasion by caricature. *Cold Comfort Farm* is usually referred to an indeterminate group of works by women novelists – Mary Webb and Sheila Kaye-Smith are among the obvious names – but it ought really to be read side-by-side with, say, *Wuthering Heights*, *Adam Bede*, *Tess of the D'Urbervilles*. For it is easy to miss what has happened by comparing symptom with symptom – romance with parody – instead of looking into the causes of the shared loss of reality.

In part it is simply the loss of a credible common world. The degree of isolation which is actual in the nineteenth-century novels can easily become, in their apparent successors, factitious. *Wuthering Heights* would not be as it is, in its real tension, if there were only the Heights and not the Grange. George Eliot and Hardy, with the difficulties we have seen, admitted and explored the tension of an increasingly intricate and interlocking society: not only the changes of urbanism and industrialism, but the new social mobility and the ideas and education of an extending culture. At its weakest, in what should be seen as a defensive reflex, the 'regional' novel, in excluding all but its region, excluded not only other places but these deep social and human forces which were explicitly active within it. There was a sustaining flight to the edges of the island, to Cornwall or to Cumberland, where this might seem more plausible. But just as Powys's Dorset, almost two generations after Hardy, is a deliberately imagined abstraction further back in time, out of time, than anything Hardy described, so, in these more carefully and often passionately observed landscapes there is an exclusion of what, to sustain the natural metaphor and the contrast with the cities, has to be seen as alien. Where it is explicitly included, as in Francis Brett-Young, it is only as a starting-point, a base from which to explore the unspoiled; compare *Mr Lucton's Freedom*. The loved places are the 'unspoiled' places, and no group agrees with this more readily than those who lived in the 'spoiled'.

At times this is innocent, at least in intention; in a way the more complete the imaginative exclusion the more convincing the simple concentration. But there is in some cases a very different undercurrent: socially very similar to some elements of the reception of evacuated children from the bombed cities in the Second War. Townspeople are seen, under this spell of pastures, as louts and brats: not only in the obvious forms of litter and damage and noise, but also in the deeper social forms of a hatred of the mob, of the unions, of the subverters of 'Old England'. This would be more negotiable if within the rural mode the exclusion of real changes, moving in and beside the same pastures, were not so complete. But rural life had to do service as more than an image of natural passions. It became the pretty seat, also, of unconscious reaction, and then, with a harsher edge, of that conscious reaction which was either a militant resident Toryism, or, in one or two significant cases, an approach to and association with fascism.

The surviving rural England deserved much better than that. On the whole it didn't get it in novels, though to see the regional novel at its best we can read Constance Holme, and find in *The Lonely Plough* a significant tension between the mode she describes as 'the green gates of vision' – an authentic but specialized survival of the green language of Clare – and a rather sharp, placing, informed observation of people and events which though its objects are rural belongs in vision and tone to another social world: the language of the middle-class observer.

But description of country places and people found its most successful mode in journals and memoirs. When we read W. H. Hudson, in *A Shepherd's Life* or *Far Away and Long Ago*, we find a strong and genuine simplicity and intensity of vision, which is always modulated by thought. As we read the earth imagery of Meredith and Forster and Lawrence, or the simple animism of some of the Georgians, we can do no better than re-read Hudson's chapter on 'A Boy's Animism' in *Far Away and Long Ago*, where the strength of the impulse, vulnerable as it always is to a strained urban wit, is so convincingly recorded, reconsidered, modestly weighed, that instead of uncritical surrender, or uncritical rejection and parody, we find ourselves making connections with experiences which many of us have had and can recall: experiences that need to be described and looked at with Hudson's kind of sense.

This is the right way also to re-read the Georgians. There is so much there that is vulnerable, but the critical definition needs to be made with great care. There are the obvious and memorable weaknesses, in the mode we have seen taking its form in Meredith. In Abercrombie, for example:

> As an unheeded bramble's reach she crost
> Her breast a spiny sinew did accost
> With eager thorns, tearing her dress to seize
> And harm her hidden white virginities.

The larger gestures of the bramble as guilt, or of the sky, as 'the great blue ceremony', are even more significant. It is what happens in John Drinkwater's *Moonlit Apples* when the apples laid in rows at the top of the house become with a certain inevitability the 'moonlit apples of dreams' and

> on orchard boughs
> They keep tryst with the moon.

It is a specific conjunction of the homely and colloquial with a kind of weak-willed fantasy. Intense observation of people and objects dissolves, without transition, into forms of fancy which in the end, indeed, are more historically significant. But it is best to look at this in the strongest part of the movement: in Edward Thomas, for example.

In his work to get his living Thomas continued, with certain changes, some of Jefferies's modes of observation (though in a less specifically working country). He understood the mode of Cobbett, though he connected more directly with the world of Stevenson and Borrow that goes back, in its simplest forms, to Gilpin. That amalgam of contradictory impulses which, held briefly in time, is the true Georgian mode is very clearly there in the prose.

> Though nearly seventy, he is staunch and straight, and spending most of his day on horseback, with his calm, large-featured, sandstone face . . .

This is developed observation; only 'staunch' is pulling the other way. But before the end of the sentence this farmer:

... suggests the thought of a Centaur ... Thirty centuries ago such a man, so marvellously in harmony with the earth, would have gone down in men's memories as a demi-god or the best-loved of the fauns ... His jesting bathes the room or the lane in the light of a Golden Age ...

Except (or is it except?) that he:

then turns without a sigh and, drawing a long draught of cider in the cool granary, drinks deep. He rises early and yet is as cheerful when he goes first afield as when he goes to bed.

And this, from *The Heart of England*, is the heart of the Georgian problem. The observation is so often clear and intense, but as the mode forms there is an inrush of alien imagery: that set of ideas about the 'rural' and the 'pastoral', filtered through a version of the classical tradition, which is so unlike any classical rural literature but which in the first decades of the century (with some surviving extensions to our own time) was a deep if conventional intellectual conviction: an eyeglass that was lifted, deliberately and proudly, to the honestly observing eye. Fauns, Pan, centaurs, the Golden Age, shepherds, Lycidas, swain, tryst, staunch peasants, churches, immemorial history, demi-gods, presences, the timeless rhythm of the seasons. If it had not been lived, in a discoverable development, it would be impossible to deduce this extraordinary collocation. 'Back to the Land', some of the critics of industrialism had been saying. But when the Georgian poets settled near Ledbury, and started *New Numbers*, it was something else: a flight from the cities, certainly; an honest appreciation of the beauty and rest of the country; a respect for labour. There had been the significant case of Edward Carpenter: the sensitive man who gave up privilege and a routine intellectualism for simplicity and connection with an ordinary life: a feeling for plainness, a feeling for the spirit; a feeling for democracy and socialism and popular education, which must be taken to the poor; a feeling for sexual freedom and in the same movement a displaced sexuality of nature.

Such men *came to* the country: that is the critical point. The nerves were already strained, the minds already formed. Jonson had seen Dryads in the woods of Kent, but in a conventional, unstrained form. These new men were strained; that was why they had gone. And the impulse connected and connects with the lives of so many others: the real experience of what was being shunned. If they could have gone and only looked, as at times happened, it would have been a different mode. But they had brought with them from the cities, and from the schools and universities, a version of rural history which was now extraordinarily amalgamated with a distantly translated literary interpretation. The honest past, the pagan spirit: it was not only in the Georgians, it was in two or three generations of literary intellectuals and observers that this knot was tied. And this would not have mattered so much, could not have been so persistent through many different men and modes, if it had not caught up in this only widely available literature what was seen, in and through and past this version, of a still present and working rural England.

The countryman is dying out, and when we hear his voice, as in George Bourne's *Bettesworth Book*, it is more foreign than French.

That sad and repeated note is significant because of the reference to books like Bourne's, detailed records for others. The real country population was indeed a minority; the place of agriculture had become marginal. But this other elegiac, neo-pastoral mode was set; this is what writers said to each other, or critics said to each other, quoting out of books like Bourne's.

When *New Numbers* was being started, in the cottages around Ledbury, my family on my mother's side were working on farms there, and I have heard many of them talk. It was not, to me, 'more foreign than French', and it was not at all foreign within that actual and working rural community. It was not, come to that, anything like as foreign as centaurs and the Golden Age. But while some overheard it as the locals or yokels talking, these poets overheard it – even sometimes heard rather than overheard – in a spirit of respect, almost reverence, which was then at once qualified by a massive historical regret: the loss of the fine old times. The times were getting better, my family always said: the old days were the bad days; the villages, now, were less oppressive and less deprived; there was the vote, there were the trains, there were the schools. Perhaps they were wrong;

some things were outside their experience. But they were not and are not figures of decline. The crisis of rural Britain, which indeed they lived through in its actual consequences, was not this crisis that had been projected from the cities and the universities. It was a crisis of wages, conditions, prices; of the use of land and work on the land. This was of course overheard, as complaint or grumbling, often finding sympathy. But it was in a different dimension from the loss of the Dryads, or from finding them either. The fact is – and it is a real loss both ways – they spoke mainly among themselves, and the Georgian observers, travelling and overhearing, spoke mainly among *themselves*; that was the kind of society it was.

The historical stereotype left many literary signs. I think, for example, of Edward Thomas's *Lob*. Here, characteristically, the poet sees:

> An old man's face, by life and weather cut
> And coloured – rough, brown, sweet as any nut

but loses contact. Trying to find the man again, asking among those who might have known 'my ancient', he is eventually told, by a squire's son, of an old figure:

> ... English as this gate, these flowers, this mire,

who has given the flowers their local names, who invented the local sayings, who died at Waterloo, Hastings, Agincourt, Sedgemoor, and who has borne all the country names from Robin Hood and Jack Cade to Lob-lie-by-the-fire. This is a shift, it is true, from Arnold's Scholar Gipsy – the wandering intellectual – but to no less an intellectual projection: a version of history which succeeds in cancelling history. All countrymen, of all conditions and periods, are merged into a singular legendary figure. The varied idioms of specific country communities – the flowers, for example, have many local names – are reduced not only to one 'country' idiom but to a legendary, timeless inventor, who is more readily seen than any actual people. And this is the point at which the Georgian imagination broke down: the respect of authentic observation overcome by a sub-intellectual fantasy: a working man becoming 'my ancient' and then the casual figure of a dream of England, in which rural labour and rural revolt, foreign wars and internal dynastic wars, history, legend and literature, are indiscriminately enfolded into a single emotional gesture. Lob or Lud, immemorial peasant or yeoman or labourer: the figure was now fixed and its name was Old England. The self-regarding patriotism of the high English imperialist period found this sweetest and most insidious of its forms in a version of the rural past.

It is crucially different from, say, Hardy:

> Only thin smoke without flame
> From the heaps of couch-grass;
> Yet this will go onward the same
> Though dynasties pass.

That is the feeling of the persistence of land work through what seem the distant accidents of political history. But the Georgian version used rural England as an image for its own internal feelings and ideas.

There was much of this oblique elaboration in the period, from many seemingly different sources. There was that uncritical, abstracting literary anthropology, within which folktales and legends became part of an unlocalized, unhistorical past; or the uncritical interest in myth, which made the land and the people a scene and characters into which anything could be projected, with or without the inclusion of scraps of a classical education. There was an extraordinary development of country-based fantasy, from Barrie and Kenneth Grahame through J. C. Powys and T. H. White and now to Tolkien. There was the abstract and limiting definition of 'folksong', which in Cecil Sharp was based on the full rural myth of the 'remnants' of the 'peasantry', and which specifically excluded, as not of the 'folk', the persistent songs of the industrial and urban working people, who did not fit the image but who were continuing to create, in an authentic popular culture, what it suited this period and this class to pretend was a lost world. It is then not only that the real land and its people were falsified; a traditional and surviving rural England was scribbled over and almost hidden from sight by what is really a suburban and half-educated scrawl.

That is the damage which can never be forgotten. But it is ironic that some of it was done by men who did look and learn in rural England, and who, like Edward Thomas, had so much genuine feeling in them. Thomas said himself of the first *Georgian Anthology*:

It shows much beauty, strength and mystery, and some magic – much aspiration, less defiance, no revolt – and it brings out with great cleverness many sides of the modern love of the simple and primitive, as seen in children, peasants, savages, early men, animals and Nature in general.

It could hardly be put in a more double-edged way than that. Yet the mood of *Lob* was not isolated; we can even see it in formation. The town boy is taken to the country and sees a woman in a market-cart:

She with her cheerful and shrewd slow way was as strange and attractive as any poet's or romancer's woman became afterwards, as far away from my world.

Watching and taking part in work, he sees, in his wife's words:

the slow experienced labourers, whose knowledge had come to them as the acorns come to the oaks, whose skill had come as the swallows' skill, who are satisfied in their hard life as are the oaks and swallows in theirs.

Thus real respect grew into a form of praise which excluded human learning and which reduced the labourers from human to 'natural' status. Again, later on his travels, he observed:

The mower, the man hoeing his onion-bed ... these the very loneliness of the road has prepared us for turning into creatures of dream ... They are no more real than the men and women of pastoral ... The most credible inhabitants are Mertilla, Florimel, Corin, Amaryllis, Dorilus, Doron, Daphnis, Silvia and Aminta, and shepherds singing to their flocks ...

If this were all, we could forget it. But a more actual response is included:

> The steep farm roof,
> With tiles duskily glowing ...

– a feeling of peace and settlement which again, as if inevitably, is caught back into the stereotype:

> since
> This England, Old already, was called Merry.

The interest again and again in the poems is the way in which a thing seen is captured by these external preconceptions:

> They have taken the gable from the roof of clay
> On the long swede pile. They have let in the sun
> To the white and gold and purple of curled fronds
> Unsunned.

But even while this is seen and remembered it is compared to going down into an Egyptian tomb, where '. . . dreamless long-dead Amen-hotep lies'. A modern critic has said, apparently as praise, that 'the unobtrusive signs accumulate, and finally one is aware that the outward scene is accessory to an inner theatre'. Accessory indeed, for what has really to be said is that the observed details are again and again convincing, and that it is the conventions of the 'inner theatre' that come near to destroying them. Thomas put down in his notebook:

Grass of the rising aftermath or 'lattermath'/beautifully green after a quickening rain . . .

By the time of the poem this is in doubtful parenthesis:

> Drenched perfect green again. 'The lattermath
> Will be a fine one.' So the stranger said,
> A wandering man. Albeit I stood at rest
> Flushed with desire I was.

There is a more successful example of the same process of development, from a diary note on 'old man's beard' to the poem *Old Man* where the plant becomes memory and loss. The 'inner theatre' was stuffed with old tales and costumes, but observation and feeling kept struggling through it: in *The Source*; in *Hay-making*, so finely observed and described, the picture of a world out of time –

> older than Clare and Cobbett, Morland and Crome

– a reference that comes with a familiar inevitability but that is now seen and known as an aspiration, the real aspiration: 'All of us gone out of the reach of change'. The feeling is there again in *As the Team's Head-Brass*: a finely observed land; the scraps of convincing talk:

                    and for the last time
          I watched the clods crumble and topple over
          After the ploughshare and the stumbling team.

'Last' because Thomas has to go back to the war; the experience
that imprinted this memory of ordinary labour and peace.

   In *February Afternoon*, listening to the starlings, his feelings
are in tension between this sense of timelessness –

                    Men heard this roar ...
                    A thousand years ago even as now

– and the sense of war in which, in a different sense 'Time swims
before me'. Past the conventional props and allusions there is a
deeper sense of loss, as in *I never saw that land before*: the
imagined and the real country –

                    The cattle, the grass, the bare ash-trees ...
                    ... The blackthorns down along the brook
                    With wounds yellow as crocuses
                    Where yesterday the labourer's hook
                    Had sliced them cleanly

– and in and through them the real uncertainty:

                    I neither expected anything
                    Nor yet remembered; but some goal
                    I touched then ...

There is a sense of being driven back to a hidden language, 'a
language not to be betrayed', an inexpressible alienation. This
deeper and more complicated feeling is there, finally, in *For
These*, where the conventional images of the Georgian retreat:
'an acre of land between the shore and the hills', the house, the
garden – are rehearsed yet in the end rejected:

                    For these I ask not, but, neither too late
                    Nor yet too early, for what men call content,
                    And also that something may be sent
                    To be contented with I ask of fate.

That, at the limit, is the harder and more necessary aspiration.
   The underlying pattern is then clear. A critique of a whole
dimension of modern life, and with it many necessary general
questions, was expressed but also reduced to a convention, which

took the form of a detailed version of a part-imagined, part-observed rural England. It is a convention that has since held the shape of many lives. All through our own century we have had country writing that moves, at times grossly, at times imperceptibly, from record to convention and back again, until these seem inextricable. This is so even in what seem the plainest kind: the memoirs and journals. To read George Bourne is to read this fusion of detailed record, as in *The Wheelwright's Shop* with its notation of a craft, and a conventionally foreshortened version of history, as in *Change in the Village*. There are some irreplaceable records, like Flora Thompson's *Lark Rise to Candleford* and Ronald Blythe's recent *Akenfield*. These are more limited personal accounts, like Adrian Bell's *Corduroy*, *Silver Ley* and *Cherry Tree*. But then, one part record, two parts ideology, there are the conventional books of which Massingham's *The English Countryman* is the readiest example. Very few country writers, in the twentieth century, have wholly escaped this strange formation in which observation, myth, record and half-history are so deeply entwined. One of the best recorders, George Ewart Evans, is the man from whose book I took the remark about the continuity from Virgil, and the irony of that is for me, in the end, deeply saddening. Writers I share so much with, in experience and memory, are in an instant of allusion, of a different way of seeing history, the strangers they ought not to be. And the full depth of the irony is that the real history, in all that we know of it, would support so much more of the real observation, the authentic feeling, that these writers keep alive.

The matter can be put to the test in a simple way. If we read any issue of that remarkable journal *The Countryman*, of which the circulation is in itself a significant index, we find, in a single convention, these different elements that have been bound together. It is impossible to read any issue without learning something about trees, birds, animals; not just natural history either, but many of the real processes of work. Yet bound in with these is a very different game: a middle-class notation of quaint old countrymen's sayings, in that conventionally strangled mummerset orthography: the natives overheard. Who then are the countrymen, within the convention? Employers of labour, hirers of servants, observers of badgers, growers of fruit. It is of course a class formation; a class that almost captured the idea of the country. An anthology, *The Countryman Book*, is the most perfect record I know of what country writing, within this convention, has been made to become: the fine observation and record; the out-of-doors reminiscences of Prime Ministers; the community histories; the old recipes; the stories of witches and superstitions; authors' country cottages; comic rustic sayings; fine photographs and drawings. Faced with this extraordinary amalgam, we might be tempted to give up. A country, finally, would have been absorbed by a class: all the real things going in with it.

But that is not quite the whole story. There were other voices. Alfred Williams of Swindon wrote about the country while working in a railway depot. The connections he made were more actual and more general, and he observed of 'dialect':

> Townspeople do not speak it but like to read it ... villagers speak it but do not like to read it.

More significantly, and by great good fortune, we have the autobiography of a modern farm labourer: Fred Kitchen's *Brother to the Ox* (1939). Even that is prefaced, at the publisher's request, by an absurd commendatory letter from the Duke of Portland, in the manner of the old patronage of the peasant poets. But Fred Kitchen can write for himself. What is most remarkable, to anyone who has been reading within the middle-class rural convention, is the plain record of all kinds of country work and country conditions, the authentic love of fields and living creatures, without any of the statutory gestures about the past or pastoral. Fred Kitchen lives in country cottages and speaks about them as most country people do, including the damp and the rats. He lives on a mining-village estate and gives a shrewd and positive account of modern urban community. He describes work on the railway and in a coking-factory; though he chooses farmwork again there is a felt continuity between the different kinds of labour, which the convention has obscured. And he sees the observers the other way round, like the parson who when told that Kitchen liked reading, questioned him but then told him, not very kindly, to read the classics; Kitchen searches a library for *The Classics* but has to go back to reading what he can pick up, including Dickens and George Eliot. Again when he touches the cultivated world he is in a position to observe:

Artists have drawn some pleasing pictures of the shepherd leading his flock on the grassy uplands, or gazing pensively at a setting sun, but we have no picture of the shepherd in the muddy turnip field; of him and his lad sliding about in the muddy sheep-pen with skeps of sliced turnips; or the lad, bending down to clean out the troughs, receiving a gallant charge in the rear from a too-playful tup . . . That then is the picture of the shepherd as I saw him; and though he had a shepherd-hut in the picture, it could only be used as a shelter at mealtimes.

In its real record, the hard days with the good days, the frustrations with the satisfactions, *Brother to the Ox* is the true voice of the surviving countryman; surviving in a mainly urban and industrial world and moving in and out of it with the real connections of labour and community. What is impressive is not only the absence of the myths, the allusions and the false history. It is the real sense of context: the ways in which men without land or money move from one job to another, in a changing economy; experiencing directly what is ordinarily abstracted even in the true history. This is the recognizable world of the intelligently observant twentieth-century worker, who is in this case a farm labourer for most but not all his working life. The miner, the cokeworker, the navvy stand beside him; shrewdly observed, without class preconceptions. And it is then significant that after years of reading on his own Fred Kitchen was encouraged to write in a class of the Workers Educational Association, which to serve all such men, in mine or factory or farm, had been begun, as it happened, in the towns.

Brother to the Ox, one of the very few direct and unmediated accounts of a rural labourer's life, had in this sense to wait for the twentieth century and for a different historical process. But that, after all, is how most working countrymen still see their history; from the unregretted hiring-fairs to which Kitchen went as a boy, to the Agricultural Wages Act and that continuing struggle to get a decent living from landwork for the majority with neither land nor capital. A particular history, meticulously observed, joins, as it must, with a common history.

It is easy to separate the country and the city and then their modes of literature: the rural or regional; the urban or metropolitan. The existence of just these separated modes, in the twentieth century, is significant in itself, as a way of responding to a connected history. But there are always some writers who insist on the connections, and among these are a few who see the transition itself as decisive, in a complex interaction and conflict of values.

It is useful, in this sense, to compare D. H. Lawrence and Lewis Grassic Gibbon. Lawrence's work is so much wider in range and so much better known that in some respects the comparison is difficult. But each writer gave himself, with particular intensity, to a version of the movement from country to city, and each, in active ways, was conscious of crisis: of a difficult borderland and of frontiers that had to be crossed.

Lawrence grew up in what he called 'a queer jumble of the old England and the new': the mining villages among farming country.

The life was a curious cross between industrialism and the old agricultural England of Shakespeare and Milton and Fielding and George Eliot.

It is interesting and characteristic that the 'old England' is seen through writers. But Lawrence lived on a border which was more than that between farms and mines. In his own development, which he writes again and again, he was on a cultural border. The choice was not only between mine and farm, but between both and the opening world of education and art. In this, directly, he is a successor of George Eliot and Hardy, but the crisis of mobility, and the history of which it is a part, are in the end very differently seen.

In *Sons and Lovers* the two landscapes, the two kinds of work, the two ways of life, are directly evoked, but within them the conflict is internal and subjective; it is a history of growing up and going away; of the struggle for identity and the capacity for relationship within the struggle of his parents and the world that frustrates them. The difficult and absorbing relationship with his mother is so close that in the end it overwhelms the more general condition that has also been evoked. In his next novel, *The Rainbow*, he begins with the general condition, but in a particular version which can never wholly be separated from what he had learned in his own family. He follows the Brangwen family through several generations to the familiar crisis, in Ursula, of education, relationship and identity. But the forms of this crisis throw their pressures back into the way the history is seen.

The opening chapter of *The Rainbow* is very moving to read, but if it is read with any consciousness of how the history had happened, and of earlier responses to it, it is at once original and surprising. There is the famous invocation of natural life in the farming generations:

Heaven and earth was teeming around them, and how should this cease? ... They knew the intercourse between heaven and earth, sunshine drawn into the breast and bowels, the rain sucked up in the daytime, nakedness that comes under the wind in autumn ... Their life and inter-relations were such: feeling the pulse and body of the soil, that opened to the furrow for the grain and became smooth and supple after their ploughing, and clung to their feet with a weight that pulled like desire ... They mounted their horses, and held life between the grip of their knees ...

This mode will be recognized. It is the sexual imagery of the earth and of working the land which runs from Meredith through the regional novelist, But, more particularly, it is male sexual imagery, and this is decisive in the version of the history.

It was enough for the men, that the earth heaved and opened its furrows to them ... But the woman wanted another form of life than this, something that was not blood-intimacy ... She stood to see the far-off world of cities and governments and the active scope of man ...

She faced outwards to where men moved dominant and creative, having turned their back on the pulsing heat of creation.

Thus the farming life is already a metaphor, but a metaphor given historical standing, for a particular kind of being: active, physical, unconscious: the body as opposed to the mind; inseparable from the processes of nature. Other men have changed this kind of living, to the 'world of cities and governments', 'to enlarge their own scope and range and freedom'. Looking out from what she sees as a limited natural environment, the woman encourages her children to education:

It was this, this education, this higher form of being, that the mother wished to give to her children, so that they too could live the supreme life on earth.

But this feeling is already entangled with class: the lives of the vicar and the curate, the squire's lady, which the woman sees as superior:

Her children, at least the children of her heart, had the complete nature that should take place in equality with the living, vital people in the land, not be left behind obscure among the labourers.

This is presented in the apparent form of an historical narrative, though it is difficult not to see it as a projection of the mother's attitudes as Lawrence had directly described them in *Sons and Lovers*. But what is more interesting is that so many of the real tensions of the history are creatively reworked into this particular form. Vitality is seen in both directions at once; in the unreflecting life of active physical work, and in the exploring mind. The call to that exploration is irresistible, but following it leads through a wasteland of ugliness and emptiness: the industrial system and its mechanical habits of mind. What will eventually replace that is a new kind of living, breaking from within this harsh, disintegrated and alienated world:

new, clean naked bodies would issue to a new germination, to a new growth.

Yet what Lawrence has to say can never be reduced to an argument. An historical scheme is important to him, and in various forms is continually reintroduced, but what he has mainly to say is about life and death in relationships, with social and historical forces present but reworked into forms of life and death. Consistently, however, industrialism and its forms of property and possession are seen as the signs of death. Yet what is opposed to them is not, in the run of his work, a farming community; it is rather a primitivism, at times given some social or historical base, as in the Indians of New Mexico, but more often and more significantly accessible as a form of direct living in contact with natural processes – animals and birds and flowers and trees but also the human body, the naked exploration and relationship.

The apparently familiar reflex to the 'old agricultural England' must then be seen as, though present, a minor theme. It is the way the history conventionally came, but it is only a form, at times misleading, of his essentially different emphasis. This can best be seen if we look at what he has to say about the city:

The great city means beauty, dignity and a certain splendour. This is the side of the Englishman that has been thwarted and shockingly betrayed.

Or again:

We live in towns from choice, when we subscribe to our great civilized form. The nostalgia for the country is not *so* important. What is important is that our towns are *false* towns – every street a blow, every corner a stab.

And this must be set alongside his more conventional insistence:

The real tragedy of England, as I see it, is the tragedy of ugliness. The country is so lovely: the man-made England is so vile.

For it is not the town but the false town that is the symptom of ugliness, and the root of its falseness is the system and spirit of possessive individualism, which has

frustrated that instinct of community which would make us unite in pride and dignity in the bigger gesture of the citizen, not the cottager.

His praise of cities, his complaint that 'the English character has failed to develop the real *urban* side of a man, the civic side', is not confined to the Italian cities on which he often draws for examples. He says, even:

The new cities of America are much more genuine cities, in the Roman sense, than is London or Manchester.

And his indictment of English cities follows a familiar nineteenth-century mode:

Nottingham is a vast place sprawling towards a million, and it is nothing more than an amorphous agglomeration. There *is* no Nottingham, in the sense that there is Siena.

The conclusion is reconstruction:

Pull down my native village to the last brick. Plan a nucleus. Fix the focus. Make a handsome gesture of radiation from the focus. And then put up big buildings, handsome, that sweep to a civic centre.

It is significant that one of the periodicals in which this programme first appeared was the *Architectural Review*. But of course it is difficult to reconcile this constructive and urban emphasis with his deep and prolonged insistence on the recovery of natural physical contact and the simplest living processes. It is difficult to reconcile because this is not in the end an argument, a position; it is the creative record of so many impulses, in the contradictory pressures of the time. Lawrence saw almost everything with a passionate but tearing insistence. He was pulled, deeply, between a physical commitment, which he described more intensely and convincingly than anyone in his generation, and an intellectual commitment, which made him respond and reason in a critical world. There is the world of the flower, as he so often described it, but there is also the world of the cell under the microscope, giving a new insight into the deepest living processes. The social contradictions – unconscious being, conscious community – are intense and severe.

It can be said that he reduced these contradictions to an emphasis on the discovery of primary relationship, but in *Women in Love*, of which this is apparently most true, the pressures of other dimensions are still close and the discovery, as a result, is to the end problematical. *Lady Chatterley's Lover* is a necessary physical discovery, and this is linked with a rejection of the ugliness of the industrial town and a care for the direct tending of natural life. Yet the discovery is not the climax, and the problem is still how this flame of life can be kept burning, in a necessary working world. In a very later *Autobiographical Fragment*, he turned, in one of the modes of his period, to a dream of the future. He sees his native mining village transformed:

> I knew, even while I looked at it, that it was the place where I was born, the ugly colliery townlet of dirty red brick. Even as a child, coming home from Moorgreen, I had looked up and seen the squares of miners' dwellings, built by the Company, rising from the hill-top in the afternoon light like the walls of Jerusalem, and I had wished it were a golden city . . .

It is a vision much like that of Morris, in *News from Nowhere*, and significantly, contradictorily, to the end, it is a city but also an agricultural village: a physical emphasis, 'soft and golden like the golden flesh of a city'.

What Lawrence concentrated in his work was that unresolved complex of impulses and attachments of which, in the twentieth century, the relation of country and city, as states of mind and feeling, was the most evidently available form. If we go from reading him to reading Grassic Gibbon, in *A Scots Quair*, we find many resemblances but in the end one significant difference; indeed a difference that is crucial for the subsequent progress of just these ideas. What Lawrence again and again rejects, though the fact that he is continually drawn to consider it is equally significant, is the idea and the practice of social agencies of change. Where Lawrence hesitates, always, is between an idea of regeneration and an idea of revolution. He stresses the future much more than the past, and the change is to be absolute, root and branch. But he sees available revolutionary movements as simply fights about property; he wants a different vision, a new sense of life, before he commits himself; otherwise it will be not regeneration but a final collapse.

Grassic Gibbon's *Scots Quair* is a trilogy which moves through the classical historical process from country to city. It begins on a small upland farm and ends in the streets of the hunger marches. The first book, *Sunset Song*, is in its way a classic statement of what is seen as the dissolution of the peasantry. And it is significant that Grassic Gibbon saw the history through this idea. The long transformation of rural England, which had

earlier than anywhere else forced the dissolution of a true peasantry and replaced it with the rent-and-wage formations of a
capitalist agriculture, had left, on its edges, socially distinguishable areas: in Ireland, in parts of Scotland, in parts of Wales.
If we read the literature of Ireland and Scotland and Wales, into
the twentieth century, we find ways of life that are hardly
present in the English villages after the eighteenth-century
changes. But this difference can be exaggerated. It has as much to
do with a system of absentee and alien landlords, and with a
strongly surviving national and community sense, as with the
economic differences which are accentuated by the facts of
marginal land. What has never quite happened in any of these
countries, though in Scotland and Wales the penetration has been
greater (and extensive industrialization of parts of the countries
has brought its own changes), is the social integration, however
bitterly contested, of the English capitalist rural order. Different
versions of community have persisted longer, nourished by and
nourishing specific national feelings. It is not so much a peasantry; it is a subordinated and relatively isolated rural community,
which is conscious, in old and new ways, of its hard but independent life. To read the Irish and Welsh rural writers, over
the whole emotional range from the picturesque to the bitter, is
to find, in all its forms, creative and destructive, a spiritual self-
subsistence which much more than the actual system of ownership is the decisive social mode.

It is this, also, which Grassic Gibbon shows, in an agricultural
system which follows the familiar pattern of rents, leases and the
estates of the gentry. Indeed he begins with a history which
shows this standard evolution. But within it there is a different
social idea: that of 'the crofters dour folk of the old Pict stock',
and it is their spirit that survives in the small mixed-farmers on
coarse land. That version of a spiritual history, the effective
continuity from prehistoric times that is evoked in responses
to the standing stones, is emotionally dominant through the
tracing of a twentieth-century community that is seen as being
finished by the First World War. The bitter memories of the
clearances, the Highland laments, the legends of prehistory are
woven into a cloth that both covers and defies poverty. This is a
characteristic nationalist emphasis: a self-definition, for con-

temporary reasons, which draws on any elements, however improbable, that can be made to inhere in a particular land. It is successful here because it is created in a very specific and powerful prose, drawing on local rhythms and words. This creates a lively contemporary world, still spiritually self-subsistent, in the very process of absorbing familiar elements of the more dependent rural retrospect. Even the Golden Age is there:

The hunters had roamed these hills, naked and bright, in a Golden Age, without fear or hope or hate or love, living high in the race of the wind and the race of life.

It is what Lawrence had imagined and wanted to recreate, against what Grassic Gibbon calls 'all the dark, mad hopes'. But the strength of *Sunset Song* is not in that kind of gesture; it is the strength of the living people: Chae Strachan, Long Rob, Chris Guthrie. The demands of the war reach in and break the settlement, and the lament for 'the Last of the Peasants, the last of the Old Scots folk' is a way to mourn, when mourning has to be done.

But what is exciting is that in the subsequent move to borough and city the spiritual inheritance is seen as surviving, in the radically altered conditions. A new and predatory system has taken the people for its wars, displaced them from their land, but:

need we doubt which side the battle they would range themselves did they live today?

This is a decisively different structure of feeling. The spiritual feeling for the land and for labour, the 'pagan' emphasis which is always latent in the imagery of the earth (very similar, through its different rhythms, to the Lawrence of the beginning of *The Rainbow*), is made available and is stressed in the new struggles: through the General Strike, in the period of *Cloud Howe*, to the time of the hunger marches in the period of *Grey Granite*. Even the legends sustain the transition, for their spiritual emphasis makes it possible to reject a Church that has openly sided with property and oppression. More historically and more convincingly, the radical independence of the small farmers, the craftsmen and the labourers is seen as transitional to the militancy of the industrial workers. The shape of a whole history is then decisively transformed.

Chris Guthrie, the child of the land, sees change as fate, that 'might be stayed by none of the dreams of men'; only the land endures. But her son is a revolutionary: unidealized; the difficulties and the weaknesses faced, in a narrative that more clearly than in any other novel embodies the active labour movement of the thirties.

It is this transition that makes the interesting comparison with Lawrence, and with a wide area of the literature of rural loss and memory. For it is not only a question of rearranging an idea. It is a way of drawing attention to an actual phase of our history which has gone largely unrecorded but which is undoubtedly there, in the long transition. The displaced labourers and craftsmen and small farmers did not learn radicalism when they came to the cities. They learned, in altering conditions, new kinds of organization, new directing ideas, which confirmed and extended a long spirit of bitterness, independence, and aspiration.

It is a critical divergence in the tradition as a whole. The men and women who came from the country to the cities did not need to be told what they had lost, any more than they needed to be told what they might struggle to gain in their new world. But then it mattered very much whether an experience of the country – in its whole reality, from a love of the land and its natural pleasures to the imposed pains of deprivation, heavy and low-paid labour, loss of work and a place–was ranged for or against them, as they struggled to readjust. A selection of the experience – the view of the landlord or the resident, the 'pastoral' or the 'traditional' descriptions – was in fact made and used, as an abstract idea, against their children and their children's children: against democracy, against education, against the labour movement. In this particular modern form, the rural retrospect became explicitly reactionary, and given the break of continuity there have been very few voices on the other side. That is why Grassic Gibbon is especially important, since he speaks for many who never got to speak for themselves in recorded ways.

This suggests also, as we look back at Lawrence, the relevant question: important just because of his genius. With the simple rural retrospect he had, as we have seen, only conventional dealings. He pushed beyond it to ideas of natural independence and renewal, and he saw quite clearly as an enemy a materialist and capitalist industrial system. But it is characteristic and significant that he then aligned the ideas of human independence and renewal – the ideas of nature itself – with an opposition to democracy, to education, to the labour movement: a restless, often contradictory opposition: at its sourest between the war years and the middle twenties: re-thought and in some ways amended, with more real sense of connection, in the reflective essays of his last years. His is a knot too tight to untie now: the knot of a life under overwhelming contradictions and pressures. But as I have watched it settle into what is now a convention – in literary education especially – I have felt it as an outrage, in a continuing crisis and on a persistent border. The song of the land, the song of rural labour, the song of delight in the many forms of life with which we all share our physical world, is too important and too moving to be tamely given up, in an embittered betrayal, to the confident enemies of all significant and actual independence and renewal.

23   The City and the Future

Out of an experience of the cities came an experience of the future. At a crisis of metropolitan experience, stories of the future went through a qualitative change. There were traditional models for this kind of projection. In all recorded literature there had been the land after death: a paradise or a hell. In the centuries of exploration and voyaging, new societies were discovered, for promise or for warning, in new lands: often islands: often the happy island, itself a shaping element in the myth. But within metropolitan experience these models, though widely drawn on, were eventually transformed. Man did not go to his destiny, or discover his fortunate place; he saw, in pride or error, his own capacity for collective transformation of himself and of his world.

As early as the eighteenth century, Louis Sébastien Mercier wrote both a contemporary topographical *Tableau de Paris* (1782–9) and a story of the secular future, *L'An 2440* (1770). But it was in the late nineteenth century, and significantly in London, that the deep transformation occurred. We can see it in writers as different as William Morris and H. G. Wells. Each, in his own way, draws on the transforming experience of contemporary London, then at the centre of social and literary attention. Each, again in his own way, draws on the new collective consciousness which is the social product of the urban experience even where its impulse is its criticism and rejection. Morris in *News from Nowhere* (1890) has his observer wake, during a restless night after a political argument, and find himself in the London of the twenty-first century. Two features are then significant: the kind of London Morris foresaw, which is a qualitative break; and the social ideas and feelings that created it, which are continuous with the socialist movement of his own day. If we look only at that imagined London, we find the dreaming and often backward-looking Morris:

> The soap-works with their smoke-vomiting chimneys were gone; the engineer's works gone; the leadworks gone; and no sound of riveting and hammering came down the west wind from Thorney-croft's. Then the bridge? I had perhaps dreamed of such a bridge, but never seen such an one out of an illustrated manuscript . . .
> . . . I opened my eyes to the sunlight again and looked round me, and cried out among the whispering trees and odorous blossoms, 'Trafalgar Square!'

London has been decentralized, keeping some of the best older parts but restoring some of the slum areas to separate small towns and villages. The industrial manufacturing cities have 'like the brick and mortar desert of London, disappeared'. Most of the smaller towns have survived, with their centres cleared; the suburbs 'have melted away into the general coun-try'. This is a combination of what is essentially restoration, turning back history and drawing on medieval and rural patterns, and what was to express itself, formally, as town-planning, the creation of urban order and control. It is an imagined old London, before industrialism and the metropolitan expansion, and a projected new London, in the contemporary sense of the garden city. These contradictory impulses are never wholly resolved, and indeed cannot be resolved without con-sidering what is offered, throughout, as the directing spirit; the new social idea. For it is from the struggling misery of nineteenth-century London, and from the socialist movement that emerged as a response to it, that the energies of change are seen as being generated: energies of angry rejection; energies of new cooperation and trust. The new social movement, once only a vision becomes hardened in struggle, as in the experience of Bloody Sunday in Trafalgar Square, and it then finds organizers who can take it through the necessary civil war to the new and peaceful society.

We have only to compare this with, say, Thomson's *Doom of a City* and *City of Dreadful Night* to see the essential change. The judgements are similar, as is the narrative convention. But what has entered and altered the experience is just this historical sense of the growth of a movement. Thomson's social criticism is as harsh, but his observer remains isolated. In Morris the negative energy has found a positive cause.

Wells's vision is harsher. He has added not only an historical but an evolutionary dimension. As he said of *When the Sleeper Awakes*, 1899 (which had developed the formal narrative mode of Thomson or Morris, but taken it, following Edward Bellamy, into a further emphasis of historical movement), it is

essentially an exaggeration of contemporary tendencies: higher buildings, bigger towns, wickeder capitalists and labour more downtrodden than ever and more desperate.

But more specifically, as in *A Story of the Days to Come* (1899), there is a direct extension of an older vision of the city:

a vast lunatic growth, producing a deepening torrent of savagery below, and above ever more flimsy gentility and silly wastefulness.

This is the vision that had been given an evolutionary dimension in *The Time Machine* (1899), when the 'savagery below', of the working poor, has evolved into the blind and brutal Morlocks, and the flimsy silliness of the rich has evolved into the doll-like Eloi, the playthings who are also the Morlocks' food. This image often recurs in different forms: the 'nether world' of Gissing has become the underground area of the enslaved workers. The sombre vision of man divided into brute labour and trivial consumption, and then of the city shaped physically to embody these worlds, is expressed again and again. This way of seeing was to have a great influence. One of its most remarkable successors is Lang's film *Metropolis*, in the nineteen-twenties.

Wells's sombre vision is then the counterpart of Morris's gentler and more idyllic vision. But just as Morris's ideal cannot be separated from his sense of a new social movement, so Wells's apocalypse cannot be separated from his sense of a new social idea. Each, in its varying forms, has come from the city experience. In Wells the solution is only in part technology, though it is emphatically that: new means of communication and transport will dissolve the hideous concentration of nineteenth-century industrial and metropolitan development; new physical and social settlements will then become practically available. But this depends fundamentally on a new sense of society – what Wells calls 'human ecology': a new collective consciousness, scientific and social, which is capable of taking control of an environment in a total way and directing it to human achievement. This dimension of thought is new, and it is provoked by observation of what has been done to men and animals, to the country and the city, by unplanned and ignorant and aggressive development. The new city, when it comes, will be a new world, directed by the new kind of science.

It is important to see these responses of Morris and Wells in this context of the crisis of metropolitan and industrial civilization. Their views have often been described as if they were idle dreaming or voluntary and arrogant projection. Yet they were nearer a real crisis which has both continued and deepened than some subsequent writers who merely reacted against them.

Huxley's *Brave New World* (1931) and Orwell's *Nineteen Eighty-Four* (1949) are still often seen as necessary correctives of the Wellsian response. But they are also 'correctives' of the Morris response, and indeed of that whole positive movement of social change. Huxley shows a world which has reached a Morris kind of ease by Wellsian means (scientific breeding, improved production and transport, drugs, a scientific social order). He diagnoses its emptiness and contrasts it with a primitive vision: a new version, owing something to Lawrence, of a simple rural vitality, not innocent now but savage; the rhythms of the blood. Orwell cuts the vision to pieces by showing the socialist movement reaching its climax in Ingsoc, with its totalitarian system of lying, torture and thought police, and with the city in which it is established dirty, half-broken, reduced to perpetual wars. There have been many grounds for these reactions, in the twentieth-century, but it is significant that the central crisis, to which Morris and Wells so powerfully responded, is then to an important extent overlooked. The movements of change, rather than the conditions that provoked them, have become the centres of critical interest. In the satisfactions of an often justified criticism, the crisis itself can come to seem secondary. Orwell, as it happens, had in many ways followed Gissing: in his deliberate explorations of urban squalor, to which he responded with some of the same anxious distaste but in the end with a much finer and more generous humanity: a resolution that reached its climax in his celebration of Barcelona, the revolutionary city. In his deep disillusion with the development of socialism, he returned, in his later work, as in *Coming up for Air* (1939) to a vision of the country, the old unspoiled country, as a place of human retreat and rest, an innocence which the new civilization, capitalist or socialist, was aggressively destroying. The shabby, ugly, exposed and lonely city of *Nineteen Eighty-Four* is the result of a perversion of the collective idea.

These were important shifts within a movement of ideas. Yet all the time the crisis itself was becoming more acute and more widespread. What has been, in the early nineteenth century, a primarily English phenomenon, was becoming international and in a sense universal, extending to industrialized Western Europe and North America in the late nineteenth and early twentieth centuries, and in the first half of the twentieth century extending to Asia and Latin America. In the United States, often now seen as a model of metropolitan civilization, the rural population still exceeded the urban as late as 1910, and was only surpassed by it between the wars. In the world as a whole, the population living in towns (over five thousand inhabitants) rose between 1850 and 1950 from seven to almost thirty per cent. More significantly, in the first half of the twentieth century the population living in cities (over a hundred thousand inhabitants) rose at the rate of two hundred and fifty per cent. In many parts of the world, older cities moved into the metropolitan phase, during a period of rapid increase in total population. It was not only a fundamental transformation in the pattern of human settlement. It was also a new kind of exposure: to problems of the relations between population and food; to problems of land-use and pollution; and, deeply affecting the imagination, to kinds of physical mass attack, as in the obliteration bombing of the Second World War and, at its peak, the destruction of cities by atomic bombs. James Thomson had imagined a natural storm which destroyed the city of the stone people. Wells had imagined a Martian attack on London, with the 'Black Smoke' and the 'Heat Ray': the paralysed inhabitants of the city exposed to this crushing destruction are saved only by the accident of differential bacterial infection. In an epoch of wars, rising populations and international social crisis the image of the city then went through a further rapid development.

This is most evident in what we now call science fiction: the linear descendant of Wells's response to the city. And there was an added element, also developed from Wells: the alternative civilizations of other planets and solar systems. James Thomson, looking from the city to the stars, had written:

> If we could near them with the flight unflown,
> We should but find them worlds as sad as this,
> Or suns as self-consuming as our own
> Enringed by planet worlds as much amiss.

In explicit scientific romance, the opposite feeling – the stars as the new frontier, for the expansion and progress of man – has been an evident element. Glittering cities have been imagined, on a thousand planets, with every kind of technical wonder. (A representative example, drawing directly on Wellsian ideas, is Brian Aldiss's *The Underprivileged*; there is also Arthur C. Clarke's *The City and the Stars*.) There has been also a significant imagining of civilizations which have evolved beyond their urban and technical phases: people living in what one can recognize as the old pastoral places – open country, small villages – but possessing great power because they have internalized the communication and productive capacities of the urban-scientific-industrial phase (Don A. Stuart's *Forgetfulness* is one of many possible examples). Every element of the long history, between country and city, has been projected in these ways.

Yet it is important to notice also a deeply pessimistic projection of the city itself. It is by now a convention. An anthology of future stories, edited by Damon Knight under the conventional title *Cities of Wonder*, contains several examples which are in effect linear descendants of the urban fiction of the nineteenth century and its transmutation through Wells. There is J. G. Ballard's *Billennium*, for example, in which

ninetyfive per cent of the population was permanently trapped in vast urban conurbations ... The countryside, as such, no longer existed. Every single square foot of ground sprouted a crop of one type or another. The one-time fields and meadows of the world were, in effect, factory floors.

Or there is the city largely destroyed by bombing and radiation, in Walter M. Miller's *Dumb Waiter*: still functioning physically by electronic control from the Central Service Co-ordinator but a dangerous place for men to re-enter and try to salvage. There is the city which to solve its own internal problems of water, food, power and waste-disposal has become, in Henry Ruttner's *Jesting Pilot*, 'so artificial that nobody could use it', and the survival of its inhabitants is ensured only by collective hypnosis. Such self-enclosed automatic cities, in which the inhabitants cannot believe in a world outside the walls, have been imagined again and again, often with the theme of an attempt to break out into the wild country beyond. An early example is E. M. Forster's *The Machine Stops*, which ends with 'the whole city . . . broken like a honeycomb' by a crashing airship, while outside 'in the mist and the fens' other people, the Homeless, wait to take over, but not to rebuild the destructive machine. Or there is the city which has become an organism, as in Robert Abernethy's *Single Combat*:

For three hundred years the city had been growing . . . like a cancer budding from a few wild cells . . . As it grew it drew nourishment from a hundred, a thousand miles of hinterland; for it the land yielded up its fatness and the forests were mown like grain, and men and animals lived also to feed its ever-increasing hunger . . . As it fed it voided its wastes into the sea and breathed its poisons into the air, and grew fouler as it grew more mighty. It developed by degrees a central nervous system of strung wires and buried cables . . . It evolved from an invertebrate enormity of wild growth to a higher creature having tangible attributes that go with the subjective concepts of *will* and *purpose* and *consciousness* . . .

Finally, on voyages to Utopia and elsewhere in the galaxy, there are the flying cities of James Blish's *Earthman, Come Home*, moving out into new worlds but recapitulating within their total environments every phase of human history.

These fictions of cities of the future interact, in the mind, with the long fictions of pastoral. But whereas, in the development of pastoral, there was a movement away from the realities of country life, in this city fiction there is an evident overlap with quite different work: in urban sociology and planning; in studies of the government of cities; in work on the physical environment of an industrial and metropolitan civilization: in all of which, though with variations of emphasis, the problems of the city – from traffic to pollution, from social to psychological effects – are often seen as overwhelming and as, in some views, insoluble.

It is a strange situation, because this coexists not only with a still rapid and often unplanned metropolitan growth, but with a specific planning on an ever larger scale: linear cities of up to a hundred miles; new cities conceived and built with an established confidence of mapping and projection. There is an evident unevenness in the dominant consciousness. In a sense, it seems, everything about the city – from the magnificent to the apocalyptic – can be believed at once. One source of this unevenness is the complexity of the pressures and the problems. But another source, less easily traced, is the abstraction of the city, as a huge isolated problem, and the traditional images have done much to support this. For what we need to notice, as we look at the facts and the images of the city, is that both have been developed within a wider world history, in which, in a surprising new dimension, both the city and the country have been given new and at first scarcely recognized definitions.

In current descriptions of the world, the major industrial societies are often described as 'metropolitan'. At first glance this can be taken as a simple description of their internal development, in which the metropolitan cities have become dominant. But when we look at it more closely, in its real historical development, we find that what is meant is an extension to the whole world of that division of functions which in the nineteenth century was a division of functions within a single state. The 'metropolitan' societies of Western Europe and North America are the 'advanced', 'developed', industrialized states; centres of economic, political and cultural power. In sharp contrast with them, though there are many intermediate stages, are other societies which are seen as 'underdeveloped': still mainly agricultural or 'under-industrialized'. The 'metropolitan' states, through a system of trade, but also through a complex of economic and political controls, draw food and, more critically, raw materials from these areas of supply, this effective hinterland, that is also the greater part of the earth's surface and that contains the great majority of its peoples. Thus a model of city and country, in economic and political relationships, has gone beyond the boundaries of the nation-state, and is seen but also challenged as a model of the world.

It is very significant that in its modern forms this began in England. Much of the real history of city and country, within England itself, is from an early date a history of the extension of a dominant model of capitalist development to include other regions of the world. And this was not, as it is now sometimes seen, a case of 'development' here, 'failure to develop' elsewhere. What was happening in the 'city', the 'metropolitan' economy, determined and was determined by what was made to happen in the 'country'; first the local hinterland and then the vast regions beyond it, in other people's lands. What happened in England has since been happening ever more widely, in new dependent relationships between all the industrialized nations and all the other 'undeveloped' but economically important lands. Thus one of the last models of 'city and country' is the system we now know as imperialism.

European expansion into the rest of the world had already, in the sixteenth and seventeenth centuries, brought back significant wealth, which found its way into the internal system. Important parts of the country-house system, from the sixteenth to the eighteenth centuries, were built on the profits of that trade. Spices, sugar, tea, coffee, tobacco, gold and silver: these fed, as mercantile profits, into an English social order, over and above the profits on English stock and crops. It was still mainly, at that stage, a profit of trading: bringing goods from one kind of economy to another, though often with physical force to back this up. The country-houses which were the apex of a local system of exploitation then had many connections to these distant lands. But another process was already under way: another kind of 'improvement'. Demand for these valued and exotic commodities was steadily rising, and the European societies and their emigrant settlers were beginning to organize increased production. To do this, in tropical regions, they began organizing 'labour': that polite term for the slave trade from Africa – anything from three million slaves in the seventeenth century to seven million in the eighteenth. The new rural economy of the tropical plantations – sugar, coffee, cotton – was built by this trade in flesh, and once again the profits fed back into the country-house system: not only the profits on the commodities but until the end of the eighteenth century the profits on slaves. In 1700 fifteen per cent of British commerce was with the colonies. In 1775 it was as much as a third. In an intricate process of economic interaction, supported by wars between the trading nations for control of the areas of supply, an organized colonial system and the development of an industrial economy changed the nature of British society.

The unprecedented events of the nineteenth century, in which Britain became a predominantly industrial and urban society, with its agriculture declining to marginal status, are inexplicable and would have been impossible without this colonial development. There was a massive export of the new industrial production. Much of the trade of the world was carried and serviced by Britain, from its dominant position in shipping, banking and insurance, the new 'City' of London. Following these profitable developments, often to the exclusion of others that might have been possible, the economy by the middle of the nineteenth century was at the point where its own population could not be fed from home production. The traditional relationship between city and country was then thoroughly rebuilt on an international scale. Distant lands became the rural areas of industrial Britain, with heavy consequent effects on its own surviving rural areas. At the same time, the drive for industrial markets and the drive for raw materials extended the effective society across half the world. Already in the eighteenth century the most important of the colonies, in North America, had achieved independence and were eventually, and even more dramatically, to follow the same paths. From the 1870s, especially, there was intense competition between the rising industrial societies, for markets, raw materials and areas of influence. This was fought out in trade and in many colonial wars. It produced, in Britain, the formal establishment of new kinds of political control over the colonial areas: the British Empire in its political sense. In the twentieth century the same rivalry was fought out in its European bases, in the First World War.

The effects of this development on the English imagination have gone deeper than can easily be traced. All the time, within it, there was the interaction at home, between country and city, that we have seen in so many examples. But from at least the mid nineteenth century, and with important instances earlier, there was this larger context within which every idea and every image was consciously and unconsciously affected. We can see in the industrial novels of the mid nineteenth century how the idea of emigration to the colonies was seized as a solution to the poverty and overcrowding of the cities. Thousands of the displaced rural workers had already gone there. Elizabeth Gaskell's *Mary Barton* ends in Canada, in a mood of rural idyll and escape as powerful as any of the earlier English images. In

Wuthering Heights, in *Great Expectations*, in *Alton Locke* and in many other novels of the period there is a way out from the struggle within English society to these distant lands; a way out that is not only the escape to a new land but as in some of the real history an acquisition of fortune to return and re-enter the struggle at a higher point. Alexander Somerville and several of the Tolpuddle Martyrs, casualties of the crisis of rural society, ended their days overseas. Many of the casualties of the urban crisis, leading Chartists among them, went the same way. The lands of the Empire were an idyllic retreat, an escape from debt or shame, or an opportunity for making a fortune. An expanding middle class found its regular careers abroad, as war and administration in the distant lands became more organized. New rural societies entered the English imagination, under the shadow of political and economic control: the plantation worlds of Kipling and Maugham and early Orwell; the trading worlds of Conrad and Joyce Cary.

From about 1880 there was then this dramatic extension of landscape and social relations. There was also a marked development of the idea of England as 'home', in that special sense in which 'home' is a memory and an ideal. Some of the images of this 'home' are of central London: the powerful, the prestigious and the consuming capital. But many are of an idea of rural England: its green peace contrasted with the tropical or arid places of actual work; its sense of belonging, of community, idealized by contrast with the tensions of colonial rule and the isolated alien settlement. We can pick up the force of this idea in many twentieth-century images of rural England. The society from which these people had come was, after all, the most urban and industrialized in the world, and it was usually in the service of just these elements that they had gone out. Perhaps this worked only to deepen the longing and the idealization. Moreover, in practical terms, the reward for service, though anticipated more often than it was gained, was a return to a rural place within this urban and industrial England: the 'residential' rural England, the 'little place in the country'; unless the service had been profitable enough to follow the older movement, to the 'country-house', the real place. The birds and trees and rivers of England; the natives speaking, more or less, one's own language:

these were the terms of many imagined and actual settlements. The country, now, was a place to retire to.

It is easy to see this in the generations of colonial officers, civil servants, plantation managers and traders. But within their own class these were the least successful. The landed aristocracy had lost much of its particular identity and its political power in the course of industrial and imperialist development. But its social imagery continued to predominate. The network of income from property and speculation was now not only industrial but imperial. And as so often before it was fed into a self-consciously rural mode of display. The country-houses of late George Eliot, of Henry James and of their etiolated successors are, as we saw, the country-houses of capital rather than of land. More significantly and more ritually than ever before, a rural mode was developed, as a cultural superstructure, on the profits of industrial and imperial development. It was a mode of play: an easy realization of the old imagery of Penshurst: field sports, fishing, and above all horses; often a marginal interest in conservation and 'old country ways'.

Meanwhile there was still, within Britain, a small rural proletariat, and the farmers, as we have seen, were in increasing numbers becoming owner-occupiers: adjusting, often with difficulty, to the subordinate position of home agriculture, but with increasing efficiency drawn from the resources of a scientific and industrial society. In a minor key, some of the old real images persisted. But they were now at last outnumbered by the new images, themselves transmuted by their changing functions. The quiet place to retire to, or the place in which to live in a country style: these, now, were the dominant ideas, in the literature as in the history.

Yet all the time, out of their sight, there was a huge rural proletariat, in the distant lands. As Orwell, who had seen some of them, wrote in 1939:

What we always forget is that the overwhelming bulk of the British proletariat does not live in Britain, but in Asia and Africa.

This, indeed, had been the developing system. Millions of slaves; millions of indentured and contracted labourers; millions of rural workers kept at wages so low that they could barely sustain life. Out of these 'country' areas there eventually came, through blood and struggle, movements for political independence. At various stages, to protect such an order, young officers from the country-houses led other Englishmen, and the expropriated Irish and Scots and Welsh, to the colonial battles in which so many died. It is a strange fate. The unemployed man from the slums of the cities, the superfluous landless worker, the dispossessed peasant: each of these found employment in killing and disciplining the rural poor of the subordinated countries.

It is often said now, in a guilty way, that the British people as a whole benefited from the system of imperialism. If we add up the figures of the movement of wealth we cannot doubt that this is true. The rise in the general standard of living depended, in large part, on the exploitation of millions who were seen only as backward peoples, as natives. Much of the guilt and hatred and prejudice bred through those generations was still there when, ironically, unemployment in the colonies prompted a reverse migration, and following an ancient pattern the displaced from the 'country' areas came, following the wealth and the stories of wealth, to the 'metropolitan' centre, where they were at once pushed in, overcrowded, among the indigenous poor, as had happened throughout in the development of the cities. Yet we have always to remember that the total wealth which came back, and which is still coming back, was not evenly distributed. London was at one of its peaks as an imperialist city when it created its desperate centre of poverty and misery in the East End. For wealth from the Empire, channelled through so few hands, was a critical source of the political and economic power which the same ruling class continued to exercise. The advantages of living in a developed industrial society, even at the lower ends of the scale, were of course more widely diffused. Even then, internally, these workers were directly exploited. But for many of these advantages British workers had to pay: with blood in repeated wars which had little or nothing to do with their immediate interests; and in deeper ways, in confusion, loss of direction, deformation of the spirit. It is the story of the city and the country in its harshest form, and now on an unimaginably complex scale.

It is now widely believed in Britain that this system has

ended. But political imperialism was only ever a stage. It was preceded by economic and trading controls, backed where necessary by force. It has been effectively succeeded by economic, monetary and commercial controls which again, at every point that resistance mounts, are at once supported by political, cultural and military intervention. The dominant relationships are still, in this sense, of a city and a country, at the point of maximum exploitation.

What is offered as an idea, to hide this exploitation, is a modern version of the old idea of 'improvement': a scale of human societies which theoretically culminates in universal industrialization. All the 'country' will become 'city': that is the logic of its development: a simple linear scale, along which degrees of 'development' and 'underdevelopment' can be marked. But the reality is quite different. Many of the 'underdeveloped' societies have been developed, precisely, for the needs of the 'metropolitan' countries. Peoples who once practised a subsistence agriculture have been changed, by economic and political force, to plantation economies, mining areas, single-crop markets. The setting of prices, on which these areas specialized to metropolitan needs must try to live, is in the decisive control of the metropolitan commodity markets. Massive investment in this kind of supply, and in its kind of economic and political infrastructure, brings in from these specialized 'rural' areas a constant flow of wealth which then further accentuates the dominating interrelations. It is essentially the same whether the crop is coffee or copper, rubber or tin, cocoa or cotton or oil. And what is called 'aid', to the poor countries, is with few exceptions an accentuation of this process: the development of their economies towards metropolitan needs; the preservation of markets and spheres of influence; or the continuation of indirect political control – sustaining a collaborating régime; opposing, if necessary by military intervention, all developments which would give these societies an independent and primarily self-directed development. Much of the history of the world, in the middle years of the twentieth century, is this decisive relationship and its turbulent consequences. It is ideologically overlaid by the abstract idea of 'development': a poor country is 'on its way' to being a rich one, just as in industrial Britain, in the nineteenth century, a poor man could be seen as someone who given the right ideas and effort was 'on his way' to being a rich man, but was for the time being at a lower stage of this development. But the facts are that the gap is widening, and that its consequences are so extensive that they are deciding the history of the world.

Within this vast action, the older images of city and country seem to fall away. But some are still relevant; the history and the ideas are relevant. We can still, any day, find rural literature, of the most traditional kinds, but we have to go farther and farther afield for it. We find stories of distant lands, but we can then recognize in them some of our own traditional experiences. The local details are different, as is natural among different peoples, but many of the historical experiences are essentially similar. If we read Yashar Kemal's fine novel of the migrant pickers in Anatolia, *The Wind from the Plain*, we can see a form of the experience which so many of our own people shared: a community that has become available labour for a speculative seasonal enterprise elsewhere: the hardships of the long walk; the familiar cheating at the end of it. We can read of the conflict between two kinds of people, two ways of rural life, in James Ngugi's *The River Between* (1965). There is the village world of Elechi Amadi's *The Concubine* (1966), and the riceland of Guyana in Wilson Harris's *The Far Journey of Oudin* (1961). There is the rural life of southern India in R. K. Narayan's *Swami and Friends* (1935), and the rural conflict of Mulk Raj Anand's *The Village* (1939).

Many of these stories include characteristic internal themes: struggles with landlords; failures of crops and debts; the penetration of capital into peasant communities. These, in all the variations of different societies and traditions, are internal tensions that we can recognize as characteristic forms, often from very far back in our history. But their most pressing interest, for us, is when they touch the imperialist and colonial experience. In Britain itself, within the home islands, the colonial process is so far back that it is in effect unrecorded, though there are late consequences of it in the rural literature of Scotland and Wales and especially of Ireland. It has become part of the long settlement which is idealized as Old England or the natural economy:

the product of centuries of successive penetration and domination. What is important in this modern literature of the colonial peoples is that we can see the history happening, see it being made, from the base of an England which, within our own literature, has been so differently described.

Thus there are bitterly remembered experiences at the receiving end of the process which made the fortunes that were converted, in England, into country-houses and that style of life: experiences on the sugar-plantations and in the slave-trade. There are many direct accounts of this developing process, at its most organized and expansive stage. We are already familiar with the work of Englishmen who experienced the tensions of this process: E. M. Forster's *Passage to India*, Orwell's *Burmese Days*, Joyce Cary's important African novels, *Aissa Saved*, *The African Witch*, *Mister Johnson*. Characterically these are liberal ways of seeing the experience, in the critical and self-questioning generation after Kipling. But we have only to go across to the Indian and African and West Indian writers to get a different and necessary perspective. The tea plantation is seen from the other side in Mulk Raj Anand's *Two Leaves and a Bud* (1937). Chinua Achebe's *Things Fall Apart* (1958) ends with a white man collecting material for a book on 'The Pacification of the Primitive Tribes of the Lower Niger', and this ironic challenge is telling because we have all read such accounts, but now see the process from within a rural community as the white men – missionaries, district officers – arrive with their mercenary soldiers and police. What is impressive about *Things Fall Apart* is that as in some English literature of rural change, as late as Hardy, the internal tensions of the society are made clear, so that we can understand the modes of the penetration which would in any case, in its process of expansion, have come. The first converts to the alien religion are the marginal people of the traditional society. The alien law and religion are bitterly resented and resisted, but the trading-station, in palm-oil, is welcomed, as an addition to the slash-and-burn subsistence farming of yams. The strongest man, Okonkwo, is destroyed in a very complicated process of internal contradictions and external invasion.

We can see the same complications, at a later stage and in

different societies, in the resistance movements of the country people against English power, in the Kenya of James Ngugi's *Weep Not, Child* and *A Grain of Wheat*, or in the Malaya of Han Suyin's *And The Rain My Drink*. What has been officially presented, to English readers, as savagery followed by terrorism, is seen in its real terms: so many different rural societies – unidealized, containing their own tensions – invaded and transformed by an uncomprehending and often brutal alien system. It is significant that the idealization of the peasant, in the modern English middle-class tradition, was not extended, when it might have mattered, to the peasants, the plantation-workers, the coolies of these occupied societies. Yet in a new and universal sense this was the penetration, transformation and subjugation of 'the country' by 'the city': long-established rural communities uprooted and redirected by the military and economic power of a developing metropolitan imperialism. Nor is this only a process of the past or the recent past; we have only to read, from South Africa, the writings of Ezekiel Mphahlele.

But what we then also see is the more complicated secondary process. In the most general sense, underlying the description of the imperialist nations as 'metropolitan', the image of the country penetrated, transformed and subjugated by the city, learning to fight back in old and new ways, can be seen to hold. But one of the effects of imperialist dominance was the initiation, within the dominated societies, of processes which then follow, internally, the lines of the alien development. An internal history of country and city occurs, often very dramatically, within the colonial and neo-colonial societies. This is particularly ironic, since the city, in Western thought, is now so regularly associated with its own most modern kinds of development, while in fact, on a world scale, the most remarkable growth of cities in the twentieth century has been in the 'underdeveloped' and 'developing' continents. Within the industrialized societies, urbanization has continued, though in societies like Britain the proportions for some time have become relatively stable. Indeed there has been some important movement away from the city in the older sense, as city centres are cleared for commercial and administrative development; or as suburbs, new towns and industrial estates are developed in rural and semi-rural areas as parts of a policy of relative dispersal. The concentrated city is in the process of being replaced, in the industrial societies, by what is in effect a transport network: the conurbation, the city region, the London-Birmingham axis. The city thus passes into its tertiary development, when it becomes in effect a province or even a state.

Meanwhile, at the other end of the imperialist process, intensely overcrowded cities are developing as a direct result of the imposed economic development and its internal consequences. Beginning as centres of colonial trade and administration, these cities have drawn in, as in our own history, the surplus people and the uprooted labourers of the rural areas. This is a long-term and continuing process, intensified by rapid rises in general population. Familiar problems of the chaotically expanding city recur, across the world, in many of the poorest countries. People who speak of the crisis of cities with London or New York or Los Angeles in mind ought to think also of the deeper crises of Calcutta or Manila or a hundred other cities across Asia and Africa and Latin America. A displaced and formerly rural population is moving and drifting towards the centres of a money economy which is directed by interests very far from their own. The last image of the city, in the ex-colonial and neo-colonial world, is the political capital or the trading port surrounded by the shanty-towns, the barriadas, which often grow at incredible speed. In Peru, as I write, a few acres of desert have become, in a fortnight, a 'city' of thirty thousand people, and this is only a particular example, in the long interaction between altered and broken rural communities and a process of capitalist agriculture and industrialization sometimes internally, more often externally directed.

It is then too late for the rich industrial societies to give warnings about the consequences of this dramatic process. There is a false conservationist and reactionary emphasis which would in effect, as Hardy observed of rural England, have the developing societies stay as they are, picturesque and poor, for the benefit of observers. Even when this is more serious, as in the reasonable emphasis on the full human consequences, it is in bad faith if it argues that the process should stop at anything like the present levels of relative advantage and disadvantage. For what has to be recognized, not only as an historical but as contemporary fact, is that the lines of development, in their intended and unintended consequences, run back to the centres of imperialist economic, political and military power. The shattered rural societies include not only the economies of Latin America but the bombed and burned devastation of Vietnam. Independent development, which has to be bitterly fought for, then offers the only chance of any possible growth in the interest of the majority. And while it is true that if we add up all the developments, or the failures to develop, the global crisis is terrifying, it is a process that cannot be stopped in any one of its sectors. The decisive changes, indeed, if they are to come at all, will have to come from within the 'metropolitan' countries, whose power now distorts the whole process and makes any genuine system of common interest and control impossible. Yet when we look at the power and impetus of the metropolitan drives, often indeed accelerated by their own internal crises, we cannot be in any doubt that a different direction, if it is to be found, will necessarily involve revolutionary change. The depth of the crisis, and the power of those who continue to dominate it, are too great for any easier or more congenial way.

Within this now vast mobility, which is the daily history of our world, literature continues to embody the almost infinitely varied experiences and interpretations. We can remember our own early literature of mobility and of the corrupting process of cities, and see many of its themes reappearing in African, Asian and West Indian literature, itself written, characteristically, in the metropolitan languages which are themselves among the consequences of mobility. We can read of the restless villages of so many far countries: in Nkem Nwankwo's *Danda*, in George Lamming's *In the Castle of My Skin*. A mixed language, learned in the mobility, comes through in V. S. Reid's *New Day*. And Chinua Achebe, who in *Things Fall Apart* and *Arrow of God* showed the arrival of the alien system in the villages, shows us the complicated process of educational mobility and new kinds of work in the city in *No Longer at Ease* and *Man of the People*. Yet we have got so used to thinking of common experiences through the alienating screens of foreignness and race that all too often we take the particularity of these stories as merely exotic. A social process is happening there, in an initially unfamiliar society, and that is its importance. But as we gain perspective, from the long history of the literature of country and city, we see how much, at different times and in different places, it is a connecting process, in what has to be seen ultimately as a common history.

(i)

The country and the city are changing historical realities, both in themselves and in their interrelations. Moreover, in our own world, they represent only two kinds of settlement. Our real social experience is not only of the country and the city, in their most singular forms, but of many kinds of intermediate and new kinds of social and physical organization.

Yet the ideas and the images of country and city retain their great force. This persistence has a significance matched only by the fact of the great actual variation, social and historical, of the ideas themselves. Clearly the contrast of country and city is one of the major forms in which we become conscious of a central part of our experience and of the crises of our society. But when this is so, the temptation is to reduce the historical variety of the forms of interpretation to what are loosely called symbols or archetypes: to abstract even these most evidently social forms and to give them a primarily psychological or metaphysical status. This reduction often happens when we find certain major forms and images and ideas persisting through periods of great change. Yet if we can see that the persistence depends on the forms and images and ideas being changed, though often subtly, internally and at times unconsciously, we can see also that the persistence indicates some permanent or effectively permanent need, to which the changing interpretations speak. I believe that there is indeed such a need, and that it is created by the processes of a particular history. But if we do not see these processes, or see them only incidentally, we fall back on modes of thought which seem able to create the permanence without the history. We may find emotional or intellectual satisfaction in this, but we have then dealt with only half the problem, for in all such major interpretations it is the co-existence of persistence and change which is really striking and interesting, and which we have to account for without reducing either fact to a form of the other. Or, to put it more theoretically, we have to be able to explain, in related terms, both the persistence and the historicity of concepts.

The ideas of the city and the country are among the major cases to which this problem applies. It is clear, for example, that an idea derived from experience of a medieval city cannot be taken, in a merely nominal continuity, as an idea about a twentieth-century metropolis, any more than a pastoral idea of rural Boeotia can be taken as a relevant interpretation of modern Norfolk. But equally we cannot say that the idea of pastoral innocence, or of the city as a civilizing agency, coming up, as each does, in so many periods and forms, is a simple illusion which has only to be exposed or contradicted. Exposure and contradiction are often critically necessary, but if we keep only to the ideas we are already aware of this, in the comparable persistence of ideas of rural idiocy or the city as a place of corruption. We then find ourselves facing the further questions: what kinds of experience do the ideas appear to interpret, and why do certain forms occur or recur at this period or at that?

To answer these questions we need to trace, historically and critically, the various forms of the ideas. But it is useful, also, to stop at certain points and take particular cross-sections: to ask not only what is happening, in a period, to ideas of the country and the city, but also with what other ideas, in a more general structure, such ideas are associated. For example we have to notice the regular sixteenth- and seventeenth-century association of ideas of the city with money and law; the eighteenth-century association with wealth and luxury; the persistent association, reaching a climax in the late eighteenth and nineteenth centuries, with the mob and the masses; the nineteenth- and twentieth-century association with mobility and isolation. Each of these ideas has a certain persistence, but isolation, for example, only emerges as a major theme during the metropolitan phase of development, while the response to the city as money ranges from isolated kinds of corruption and intrigue to perception of a commercial and political system. There are similar radical differences in associations with ideas of the country: the idea of settlement, for example, as compared with the idea of rural retreat, which implies mobility. Each idea can be found in very different periods, and seems to depend on class variations, whereas the other obvious contrast, between an idea or cultivated country, cultivation being honest growth, and the idea of wild or unspoiled country, not cultivation but isolated nature, has a clearer historical perspective, since the latter so evidently involves response to a whole way of life largely determined elsewhere. The degree to which the fact of labour is included, in observing a working country, is similarly, as we have seen, historically conditioned. Yet even within a period, we can see how in an idea like that of the Golden Age an apparent similarity turns out, on analysis, to cover different real ideas, as in its alternative uses by an aristocracy, by small proprietors and by the landless. Often in these cases of association and internal variation, it matters more what else is being said than what is being said about the country; just as in the nineteenth and twentieth centuries it often matters more what else is being said than what is being said, in conventional ways, about the city.

This complexity goes very deep. It is useful, for example, to see three main periods of rural complaint in which a happier past is explicitly invoked: the late sixteenth and early seventeenth centuries; the late eighteenth and early nineteenth; the late nineteenth and early twentieth. And it is then clear enough that each of these corresponds to a period of exceptional change in the rural economy, which we find directly reflected in varying ways. But it is not only that each of these reflections comes to include other social and metaphysical ideas. It is also that the convention of the country as a settled way of life disturbed by unwanted and external change has been complicated, in our own century, by very similar ideas about towns and cities. The complaints of rural change might come from threatened small proprietors, or from commoners, or even, in the twentieth century, from a class of landlords, but it is fascinating to hear some of the same phrases – destruction of a local community, the driving out of small men, indifference to settled and customary ways – in the innumerable campaigns about the effects of redevelopment, urban planning, airport and motorway systems, in so many twentieth-century towns and even, very strongly, in parts of London. I have heard a defence of Covent Garden, against plans for development, which repeated in almost every particular the defence of the commons in the period of parliamentary enclosures. Clearly ideas of the country and the city have specific contents and histories, but just as clearly, at times, they are forms of isolation and identification of more general processes. People have often said 'the city' when they meant capitalism or bureaucracy or centralized power, while 'the country', as we have seen, has at times meant everything from independence to deprivation, and from the powers of an active imagination to a form of release from consciousness. At every point we need to put these ideas to the historical realities: at times to be confirmed, at times denied. But also, as we see the whole process, we need to put the historical realities to the ideas, for at times these express, not only in disguise and displacement but in effective mediation or in offered and sometimes effective transcendence, human interests and purposes for which there is no other immediately available vocabulary. It is not only an absence or distance of more specific terms and concepts; it is that in country and city, physically present and substantial, the experience finds material which gives body to the thoughts.

I have traced what I believe to be these major processes, in their major variations, within a single literature and society: a literature, English, which is perhaps richer than any other in the full range of its themes of country and city; and a society which went through a process of historical development, in rural and then industrial and urban economies and communities, very early and very thoroughly; still a particular history but one which has also become, in some central ways, a dominant mode of development in many parts of the world. Each of the phases of this history can be looked at more deeply in itself, and there are still other ways of describing the sequence, the interaction and the development. There is an obvious need for more comparative studies: there is already rich material in French and Russian literature, where both the country and the city have related but specific major meanings; in German thought and literature, where the idea of the city as a cultural centre followed an especially positive course; in American literature and culture, where the speed and scale of the process have created very powerful and at times universal ideas and images; in Italian culture, not only as a source, but in the dramatic character of its contemporary transition; in the literatures, as we have seen, of the developing world, where other ways of seeing a related process have been becoming articulate. All this, it is hoped and can be expected, will be specifically and comparatively studied.

(ii)

But it is not, was not, ever a question of study alone. The very fact that the historical process, in some of its main features, is now effectively international, means that we have more than material for interesting comparisons. We are touching, and know that we are touching, forms of a general crisis. Looking back, for example, on the English history, and especially on its culmination in imperialism, I can see in this process of the altering relations of country and city the driving force of a mode of production which has indeed transformed the world. I am then very willing to see the city as capitalism, as so many now do, if I can say also that this mode of production began, specifically, in the English rural economy, and produced, there, many of the characteristic effects – increases of production, physical reordering of a totally available world, displacement of customary settlements, a human remnant and force which became a proletariat – which have since been seen, in many extending forms, in cities and colonies and in an international system as a whole. It then does not surprise me that the complaints in Covent Garden echo the complaints of the commoners, since the forces of improvement and development, in those specific forms – an amalgam of financial and political power which is pursuing different ends from those of any local community but which has its own and specific internal rationale – are in a fundamental sense similar, as phases of capitalist enterprise.

What the oil companies do, what the mining companies do, is what landlords did, what plantation owners did and do. And many have gone along with them, seeing the land and its properties as available for profitable exploitation: so clear a profit that the quite different needs of local settlement and community are overridden, often ruthlessly. Difficult and complex as this process is, since the increases in production and the increases in new forms of work and wealth are undoubtedly real, it is usually more necessary to see this kind of contrast – between forms of settlement and forms of exploitation – than to see the more conventional contrast between agricultural and industrial development: the country as cooperation with nature, the city and industry as overriding and transforming it. There is a visible qualitative difference between the results of farming and the results of mining, but if we see only this contrast we see only some of the results. The effects on human settlements, and on customary or locally self-determined ways of life, are often very similar. The land, for its fertility or for its ore, is in both cases abstractly seen. It is used in an enterprise which overrides, for the time being, all other considerations. Since the dramatic physical transformations of the Industrial Revolution we have found it easy to forget how profoundly and still visibly agriculture altered the land. Some of the earliest and most remarkable environmental effects, negative as well as positive, followed from agricultural practice: making land fertile but also, in places, overgrazing it to a desert; clearing good land but also, in places, with the felling of trees, destroying it or creating erosion. Some of these uses preceded any capitalist order, but the capitalist mode of production is still, in world history, the most effective and powerful agency for all these kinds of physical and social transformation. The city is only one if now conventional way of seeing this kind of change; and the country, as almost all of us now know it, is undoubtedly another. Indeed the change from admiration of cultivated country to the intense attachment to 'unspoiled' places is a precise record of this persistent process and its effects at one of its most active stages.

But we must then also make a distinction between such techniques of production and the *mode* of production which is their particular social form. We call the technical changes improvement and progress, welcome some of their effects and deplore others, and can feel either numbed or divided; a state of mind in which, again and again, the most abstract and illusory ideas of a natural rural way of life tempt or at least charm us. Or we can fall back on saying that this is the human condition: the irresolvable choice between a necessary materialism and a necessary humanity. Often we try to resolve it by dividing work and leisure, or society and the individual, or city and country, not only in our minds but in suburbs and garden cities, town houses and country cottages, the week and the weekend. But we then usually find that the directors of the improvements, the captains of the change, have arrived earlier and settled deeper; have made, in fact, a more successful self-division. The country-house, as we saw, was one of the first forms of this temporary resolution, and in the nineteenth century as many were built by the new lords of capitalist production as survived, improved, from the old lords, sometimes their ancestors, of the agrarian change. It remains remarkable that so much of this settlement has been physically imitated, down to details of semi-detached villas and styles of leisure and weekends. An immensely productive capitalism, in all its stages, has extended both the resources and the modes which, however unevenly, provide and contain forms of response to its effects.

It is then often difficult, past this continuing process which contains the substance of so much of our lives, to recognize, adequately, the specific character of the capitalist mode of production, which is not the use of machines or techniques of improvement, but their minority ownership. Indeed as the persistent concentration of ownership, first of the land, then of all major means of production, was built into a system and a state, with many kinds of political and cultural mediation, it was easy for the perception to diminish though the fact was increasing. Many modern ruralists, many urban conservationists, see 'the state' or 'the planners' as their essential enemy, when it is quite evident that what the state is administering and the planners serving is an economic system which is capitalist in all its main intentions, procedures and criteria. The motorway system, the housing clearance, the office-block and supermarket replacing streets of homes and shops, may materialize in the form of a social plan, but there is no case in which the priorities of a capitalist system have not, from the beginning, been built in. It may be simple industrial development or mining: the decision will have been made originally and will be finally determined by owners calculating profit. The road system will include their needs and preferences for modes of distribution and transport, and these are given priority, either as in the case of lorries against railways or as in the more general situation in which the land itself is looked on, abstractedly, as a transport network, just as it is looked on elsewhere, again abstractly, as an opportunity for production. Housing clearance and housing shortage are alike related to the altered distribution of human settlement which has followed from a set of minority decisions about where work will be made available, by the criteria of profit and internal convenience. What are called regional policies are remedial efforts within these priorities rather than decisively against them. The industrial-agricultural balance, in all its physical forms of town-and-country relations, is the product, however mediated, of a set of decisions about capital investment made by the minority which controls capital and which determines its use by calculations of profit.

When we have lived long enough with such a system it is difficult not to mistake it for a necessary and practical reality, whatever elements of its process we may find objectionable. But it is not only that the specific histories of country and city, and of their immediate interrelations, have been determined, in Britain, by capitalism. It is that the total character of what we know as modern society has been similarly determined. The competitive indifference or the sense of isolation in the cities can be seen as bearing a profound relation to the kinds of social competition and alienation which just such a system promotes. These experiences are never exclusive, since within the pressures and limits people make other settlements and attachments and try to live by other values. But the central drive is still there.

Again, enough of us now, for a long enough period, have been living in cities for new kinds of communication to become necessary, and these in their turn reveal both the extension and mobility of the urban and industrial process and the appropriation and exploitation of the same media for capitalist purposes. I do not only mean advertising, though that is a specific deformation of the capitalist city. Nor do I mean only the minority ownership and purposes of the press. I mean the conversion of a necessary social mode into specific forms. It is very striking that in response to the city and to a more deeply interrelated society and world we have developed habitual responses to information, in an altered sense. The morning newspaper, the early radio programme, the evening television, are in this sense forms of orientation in which our central social sense is both sought and in specific and limited ways confirmed.

Wordsworth saw that when we become uncertain in a world of apparent strangers who yet, decisively, have a common effect on us, and when forces that will alter our lives are moving all around us in apparently external and unrecognizable forms, we can retreat, for security, into a deep subjectivity, or we can look around us for social pictures, social signs, social messages, to which, characteristically, we try to relate as individuals but so as to discover, in some form, community. Much of the content of modern communications is this kind of substitute for directly discoverable and transitive relations to the world. It can be properly related to the scale and complexity of modern society, of which the city is always the most evident example. But it has become general, reaching to the most remote rural regions. It is a form of shared consciousness rather than merely a set of techniques. And as a form of consciousness it is not to be understood by rhetorical analogies like the 'global village'. Nothing could be less like the experience of any kind of village or settled active community. For in its main uses it is a form of unevenly shared consciousness of persistently external events. It is what appears to happen, in these powerfully transmitted and mediated ways, in a world with which we have no other perceptible connections but which we feel is at once central and marginal to our lives. This paradoxical set of one-way relationships, in itself determining what we take to be relevant information and news, is then a specific form of consciousness which is inherent in the dominant mode of production, in which, in remarkably similar ways, our skills, our energies, our daily ordering of our lives, our perceptions of the shape of a lifetime, are to a critical extent defined and determined by external formulations of a necessary reality: that external, willed reality – external because its means are in minority hands – from which, in so much of our lives, we seem to have no option but to learn.

Underlying social relations often manifest themselves in these habitual and conventional ways. The communications system is not only the information network but also the transport network. The city, obviously, has always been associated with concentration of traffic. Notoriously, in modern transport systems, this is still the case, and the problem often seems insoluble. But traffic is not only a technique; it is a form of consciousness and a form of social relations. I do not mean only the obvious derivation of so many problems of traffic from a series of decisions about the location of work and the centralization of political power; decisions which were never, in any real sense, socially made, but which were imposed by the priorities of a mode of production. I mean also the forms of modern traffic. It is impossible to read the early descriptions of crowded metropolitan streets – the people as isolated atoms, flowing this way and that; a common stream of separated identities and directions – without seeing, past them, this mode of relationship embodied in the modern car: private, enclosed, an individual vehicle in a pressing and merely aggregated common flow; certain underlying conventions of external control but within them the passing of rapid signals of warning, avoidance, concession, irritation, as we pursue our ultimately separate ways but in a common mode. And this is no longer only a feature of the city, though it is most evident there. Over a whole network of the land, this is how, at one level, we relate; indeed it is one form of settlement, intersecting and often deeply affecting what we think of as settlements – cities, towns, villages – in an older mode.

In all these actual social relations and forms of consciousness, ideas of the country and the city, often of an older kind, continue to act as partial interpreters. But we do not always see that in their main bearings they are forms of response to a social system as a whole. Most obviously since the Industrial Revolution, but in my view also since the beginning of the capitalist agrarian mode of production, our powerful images of country and city have been ways of responding to a whole social development. This is why, in the end, we must not limit ourselves to their contrast but go on to see their interrelations and through these the real shape of the underlying crisis.

It is significant, for example, that the common image of the country is now an image of the past, and the common image of the city an image of the future. That leaves, if we isolate them, an undefined present. The pull of the idea of the country is towards old ways, human ways, natural ways. The pull of the idea of the city is towards progress, modernization, development. In what is then a tension, a present experienced as tension, we use the contrast of country and city to ratify an unresolved division and conflict of impulses, which it might be better to face in its own terms.

Aspects of the history of the ideas can then help us. We have seen how often an idea of the country is an idea of childhood: not only the local memories, or the ideally shared communal memory, but the feel of childhood: of delighted absorption in our own world, from which, eventually, in the course of growing up, we are distanced and separated, so that it and the world become things we observe. In Wordsworth and Clare, and in many other writers, this structure of feeling is powerfully expressed, and we have seen how often it is then converted into illusory ideas of the rural past: those successive and endlessly recessive 'happy Englands of my boyhood'. But what is interesting now is that we have had enough stories and memories of urban childhoods to perceive the same pattern. The old urban working-class community; the delights of corner-shops, gas lamps, horsecabs, trams, piestalls: all gone, it seems, in successive generations. These urban ways and objects seem to have, in the literature, the same real emotional substance as the brooks, commons, hedges, cottages, festivals of the rural scene. And the point of saying this is not to disprove or devalue either kind of feeling. It is to see the real change that is being written about, as we discern its common process.

For what is at issue, in all these cases, is a growth and alteration of consciousness: a history repeated in many lives and many places which is fundamentally an alteration of perception and relationship. What was once close, absorbing, accepted, familiar, internally experienced becomes separate, distinguishable, critical, changing, externally observed. In common or backstreet, village or city quarter, this process happens. We can say, of course, that it is an inevitable process; that this growth of adult consciousness is profoundly necessary, if only to see that these valued worlds were and are being created by men. But we have to say also that the village or backstreet of a child is not and cannot be the village or backstreet of the contemporary working adult. Great confusion is caused if the real childhood memory is projected, unqualified, as history. Yet what we have finally to say is that we live in a world in which the dominant mode of production and social relationships teaches, impresses, offers to make normal and even rigid, modes of detached, separated, external perception and action: modes of using and consuming rather than accepting and enjoying people and things. The structure of feeling of the memoirs is then significant and indispensable as a response to this specific social deformation. Yet this importance can only be recognized when we have made the historical judgement: not only that these are childhood views, which contemporary adult experience contradicts or qualifies; but that a process of human growth has in itself been deformed, by these deep internal directions of what an adult consciousness must be, in this kind of using, consuming, abstracting world. It is not so much the old village or the old backstreet that is significant. It is the perception and affirmation of a world in which one is not necessarily a stranger and an agent, but can be a member, a discoverer, in a shared source of life. Taken alone, of course, this is never enough. Indeed its displacement to fantasies about old villages and old backstreets can diminish even its immediate significance. To make an adult, working world of that kind would involve sharp critical consciousness and long active agency. Yet we can see here, in a central example, the true aetiology of some of the powerful images of country and city, when unalienated experience is the rural past and realistic experience is the urban future. If we take only the images, we can swing from one to the other, but without illumination. For we have really to look, in country and city alike, at the real social processes of alienation, separation, externality, abstraction. And we have to do this not only critically, in the necessary history of rural and urban capitalism, but substantially, by affirming the experiences which in many millions of lives are discovered and rediscovered, very often under pressure: experiences of directness, connection, mutuality, sharing, which alone can define, in the end, what the real deformation may be.

In the late nineteen-forties I knew that I was at last separated from the village in which I had grown up. I began to write what I thought this experience was, in the seven versions that eventually became the novel *Border Country*. It wasn't only, through those versions, that I found myself connecting the experience to a more general history of physical and social mobility, and beyond that to a crisis of education and class which when I had worked it through I went back and read, as if for the first time, in George Eliot and Hardy and Lawrence. It was also that I had to look at the village again, and to set up some tension between my childhood memories and the adult working experience of my father's generation. But even that was not enough. Many people have assumed that Harry Price, the signalman with his gardens, was a portrait of my father; but this is not really so. I found that to get the real movement I had to divide and contrast what I had seen in my father as conflicting impulses and modes. I had to imagine another character. Morgan Rosser, the politician and dealer, who in his relation to Harry Price could express and work through what I believed I had seen as an internal conflict. The modes of contemplation and of action, of absorbed work and of mobile and critical change, had to be expressed in a relationship if the complicated development of the life of the village was to be fully expressed. Beyond this again was the son, the observer, more specifically removed; bound to these two modes, these two figures of a father, and taking that continuing action into his work in the city.

I used the same method, of dividing and then connecting to express this internal crisis, in a novel of the city, *Second Generation*, which was essentially the same movement, in a different environment. That was an image of traffic, of relationships as traffic and of persistent attempts to find other relationships, as clearly as in *Border Country*, with its simpler form of the country railway and its changes. That is how I have seen the whole problem since, in more general ways. The experience that went into the novels became the questions I put to the tradition.

But at one time, while writing *Border Country*, I felt a sudden sadness, apparently separate from my theme. I felt, because I think I had been told, that the rural experience, the working country, had gone; that in Britain it was only a marginal thing, and that as time went by this would be so everywhere. I accepted this, at one level, for much longer than now seems possible. It was one of the impulses, I can see now, that kept sending me back to old rural literature and history. And I cannot clearly remember when I suddenly realized that it was not really true at all. Even while I was showing in the novels a different and persistent experience, this idea had stuck. When at last I saw that it was false I knew I had to look for its sources. These were not only, as might be supposed, the sentimental ruralists, though just because of my experience I had to face them. They were also, and more critically, the brisk metropolitan progressives, many of them supposedly internationalists and socialists, whose contempt for rural societies was matched only by their confidence in an urban industrial future which they were about in one way or another – modernization, the white heat of technology, revolution – to convert into socialism. There are so many writers and thinkers, still, of each of these kinds, that it takes a long time, a long effort, to look round and say that their common idea of a lost rural economy is false.

Is it then not false? Is it not obvious that in Britain a working agriculture is marginal? That was the first mode of error I learned to perceive: an unnoticed persistence, in the old imperialist countries, of a kind of abstract chauvinism: that what happened to them was what was happening or would happen to everyone. Still most countries in the world were predominantly rural, but within the imperialist division of the world they did not really count, were not in important ways there. Even those who saw that they were exploited, within the imperialist division of the world, did not necessarily go on to see that in and through this condition and its struggles a working agriculture, a rural economy in any of its possible forms, simply had to persist: in the exploited countries themselves and, if some elements of the exploitation were to be diminished, in what had been abstractly thought of as the developed metropolitan countries. Perhaps more of us now know this. The facts of the food and population crisis have been widely and properly publicized. If we are to survive at all, we shall have to develop and extend our working agricultures. The common idea of a lost rural world is then not only an abstraction of this or that stage in a continuing history (and many of the stages we can be glad have gone or are going). It is in direct contradiction to any effective shape of our future, in which work on the land will have to become more rather than less important and central. It is one of the most striking deformations of industrial capitalism that one of our most central and urgent and necessary activities should have been so displaced, in space or in time or in both, that it can be plausibly associated only with the past or with distant lands.

Some of this, now, is changing, even within old imperialist Europe. But it is still the case that the future of agriculture is seen, here and in the third world, in mainly capitalist forms, and especially as involving massive social displacement. It could be done, and is elsewhere being done, in quite different ways. And the urgency of its doing, in ways that break with capitalism, is linked with that other complementary aspect of the crisis: the condition and the future of the cities and of industry. One of the real merits of some rural writers, often not seen because other elements are present, is an insistence on the complexity of the living natural environment. Now that the dangers to this environment have come more clearly into view, our ideas, once again, have to shift. Some of the darkest images of the city have to be faced as quite literal futures. An insane over-confidence in the specialized powers of metropolitan industrialism has brought us to the point where however we precisely assess it the risk to human survival is becoming evident, or if we survive, as I think we shall, there is the clear impossibility of continuing as we are.

It is necessary to say this, in the deepening crisis of modern metropolitan and industrial living, and in the more serious crisis of persistent and intractable poverty in the rest of the world, even while we know it can easily be diverted into yet another rural threnody, or into a cynical fatalism. It is important to remember how much damage to the environment was and is being done by the capitalist mode of progressive agriculture; this is not a crisis of manufacturing industry alone. Similarly we need to acknowledge that recognition of the crisis, and almost all possible ways of resolving it, are functions of consciousness: of a flexible and highly mobile capacity to observe and intervene: in techniques and modes of planning and conservation, but even more critically in the area which will really decide our future, the area of decision itself. As we perceive a total environment, and as we register the consequences of so many abstracted and separated activities, we begin to see that all the real decisions are about modes of social interest and control. We begin to see, in fact, that the active powers of minority capital, in all its possible forms, are our most active enemies, and that they will have to be not just persuaded but defeated and superseded. The scale and connection of the necessary decisions require social powers and social resources which capitalism in any of its forms denies, opposes and alienates. The different social consciousness of the dispossessed labourers and of the urban workers, born in protest and despair, has to come through in new ways as a collectively responsible society. Neither will the city save the country nor the country the city. Rather the long struggle within both will become a general struggle, as in a sense it has always been.

We have more to work with than we ordinarily acknowledge. Rural England is said to be a thing of the past, and of course the changes are evident. But if we look up from the idea and back at the country we see how much is still present, even in this exceptionally industrialized and urbanized nation. Four-fifths of our land surface: the cultivated land, much of it better kept than it has ever been; the wild land, made more accessible, in a complicated process of pressure and openness. Most of the natural and working experiences which have been so powerfully celebrated in our rural literature are still directly available. It is still in so many places a beautiful country, and many of us can work in different ways, to keep and enhance it. I have had the luck to thin a wood and watch the cowslips and bluebells and foxgloves come back; to repair and rebuild old drystone walls; to hedge and ditch, after long neglect, and to see from skilled men how the jobs should be done. And if we look up from the idea of the city, we find in and through the extraordinary pressures a good deal of caring and intelligent work to make the cities cleaner and finer, to bring out and to build their best qualities. To know any of this directly is to know also, very closely, the constant threat of deliberate and indifferent destruction. But each process is a fact; in the best and in the worst there is neither a lost nor a won cause; it is an active, immediate and persistent struggle. It is also, as we shall see, a very complicated struggle, reaching into every part of our lives.

(iv)

I have been arguing that capitalism, as a mode of production, is the basic process of most of what we know as the history of country and city. Its abstracted economic drives, its fundamental priorities in social relations, its criteria of growth and of profit and loss, have over several centuries altered our country and created our kinds of city. In its final forms of imperialism it has altered our world.

Seeing the history in this way, I am then of course convinced that resistance to capitalism is the decisive form of the necessary human defence. Many particular defences stop short of seeing this decisive process, and need to be challenged to take the ideas and the feelings right through. Many others, however, get through as defences, as forms of opposition to what is called the modern world, in which capitalism or technology may well be included, but with no specificity: the reflex indeed being fundamentally defensive, with no available confidence in any different way of life, or with such confidence replaced by utopian or apocalyptic visions, none of which can connect with any immediate social practice or movement. And what serious movement, it is asked, could there be? Look at socialism or communism: historically the enemies of capitalism, but in detail and often in principle, in matters of the country and the city, continuing and even intensifying some of the same fundamental processes.

This is a genuine historical and political difficulty. Trotsky said that the history of capitalism was the history of the victory of town over country. He then proceeded, in the critical first years of the Russian Revolution, to outline a programme for just such a victory, on a massive scale, as a way of defeating capitalism and preserving socialism. Stalin carried through very much that programme, on a scale and with a brutality which made that 'victory' over the peasants one of the most terrible phases in the whole history of rural society. The local needs and priorities were desperate: a shattered economy and an appalling food shortage; rural capitalism, in new forms, undoubtedly spreading. But the way it was done, and the spirit in which it was done, were not only brutal; they drew on one element of an ambiguity in Marxism which in its turn had massive consequences on the character of the society as a whole.

Engels, as we saw, was among the first to see the modern city as a social and physical consequence of capitalism: built and living in its modes. He added, later, the decisive idea that the very processes of disturbance and exposure, in these particular forms, had created a proletarian and a socialist movement which could end capitalism and create different social relations and different kinds of human settlement. In the *Communist Manifesto* Marx and Engels argued that 'the bourgeoisie has subjected the country to the rule of the towns . . . has created enormous cities . . . has made barbarian and semi-barbarian countries dependent on the civilized ones': the familiar history of capitalism and imperialism. They argued that these relations of centralization and dependence had created the conditions for revolution, and in one sense they were right.

But there was an ambiguity at the core of the argument. They denounced what was being done in the tearing progress of capitalism and imperialism; they insisted that men must struggle to supersede it, and they showed us some ways. But implicit in the denunciation was another set of value-judgements: the bourgeoisie had 'rescued a considerable part of the population from the idiocy of rural life'; the subjected nations were 'barbarian and semi-barbarian', the dominating powers 'civilized'. It was then on this kind of confidence in the singular values of modernization and civilization that a major distortion in the history of communism was erected. The exposed urban proletariat would learn and create new and higher forms of society: if that was all that had been said it would have been very different. But if the forms of bourgeois development contained, with whatever contradiction, values higher than 'rural idiocy' or 'barbarism', then almost any programme, in the name of the urban proletariat, could be justified and imposed. The terrible irony has been that the real processes of absolute urban and industrial priority, and of the related priority of the advanced and civilized nations, worked through not only to damage the 'rural idiots' and the colonial 'barbarians and semi-barbarians', but to damage, at the heart, the urban proletarians themselves, and the advanced and civilized societies over which, in their turn, the priorities exercised their domination, in a strange dialectical twist. To see exposure creating revolution was one thing; to see more of the same producing more of something quite different was at best an apocalyptic hope.

This difficulty worked itself through, in a surprising way, in our own century. Revolutions came not in the 'developed' but in the 'undeveloped' countries. The Chinese revolution, defeated in the cities, went to the country and gained its ultimate strength. The Cuban Revolution went from the city to the country, where its force was formed. In a whole epoch of national and social liberation struggles, the exploited rural and colonial populations became the main sources of continued revolt. In the famous Chinese phrase about world revolution, the 'countryside' was surrounding the 'cities'. Thus the 'rural idiots' and the 'barbarians and semi-barbarians' have been, for the last forty years, the main revolutionary force in the world.

We can then look back, from this real historical experience, to one of the underlying forms of the idea of revolution. In some of the fundamental thinking of the socialist tradition, including that of Marx and Engels, there is a formulation which is at once the most exciting, the most relevant and yet the most undeveloped in the whole revolutionary argument. Engels wrote of socialism as 'abolishing the contrast between town and country, which has been brought to its extreme point by present-day capitalist society'. Marx and Engels wrote that the housing question could never be solved while 'modern big cities' were maintained, and that only with socialism could we restore 'the intimate connection between industrial and agricultural production'. The utopian socialists had made many proposals for new kinds of balanced communities and societies; William Morris, as we saw, continued to think in this way. But under many pressures, in the twentieth century, from the sheer physical drive of developing capitalism and imperialism to the class habits of thought of metropolitan socialist intellectuals, this extraordinary emphasis was virtually lost. Its phrases were remembered, but as an old, impractical, childish dream. Yet it is an emphasis that is now being revived. It has been stated as a direction of policy in the Chinese Revolution. And it has been significantly revived, among Western revolutionary socialists, as a response to the crisis of industrial civilization and what is seen as megalopolis.

It can be restated theoretically. The division and opposition of city and country, industry and agriculture, in their modern forms, are the critical culmination of the division and specialization of labour which, though it did not begin with capitalism, was developed under it to an extraordinary and transforming degree. Other forms of the same fundamental division are the separation between mental and manual labour, between administration and operation, between politics and social life. The symptoms of this division can be found at every point in what is now our common life: in the idea and practice of social classes; in conventional definitions of work and of education; in the physical distribution of settlements; and in temporal organization of the day, the week, the year, the lifetime. Much of the creative thinking of our time is an attempt to re-examine each of these concepts and practices. It is based on the conviction that the system which generates and is composed by them is intolerable and will not survive. In many areas of this thinking there is not only analytic but programmatic response: on new forms of decision-making, new kinds of education, new definitions and practices of work, new kinds of settlement and land-use.

I can now look back a generation, to the immediate postwar years, and remember my feeling that except for certain simple kinds of idealizing retrospect there was no main current of thought in the world which had not been incorporated within the fundamental forms of the capitalist and imperialist system. Orthodox communism and orthodox social-democracy – its traditional opponents – indeed showed many features of this system in their most powerful forms, all the more dangerously because they had been fused with continuing aspirations to social liberation and development. But to feel this was to be pressed back towards the extreme subjectivism and fatalism

366

which then, and for a generation, dominated our thought. Many descriptions of our current crisis were and still are cast within these subjectivist and fatalist forms.

Yet a deeper change has now become quite evident. All the conventional priorities are again being questioned. Other kinds of social response and social analysis have worked their way through, until in often confused and still unfinished forms they hold a certain initiative. The theoretical if not practical confidence of defenders of the existing system has gone. The position in ideas is again quite open, ironically at the very time when the practical pressures are almost overwhelming.

This change of basic ideas and questions, especially in the socialist and revolutionary movements, has been for me the connection which I have been seeking for so long, through the local forms of a particular and personal crisis, and through the extended inquiry which has taken many forms but which has come through as this inquiry into the country and the city. They are the many questions that were a single question, that once moved like light: a personal experience, for the reasons I described, but now also a social experience, which connects me, increasingly, with so many others. This is the position, the sense of shape, for which I have worked. Yet it is still, even now, only beginning to form. It is what is being done and is to do, rather than anything that has been finally done.

For there is nothing now more urgent than to take the fundamental idea, the problem of overcoming the division of labour, to the tests of rigorous analysis, rigorous proposal and rigorous practice. It can be done only in new forms of cooperative effort. If what is visible already as the outlines of a movement is to come through with the necessary understanding and strength, we shall have to say what in detail can be practically done, over a vast range from regional and investment planning to a thousand processes in work, education, and community. The negative effects will continue to show themselves, in a powerful and apparently irresistible pressure: physical effects on the environment: a simultaneous crisis of overcrowded cities and a depopulating countryside, not only within but between nations; physical and nervous stresses of certain characteristic kinds of work and characteristic kinds of career; the widening gap between the rich and poor of the world, within the threatening crisis of population and resources; the similarly widening gap between concern and decision, in a world in which all the fallout, military, technical and social, is in the end inescapable. And to see the negative effects, with whatever urgency, can be to paralyse the will. The last recess of the division of labour is this recess within ourselves, where what we want and what we believe we can do seem impassably divided.

We can overcome division only by refusing to be divided. That is a personal decision but then a social action. I can only record what I have myself learned. Others will learn it quite differently. But I grew up, as I said, where the division was visible, in a land and then in a family. I moved from country to city, and now live and work in both. I learned, in many forms, the shapes of this history, its ideas and its images, in the society and the literature which had earliest and most thoroughly experienced a change that was to become universal or at least an offered model for universal development. This left, in my mind, every kind of question and intricacy, and I had slowly to retrace the experience, in myself and in the record, as a way of gaining the present and the future through a different understanding of the shaping and fascinating past.

It was always a limited inquiry: the country and the city within a single tradition. But it has brought me to the point where I can offer its meanings, its implications and its connections to others: for discussion and amendment; for many kinds of possible cooperative work; but above all for an emphasis – the sense of an experience and of ways of changing it – in the many countries and cities where we live.

Appendix

'Country', as a word, is derived from *contra* (against, opposite) and has the original sense of land spread out over against the observer. In the thirteenth century it acquired its modern meanings of a tract or region, and of a land or nation. In Tindale in 1526 it is contrasted with the city: 'tolde it in the cyte, and in the countre' (Mark v, 14). 'City' had by this time become normal usage for a large town, though derived from *civitas*, which was in its turn derived from *civis* (a citizen in the sense of a national). *Civitas* had meant community, and was so applied to the tribes of Gaul; later it was the name of an ecclesiastical district. In Old English it became interchangeable with *burh* and was more commonly used in this sense than *urbs*, which had been nearer the modern sense. In Middle English it became common and in the reign of Henry VIII was made equivalent to the seat of a cathedral, a usage since surpassed.

From the late sixteenth century, as the general history would lead one to expect, there are more frequent and more pointed contrasts of 'city' and 'country'. 'Countryman' and 'country people' in the rural sense date from this period, as do 'country-house' and 'country-seat'. 'Countryfied' follows in the mid-seventeenth century; 'bumpkin' and 'country bumpkin' from the same period. 'Countryside' is an eighteenth- to nineteenth-century development, in its modern sense. 'Rural' and 'rustic' are present as physical descriptions from the fifteenth century but acquire social implications, mainly specializing in 'rustic' and 'rusticity' from the late sixteenth century. 'Urbane' similarly extended from its sixteenth-century physical sense to its modern social implications, first recorded in the early seventeenth century.

'Metropolis' had been the chief town or the seat of a bishop from the sixteenth century; 'metropolitan' is still mainly physical until the eighteenth century, when it begins to take on its modern social implications. 'Suburban', similarly, has a physical sense from the early seventeenth century, and a social sense from the early nineteenth.

'Farm' was originally a fixed payment, then from the sixteenth century, by extension, a holding of land on lease, and so to the modern meaning. 'Commuter' is a late nineteenth-century railway term, from the ticket bought at a commuted rate. 'Conurbation' first appears in the mid-twentieth century. 'Pastoral', with a root sense of feeding, as in 'pasture', is in common use for shepherds from the fourteenth century, and has an almost contemporary analogical meaning for priests. 'Pastoral' in its social and literary sense comes from the late sixteenth century, which can be seen as the decisive period in the formation of the structure of meanings in the words which describe my main theme.

References

Page   1. COUNTRY AND CITY

14 *Composed upon Westminster Bridge, Sept 3, 1803*, in *The Poetical Works of William Wordsworth*; ed. E. de Selincourt and H. Darbishire; Oxford, 1940–49; Vol. III.

16 *Tour Through the Whole Island of Great Britain*; Daniel Defoe; ed. G. D. H. Cole and D. C. Browning; Everyman Revised Edition (1962); 83.

16 Cit. *Sheep and Turnips; being the life and times of Arthur Young*; A. Defries; 1938; 150–51.

16 *Tour*; 87.

16 Op. cit., 177–8.

16–17 *Rural Rides*; William Cobbett; ed. G. D. H. and M. Cole; 3 vols.; Oxford, 1930; 76.

2. A PROBLEM OF PERSPECTIVE

18 *The Pattern under the Plough*; G. Ewart Evans; London, 1966; 17.

18 *Culture and Environment*; F. R. Leavis and Denys Thompson; London, 1933; 87.

18 *Change in the Village*; George Sturt (George Bourne); London, 1912; 7.

19 *Helpstone*; John Clare; in *Poems*, ed. J. W. Tibble; 2 vols.; London, 1935.

19 *The Village*; George Crabbe; in *Poetical Works of George Crabbe*; ed. A. J. and R. M. Carlyle; Oxford, 1914.

19 *The Deserted Village*; Oliver Goldsmith; in *Complete Poetical Works*; ed. A. Dobson; Oxford, 1906.

20 *The City Madam*; Philip Massinger; Act IV, sc. iv.

20–21 *Utopia*; ed. J. H. Lupton; Oxford, 1895; 39–40.

21 *Selected Letters of Innocent III*; ed. Cheney and Semple; Edinburgh, 1953.

3. PASTORAL AND COUNTER-PASTORAL

23 *The Village*; op. cit.

24 The evidence for this amendment is in Boswell's *Life of Samuel*

Page

    Johnson; ed. J. W. Crocker; London, 1831; Vol. V, 55.

24 *Works*; Hesiod; ed. and trans. H. G. Evelyn White; London, 1914 (repr. 1954); 11.

25 *The Greek Bucolic Poets*; ed. and trans. A. S. F. Gow; Cambridge, 1953; 30.

25 ibid., 39–40.

26 ibid., 47.

26 *Oxford Book of Greek Verse in Translation*; T. F. Higham and C. M. Bowra; Oxford, 1938; 144–5.

26 *A Book of Greek Verse*; W. Headlam; Cambridge, 1907; 213.

26–27 *The Eclogues of Virgil*; trans. C. Day Lewis; London, 1963; 11.

27 ibid., 11.

27 ibid., 41.

28 *Georgics*, II, 459–501 *passim*.

28 *Eclogues*, op. cit., 23–4.

29 *Odes of Horace*; trans. A. D. Godley; London, 1898.

29 There are some exceptions to this conventional excision. Miss Elizabeth Duthie has drawn my attention to examples in *Poems on Several Occasions* by Jonathan Smedley (1730) and in *Poems* by William Somerville (1727).

30 *Select Poetry and Prose of S. T. Coleridge*; ed. S. Potter; London, 1950; 58.

30 Pope: Twickenham Edition, Vol. 1; 27.

30 *The Village*; op. cit.

31 ibid.

32 Op. cit., 26.

32 *The Arte of English Poesie*; G. Puttenham; ed. G. D. Willcock and A. Walker; Cambridge, 1936; 38.

34 *The Ploughman's Song*; in *Oxford Book of 16th Century Verse*; ed. E. K. Chambers; Oxford, 1932; 410.

34 *The Passionate Shepherd to his Love*; in Marlowe's *Poems*; ed. M. Maclean; London, 1968; 257.

34 *The Nymph's Reply to the Shepherd*; in *Poems of Sir Walter Raleigh*; ed. Agnes M. C. Latham; London, 1929; 40.

35 *The Works of Michael Drayton*; ed. J. William Hebel; Oxford, 1931; Vol. II, 363.

35–36 In *Oxford Book of 17th Century Verse*; ed. H. J. C. Grierson and G. Bullough; Oxford, 1934; 954.

36 *Poems of Abraham Cowley*; ed. A. R. Waller; Cambridge, 1905; 88.

36 In *Oxford Book of 17th Century Verse*; op. cit., 798.

37 *Poems of Richard Lovelace*; ed. C. H. Wilkinson; Oxford, 1930; 58.

37 *The Choice* in *Poems*; London, 1792.

37 *Ode on Solitude*; Pope, op. cit., Vol. VI.

38 *A Cure for the Spleen*; in *Oxford Book*, op. cit., 286.

38–39 In *Oxford Book of 17th Century Verse*; op. cit., 713.

Page

39 *Ode upon occasion of His Majesty's Proclamation in the year 1630.
    Commanding the Gentry to reside upon their estates in the Countrey.*
    In *Oxford Book*, op. cit., 448.

39 *The Readie and Easie Way to Establish a Free Commonwealth*;
    John Milton; London, 1660 (second – revised – edition); repr.
    Prose of Milton; ed. R. Garnett; London, 1921; 156.

40 *To Sir Robert Wroth* and *To Penshurst* were first published in *The
    Forrest* (1616) and are reprinted in *Ben Jonson, Works*; ed. C. H.
    Herford and P. and E. Simpson; Oxford, 1925–52; Vol. VII.

40 ibid.

41 ibid.

41 In *Poems of Thomas Carew*; ed. R. Dunlop; Oxford, 1949.

41 Op. cit., ll. 27–30.

42 Op. cit., ll. 23–8.

42 Op. cit., ll. 65–9.

43 Luxemburg: Socialism and the Churches; cit. A. Cunningham:
    Catholics and the Left; London, 1966; pp. 83–4.

43 ibid., *The Failure of the Christian Revolution.*

44 Op. cit., ll. 41–5.

45 *The Garden*; in *Poems and Letters of Andrew Marvell*; ed. H. M.
    Margoliouth; rev. ed. P. Legouis and E. F. Duncan-Jones;
    Oxford, 1971; Vol. I.

45 *The Thresher's Labour*; in *Poems on Several Occasions*; Stephen
    Duck; London, 1736.

46 Op. cit., ll. 1–2 and 5–10.

46 In *The Poetical Works of Robert Herrick*; ed. F. W. Moorman;
    Oxford, 1921; 100.

47 ibid.

4. GOLDEN AGES

49 Herrick, op. cit.

50 *Manifesto of the Communist Party*; K. Marx and F. Engels;
    London, 1934; 14.

51 Cit. *Studies in the Development of Capitalism*; M. H. Dobb;
    London, 1946; 44.

55 *Little Saxham Parish Registers, 1559–1850*; Woodbridge, 1907.

56 *Volpone*, Act I, sc. i.

56 Cit. *A People's History of England*; A. L. Morton; London, 1938;
    119.

57 Translated in Wilkinson, L. P.; *The Georgics of Virgil*; Cam-
    bridge, 1969.

57 In *Works of Edmund Spenser*; ed. Osgood and Lotspeich; Balti-
    more, 1932–49; *Minor Poems*, Vol. II, 110.

57 G. Chapman: *Dramatic Works*, Vol. III; London, 1873; 117.

58 *Utopia*; op. cit., 35–6.

58 ibid., 39–40.

58 ibid., 42.
59 ibid., 43.

5. TOWN AND COUNTRY

62 *Juvenal: the Sixteen Satires*; trans. P. Green; London, 1967; 88.
62 ibid., 269.
62 ibid., 75.
62 ibid., 127.
62 ibid., 127.
63 ibid., 87.
63 ibid., 286–7.
64 *Description of England*; William Harrison; ed. F. Furnivall; London, 1887; 131.
65 *Select Works of Robert Crowley (Crole)*; ed. J. M. Cowper; London, 1871.
65 *The Devil is an Ass*; Act II, sc. i.
68 *The Man of Mode*; George Etherege; London, 1676; Act V, sc. ii, ll. 217–18.
68 ibid., ll. 492–3.
69 *The Relapse*; John Vanbrugh; London, 1696; Act III, sc. iii, ll. 1–10.
69 *The Man of Mode*, Act IV, sc. ii, ll. 217–18.
69 *The Way of the World*; William Congreve, London, 1700; Act V, sc. i, ll. 550–2.
70 *The Plain Dealer*; William Wycherley; London, 1676; Act V, sc. iii, ll. 183–6.

6. THEIR DESTINY THEIR CHOICE

72 *Upon Appleton House* in Marvell, ed. cit.
73 ibid.
73 ibid.
74 ibid.
74 ibid.
74 ibid.
75 ibid.
75 ibid.
75 *Horatian Ode*, in Marvell, ed. cit.
76 *Epistle to Bathurst*; in Twickenham ed., Vol. III, ii; 111.
76 *Epistle to Burlington*; ibid., 154–5.
77 *To Bathurst*; ibid., 118–19.
77 *To Burlington*; ibid., 142.

7. THE MORALITY OF IMPROVEMENT

81 *Tom Jones*; Bk. VI, ch. vii.
82 ibid., Bk. VI, ch. iii.

Page
82 ibid.
83 ibid., Bk. XVIII, ch. xiii.
83 *Clarissa*, Vol. I, Letters 13 and 17.
83 *Tom Jones*, Bk. VI, ch. vii.
86 *Annals of Agriculture*, XXVI, 214.

8. NATURE'S THREADS

87 *The Deserted Village*, op. cit., ll. 397–8.
87 *The Seasons*; in *Complete Poetical Works of James Thomson*; ed.
    J. L. Robertson; Oxford, 1908; 48–9.
88 ibid., 13n.
88 ibid., *Autumn*, ll. 1235–8.
88 ibid., *Winter*, ll. 663–5.
88 ibid., *Castle of Indolence*, I, vi; 255.
88 ibid., II, xxvii; 288.
88 ibid., *Spring*, ll. 67 and 74–7.
89 ibid., *Summer*, ll. 1442 and 1448–56; cf. 106n.
89 ibid., 119n.
89 ibid., ll. 1764–7.
90 ibid., *Autumn*, ll. 162–4.
90 ibid., ll. 169–74.
90 ibid., ll. 350–52.
90 ibid., *Summer*, ll. 516–17 and 522.
90 ibid., *Autumn*, ll. 970–73.
91 ibid., ll. 1003–5 and 1031.
91 *Yardley Oak*, ll. 80–85, in *The Late Augustans: Longer Poems of
    the Later Eighteenth Century*; ed. D. Davie; London, 1958; 95.
92 *A Thanksgiving*; in Herrick, op. cit.
93 *The School Mistress*, ll. 1–2; in *Poetical Works of William Shen-
    stone*; ed. G. Gilfillan; Edinburgh, 1854.
93–94 *Rural Elegance*; in Shenstone, op. cit.
94 *Elegy written in a country churchyard*, vv. 9, 19 and 13, in Davie,
    op. cit.
95 *The Deserted Village*, op. cit., ll. 57–8.
95 ibid., ll. 63–4.
95 *Dedication to The Deserted Village*; cit. *New Essays by Oliver
    Goldsmith*; ed. R. S. Crane; Chicago, 1927; 120n.
96 Cf. Crane, op. cit.
96 Repr. as *The Revolution in Low Life*; in Crane, op. cit., 120.
96 *The Deserted Village*, ll. 39 and 275–8.
96 ibid., ll. 305–8.
96 ibid., ll. 309–10.
97 ibid., l. 342.
97 ibid., ll. 1–4.
97 ibid., ll. 5–6.

Page
97 ibid., ll. 9–14.
97 ibid., ll. 17–18.
98 ibid., ll. 31–2.
98 ibid., ll. 105–6.
98 ibid., ll. 95–6.
98 ibid., ll. 407–14.
99 ibid., ll. 39–46.
100 ibid., ll. 421–2.
100 ibid., ll. 427–30.
101 *The Country Justice*, Part I, II, 17–20; in Davie, op. cit., 71–92.
101 ibid., Part I, II, ll. 31–54 *passim* and l. 80.
101 ibid., ll. 61–4.
102 ibid., ll. 73–4.
102 ibid., ll. 167–8.
102 ibid., Part II, ll. 35–60.
103 ibid., ll. 95–6 and 99–100.
103 ibid., ll. 123–34 *passim*.
103 ibid., l. 115.
106 *Notes towards the Definition of Culture*; T. S. Eliot; London,
    1948; 52.
108 *The Village*, op. cit.

9. BRED TO TILL THE EARTH

110 *The Village*, op. cit., Bk. II.
110 ibid., Bk. I.
110–11 *The Thresher's Labour*, op. cit.
111–12 ibid.
112 *On Poverty*, op. cit.
112 *Gratitude*, op. cit.
113 *On Richmond Park*, op. cit.
113 *The Village*, op. cit.
114 ibid.
115 ibid.
115 ibid.
116 ibid.
117 ibid.
119 ibid.

10. ENCLOSURES, COMMONS AND COMMUNITIES

123 'The Agricultural Revolution in English History: a reconsidera-
    tion', in *Essays in Agrarian History*, ed. Minchinton; Vol. 2;
    Newton Abbot, 1968.
125 *Opinions of William Cobbett*; ed. G. D. H. Cole; London, 1944;
    86.
125 *Memoir of Thomas Bewick*; London, 1961; 27–8.

Page

126 ibid., 28 and 29.

126 ibid., 32.

128 Cf. *Village Life in the 18th Century*, G. E. Fussell; Worcester, 1948; ch. ii.

130 *Joseph Ashby of Tysoe*; M. K. Ashby; Cambridge, 1961; ch. xix.

132 *Culture and Anarchy*, ch. iii.

II. THREE AROUND FARNHAM

135–36 *Rural Rides*, op. cit., 13 and 15.

136 ibid., 17 and 233.

137 ibid., 207, 221, 34.

137–38 ibid., 311, 313, 313–14.

138–39 ibid., 65–6, 67.

140 ibid., 313.

142 *Persuasion*, chs. i, iii, and v.

144 'Economic Functions of English Landowners in the 17th and 18th Centuries', in *Essays in Agrarian History*, ed. Minchinton; Vol. I; Newton Abbot, 1968.

146 The Great Society, cit. Morton, op. cit., 119; Stephen Duck; and cit. *The Making of the English Working Class*; E. P. Thompson; London, 1963; ch. vii.

147 In *Writings of Gilbert White of Selborne*; ed. H. J. Massingham; London, 1938; 63–4.

147–48 ibid., 300–301.

12. PLEASING PROSPECTS

150 *The Civilization of the Renaissance in Italy*; J. Burckhardt; trans. Middlemore; London, 1929; 296.

152 *Paradise Lost*, Bk. IV.

153 *Upon Appleton House*, op. cit.

153 Pope; cit. *English Landscaping and Literature*; E. Malins; London, 1966.

153 *Poems of Charles Cotton*; ed. Buxton; London, 1958.

153 *Mansfield Park*, ch. xxv.

155 *Clandestine Marriage*, Act II, sc. ii.

155 *Headlong Hall*, ch. vi.

155 *The Fleece*, Bk. II; *Poems of John Dyer*; ed. E. Thomas; London, 1903.

155–56 *Grongar Hill*, op. cit.

156 *Spring*, op. cit., ll. 950–51.

156 *The Task*, Bk. I.

157 *Frost at Midnight*; op. cit.

158 Cit. *The Picturesque*; C. Hussey; London, 1927; 128.

158 *Prelude*, Bk. II (1850).

159 Cit. Hussey, op. cit., 86, 87.

159 *Correspondence of Thomas Gray*; ed. Paget Toynbee and L. Whibble; Oxford, 1935; rev. 1971; Vol. I, 128.

159 *Hymn before Sunrise, in the Vale of Chamouni*, 1802, in Coleridge, op. cit.

159 Johnson, cit. Hussey, op. cit., 112.

160 *Prelude*, Bk. XII (1850).

160 Johnson, cit. Hussey, op. cit., 113.

161 *Prelude*, Bk. XIV (1850).

161 ibid.

161 *Michael*; in Wordsworth, op. cit., Vol. II.

161 ibid.

162 *The Old Cumberland Beggar*; op. cit., Vol. IV.

163 *Prelude*, Bk. VIII (1805).

163 ibid., Bk. VII (1805).

163 ibid., Bk. VIII (1805).

163 ibid., Bk. VIII (1805).

164 *Frost at Midnight*, op. cit.

164 *Dejection*, op. cit.

164 *Pastoral Poesy*; in *Poems of John Clare*; ed. J. W. Tibble, 2 vols., London, 1935; Vol. II.

164–65 *Lines Written a few Miles above Tintern Abbey*; op. cit., Vol. II.

165 *Prelude*, Bk. XIV.

165 *Spring*, op. cit.

165 Cit. *Selected Poems of John Clare*; introd. G. Grigson, 1950; 11.

166 Cit. *The Rural Muse*; R. Unwin; London, 1954; 78.

167 *The Poetical Works of Robert Bloomfield and Henry Kirke White*; London, 1871; 27–8.

167 Cit. Unwin, op. cit., 48 and 105.

168 *The Farmer's Boy: Spring*; op. cit., 28.

168 ibid., *Autumn*; 66.

169 *The Shepherd's Calendar*; ed. E. Robinson and G. Summerfield; London, 1964.

169–70 *The Village Minstrel*, op. cit.

170 *The Revolution in Low Life*; op. cit., 123.

170 *Helpstone*; op. cit.

171 ibid.

171 ibid.

172 *The Village Minstrel*, CVI; op. cit.

172 *Joys of Childhood*; op. cit.

173 *Pastoral Poesy*; op. cit.

174 *The Progress of Rhyme*; op. cit.

174 *I am*; op. cit.

176 *Town Eclogues*; C. Jenner; London, 1772; Eclogue IV, *The Poet*;
    27–8.

177 Thomson, op. cit., 180, 209.

177 ibid., 106, 137–8.

178 ibid., 178–9.

178 *Verses on the Death of Adrienne Lecouvreur* (*La Mort de Mlle
    Lecouvreur, célèbre actrice*); trans. in *Voltaire*; H. N. Brailsford;
    Oxford, 1935; 54.

179 Cf. *The Crowd in History*; G. Rudé; New York, 1964.

179 *Inquiry into the Cause of the Late Increase of Robbers*; London,
    1751; 76.

180 *Four Letters to the Earl of Shelburne*; London, 2nd ed., 1783; 44.

181 *The Farmer's Letters to the People of England*; 2nd ed., 1771;
    353–4.

182 Cit. *London Life in the XVIIIth Century*; M. D. George;
    London, 1925; 323.

183 *London*; in *Poems of Blake*; ed. Binyon; London, 1931; 59.

183 ibid.

185 *The Prelude, a parallel text*; ed. J. C. Maxwell; London, 1971;
    256.

185 ibid., 339.

185 ibid., 499.

185 ibid., 260–61.

185 Thomson, op. cit., *Autumn*, l. 1301.

185 *Prelude*; ed. cit., 259, 261.

186 ibid., 286.

187 ibid., 292.

187 ibid., 343.

188 *Composed upon Westminster Bridge*; op. cit., Vol. III.

15. PEOPLE OF THE CITY

189 *Hard Times*; Book the First, ch. v.

192 *Dombey and Son*; ch. xlvii.

193–94 *Little Dorrit*; Book the First, ch. xxi.

194 ibid., ch. xv.

194 ibid., ch. xxvii.

195 *Dombey and Son*, ch. xiii.

195 ibid., ch. iii.

196 ibid., ch. xxxiii.

196–97 ibid., ch. xlviii.

197 ibid.

197–98 *Little Dorritt*; Book the Second; ch. xxxiv.

198 *Dombey and Son*; ch. i.

198–99 ibid., ch. vi.

Page

199–200 ibid., ch. xv.

200 ibid., ch. xx.

201 ibid., ch. xv.

16. KNOWABLE COMMUNITIES

204 *George Eliot's Life*; ed. J. W. Cross; Edinburgh and London, 1885; 254.

204 *Adam Bede*; ch. xxxii.

205 ibid., ch. vii.

205 ibid., ch. xii.

209–10 *The Mill on the Floss*; Bk. IV, ch. iii.

210–11 *Adam Bede*; ch. xvii.

211 ibid., ch. liii.

213 *Doctor Thorne*, ch. i.

216–17 *Adam Bede*; ch. lii.

218 *Felix Holt the Radical: Introduction*.

17. THE SHADOWED COUNTRY

222 Cf. *Captain Swing*; E. J. Hobsbawm and G. Rudé: London, 1969; ch. ii.

223 *To Penshurst*; op. cit.

224 Cit. Hobsbawm and Rudé, op. cit., 138.

224 ibid., 298.

226 *The Agricultural Revolution*; G. E. Mingay and J. D. Chambers; London, 1966; 166–7.

226 'The Land Market in the 19th Century' in *Essays in Agrarian History*, ed. Minchinton; Vol. 2; Newton Abbot, 1968.

230 *The Whistler at the Plough*; Alexander Somerville; Manchester, 1852; 383–4.

230 ibid., 387.

231 ibid., 388.

231 *Autobiography of Joseph Arch*; London, 1966; 43.

232 *The Times*, 14 November 1872.

232 Cit. *Richard Jefferies, Man of the Fields*; ed. S. J. Looker and C. Porteous; London, 1965; 4 and 6.

234 Preface to *Hodge and his Masters*.

236 *One of the New Voters*; repr. *The Open Air*; London, 1885.

236–37 'Thoughts on the Labour Question'; *Pall Mall Gazette*, 10 November 1891.

237 In *The Hills and the Vale*; London, 1909.

238 'Primrose Gold in Our Villages'; *Pall Mall Gazette*, 8 June 1887; repr. *Field and Farm*; ed. S. J. Looker; London, 1957.

241 In *Preface* to *Cakes and Ale*; 1970.

243 *Tess of the D'Urbervilles*, ch. iii.

244 *The Return of the Native*; Book Third, ch. ii.

244 ibid.

245 ibid.

248 *Tess of the D'Urbervilles*; ch. xx.

249 ibid.

250 ibid., ch. xxv.

250 ibid.

251 Repr. in *Hardy's Personal Writings*; ed. H. Orel; London, 1967; 181.

251 From the Preface to *Far from the Madding Crowd*.

251–52 *Tess of the D'Urbervilles*; ch. li.

252–53 ibid., ch. xxx.

256 ibid., ch. xlvii.

256–57 ibid., ch. xlviii.

257 *The Woodlanders*; ch. xliv.

257–58 *Tess of the D'Urbervilles*, ch. xliii.

19. CITIES OF DARKNESS AND OF LIGHT

259 *The Early Life of Thomas Hardy*; F. E. Hardy; London, 1928; 271.

259 Journal of 1831, cit. *Thomas Carlyle*; J. A. Froude; London, 1882; Vol. II, ch. ix.

259 Cit. Froude, op. cit., Vol. II, ch. ix.

260 *The Condition of the Working Class in England in 1844*; F. Engels; trans. F. K. Wischnewetzky; London, 1934; 24.

260 *Early Life*; 179.

260 ibid., 171.

261 ibid. 129.

262–63 Repr. in *Mayhew's Characters*; ed. P. Quennell; London, 1969; 96.

263 ibid., 176.

263 Cit. *The Unknown Mayhew*; ed. Thompson and Yeo; London, 1971.

264 Cit. *Elizabeth Gaskell*; A. B. Hopkins; London, 1952; 77.

266 *Taxes and Contributions*; cit. George, op. cit., 64.

266 *A Picture of England*; W. Archenholz; Dublin, 1791.

268 *The Nether World*; London, 1889; 23–4.

269 ibid., 58–9.

269 *Introduction to Oliver Twist*; Gissing, G.; Rochester Edition, 1900; xvii.

269 *Introduction to Bleak House*; Rochester Edition, 1900; xiv.

269 ibid. xx.

269–70 *Demos*; London, 1886; 178.

Page

271 *Working Class Stories of the 1890s*; ed. P. J. Keating; London, 1971; 29.

274 Archenholz, op. cit.

274 Cit. *Great London*; C. Trent; London, 1965; 200.

275 *European Life and Manners*; Colman; Boston, 1849; Vol. I, 155.

275 *The Geographical Distribution of British Intellect*; A. Conan Doyle in *The Nineteenth Century*, August 1888.

276 Cit. *Victorian Cities*; Asa Briggs; London, 1963; 17, 358.

276 *Tono-Bungay*, Book the First, ch. 1 and Book the Second, ch. 1.

278 Engels, op. cit., xviii; *Preface* of 11 January 1892.

20.   THE FIGURE IN THE CITY

280 *London*, op. cit., 59.

280 *Prelude*, op. cit., 286.

280 Cf. ''Tis solitude in cities, crowds all move like living death'; Clare, *Child Harold*, Canto Third, xxvi.

280 *Dombey and Son*; ch. xlviii.

280-81 *Mary Barton*; ch. vi.

281 *Short Poems in Prose*; in *The Essence of Laughter*; ed. P. Quennell; New York, 1956; 139.

281 ibid., 140.

282 Cf. *Baudelaire*; M. Turnell; London, 1953; 193.

282 *Introduction to Bleak House*; ed. cit., xx.

282 *Demos*; 178.

283 *The Nether World*; 59.

283 *Poems and Some Letters of James Thomson*; ed. A. Ridler; London, 1963; 12.

284 ibid., 13.

284 ibid., 25.

284 ibid., 21.

284 ibid., 23.

284 ibid., 25.

285 ibid., 31.

285 ibid., 39.

285 ibid., 52.

285 ibid., 180.

285 ibid., 184-5.

286 ibid., 191.

286 ibid., 192.

286 ibid., 195.

286-87 ibid., 196-7.

287 *The Waste Land*; in *Collected Poems, 1909-35*; London, 1944; 63.

288 'Preludes'; op. cit., 21.

288 *Preludes*; op. cit., 22.

288-89 'Morning at the Window'; op. cit., 27.

Page

289 *Choruses from 'The Rock'*; op. cit., 166–7.

289–90 *Four Quartets*; London, 1944; 38.

290 *Orlando*; London (1942); 176–7.

291 *Prelude*; op. cit., 286.

291–92 *Ulysses*; London (1947); 50.

292–93 ibid., 50–51.

293 ibid., 144 and 153.

294 *Early Life*; 271.

21. SURVIVING COUNTRYMEN

300 'The Natural History of German Life'; *Westminster Review*, 1856.

300–1 *Poetical Works of George Meredith*; ed. G. M. Trevelyan; London, 1912; 176–7.

301 ibid., 154.

301 ibid., *Hard Weather*; 320.

301 Sorley, cit. *George Meredith*; J. Lindsay; London, 1956; 373.

301–2 Op. cit., *Jump-to-Glory-Jane*; 372.

302 ibid., *The Flourish in February*; 328.

305 *Oxford Book of Modern Verse*; ed. W. B. Yeats; Oxford, 1936; 208.

305 ibid., 215–16.

306 *The Heart of England*; London, 1906; 73–4.

307 *The Country*; London, 1913; 21.

308 *Collected Poems of Edward Thomas*; London, 1961; 54.

308 ibid., 55.

309 'In Time of the "Breaking of the Nations"'; in *Selected Poems of Thomas Hardy*, ed. G. M. Young; 1940; 67.

309 Cf. David Harker, Introduction to reprint of *Rhymes of Northern Bards*; Newcastle, 1971; xlix-l.

310 *Daily Chronicle*, 14 January 1913.

310 *The Childhood of Edward Thomas*; London, 1938; 53.

310 *World Without End*; Helen Thomas; London, 1956; 107.

310 *The Heart of England*; London, 1906; 62–3.

310 *Poems*, op. cit., 25.

311 ibid., 27.

311 *New Bearings in English Poetry*; F. R. Leavis; London, 1936; 69.

311 Cit. *Edward Thomas*; W. Cooke; London, 1970; 106.

311 *Collected Poems*, 69.

311 ibid., 71–2.

312 ibid., 30.

312 ibid., 108.

312 ibid., 100.

312 Cit. Cooke, op. cit., 224–5.

314 Cf. *Alfred Williams, his life and world*; L. Clark; Newton Abbot, 1969.

315 *Brother to the Ox*; F. Kitchen; London, 1940; 125.

316 *Phoenix*; London, 1936; 135.
317 *The Rainbow*; London (1949); 7–8.
317–18 ibid., 8–9.
318 ibid., 10.
318 ibid., 496.
318 *Phoenix*; 139.
319 *Letters to Bertrand Russell*; ed. H. Moore; London, 1948; 80.
319 *Phoenix*; 137.
319 ibid., 139.
320 ibid., 139.
320 ibid., 140,
321 ibid., 829.
322 *A Scots Quair*; London, 1950; 17.
323 ibid., 300.
323 ibid., 193.
324 ibid., 496.

23. THE CITY AND THE FUTURE

327 *News from Nowhere* in Morris Centenary Edition; ed. G. D. H.
    Cole; London, 1946; 8.
327 ibid., 39.
327 ibid., 64.
328 *Experiment in Autobiography*; London, 1969; Vol. II; 645.
328 *Complete Short Stories of H. G. Wells*; London, 1948; 786.
331 Thomson, op. cit., 199.
331 *Cities of Wonder*; ed. D. Knight; London, 1970; 92.
332 ibid., 64.
332 ibid., 186.
332 ibid., 15–16.

24. THE NEW METROPOLIS

338 *Collected Essays, Journalism and Letters of George Orwell*; London,
    1968; Vol. I; 397.

25. CITIES AND COUNTRIES

363 Cf. *The Prophet Unarmed*; I. Deutscher; London, 1959.
364 *Manifesto*; ed. cit., 13–14.
364 ibid., 14.

Selected Bibliography

A: *Literature* (i) Chs. i–viii; (ii) Chs. ix–xvii; (iii) Chs. xviii–xxv
B: *History and Related Studies*
C: *Studies of Literature, Art and Ideas*
Note: the place of publication is London unless otherwise shown.
   Italicized names indicate editors.

A: LITERATURE

(i)

Hesiod, *Works and Days*, ed. Sinclair, T. A., 1932
Theocritus, *Works*, ed. Gow, A. S. F., Cambridge, 1952
Edmonds, J. M., The Greek Bucolic Poets, 1912
Gow, A. S. F., The Greek Bucolic Poets, Cambridge 1953
Headlam, W., A Book of Greek Verse, Cambridge, 1907
*Higham, T. F. and Bowra, C. M., Oxford Book of Greek Verse in
   Translation*, Oxford, 1938
Virgil, *Eclogues*, trans. Day Lewis, C., 1963
Virgil, *Georgics*, trans. Day Lewis, C., 1940
Horace, *Odes*, trans. Godley, A. D., 1898
Juvenal, *Sixteen Satires*, trans. Green, P., 1967
Knott, T. A. and Fowler, D. C., Piers the Plowman, Baltimore, 1952
Pollard, A. W., English Miracle Plays, Moralities and Interludes,
   Oxford rev. 1927
More, T., *Utopia*, ed. Sampson, G. and Guthkelch, A., 1910
Sannazaro, G., *Arcadia*, Napoli, (1966)
Tasso, T., *Aminta*, ed. Sozzi, B. T., Padova, (1957)
Politianus, A., *Rusticus*, 1672
Alamanni, L., *La Coltivazione*, 1780
Sidney, P., *Arcadia*, ed. Baker, E. A., 1907
Bastard, T., *Chrestoleros*, repr. Grosart, A. B., 1880
Crole, R. (Crowley), *Select Works*, ed. Cowper, J. M., 1872
Jonson, B., *Works*, ed. Herford, C. H. and Simpson, P. E., Oxford,
   1925–52
Marlowe, C., *Works*, ed. Case, R. H., 1933
Middleton, T., *Plays*, ed. Swinburne, A. C. and Ellis, H., 1887–90
Spenser, E., *The Shepheardes Calendar*, ed., Herford, C. H., 1895

385

Rapin, R., *Dissertatio de Carmine Pastorali Eclogae Sacrae*, Paris, 1659

Creech, T., *The Idylliums of Theocritus with Rapin's Discourse of Pastorals*, 1684

Fontenelle, B., *Discours sur la nature de l'églogue*, Paris, 1688.

Motteux, P. A., *Of Pastorals*, 1695.

Carew, T., *Poems*, ed. Dunlap, R., Oxford, 1949

Herrick, R., *Poetical Works*, ed. Moorman, F. W., Oxford, 1921

Marvell, A., *Poems and Letters*, ed. Margoliouth, H. M., Oxford, 1952

Massinger, P., *Plays*, ed. Symons, A., 1887–9.

Milton, J., *The Readie and Easie Way to Establish a Free Commonwealth*, 2nd rev. ed., 1660

Milton, J., *Complete Poetry and Selected Prose*, ed. Visiak, E. H., New York, 1938

Pomfret, J., *Poems*, 1792

Chambers, E. K., *Oxford Book of 16th Century Verse*, Oxford, 1932

Kermode, J. F., *English Pastoral Poetry, from the beginnings to Marvell*, 1952

Grierson, H. J. C. and Bullough, G., *Oxford Book of 17th Century Verse*, Oxford, 1934

Smith, D.N., *Oxford Book of 18th Century Verse*, Oxford, 1926

Fausset, H. I'A., *Minor Poets of the 18th Century*, 1930

Davie, D., *The Late Augustans: Longer Poems of the Later 18th Century*, 1958

Congreve, W., *Works*, ed. Bateson, F. W., Oxford, 1930

Etherege, G., *Works*, ed. Brett-Smith, H. F. B., Oxford, 1927

Vanbrugh, J., *Complete Works*, ed. Dobrée, B. and Webb, G., 1927

Wycherley, W., *Plays*, ed. Ward, W. C., 1888

Nettleton, G. H. and Case, A., *British Dramatists from Dryden to Sheridan*, 1939

Pope, A., *Poems*, ed. Butt, J., Vols. I, III.ii, IV; 1961, 1951, 1953

Defoe, D., *Novels and Selected Writings*, Oxford, 1927–8

Fielding, H., *Novels*, Oxford, 1926

Richardson, S., *Novels*, Oxford, 1930

Cole, G. D. H., *Defoe's Tour Thro' the Whole Island of Great Britain*, 1927

Cowper, W., *Poems*, ed. Fausset, H. I'A., 1931

Duck, S., *Poems on Several Occasions*, 1736

Dyer, J., *Poems*, ed. Thomas, E., 1903

Goldsmith, O., *Complete Poetical Works*, ed. Dobson, A., Oxford, 1906

Gray, T. and Collins, W., *Poetical Works*, ed. Poole, A. L., rev. Whibley, L., Oxford, 1937

Langhorne, J., *Poetical Works*, ed. Langhorne, J. T., 1804

Philips, A., *Poems*, ed. Segar, M. G., Oxford, 1937

Shenstone, W., *Poetical Works*, ed. Gilfillan, W., Edinburgh, 1854

Young, A., *A Farmer's Letters to the People of England*, 1768

Young, A., *Autobiography*, ed. Betham-Edwards, M., 1898

Addison, J. *Essays*, ed. Frazer, J. G., 1915

Austen, J., *Novels*, ed., Chapman, R. W., 1923–54

Bewick, T., *Memoir Written by Himself, 1882–8*, repr., 1961

Blake, W., *Complete Poetry*, ed. Hillyer, R. S., New York, 1941

Bloomfield, R., *Poetical Works (of Robert Bloomfield and Henry Kirke-White)*, 1871

Clare, J., *Poems*, ed. Tibble, J. W., 1935

Cobbett, W., *Rural Rides*, ed. Cole, G. D. H. and M., Oxford, 1930

Coleridge, S. T., *Poetical Works*, ed. Coleridge, E. H., Oxford, 1912

Coleridge S. T., *Select Poetry and Prose*, ed. Potter, S., 1933

Constable, J., *Lectures at the Royal Institution*, 1836

Crabbe, G., *Poetical Works*, ed. Carlyle, A. J. and R. M., Oxford, 1914

Evelyn, J., *Diary*, ed. Beer, E. de S., Oxford, 1955

Galt, J., *Annals of the Parish*, ed. Gordon, G. S., 1908

Gilpin, W., *Observations*, 6 vols, 1782–98; *Three Essays*, 1792

Jenner, C., *Town Eclogues*, 1772

Johnson, S., *Prose and Poetry*, ed. Chapman, R. W., 1922

Boswell, J., *Life of Samuel Johnson*, ed. Hill, G. B., rev. Powell, L. F., Oxford, 1934–50

Kent, N., *Hints to Gentlemen of Landed Property*, 1775

Lillo, J., *The London Merchant*, ed. Ward, A. W., Oxford, 1906

Peacock, T. L., *Novels*, ed. Garnett, D., 1948

Repton, H., *An Enquiry into the Changes in Landscape Gardening*, 1806

White, G., *Writings*, ed. Massingham, H. J., 1938

Wordsworth, W., *Poetical Works*, ed. Selincourt, E. de and Darbishire, H., Oxford, 1940–49

Maxwell, J. C., The Prelude: a parallel text, 1971

Arch, J., *Life*, 1898

Brontë, C., *Shirley*, 1849

Brontë, E., *Wuthering Heights*, 1847

Dickens, C., *Old Curiosity Shop*, 1841; *Nicholas Nickleby*, 1839; *Dombey and Son*, 1848; *Hard Times*, 1854; *Little Dorrit*, 1857; *Our Mutual Friend*, 1865

Disraeli, B., *Coningsby*, 1844; *Sybil*, 1845

Dolby, T., *Floreston*, 1839

Eliot, G., *Adam Bede*, Edinburgh, 1959; *Mill on the Floss*, Edinburgh, 1860; *Felix Holt*, 1866; *Middlemarch*, Edinburgh, 1871–3; *Daniel Deronda*, Edinburgh, 1876

Cross, J. W., *Life of George Eliot*, Edinburgh, 1885

Gaskell, E., *Mary Barton*, 1848; *Cranford*, 1853; *North and South*, 1855; *Wives and Daughters*, 1866

Jefferies, R., *Hodge and his Masters*, 1880; *The Dewy Morn*, 1884; *The Life of the Fields*, 1884; *After London*, 1885; *The Open Air*, 1885; *Amaryllis at the Fair*, 1887; *Toilers of the Field*, 1892

Looker, S. J., *Richard Jefferies: Field and Farm*, 1957

Thomas, E., *Hills and the Vale: Richard Jefferies*, 1909
Kingsley, C., *Yeast*, 1851; *Alton Locke*, 1852
Somerville, A., *Autobiography of a Working Man*, 1848; *The Whistler at the Plough*, Manchester, 1852
Surtees, R. S., *Jaunts and Jollities*, 1838
Trollope, A., *Doctor Thorne*, 1858
Trollope, A., *The Barsetshire Novels*, ed. Harrison, F., 1906–28
Watson, J., *Confessions of a Poacher*, 1890; *Poachers and Poaching*, 1891

(iii)

Barnes, W., *Poems of Rural Life, in the Dorset Dialect*, 1844
Besant, W., *Children of Gibeon*, 1886
Booth, W., *In Darkest England*, 1890
Carlyle, T., *Collected Works*, 1857–8
Conan-Doyle, A., *Memoirs of Sherlock Holmes*, 1894
Egan., P., *Life in London*, 1821
Gissing, G., *Workers in the Dawn*, 1880; *The Unclassed*, 1884; *Demos*, 1886; *The Nether World*, 1889; *New Grub Street*, 1891; *Born in Exile*, 1892; *In the Year of Jubilee*, 1894
Gallienne, R. le, *English Poems*, 1892
Greenwood, J. A., *Night in a Workhouse*, 1866
Hardy, T., *Under the Greenwood Tree*, 1872; *Far From the Madding Crowd*, 1874; *The Return of the Native*, 1878; *The Mayor of Casterbridge*, 1886; *The Woodlanders*, 1887; *Tess of the D'Urbervilles*, 1891; *Jude the Obscure*, 1896
Orel, H., *Thomas Hardy: Personal Writings*, 1967
Hardy, F. E., *The Early Life of Thomas Hardy*, 1928
Hollingshead, J., *Ragged London in 1861*, 1961
Keating, P. J., *Working-class Stories of the 1890s*, 1971
Mayhew, A., *Kitty Lamere*, 1855; *Paved with Gold*, 1858
Mayhew, A. and H., *The Greatest Plague of Life*, 1847; *Living for Appearances*, 1855
Morris, W., *News from Nowhere*, 1891
Morrison, A., *Tales of Mean Streets*, 1894; *A Child of the Jago*, 1896
Pall Mall Gazette, 1885
Rutherford, M., *The Revolution in Tanner's Lane*, 1887
Sims, G., *How the Poor Live*, 1883
Wells, H. G., *The Time Machine*, 1895; *The War of the Worlds*, 1898; *Tono-Bungay*, 1909; *Experiment in Autobiography*, 1934; *Complete Short Stories*, 1927
Borrow, G., *Wild Wales*, 1862
Kilvert, F., *Diary, 1870–79*; (1938–40)
Stevenson, R. L., *Inland Voyage*, 1878; *Travels with a Donkey in the Cevennes*, 1879
Baudelaire, C. P., *Oeuvres*, Paris, 1954
Dostoievsky, F., *Crime and Punishment*, 1886

Kafka, F., *The Trial*, 1956; *The Castle*, 1953

Mercier, L-S., *Tableau de Paris*, 1929; *L'An 2440*, Neuchâtel, 1772

Thomson, J., *Poems and Some Letters*, 1963

Abercrombie, L., *Collected Poems*, 1930

Barrie, J. M., *A Window in Thrums*, 1889

Bourne, G., *Memoirs of a Surrey Labourer*, 1907; *Change in the Village*, 1912; *The Wheelwright's Shop*, Cambridge, 1923

Bell, A., *Corduroy*, 1930; *Silver Ley*, 1931; *Cherry Tree*, 1932

Bell, A., *The Open Air*, 1936

Blythe, R., *Akenfield*, 1969

Carpenter, E., *Towards Democracy*, 1885; *Civilization, its Cause and Cure*, 1889

Christie, A., *The Body in the Library*, 1942

Drinkwater, J., *Collected Poems*, 1923

Eliot, T. S., *Collected Poems*, 1936; *Idea of a Christian Society*, 1939; *Four Quartets*, 1944; *Notes towards the definition of Culture*, 1948

Evans, G. E., *The Pattern under the Plough*, 1966

Forster, E. M., *The Longest Journey*, 1907; *Howard's End*, 1910; *A Passage to India*, 1924

Gibbon, L. G., *A Scots Quair*, 1950

Gibbons, S., *Cold Comfort Farm*, 1938

Grahame, K., *The Wind in the Willows*, 1908

Holme, C., *The Lonely Plough*, 1914

Hudson, W. H., *A Shepherd's Life*, 1910; *Far Away and Long Ago*, 1918

James, H., *Portrait of a Lady*, 1881; *The Spoils of Poynton*, 1897; *The Golden Bowl*, 1904

Joyce, J., *Dubliners*, 1914; *Portrait of the Artist as a Young Man*, 1916; *Ulysses*, 1922; *Finnegans Wake*, 1939

Kitchen, F., *Brother to the Ox*, 1939

Lawrence, D. H., *Sons and Lovers*, 1913; *The Rainbow*, 1915; *Women in Love*, 1921; *Lady Chatterley's Lover*, (1961); *Phoenix*, 1936; *Phoenix II*, 1968

Marsh, E., *Georgian Poetry*, 1911–22

Martin, E. W., *The Secret People*, 1954

Massingham, H., *The English Countryman*, 1942

Meredith, G., *The Ordeal of Richard Feverel*, 1859; *Rhoda Fleming*, 1865; *Poems and Lyrics of the Joy of Earth*, 1883; *A Reading of Earth*, 1888

Phillpotts, E., *Dartmoor Omnibus*, 1933

Powys, J. C., *A Glastonbury Romance*, 1933

Powys, T. F., *Fables*, 1929; *Mr Weston's Good Wine*, 1927

Sayers, D. L., *The Nine Tailors*, 1934

Scott, J. R., *The Countryman Book*, 1948

Thomas, E., *Collected Poems*, 1936

Thompson, F., *Lark Rise to Candleford*, 1945

Tolkien, J. R., *Lord of the Rings*, 1966

White, T. H., *The Sword in the Stone*, 1938

Williamson, H., *Collected Nature Stories*, 1970

Woolf, V., *Mrs Dalloway*, 1925; *To the Lighthouse*, 1927; *Orlando*, 1929; *The Waves*, 1931; *Between the Acts*, 1941

Young, F. B., *Mr Lucton's Freedom*, 1940

Aldiss, B., *Omnibus*, 1969

Clarke, A. C., *The City and the Stars*, 1957

Han Suyin, *And the Rain my Drink*, 1956

Huxley, A., *Brave New World*, 1932

Knight, D., *Cities of Wonder*, 1970

Orwell, G., *Down and Out in Paris and London*, 1933; *Burmese Days*, 1934; *A Clergyman's Daughter*, 1935; *Keep the Aspidistra Flying*, 1936; *The Road to Wigan Pier*, 1937; *Coming up for Air*, 1939; *Animal Farm*, 1945; *Nineteen Eighty-Four*, 1949; *Collected Essays, Journalism and Letters*, 1969

Tressall, R., *The Ragged Trousered Philanthropists*, 1927

Achebe, C., *Things Fall Apart*, 1958; *Arrow of God*, 1964; *No Longer at Ease*, 1960; *Man of the People*, 1966

Amadi, E., *The Concubine*, 1966

Anand, M. R., *Two Leaves and a Bud*, 1937; *The Village*, 1939

Cary, J., *Aissa Saved*, 1932; *The African Witch*, 1936; *Mister Johnson*, 1939

Harris, W., *The Far Journey of Oudin*, 1961

Kemel, Y., *The Wind from the Plain*, 1964; *Anatolian Tales*, 1968

Lamming, G., *In the Castle of My Skin*, 1953

Mphahlele, E., *Man Must Live*, Cape Town, 1946

Narayan, R. K., *Swami and Friends*, 1935

Ngugi, J., *Weep not, Child*, 1964; *A Grain of Wheat*, 1967; *The River Between*, 1965

Nwankwo, N., *Danda*, 1964

Reid, V. S., *New Day*, 1950

B: HISTORY AND RELATED STUDIES

Archenholz, J. W. von., *A Picture of England*, Dublin, 1790

Ashley, M. R., *Joseph Ashley of Tysoe*, 1961

Bennett, H. S., *Life on the English Manor, 1150–1400*, 1937

Bloch, M., *La Société Féodale*, Paris, 1940

Briggs, A., *Victorian Cities*, 1963

Beresford, M. W., *New Towns of the Middle Ages*, 1967

Bonser, K. J., *The Drovers*, 1970

Booth, C., *Life and Labour of the People in London*, 1889–1903

Caird, J., *English Agriculture in 1850–51*, 1852; *The British Land Question*, 1881

Chambers, J. D. and Mingay, G. E., *The Agricultural Revolution, 1750–1880*, 1966

Clapham, J. H., *Economic History of Modern Britain*, Cambridge, 1927

Coulton, G. C., *Social Life in Britain from the Conquest to the Reformation*, 1918

Deane, P. M. and Cole, W. A., *British Economic Growth, 1688–1959*, Cambridge, 1962

Defries, A., *Sheep and Turnips, being the Life and Times of Arthur Young*, 1938

Dickinson, R. E., *The West European City*, 1951

Dobb, M. H., *Studies in the Development of Capitalism*, 1946

Engels, F., *The Condition of the Working Class in England, 1844*, 1892

Fairbrother, N., *New Lives, New Landscapes*, 1970

Fussell, G. E., *Village Life in the 18th Century*, 1948; *The English Rural Labourer*, 1949

Fussell, G. E. and K. R., *The English Countryman*, 1955

Hammond, J. L., and B., *The Village Labourer*, 1911; *The Skilled Labourer*, 1919

Hasbach, W., *A History of the English Agricultural Labourer*, 1908

Handlin, O. and Burchard, J., *The Historian and the City*, Cambridge, Mass., 1966

Hobsbawm, E. J., *The Age of Revolution*, 1962; *Industry and Empire*, 1968

Hobsbawm, E. J., and Rudé, G., *Captain Swing*, 1969

Habakkuk, H. J., *American and British Technology in the 19th Century*, 1962

Harden, D. B., *Dark Age England*, 1956

Hoskins, W. G., *The Making of the English Landscape*, 1957

Howitt, W., *The Rural Life of England*, 1838

Jones, E., *Towns and Cities*, 1966

Marshall, W., *Rural Economy*, 1787–98

Marx, K., *Capital*, 1887

Mayhew, H., *London Labour and the London Poor*, 1861

Minchinton, W. E., ed., *Essays in Agrarian History*, 2 vols., Newton Abbot, 1968

Mingay, G. E., *English Landed Society in the 18th Century*, 1963

Mumford, L., *The Culture of Cities*, 1938; *Technics and Civilisation*, 1938

Orwin, C. S. and Whetham, E. H., *History of British Agriculture, 1846–1914*, 1964

Peacock, A. J., *Bread or Blood*, 1965

Pirenne, N., *Medieval Cities*, New York, 1925

Prothero, R. (Ernle), *English Farming Past and Present*, 6th edn., rev. Hall, D., and introd. Fussell, G. E. and McGregor, O. R., 1961

Rosenau, H., *The Ideal City*, 1959

Rubinstein, S., *Historians of London*, 1968

Saville, J., *Rural Depopulation in England and Wales, 1851–1951*, 1957

Sheppard, F., *London, 1808–70; the infernal wen*, 1971

Slater, G., *The English Peasantry and the Enclosure of Common Fields*, 1907

Tawney, R. H., *The Agrarian Problem in the 16th Century*, 1912

Thirsk, J., The Agrarian History of England and Wales, Vol. IV, 1967

Thompson, E. P., *The Making of the English Working Class*, 1963

Thompson, F. M. L., *English Landed Society in the 19th Century*, 1963

Trent, C., *Greater London*, 1965

Vaughan, R., *The Age of Great Cities*, 1848

Vinogradoff, P., *Villeinage in England*, 1968

Voltaire, *Oeuvres, Vol. X*, Paris, 1877

Whitelock, D., *The Beginnings of English Society*, 1963

Young, A., *A Farmer's Letters to the People of England*, 1768; *Annals of Agriculture*, contrib.

C: STUDIES OF LITERATURE, ART AND IDEAS

Arnold, M., *Culture and Anarchy*, 1869

Barrell, J., *The Idea of Landscape and the Sense of Place*, 1972

Burckhardt, J., *The Civilisation of the Renaissance in Italy*, trans. Middlemore, 1929

Congleton, J. E., *Theories of Pastoral Poetry in England, 1684–1798*, 1952

Cooper, E. H., *The Medieval Background of English Renaissance Pastoral Literature*, Ph.D. thesis, Cambridge, 1972

Duckworth, A. M., *The Improvement of the Estate*, 1972

Empson, W., *Some Versions of Pastoral*, 1935

Hibbard, G. H., *Journal of the Warburg Institute*, XIX, 1–2 (1954)

Hill, C., *Puritanism and Revolution*, 1958

Hopkins, A. B., *Elizabeth Gaskell: her life and work*, 1952

Hussey, C., *The Picturesque: studies in a point of view*, 1927

Leavis, F. R., *The Great Tradition*, 1948

Leavis, F. R. and Thompson, D., *Culture and Environment*, 1933

Knights, L. C., *Drama and Society in the Age of Jonson*, 1937

Leavis, Q. D., *Fiction and the Reading Public*, 1932

Lindsay, J., *George Meredith*, 1956

Mack, M., *The Garden and the City*, London, 1969

Malins, E., *English Landscaping and Literature*, 1966

Rostvig, M-S., *The Happy Man*; 2 vols., Oslo, 1954 and 1958

Smith, G., *Dickens, Money and Society*; Berkeley, 1968

Unwin, R., *The Rural Muse*, 1954

Welsh, A., *The City of Dickens*, 1971

Wilkinson, L. P., *The Georgics of Virgil*, 1969

Williams, M., *Thomas Hardy and Rural England*, 1972

Index